T0270320

AIR APACHES

The True Story of the 345th Bomb Group and
Its Low, Fast, and Deadly Mission in World War II

JAY A. STOUT

STACKPOLE
BOOKS

Essex, Connecticut
Blue Ridge Summit, Pennsylvania

For Frankie, and other dear friends

STACKPOLE BOOKS

An imprint of Globe Pequot, the trade division of
The Rowman & Littlefield Publishing Group, Inc.
4501 Forbes Blvd., Ste. 200
Lanham, MD 20706
www.rowman.com

Distributed by NATIONAL BOOK NETWORK

Copyright © 2019 by Jay A. Stout

Maps by Jay A. Stout

All rights reserved. No part of this book may be reproduced in any form or by any electronic
or mechanical means, including information storage and retrieval systems, without written
permission from the publisher, except by a reviewer who may quote passages in a review.

British Library Cataloguing in Publication Information available

Library of Congress Cataloging-in-Publication Data

Names: Stout, Jay A. 1959- author.
Title: Air Apaches : the true story of the 345th Bomb Group and its low, fast, and deadly missions
   in World War II / Jay A. Stout.
Description: Lanham, MD : Stackpole Books, an imprint of The Rowman & Littlefield Publishing
   Group, Inc., [2019] | Includes bibliographical references and index.
Identifiers: LCCN 2018043728 (print) | LCCN 2018044138 (ebook) | ISBN 9780811738019
   (print) | ISBN 9780811768092 (ebook) | ISBN 9780811772686 (pbk)
Subjects: United States. Army Air Forces. Bombardment Group, 345th. | World War, 1939-
   1945—Personal narratives, American. | World War, 1939-1945—Aerial operations, American. |
   World War, 1939-1945—Campaigns—Pacific Area.
Classification: LCC D790.253 345th .S76 2019 (print) | LCC D790.253 345th (ebook) |
   940.54/4973
LC record available at https://lccn.loc.gov/2018043728
LC ebook record available at https://lccn.loc.gov/2018044138

∞™ The paper used in this publication meets the minimum requirements of American National
Standard for Information Sciences—Permanence of Paper for Printed Library Materials, ANSI/
NISO Z39.48-1992.

Contents

Foreword iv
Preface viii
Introduction xi

CHAPTER 1: "It Couldn't Be Much Worse" 1
CHAPTER 2: "That Made Him Very Happy" 26
CHAPTER 3: "The Enemy Was Taken Completely By Surprise" 45
CHAPTER 4: "The Squadron Was Attacked" 73
CHAPTER 5: "The Pilots Did Not Appear Eager" 89
CHAPTER 6: "I Turned Back to Pick Him Up" 103
CHAPTER 7: "We Think We Destroyed the Mission" 123
CHAPTER 8: "Many Strange Faces" 142
CHAPTER 9: "I Hate to See Them Go" 168
CHAPTER 10: "Torn to Death" 184
CHAPTER 11: "Love to All and Write Real Often" 204
CHAPTER 12: "A Perfect Swan Dive" 227
CHAPTER 13: "It's All for the Best, Dad" 238
CHAPTER 14: "We Seemed to Be Awfully High" 249
CHAPTER 15: "He Was Even More Handsome in His Uniform" . . 271
CHAPTER 16: "Jap Fighters Making Long Range Passes" 283
CHAPTER 17: "I Inflated My Mae West" 299
CHAPTER 18: "I Jerked and Ducked Instinctively" 311
CHAPTER 19: "He Also Flew Missions with Several
              Other Crews" 318
CHAPTER 20: "Well, I'm Done For" 332

Epilogue 347
Acknowledgments 353
Notes and References 356
Bibliography 367
Index 370

FOREWORD

CLARK FIELD ON THE ISLAND OF LUZON IN THE PHILIPPINES LOOKED very much different to my father in 1958 than it had in January 1945, when he flew B-25s with the 345th Bomb Group—the famed Air Apaches. During the war, then lieutenant Ed Bina and his crew had roared low over the runways at Clark and ripped Japanese aircraft and personnel with torrents of deadly machine-gun fire. In their wake, they left a trail of parachute-suspended fragmentation bombs that settled gently to earth before exploding with fatal ferocity.

That same airfield was where he was stationed thirteen years later. And it was where he had brought me and the rest of our family to live. Indeed, it was at Clark that I, as a young boy, barely started to grasp my father's wartime legacy as a B-25 pilot with the 345th Bomb Group's 501st Bomb Squadron: the Black Panthers. The 501st was one of four squadrons that made up the group.

During that time, the days of the Japanese occupation of Clark, while still visible, were being slowly erased by man and nature. But there was still evidence of the fighting at almost every turn. As kids, we collected spent shell casings and bullets; a long, jagged piece of shrapnel from a five-hundred-pound bomb served as a makeshift machete. Also strong in my memory are hikes to caves where the Japanese had holed up as the Americans and their allies retook Luzon. I vividly recall stepping around and over unexploded bombs, heeding my father's warnings not to touch them. And an image persists of a war-torn field at the end of the street where we lived.

The war left telltale marks. And although I was young, I knew that those marks and my dad were somehow connected.

As was typical of many of the war's veterans, my father didn't dwell on his wartime experiences. A fellow Air Apache and Dad's radio operator, James Baross, declared, "It was just something you didn't talk about." By the time my father finally retired after thirty-six years of service, he had described to me only two of his missions. Still, reminders were always there. Among others, his A-2 flight jacket hung untouched in the closet, and his B-25 flight manual was part of my book collection.

The 345th Bomb Group Association got going with purpose during the late 1970s and dedicated the group's memorial in 1985 at the National Museum of the Air Force. Dad and I visited the site shortly after the ceremony. I think it was typical of my father's humble character that he played an instrumental role in creating the memorial but never memorialized himself. Later that week we met with his lifelong friends from the war, Jay Moore and Julius Fisher. They had all flown together and were part of a much larger group of really amazing guys.

Although I learned more over the years, I still didn't fully understand what my dad—and the rest of the Air Apaches—had done. I didn't press him, and he maintained his "no talk" protocol to the end. Sadly, Colonel Ed Bina "went west" in 2005 and took most of his wartime memories with him.

Dad's passing was the spark that ignited my real passion—the history of the 345th. Although he was gone and I would never again have the opportunity to talk with him, there were other resources that put me on a path of discovery. One of the richest proved to be the 345th's annual reunions, where Air Apache veterans gathered to share their memories and rekindle lost camaraderie. Decades had passed since they had fought the Japanese, and many of them began to open up about their wartime experiences. These stories—some sad, some humorous, and some almost unbelievable—fascinated me. What made them more incredible was that these "old" men who had lived them were barely more than kids during the war.

At my second Air Apaches reunion, I was elected president of the 345th Bomb Group Association. I was the first of the "next generation" to serve in that position, and it was my ambition to save as much as I could of the history of this proud bomb group—the hard-fighting, hard-playing, and hard-living young men who had so terrorized the Japanese in the South Pacific and beyond.

Aside from talking with those veterans still surviving, I visited various archives. It was in one of these that my search circled back to my childhood at Clark Field. I found the mission summary report for the 345th's savage attack there on January 7, 1945. And there was my father's name. He had flown in his squadron's second flight of three B-25s in aircraft number 178. The squadron described the mission as "designed to deliver the coup de grâce to the Imperial Air Force in Luzon." After tallying the damage wrought against the Japanese, the report described the attack as "beautifully executed."

The paper I held in my hand had traveled miles and years from that awful war. And it helped me to further understand who my dad was and what he had really done.

I will never be able to fully recreate my father's experiences, but I piece together what I collect in order to tell at least a partial story of one of the many young Air Apaches who answered Uncle Sam's call. I had often wondered if he knew what he was getting into when he enlisted in the Army in 1942. And I found the answer in a letter he wrote to his own father from Biak in 1944. It was apparent he knew quite well. "Don't worry dad," he wrote, "everything is fine here and I'm doing exactly what I've always wanted to do." The words seemed quite forthright, coming as they did from a twenty-one-year-old kid who was flying and fighting in a very special hell.

Ed Bina was only one of the more than four thousand men who served with the 345th Air Apaches. And he was but one small part of a team that included not only other flyers but also the cooks and mechanics and clerks and many other men who helped make the group one of the best outfits of the war. And long after the fighting ended, they formed a strong association that helped them not only satisfy their desire to reconnect with old comrades but also preserve their own history. Indeed, without the efforts of the 345th Bomb Group Association the story of the Air Apaches would remain virtually untold.

The story that Jay Stout tells here isn't only about the machines, the bombs, the guns, and the technologies of that time. Nor is it about the incredible numbers of enemy ships and aircraft that the 345th destroyed or the many Japanese whom its men killed. Rather, this story is about the men who did—or made possible—all that necessary destroying and killing. And it is about the brotherhood they forged as they did it. Above all, it is about a spirit and a legacy that will endure through many more generations, even as the last of the men make their final sortie. And because this book is about men rather than machines, it is a story that will likewise endure, and it is one that recalls a sentiment captured so well by William Shakespeare:

> We few, we happy few, we band of brothers;
> For he to-day that sheds his blood with me
> Shall be my brother.

James Bina
Virginia, 2018

PREFACE

As air wars go, the one that cleared Douglas MacArthur's path across New Guinea and up through the Philippines and beyond was as grubby, rotten, and brutal as any in history. It was fought above stinking, disease-ridden jungles that—on their own—brought entire army units to their knees. And it was likewise fought above vast expanses of ocean that swallowed, without a trace, everything from aircraft to capital ships. And it was waged against an enemy who, combat aside, showed not the slightest shred of goodliness or godliness.

As an air combat veteran, I was fascinated by this particular air war. The men flew hard-worn aircraft to far-flung targets with tongue-twisting names. Some of those targets were ill-protected backwaters, but too many were fiercely defended and exacted high costs in men and machines. It was gruesome and frightening and difficult to understand. As I researched and wrote, I made discoveries that compelled me to research and write more. I consequently found stories that bordered on incredible not just from the perspective of my own modern-day military experience but in the context of what happened in the Pacific as compared to other combat theaters of World War II. For example, unlike the monsters against whom the 345th fought, the Germans did not eat their prisoners.

I wondered at what motivated the men to keep going. Strafing units like the 345th Bomb Group—the Air Apaches—made their attacks at very low altitude. If they were hit by antiaircraft fire or fighters, their odds of survival were very poor. Too often they smashed into the ground and died fiery deaths. Not once did I find an instance of a combat-damaged aircraft being abandoned by parachute.

If they were able to wrestle their stricken aircraft past the shoreline to put down on the water, they were usually captured and murdered—that is, if they didn't drown. Those crews who coaxed their damaged bombers well away from the target before ditching too often hauled themselves into life rafts never to be seen again.

And it wasn't just the aircrews who endured hardship. In fact, the flyers were granted periodic furloughs to Australia and had some expectation of returning to the States if they survived their tours of combat. On the other hand, the support personnel worked long, hard hours, days, weeks, and months without break. Although they were seldom thrust into combat, they nonetheless suffered losses from accidents, bombings, snipers, and kamikazes, not to mention disease. And they were stuck in the Pacific for the duration of the war. Although the fighting did not last so long, "the Golden Gate in '48" was not just a catchy phrase. It wasn't unreasonable—especially early in the war—to expect that the war wouldn't be won until 1948.

I deduced that my question as to what motivated the 345th's men had many answers. Certainly there was the fact that the 345th was a military organization, and the men were bound to follow orders. And no doubt the men followed those orders in part because of a sense of patriotism, or love of country. But after reading and hearing the words of the men, I came to see that the Air Apaches were driven primarily by a sense of comradely love. It was a love that grew through shared hardship and a common mission, and it was a love that was strengthened and steeled through death and loss. Ultimately, they grew bound to each other in ways that cannot be understood by those who have not served in similar circumstances.

What made the 345th's accomplishments more impressive was that the group fought its war while constantly on the move. From June 1943 until the end of the fighting in August 1945, it set itself up at nine different bases. Along the way, the Air Apaches sank 260 vessels and destroyed 367 enemy aircraft—107 of them in aerial combat. Hard to measure but perhaps most important were the many thousands of tons of war-fighting material and equipment that the group's men bombed and strafed to bits.

But this came at a cost. Aside from enduring the stinking misery that was part and parcel of making war in the tropics, the Air Apaches lost 170 aircraft and 754 men. That loss rate, more than 16 percent of the approximately 4,500 men who served with the Air Apaches, was greater than that of most units that saw combat during the war.

Consequently, there are—or were—almost innumerable stories to be told. Each of the thousands of men who served with the 345th could have written his own book. But now almost all of them are gone. Nevertheless, in readying for this project, I still collected more material than I could use. And that was disheartening to a certain degree—there was no way I could tell the story of every man, of every loss, and of every instant of terror.

Still, too much to choose from was better than not enough, and I spent a great deal of time considering what I might and might not use. Ultimately, I chose to tell the story of the 345th through the missions and recollections that were most representative of what the group did during a given period. And as much as was possible, I used the words of the men and the contemporaneous records they created. I hope that this approach has given the book a credibility and sense of immediacy that makes the 345th's experience that much more real. And in making that experience more real, I hope that I have done justice to the dedication and guts of the men who made the Air Apaches one of the deadliest bomb groups of a very deadly war.

Introduction

"I wanted wings 'till I got the Goddamn things,
Now, I don't want them anymore.
They taught me how to fly,
Then they sent me off to die,
Well I've had a belly full of war."
—U.S. ARMY AIR FORCES DRINKING SONG

WILLIAM KYSER LOOKED DOWN AT THE PILOT'S SEAT. THE CUSHION WAS still damp with the perspiration of the pilot who had flown the morning mission. In fact, the entire aircraft smelled of sweat and gunpowder and hot engines—it had landed back at Dobodura only a couple of hours earlier. Since then, the mechanics had fueled and serviced it, and an ordnance crew had stuffed it with four five-hundred-pound bombs.

Everything in New Guinea was wet or rotten or stank—or all three. The sweaty seat was a minor matter, and Kyser settled into it and situated himself behind the B-25's control yoke. To his right, his copilot shimmied between the seats and likewise sat down. Richard Whitman was a big man, new to the squadron and new to combat. When he was seated, his shoulder almost touched Kyser's.

Elsewhere in the aircraft four other men readied their positions. The navigator, Homer Stine, sat at his little desk behind the two pilots and fussed with a heavily creased chart. Farther back and out of view beyond the bomb bay, Marshall Marks checked his rack of radio equipment. And Charles Sebastian, the flight engineer and top turret gunner, arranged ammunition for his guns. Also out of view was Sam Vojnovich, the new gunner. The muted clump of footsteps and the clank of metal on metal told Kyser that he was also situating his weapons and ammunition.

Kyser double-checked the various controls and switches as well as the panel behind the control yoke. There were holes in it where instruments were missing. The paint was chipped or worn away in many places, and everything in the cockpit wore a patina of dust and hard use even though the bomber had been rolled out of the factory only a year or so earlier. Still, the tired olive green machine was functional. Worn as it was, like a reliable work truck, it could still carry its crew and its guns and a load of bombs to the target and back. Such a task didn't require shiny paint or a full complement of instruments.

The B-25's nose was painted with a name, *Here's Howe*. The aircraft had been passed down from another unit, and Kyser had no idea who Howe was or how he did things. Or even if he was still alive.

The chuffing cough of an engine coming to life caught Kyser's attention. He looked across the airfield's earthen revetments and saw propellers turning on other squadron aircraft. The clouds of oily blue smoke exhausted by the engines were quickly blown away as the propellers came up to speed. On the ground, Kyser's crew chief nodded and gave him a thumbs-up. Kyser hauled back on the control yoke and turned it one way and then the other, simultaneously stepping on the rudders. He twisted in his seat to see as much of the aircraft as possible and noted that the ailerons, elevators, and rudders responded freely to his inputs. That done, he leaned across Whitman to check the right engine, then turned back and made certain that no one stood in the arc of the left engine's propeller. He and Whitman ran through the start checklist, and a moment or so later both of *Here's Howe*'s engines added their syrupy purr to the rumble that rolled across the airfield.

Kyser's unit, the 500th Bomb Squadron, was one of four assigned to the 345th Bomb Group, which was newly arrived at Dobodura from the airfield complex at Port Moresby. On that day, December 26, 1943, the Marines were landing at Cape Gloucester on the western end of New Britain, 225 miles to the north. Earlier that morning the four squadrons of the 345th had launched a total of thirty-nine aircraft to hit Japanese positions in the hills beyond the landing beaches. It had been a textbook-perfect affair that the 345th's leadership was anxious to repeat with twenty-four aircraft on this second mission of the day.

Kyser watched a vortex of dust swirl into the muggy air behind the squadron's lead aircraft as its pilot advanced the throttles and moved onto the taxiway. His own crew chief ducked under *Here's Howe*'s wings to pull the wheel chocks and then reappeared to signal that the way was clear for Kyser to taxi from the revetment. Kyser eased the throttles forward, released the brakes, and joined the line of B-25s headed for the runway.

A few minutes later, the 500th's aircraft stopped at one of Dobodura's eleven runways. There, the crews waited only a few minutes until the takeoff time, 1300. When the hour arrived they individually taxied onto the runway at thirty-second intervals and started their takeoff runs.

When it was his turn, Kyser checked his controls again as he rolled onto the runway. Already, a whirling shroud of propeller-whipped dirt veiled the far end. Kyser aligned the big ship with the center of the runway and made certain it was tracking straight before pushing the throttles to takeoff power. The two Wright Cyclone R-2600 radial engines—mounted close to the cockpit—accelerated the aircraft with a roar that made conversation impossible.

Once airborne, with the landing gear tucking itself away, Kyser let the nose of the aircraft drop slightly toward the horizon so that the bomber picked up speed more rapidly. Ahead of him, he spotted the other aircraft in his squadron turning toward the coastline, and he maneuvered to expedite the rendezvous. At the same time, he and Whitman scanned the cockpit instruments and visually checked the engines. *Here's Howe* was performing as it should.

Charles Howard led the 500th that day, and Kyser was one of his two wingmen. Catching Howard, he slid into position just to his left. The other wingman was already joined on Howard's right side. The squadron's other three-ship flight came together slightly behind them and to the right. Ahead, orbiting over the Gona Wreck—a partially sunk Japanese transport—was the 498th Bomb Squadron, which was leading the group that day, and the 499th. Behind Howard and Kyser and the rest of the 500th, the six aircraft of the 501st Bomb Squadron made up the rear of the 345th's formation.

Once joined, the group's twenty-four B-25 Mitchells turned northwest toward Finschafen. There, they picked up an escort of P-39 fighters before arcing north toward Cape Gloucester and Borgen Bay, where elements of the 1st Marine Division were coming ashore. Killing the Japanese opposing the Marines was the objective of the 345th's flyers that day.

Kyser passed control of the aircraft to Whitman, then stretched as much as he could in the tight confines of the cockpit. He watched Whitman for a moment or two and then, assured that the other man could handle the aircraft, took in the view. The formation flew at only a couple hundred feet above the water and sped along at just under two hundred miles per hour. Kyser enjoyed the sense of speed imparted by flying so low over the wave tops; the pair of seagulls that flashed past the windscreen underscored that speed. Below, the water was a deep blue-black marked by frothy whitecaps. And although he couldn't see them, Kyser knew that man-eating sharks cruised just below the surface.

He counted the aircraft to his front, then looked out both sides to see what he could of the remainder of the formation. Just above, the little P-39s weaved back and forth. Not much higher, a layer of clouds obscured the sun. Behind Whitman, Homer Stine checked his watch and made a mark on his chart. So long as the formation stayed together, Stine's navigational savvy wasn't needed. But in the event *Here's Howe* became separated from the rest of the group, Stine would get them home.

Kyser took the controls from Whitman a short time later as Umboi Island came into view. The next checkpoint was Sakar Island. However, the 345th's formation leaned away from Sakar. Squinting skyward, Kyser spied the reason. A dogfight swirled above it. So far away, the combatants resembled a swarm of bees—friend was indistinguishable from foe. Regardless, there was no good reason to get into the thick of it, and the B-25 pilots stayed clear.

The B-25s put the island behind them with an easy right-hand turn to the southeast. So low, the pilots were careful not to drop a wing into the water. At the same time, they took special care not to run into each other. Kyser sat taller in his seat to see over *Here's Howe*'s nose and worked the throttles and flight controls instinctively. The B-25 was notable for the degree of muscle required to fly it well. Once Kyser brought the aircraft out of the turn, he exhaled, shrugged his shoulders, and dropped down with the rest of the group to only a few dozen feet above the water. The two, three-ship formations that made up each squadron came abreast of each other.

The classic panorama of an opposed amphibious invasion presented itself to the 345th's crews. Smoke from the two enemy airfields at Cape Gloucester rose to their right front. To the left was a line of five American destroyers. A Japanese bomber pulled out of its dive, and one of the ships erupted into a massive fireball. Other enemy aircraft attacked the destroyers through curtains of deadly antiaircraft fire. American fighters chased overhead and shot down the attackers they caught. Their victims fell into the sea, trailing vertical arcs of black smoke and orange flames. Ahead and below the 345th, barges and landing craft crisscrossed from the beach to their transport ships and back. The shoreline was crowded with boats, troops, and material. A Japanese dive bomber hit one of the barges, and it exploded.

Kyser spotted another enemy dive bomber in the distance; it flew a parallel path to the right of the 345th's formation. The aircraft turned and attacked the six B-25s of the 499th Bomb Squadron to his front. Bright flashes spat from the top turret of one of the bombers, and the Japanese aircraft—trailing a plume of fuel-fed fire—smashed into the water.

The 345th's B-25s, each carrying a load of four five-hundred-pound bombs, opened their bomb bay doors. Anxious to stay clear of the antiaircraft fire coming from the friendly destroyers, they edged over the landing beach. Another enemy dive bomber appeared in front of them, and several of the B-25 pilots opened fire with their nose guns.

Some of the American gunners in the boats did not recognize the 345th's B-25s for what they were. Perhaps confused by the machine-gun fire coming from the aircraft, the gunners swung their weapons around and against their countrymen. Curtains of antiaircraft fire lashed up at the 345th. The leading two squadrons went largely unscathed, but not so the 500th and the 501st.

Kyser both felt and heard the rounds that smashed into *Here's Howe*. The interphone erupted with calls from his crew telling him what he already knew: the aircraft was on fire. The right engine burned fiercely and failed to respond to its throttle. Likewise, the aircraft's controls were slack. *Here's Howe* made an abrupt, uncommanded turn to the left and fell toward the water. Whitman and Kyser both hauled back on their control yokes, but to no avail. The big copilot, his neck bulging with exertion, turned to Kyser, eyes wide with terror.

Here's Howe exploded just as it crashed into the water. A circular shockwave flattened the waves, and a fiery slick burned atop the water. Little else remained of the aircraft or its crew. In the distance, the remaining 345th crews prepared to drop their bombs.

CHAPTER ONE

"It Couldn't Be Much Worse"

GEORGE C. KENNEY, AT FIVE FEET, SIX INCHES, WAS NOT A BIG MAN. A veteran of World War I, he had served with famed American ace Eddie Rickenbacker and was himself credited with one aerial victory. Since that time, he had distinguished himself as a thinker and an innovator. He pioneered the mounting of guns onto aircraft wings and invented the parachute-retarded aerial bomb. As he advanced in rank between the world wars, he played a large role in crafting American tactics for air warfare.

But most of all, Kenney was a leader who got things done. Personable and energetic—and explosive if necessary—he did the right things at the right time to accomplish tasks that often stymied others. If something could be reasonably achieved by working through the proper processes and procedures, he used those proper processes and procedures. But if they added friction or prevented him from getting done what needed getting done, he swept them aside. This brashness earned him a few detractors but also a great many admirers.

Fortunately, Henry "Hap" Arnold, head of the United States Army Air Forces (USAAF), was an admirer. Arnold, a man of action himself, sent Kenney to take over air operations in the Southwest Pacific where he was to serve under Douglas MacArthur, the supreme commander of Allied Forces in the Southwest Pacific Area—SWAPA. Kenney arrived during early August 1942 to discover that the various air organizations in Australia and New Guinea were teetering on the edge of catastrophe.

Those air organizations were too often understrength in men and material, cobbled together with pieces and parts of other organizations, and wanting for everything. Many of the aircraft and much of the equipment was left over from the disastrous fighting in the Netherlands East Indies. Bare handfuls of heavy bombers based in Australia flew ill-coordinated and mostly ineffective raids against the Japanese after staging through Port Moresby in New Guinea.

Fighter units flew hard-worn P-39s and P-40s that were equal to their Japanese counterparts only in the most expert hands. A-24 dive bombers—the USAAF variant of the Douglas SDB—proved short-legged and slow, while B-25s, B-26s, and A-20s were more effective but not numerous enough.

Shortages of aircraft and equipment aside, Kenney found a stunning morass of inept leadership, conflicting lines of command, poor communications and logistics, bad morale, and a pervasive attitude of disinterest and resignation that bordered on dereliction. He understated the situation as "really chaotic."[1] The men in the fighting organizations were in bad health, and poorly fed and cared for. Moreover, they were undertrained for the type of flying demanded of them. There seemed little doubt that New Guinea would soon be given up to the Japanese.

It was a mess perfectly suited to Kenney's skills. "One thing was certain," he noted. "No matter what I accomplished, it would be an improvement. It couldn't be much worse."[2] He made clear to MacArthur—whom he genuinely liked—that he intended to make dramatic changes that would produce even more dramatic results. Immediately, headquarters staffs were thinned and moved closer to the fighting. Paperwork was reduced or eliminated. Australian and American aircrews—which were commingled in many of the same units—were separated. Command relationships were streamlined, and deadwood, sick, and exhausted personnel were sent home. Just as important, support organizations were ordered to support, and much-needed material and equipment was pulled from warehouses in Australia and sent to the units fighting in New Guinea.

Those fighting units received similar attention. Kenney's squadrons were so badly broken that very few aircraft were serviceable. Accordingly, he personally scrutinized the location and state of repair of individual aircraft. Such interest by the commander of an air force was unheard of. He extended his style of leadership to his men and gave them carte blanche to take any actions required to make the repairs needed to get their aircraft ready for combat.

Units were inspected, and personnel who warranted awards received them—often on the spot. Importantly, Kenney ensured that his men received better food and directed additional measures to improve their health. But foremost, he put a renewed focus on fighting the war and killing Japanese. Toward that end, he promoted and put in charge the men who were best at it.

Kenney's enthusiasm, energy, and get-it-done-yesterday attitude produced immediate results. Aside from getting the American component of his forces redesignated as the Fifth Air Force, sortie rates improved. And with more competent and aggressive leadership, the effectiveness of those sorties also increased. Rabaul, the main Japanese stronghold in the Southwest Pacific, was attacked regularly, as were all points—and shipping—in between. Kenney especially endeared himself to MacArthur as he organized his aircraft and crews to move men, equipment, and supplies to and around New Guinea in a series of brilliant campaigns that outmaneuvered the Japanese army and put it on the defensive.

Indeed, Kenney showed MacArthur that his little air force could do things that no one previously thought possible. And MacArthur rewarded him with a free hand. "He said he didn't care how my gang was handled, how they looked, how they dressed, how they behaved, or what they did do, as long as they would fight, shoot down Japs, and put bombs on the targets."[3] Of Kenney's unorthodox way of operating, MacArthur declared, "Oh, George was born three hundred years too late. He's just a natural-born pirate."[4]

Still, although much improved, the Allied air situation in the Southwest Pacific as 1942 gave way to 1943 was far from assured. Although the USAAF had more aircraft there than in any other combat theater, this was largely because it was the only theater in which fighting had been ongoing since the United States entered the war. The fact was that because the Allies had agreed that Germany should be defeated first, the bulk of the units formed at that time were being staged for combat against the Nazis.

Consequently, aircraft, men, and material from the United States dribbled into the theater only sporadically. And many of those resources were diverted out of Kenney's control and over to the critical—and desperate—Guadalcanal campaign. Existing stocks of aircraft parts were depleted, and the scores of wrecked and worn-out aircraft that could be readily cannibalized were picked clean. In fact, Kenney was running short of the sow's ears out of which he was making silk purses. What he needed were fresh units from the States—fully equipped and provisioned, fully manned and fully trained.

—◦—

Kenney got what he wanted, but not immediately. Then in training, the 345th Bombardment Group (M) was ordered into existence by the Third Air Force on September 6, 1942, and officially formed on November 11, 1942, at Columbia Army Air Base in South Carolina. A B-25 unit, its men were sourced from all over the still-growing, nationwide web of Army Air Forces training organizations. However, the initial cadre was drawn from the 309th Bombardment Group (M), which was a Columbia-based B-25 training unit. The 345th was organized into four squadrons with sixteen aircraft each: the 498th, 499th, 500th, and 501st. The unit included a broad spectrum of support elements—medical, engineering, administrative, intelligence, operations, logistics, and so forth—that were responsible for getting and keeping the group's men and aircraft ready for combat. Fully manned, the group would grow to more than a thousand men.

The group's commander, Jarred V. Crabb, was well regarded. Irving Horwitz, one of the 345th's original navigators, recalled, "He wasn't a very big man, but he made a big impression. He said, 'Anyone can fly, but not everyone can be a combat pilot. I'm not only going to teach you how to fly in combat, but I'm also going to teach you how to be an officer and a gentleman.'" Horwitz remembered that Crabb "was a real leader."[5]

The 345th's first aircraft—a mix of well-used B-25Cs and B-25Ds that were nonetheless good enough for the training that had to be done—started trickling into the unit at the end of November 1942. Crabb led the group through its standup and preparations for combat with common sense and a steady hand. Small infractions such as failing to shave earned offenders a night shivering in a pup tent rather than formal military discipline. Never did the focus shift from preparing for combat, and emphasis was put not only on good flying but on good aircraft maintenance and support functions. Indeed, under Crabb's stewardship the 345th stayed ahead of its training schedule despite the vagaries of the winter weather.

The B-25 "Mitchell"—with which the 345th was equipped through the entire war—took a while to happen. North American Aviation flew its first twin-engine bomber at the end of 1936. A portly and ugly aircraft, variously designated as the NA-21, the NA-39, and the XB-21, it generally outperformed its chief competitor, the equally unattractive Douglas B-18. However, its performance advantage was not enough to justify a price nearly double that of the Douglas offering. Consequently, North American came out of the competition with little more than expensive, hard-earned experience.

By 1938, the United States was serious about readying for the coming European conflict, and the Army Air Corps issued a specification that called for a medium bomber capable of carrying a twelve-hundred-pound payload to a distance of twelve hundred miles at an airspeed of two hundred miles per hour. Drawing from its experience with the NA-39, North American designed an aircraft, the NA-40, which showed good promise. It was bigger and faster than its predecessor and had distinctive twin vertical stabilizers. Initial tests at the start of 1939 turned up typical teething problems and additionally showed that its two eleven-hundred-horsepower Pratt & Whitney R-1830 radial engines were too small to achieve the desired performance. The NA-40 was modified with more powerful sixteen-hundred-horsepower Wright Cyclone R-2600 engines, while various fixes were applied against the other problems.

The result, the NA-40B, was a capable performer that the Army Air Corps turned down in favor of Douglas's A-20. The aircraft also failed to secure orders from overseas customers, most notably Great Britain and France. Again, North American's try for a medium-bomber contract yielded little more than hard knocks. That the prototype was destroyed in a crash on April 11, 1939, was salt in the wound.

Yet North American persisted, and the third time proved the charm. By early 1939 the Army Air Corps was in a full sprint to grow and modernize its forces. It issued a new set of specifications during March—even before the NA-40B prototype crashed—calling for a bigger, more capable medium bomber. This design had to carry a twenty-four-hundred-pound payload, twice as much as its predecessor. And it had to haul it just as far, twelve hundred miles, at an airspeed of three hundred miles per hour, which was half again as fast as the previous specification.

Their egos were bruised, but after two failed attempts North American's engineers were more experienced than ever. The company's offering, the NA-62, was the design that ultimately became famous as the B-25. The Army Air Corps was so needful of capable aircraft that it didn't even wait for North American to produce a prototype. Both the NA-62 and Martin's counterpart, which evolved into the B-26, were ordered from the design stage directly into production during September 1939. The war in Europe was finally underway, and the Army Air Corps needed good aircraft as fast as it could get them.

The type was designated the B-25 Mitchell in honor of William "Billy" Mitchell, the Army firebrand who had advocated so vigorously for a strategic air force during the 1920s at the cost of his career. North American put the aircraft into production as rapidly as possible. In so doing, changes were incorporated as needed, so long as they didn't unnecessarily disrupt the manufacturing line. One of the first and most apparent design alterations was to the shoulder-mounted wings, which initially had a gentle dihedral, or upward, sweep along their entire length. This dihedral caused handling issues, which obviously weren't expected. Consequently, after less than a dozen aircraft were produced, the outer wings, at a point just beyond the engines, were given a very slight downward inclination, or anhedral. The modification fixed the problem, and the resulting droop-winged appearance remained distinctive of the type through its entire service life.

Powered by two Wright Cyclone R-2600 radial engines, the B-25 had twin vertical stabilizers and a glazed nose that accommodated the bombardier. Its substantial, workmanlike appearance indicated its ruggedness. Although it was modified throughout its life, this look of tough and deadly competence never changed.

The Army Air Corps received its first B-25A in 1941. This initial variant, as was typical, was used chiefly to explore the type's capabilities and shortcomings. Only 40 were produced, and they were followed by the B-25B, of which 120 were delivered. This model eliminated the tail turret and added a dorsal turret and a retractable ventral turret, each equipped with two .50-caliber machine guns. It was the B-25B that Jimmy Doolittle's raiders flew against Tokyo from the USS *Hornet* on April 18, 1942.

The B-25Cs and B-25Ds that the 345th initially flew incorporated improvements that were informed by experience with the earlier models. These included upgraded variants of the same Wright R-2600 engines that powered the initial models, anti-ice and de-ice capabilities, and an observation dome for the navigator. A pair of .50-caliber machine guns was also added to the nose. Both models, the B-25C and the B-25D, were essentially identical, the only distinction being that the B-25C was manufactured in Inglewood, California, while the B-25D was produced in Kansas City, Kansas. At medium altitude, the aircraft had a maximum speed of 284 miles per hour and a cruising speed of 233 miles per hour. Those speeds declined at lower altitudes.

In truth, through the type's life, there were many variations within the production runs of each model of the B-25. This was especially true in the case of armament and fuel tanks. And myriad smaller changes were introduced that made operations and maintenance easier and more effective—not to mention the modifications that were never apparent to the crews but which eased manufacturing. Moreover, the number of field-expedient changes made by units after they received their aircraft was considerable.

A B-25 crew during that period was standardized at six personnel. The pilot, more formally known as the airplane commander, sat in the cockpit's left seat and was responsible not only for flying the aircraft but also for leading the crew. Ultimately, like the captain of a ship, he was accountable for the well-being of his aircraft and men and for what they did or did not accomplish.

The copilot sat to the pilot's right; he was typically less experienced than the pilot but was still expected to be able to handle the aircraft and crew well enough to execute the mission in the event that the pilot, for whatever reason, could not. He was the pilot's "right-hand man" and helped with crew coordination and leadership. And he periodically did the actual flying during particularly long flights so that the pilot could rest.

The navigator sat behind the pilot and copilot at a little desk that faced to the rear of the aircraft. He was responsible for knowing the aircraft's exact location at all times. He tracked its course and the current weather and gave the pilot airspeed and course updates and other information as required to get to the target and back home. During multiaircraft missions, the lead navigator was responsible for getting the formation where it needed to be, but the navigator aboard each aircraft had to be ready to chart a course in the event that his plane was forced to turn back to base or was separated from the rest of the formation by weather, enemy action, or mechanical difficulties.

The bombardier sat in the very front of the aircraft on the right side of the glazed nose and was responsible—along with the pilot—for ensuring that the aircraft's bombs hit the target. He was intimately familiar with the sighting equipment that guided the aircraft to the exact point in the sky at which the bombs had to be released in order to hit the designated aim point. And he was the onboard expert on the actual bombs, racks, fuzes, switches, and so forth. Once airborne, if there was a problem with the bombs, he was expected to fix it. He also knew how to load, aim, and fire the flexible .50-caliber machine gun installed in the nose.

The radio operator, also known as the radio-gunner, sat behind the bomb bay in the rear of the fuselage and faced the left side of the aircraft. He was responsible for the long- and short-range radios, as well as the radio navigation and landing equipment. He was an expert in Morse code. When required, particularly over the target, he usually operated the waist or tail guns—when they were later installed.

The engineer, or engineer-gunner, usually positioned himself behind the cockpit and was trained on the mechanical workings of virtually every aspect of the aircraft. Together with the pilot and copilot, he monitored the performance of all the aircraft's various components, including the engines as well as the electrical, fuel, hydraulic, oil, and pneumatic systems—among others. As required, he helped transfer fuel and troubleshoot problems and actuated switches and valves and other controls. He was also a gunner and could operate any of the crew-served weapons. Along with the pilot, he briefed and debriefed with the crew chief on the ground about an aircraft's issues or peculiarities.

The gunner usually operated the top turret or tail guns—if they were installed. He was an expert marksman and not only knew how to load, aim, and fire the guns but was additionally skilled at aircraft identification—both friendly and enemy. When guns jammed or otherwise would not fire, he put them back in service. When needed, he also helped elsewhere in the aircraft as extra muscle or another set of eyes.

As the 345th's crews gained experience with their B-25s, they sharpened their bombing techniques against targets at nearby Lake Murray, while aerial gunnery training was performed on the ranges at Myrtle Beach. Wilmer "Buck" Fowler was a gunner with the 345th's 500th Bomb Squadron and wrote to his sister about firing at a series of ground targets: "I let go with my share of 'typewriting.' The instructor was so well pleased with my marksmanship that he told me he would qualify me, even though I had only flown two [training] missions."

But things soon went badly for Fowler. "I was very well pleased with myself when, suddenly, I felt my noon chow regurgitating." Afraid of being found unfit for flying duty due to airsickness, Fowler tried to hide his condition from the instructor. He surreptitiously puked first into his handkerchief, then into his ball cap, and finally inside the front of his flying suit. As the aircraft winged for home, he was certain that his sickness had gone unnoticed. "The instructor moved to me, smiled, and said, 'I saw you, kid; but if a guy is man enough to try as hard as that to hide it, I'm sport enough not to see anything.'" Fowler got a passing mark.

In his letter, Fowler also made clear his feelings about the rationing of goods that the nation's citizenry was enduring. "The more of this I go through, the more bitter I become against slackers, complaining civilians and black market dealers. I can't imagine a person griping because he can't get gas, sugar, or meat, while we are here taking risks and struggling to keep from puking while we fly vicious circles for hours at a stretch. Sister," he continued, "I know our family doesn't mind the various rationings, and I wish all families accepted their patriotic duties as willingly."[6]

Navigation exercises took the aircrews all over the eastern half of the United States and sometimes beyond. The aircrews learned to fly alone in their own aircraft, then in small formations, before operating as full squadrons and then as an entire group. The 345th's records noted, "Combat mission problems left 'Tunis,' better known as Birmingham, Alabama, a smoking ruin."

Virtually all the group's training was performed during the winter months, and the men recalled the cold as much as anything else. William Miller was a young radio operator with the 345th's 501st Bomb Squadron. He was assigned to guard duty on the flight line during a particularly miserable night. "It rained and was cold—I had never been so cold in all my life," he said. In the distance he heard a jeep stopping at the different guard posts. "It was the new second-in-command, Lieutenant Colonel [Clinton] True. We were well-briefed on him—West Point graduate and all. A real hard nose."

The jeep squeaked to a halt near where Miller guarded his aircraft. True stepped down into the wet and started toward him. "My knees shook," Miller said. "What should I do?" In accordance with his orders, Miller shouted into the night for True to stop. "He kept coming. I put a round in the chamber [of my rifle] and shouted halt again. This time, he stopped. 'For God's sake, soldier, it's the officer of the day,' he said."

Miller ordered True to take four steps forward. He then directed him to put his identification card on the ground and to step back. "His wallet got soaking wet," Miller said. He verified True's identity, returned the card, and answered a few perfunctory questions. "That was my first meeting with our new chief, and I figured my last," Miller said.[7] Despite Miller's misgivings, True appreciated his adherence to regulations, climbed back aboard the jeep, and continued his rounds.

Indeed, the time was remembered as "a cold winter, against a background of lukewarm war news from the Pacific and Europe and Africa." The melancholy war news was tragically underwritten during the training period by a handful of accidents that claimed both men and machines, including the 499th's commanding officer, Buell Bankston, and his crew.

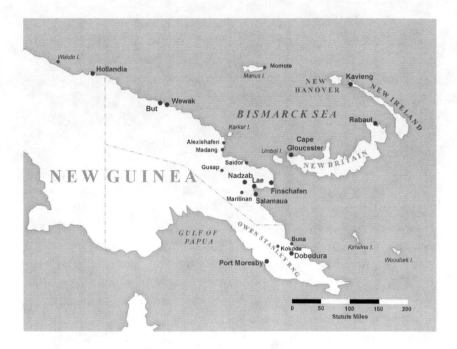

Bankston crashed his aircraft in a winter storm during a trip to Houston, where his wife was giving birth to their first child.[8]

Still, the men were well trained, well equipped, and well fed. The mess hall was noted for serving steaks "so big they hung over the edge of the plate." The 1942 Christmas feed, which included traditional turkey and dressing as well as fruit cocktail and dinner mints, was particularly memorable. And the officers had such a good time at their New Year's Eve party a few days later that the building in which they celebrated literally burned to the ground.

The training, including field maneuvers at an old Civilian Conservation Corps camp at Aiken, South Carolina, continued through the holidays and beyond at a torrid pace. During early March 1943, near the end of its scheduled training period, the 345th left Columbia for the airfield at Walterboro, South Carolina, "a hospitable whistle stop with runways," for a final few weeks of preparation.

The men generally assumed that they were destined for combat over North Africa, the Mediterranean, or Europe. Much of their training and many of their briefings focused on fighting the Germans. When they drew additional cold-weather flying gear, it seemed that orders across the Atlantic were imminent. The notion was reinforced by visits by personnel from Great Britain's Royal Air Force and receipt of the group's first factory-fresh B-25D toward the end of March—it arrived fully winterized. "Then," noted the 498th Bomb Squadron, "when the new plane's equipment was supplemented with jungle kits, even the rumor mongers were baffled. We didn't know where we were going."[9]

The possibilities were narrowed by mid-April 1943, by which time the 345th was equipped with a full complement of new B-25Ds. It was then that aircrews from the group's four squadrons—together with a small contingent of maintenance and engineering personnel—left Walterboro for Savannah Army Airfield. There, the new aircraft underwent a round of modifications and upgrades. A few days later, the crews hopscotched their B-25s across the country to Sacramento, California. At that point it was apparent that, whatever its specific destination might be, the 345th was headed to the Pacific to fight the Japanese.

While the aircraft were being modified, Buck Fowler wrote to his sister Edna from where he was staying at the Hotel Senator. He described how the three B-25s of his particular flight were named. "Here are the names: *Boom-Boom*, the flight leader; *Dittum Dattum*, our plane; *Wattum Chew*, the third. Get it? *The Three Little Fishes*. Corny? We're fighting proud of the names."[10] In fact, the three names came from the catchy and nonsensical refrain of the comedic song *Three Little Fishes*, performed by Kay Kyser and his group, which reached the top of the charts in 1939.

In the same letter, Fowler offered his sister some brotherly advice. "You are doing a good service by enlisting into the USO, but remember: Prenez garde [Take care]! Most soldiers have unethical notions about fun. They know that nobody but them knows where they are; so they are careless and irresponsible. Be very careful."

With their aircraft gone, the 345th's ground personnel busied themselves with packing material and equipment and joining additional men to the roster. The most maddening task was "placing the equipment in overseas crates and then rebuilding the crates when they didn't meet with the approval of the super-critical inspecting engineer." On April 16, the four squadrons loaded themselves and their gear aboard two trains and headed west. "Through Macon, Memphis and Little Rock we went, stopping once a day for calisthenics in some railroad yard, eating from a mess kitchen which had been established in a baggage car, dozing, reading and playing cards throughout the day and sleeping in the berths at night."[11]

The trains turned northwest at Pueblo, Colorado, and climbed through the Rockies before dropping down the other side and passing through Salt Lake City. On the seventh day the men—stiff and bleary-eyed—stumbled from the train at Camp Stoneman in Pittsburg, California, twenty miles northeast of Oakland. Then followed several more days of administrative tasks before they moved to San Francisco and boarded the SS *President Johnson*.

Launched decades earlier in 1903 as the SS *Manchuria*, the ship was the largest ever built in the United States up to that time and served as a passenger liner and freighter. During World War I it was pressed into service to ferry troops and equipment to Europe. Later renamed the SS *President Johnson*, the ship was operated by various civilian shipping lines until just before World War II, when it was pressed into government service again—as were most big commercial ships. Configured to transport thousands of men and their equipment rather than for comfort, the aging ship was dank, dark, and exceedingly crowded. The bunks were arranged in pairs, stacked three high. One wit jested that the ship hadn't been taken by King Neptune because he didn't want it.

The SS *President Johnson* slipped its moorings on May 1, 1943, and, loaded with three thousand men from various units, nosed its way under the Golden Gate Bridge, out of San Francisco Bay, and into the Pacific. The 345th's ground element was on its way to combat.

And so were its aircraft. After flying across the country the previous month, the aircrews flew their B-25s into Sacramento's McClellan Field, where they were modified once more. In particular, they were fitted with the long-range fuel tanks necessary for the next leg of their journey—a twenty-one-hundred-nautical-mile overwater flight to Hickam Field, Hawaii. While the aircraft were modified, the crews had little to do, and most of them found lodging in town, where they enjoyed what the area had to offer.

Finally, during late April and early May, the 345th's aircraft were flown to Hamilton Field, north of San Francisco. Unnecessary equipment was removed from the aircraft to save weight, as were the gunners, bombardiers, and other ancillary personnel, who were sent to Hawaii via transport aircraft. Finally, the bare-bones crews took off in the dark of very early morning to ensure a daylight arrival at Hawaii. The flights—which typically lasted twelve hours or more—were mostly uneventful, although one aircraft and its crew from the 499th Bomb Squadron was lost without a trace.

At Hickam, the long-range fuel tanks were removed, and smaller auxiliary fuel tanks were installed in the bomb bays. The gunners and bombardiers also rejoined their crews. In the meantime, the men had time off to appreciate the exotic nature of the place before starting south, usually in formations of two or three as aircraft were made ready. The crews typically flew one leg per day with Christmas Island (Kiritimati) as the first stop. Although the routes varied, the one most used included stops at Canton Island, Fiji, New Caledonia, and finally Amberley Field, near Brisbane, Australia. There, the first crews touched down on May 8, 1943.[12]

Although the segments of these routes were shorter than that from San Francisco to Hawaii, they were still long and overwater. Even a small navigational error could put a crew so far off course as to be forever lost. Likewise, mechanical failures could force a crew into the water prematurely. Throughout the course of the war, many aircraft from many units simply disappeared. For instance, the fate of the Nandi-bound crew of Clifford Bryant after they got airborne out of Tutuila Island is unknown. The 499th Bomb Squadron's report merely stated, "No word was received from the crew, nor was the airplane observed, either in flight or crashed, hence no details are known. The airplane simply failed to arrive at Nandi."

It should be noted that the Curtiss-Wright Aeronautical Corporation, the manufacturer of the B-25's R-2600 engines, was under investigation during this period. The use of shoddy material and parts, in combination with inadequate supervision and poorly performed inspections, lay at the root of performance and reliability issues. One company inspector complained, "The company was cheating on inspections all the time." Other accusations included falsification of tests and bilking of the government at the expense of the safety of aircrews.[13]

The investigating committee, headed by Senator Harry S. Truman, noted problems and helped inform changes. It found that although there were irregularities, the performance of the engines was satisfactory. On the other hand, long overwater flights such as the 345th was making to get into theater—and would make throughout the rest of the war—demanded highly reliable engines. There is little doubt that some small percentage of the group's losses was due to engine failure.

Talmadge "Tal" Epps was an engineer-gunner with the 500th Bomb Squadron and—with the rest of his crew—was flown into Amberley on a B-24 after his pilot was injured at New Caledonia in a jeep accident. After being paid and assigned to a barracks, the men traveled to nearby Ipswich, where they toured the local sights. Epps recalled that, so far from home and with combat operations imminent, they were "scared as hell inside, while pretending not to be."

Epps and several others went to a movie theater. The Australian national anthem was played, followed by "The Star Spangled Banner." "And a message flashed on the screen: 'We wish to welcome our American cousins.' This message, at that moment in my life, caused a warm glow to flood over me. The message didn't say, 'friends,' or 'good neighbors,' it said 'cousins.' I took that to mean we were family."[14]

As it developed, Amberley was not the 345th's final destination. In fact, the squadrons were ordered further north in Queensland for rest and training, and still more aircraft modifications, while they waited for the *President Johnson* to arrive in theater. The headquarters element went to Garbutt at Townsville, a major Australian base that also hosted American units. The 345th's squadrons were sent to outlying airfields—the 498th to Woodstock, the 499th and 500th to Reid River, and the 501st to Charters Towers.

In the meantime, the *President Johnson* plowed south across the Pacific while the 345th's men made themselves as comfortable as they could. Hygiene became an issue as the men constantly perspired and the limited saltwater showers were inadequate. Consequently, they stank. Many of the men couldn't stand the conditions below decks and slept topside. Ben Miller, a communications man with the 499th Bomb Squadron, recalled that a friend "used my bunk for storing his gear and mine while I slept on deck as the foul air made me sick."[15] Miller had competition, as sleeping space in the open air was limited, and men started staking their claims during the afternoons.

As soldiers always have, the men groused about the food. Especially reviled were the hardboiled eggs featured at nearly every meal. A formal calisthenics program, intended to keep the men fit and alert, was abandoned after a short time due to lack of interest. Drills of all sorts—the most unnerving being abandon-ship exercises—occupied the men, and boxing matches were held on some evenings. But aside from eating and sleeping, the men spent most of their time reading, playing cards, or gambling.

Apart from a mechanical breakdown that left the ship dead in the water one night, the voyage was mostly uneventful. However, another event, poorly documented, marked the passage. The *President Johnson's* escort was a Free French corvette, unnamed by the 345th's official history. It was separated from the *President Johnson* during a storm but ultimately rejoined the big ship and resumed its escort duties. Not long afterward it made contact with a Japanese submarine, as described by the 498th Bomb Squadron:

> *It was shortly afterward during a sub[marine] alert, that she reappeared and then we saw great mushrooming columns of water rise up behind her boiling stern and seconds later we'd get the concussion of the depth charges. While we were worrying about whether the sub would be sunk or break loose and sink us, the report came over that the valiant little corvette had destroyed her undersea enemy. Meanwhile the SS [President] Johnson almost had a casualty of another sort. The fascinated GIs had all rushed over to one rail to better watch the excitement and the old craft heeled over to an alarming degree, threatening to capsize. The captain barked some quick orders and the crisis was averted.[16]*

This event was also described by the 345th's 499th Bomb Squadron. It is unclear what actually happened—or exactly where and when, although one 498th Bomb Squadron account indicates it occurred on May 16, 1943.[17] Whether or not an enemy submarine was actually destroyed is not clear. However, the RO-102, commissioned the previous year, was operating with the Imperial Japanese Navy's Eighth Fleet out of Rabaul during this period. It made its last report on May 9, 1943, and was not heard from again.[18] Whether or not it was engaged and sunk by the *President Johnson*'s escort is unknown.

The stifling heat grew worse as the ship sailed farther into the tropical latitudes. Nevertheless, the men endured, and on May 27, 1943, the 345th finally disembarked at Brisbane. One among them didn't leave the ship on his own. Roy Sneed of the 500th Bomb Squadron had been gravely injured while representing the squadron in a boxing match. He later died on the operating table.

The *President Johnson* traded cargoes at Brisbane, while the 345th's men marched to Camp Doomben, a converted racetrack. There they were treated to a stage show by their Australian hosts and a beer bash arranged by the group's commander, Jarred Crabb. "The squadron 'wheels' got to feeling so gay they forgot all about being wheels and threw their dignity to the winds," noted the 498th Bomb Squadron. "But even an alcoholic glow couldn't keep off that winter nip in the air."[19] Indeed, the men were surprised by the dramatic temperature swings—too hot during the day and too cold at night. However, their stay at Brisbane was brief, and they climbed back aboard the *President Johnson* on May 31. After a short stop at Townsville, the ship set course for Port Moresby, New Guinea, and arrived on June 5, 1943.

The Japanese had coveted Port Moresby since early the previous year. In fact, it was the reason behind history's first aircraft carrier clash, when on May 4 and 5, 1942, American and Japanese naval forces traded over-the-horizon air strikes. Although the Americans lost a fleet carrier and the Japanese lost only a light carrier in what came to be known as the Battle of the Coral Sea, the Japanese amphibious assault on Port Moresby was turned back. It was a strategic victory for the Allies and the first of many stinging defeats for Japan.

Strategically located on New Guinea's southeastern coast, just more than three hundred miles from the Australian continent, Port Moresby was much more than a harbor town. Following the start of the war, the Australians and Americans had transformed it into an enormous ground, air, and naval complex. The Japanese wanted not only to eject the Allies from Port Moresby but also to use it as a base from which to interdict lines of communication between the United States and Australia and New Zealand. Moreover it could serve as a base from which to protect the southern approaches to Japan's forces on Rabaul.

Undeterred by their setback in the Coral Sea—and the subsequent debacle at Midway—the Japanese put troops ashore at Buna, on New Guinea's northeastern coast, during July and August 1942. Their objective was Port Moresby. From Buna they slogged nearly a hundred miles up the jungle-choked Kokoda Track and over the Owen Stanley Range. It was a remarkable feat. Still, short of supplies and their ranks thinned by fighting and disease, the Japanese were stopped by Australian infantry units only a few miles from Port Moresby during September 1942. The remaining Japanese troops—hungry, demoralized, and racked with disease—fled into the jungle. Those who could not reach Buna succumbed to starvation or one or more tropical illnesses.

By the time the 345th's men arrived at Port Moresby, the danger of a Japanese ground assault had passed, although nighttime air raids were common. The men disembarked from the now familiar *President Johnson* and climbed aboard trucks that took them over rough roads to their new homes. As they started out, swatting and slapping at all manner of biting bugs, they passed under a large sign which read, "Through these portals pass the best damn mosquito bait in the world."

The Port Moresby complex included seven operational airfields, and the 345th's four squadrons were initially assigned to three of them. The 498th and 500th were dropped off at Jackson Airfield, which was more commonly called "Seven-Mile Airdrome" because of its distance from Port Moresby. The 501st set up shop at Schwimmer, or "Fourteen-Mile Airdrome," while the 499th was taken to Durand Airfield, which was also called "Seventeen-Mile Airdrome." Later, at the end of September, the 499th vacated Durand and joined the 501st at Schwimmer.

Living conditions at all the airfields were primitive. This was underscored during the first night when many of the men, with nothing more for shelter than their pup tents, were pummeled by a driving rain. "This was the first of a great deal of wet weather to come and it was just as well we got accustomed to it at the start," noted the 498th. Happily, the next day dawned clear and bright, and the men "worked busily at unloading the ship, re-sorting the jumbled equipment which had become thoroughly mixed up among the four squadrons, and setting up our line and living areas."[20] The acquisition of larger pyramidal tents and sleeping cots a few days later greatly improved everyone's mood.

The 345th's men first encountered New Guinea's natives at Port Moresby. There the black, kinky-haired, nearly naked "fuzzy wuzzies" worked assiduously at loading and unloading cargoes and performing a myriad of menial but important tasks such as clearing brush or repairing roads. The name referred to the great, matted mops of frizzy hair that crowned their heads. It was a term of endearment used by the Australians and copied by the Americans. The fascination of the 345th's men for these strange-looking people was profound: "All feet and hair they seemed at first glance," observed the 498th Bomb Squadron. "Lord what hair—you had to see it to believe it. They were plenty fuzzy all right—those bushy heads were a regular trademark."[21]

Largely sympathetic to the Allies, the natives served in many roles. They had earlier won the hearts of the Australian people during the fighting on the Kokoda Track. During that campaign they carried supplies through the tangled brush and jungle to Australian troops and returned with the wounded. The tenderness with which they treated the injured soldiers was astonishing. An Australian medical report noted,

> *They carried stretchers over seemingly impassable barriers, with the patient reasonably comfortable. The care they give to the patient is magnificent. If night finds the stretcher still on the track, they will find a level spot and build a shelter over the patient. They will make him as comfortable as possible fetch him water and feed him if food is available, regardless of their own needs. They sleep four each side of the stretcher and if the patient moves or requires any attention during the night, this is given instantly. These were the deeds of the "Fuzzy Wuzzy Angels."*[22]

Balancing the admirable service of the natives was the fact, outlined in the same report, that the desertion rate was sometimes high; disease and overwork were mitigating factors. Also, some natives served the Japanese, for which the Australian army meted out harsh punishment; more than two hundred natives were executed.[23] Moreover, the fuzzy wuzzies were sometimes a nuisance, committing petty theft and other small offenses. Still, the Allies were better off because of the service they provided.

The more removed the natives were from the influence of civilization, the more primitive they were. Ben Miller recalled a visit to a village a few miles from Durand Airfield. "The grass-skirted native women were unlike the Hollywood version. They had open sores, were covered with flies and had lumpy tattoos under their skin. The men didn't smile and carried weapons with barbed tips. Having seen enough, we didn't linger, but hightailed it."[24]

As the 345th's ground elements put tools and equipment into place at their new airfields and otherwise readied for action, the aircrews left Australia for Port Moresby beginning on June 20, 1943. Tal Epps, who had been so impressed by the Australians at Ipswich, was among the 500th Bomb Squadron's aircrews at Reid River. "Our plane and full crew—with our new pilot, Second Lieutenant [Lee] Ow—was the last to leave the field," he said. "A jeep drove alongside our plane and signaled the pilot to cut the engines."

Ow shut the aircraft down and conferred briefly with the other man—the squadron's assistant operations officer—before calling for Epps. "I was instructed to take my bags and go with the driver of the jeep to take charge of some equipment that was being shipped by boat to Port Moresby." Epps wasn't happy about the abrupt change of plans or the idea of traveling to New Guinea by ship, but he grabbed his gear, climbed down from the B-25, and was driven away.

The arrival of the group's aircraft at the Port Moresby airfields was marked by many bear hugs and much back slapping as the air and ground elements were together again for the first time since parting at Walterboro, South Carolina. Everyone buckled down, and within days the 345th's men were ready for the combat for which they had trained with such vigor.

In truth, the 345th's first missions were anticlimactic. George Kenney's Fifth Air Force was not as hard-pressed as it had been several months earlier, and he was consequently able to introduce his brand-new bomb group to combat gradually. Accordingly, the 345th was tasked with air-dropping supplies to Australia's 3rd Division, which was engaged in vicious fighting west of Salamaua. Seizing Salamaua, a major Japanese staging base situated on a polyp-shaped peninsula on the northern coast of New Guinea, was a key element of MacArthur's plan to advance northwest across the top of the island. Keeping the Australians well provisioned, a luxury that their desperate Japanese enemies did not enjoy, was critical to the effort.

The 345th's squadrons took off from their Port Moresby airfields almost daily and climbed north, across the rugged Owen Stanley Range. Once clear of the mountains, they descended over poorly charted terrain west of Salamaua, where one set of peaks and valleys resembled the next. Although enemy fire was usually light or nonexistent, the combination of unforgiving terrain and unpredictable—and often violent—weather made the flying quite dangerous. Still, the 345th and other units dropped tons of canisters stuffed with desperately needed material.

While the 345th was getting its teeth into the bit, Tal Epps finally arrived at Jackson Airfield after being pulled from Lee Ow's aircraft in Australia a week earlier. He was no worse for wear after a four-day voyage aboard a Dutch freighter and had safely delivered the equipment put into his custody. But bad news waited for him. "I was informed that Lieutenant Ow and all of our crew had disappeared while flying a mission to resupply Australian troops." Indeed, Ow had crashed on June 27, 1943. The missing air crew report noted, "The airplane was last seen by other crews of this organization to enter a cloud in the valley of the Pilimung vicinity and was never seen again."

In fact, the crash site was discovered the very next day by an Australian infantry brigade five miles from Pilimung. The Australian report declared, "Natives state that they had 'planted the three masters' about twenty feet from where the airplane had crashed, and investigation showed the graves were in good order. No evidence was found of a fourth body."[25] Ow had been flying without a copilot and with only a navigator, gunner, and radioman. Ow and his crew had the sad distinction of being the 345th's first combat casualties.

Although it continued to air-drop supplies, the 345th started dropping bombs and killing Japanese in earnest beginning at the start of July 1943. Most of the missions that month were flown against Salamaua, its airfield, and other nearby targets. American forces made an amphibious landing at Nassau Bay, about fifteen miles southeast of Salamaua, beginning on June 30 and advanced northwest along the coast as their Australian allies attacked from the interior. The Fifth Air Force—including the 345th—was tasked with reducing the capacity of the Japanese to fight.

Accomplishing that task came at a cost, and during this period the 345th suffered its first loss directly attributable to enemy fire. On July 13, the group sent thirty-six B-25s to hit antiaircraft positions at Salamaua. They were joined by another B-25 squadron from the 38th Bomb Group. The takeoff and rendezvous out of Port Moresby were uneventful, as was the flight north over the Owen Stanley Range. An escort of fighters was slated to join the group over the American airfield complex at Dobodura; however, the B-25s were forced to circle for half an hour before they arrived.

The formation pressed on to Salamaua with its fighter escort, and the individual squadrons separated for their assigned targets as they neared the peninsula. Lieutenant Alden Thompson led the 499th Bomb Squadron and, as reported by the squadron's mission report, "saw the wall of ack-ack [antiaircraft fire] in front, but he continued the run." The bomb run was described as "perfect," but so was the aim of the Japanese gunners. "Just as Lieutenant Thompson's bombs were released, his ship was hit by A/A [antiaircraft] fire between the right engine nacelle and the fuselage." The engine caught fire immediately, as did the navigator's position. Thompson let the nose of the aircraft drop as he wrestled it over the water.

The aircraft was doomed. Thompson's two wingmen, Jack George and George Cooper, escorted him away from Salamaua. Jack George's aircraft was also badly damaged, but he and Cooper stayed with the stricken B-25 until Thompson "made a safe and clean landing on the water using no flaps." Notwithstanding the "safe and clean landing," the aircraft sank quickly and took Thompson's wounded bombardier, John Yarborough, with it. The rest of the crew flailed their way clear of the sinking wreckage, and "Lieutenant Cooper saw five of the crew swimming in the water and observed five Australian soldiers on the beach directing two natives who were launching two dugout canoes."

The canoes never reached Thompson's men. It was many hours before Thompson and the rest of his crew paddled through the rough water to shore. Along the way, another badly injured crewman, Lawrence Davis, died and was left to slip beneath the waves. When they finally splashed ashore, Thompson and his men made contact with an Australian unit and were returned to Port Moresby within a few days.

The bombing missions that the 345th flew during this time were executed using the same tactics in which the men had trained in the States and, more recently, in Australia. They were flown at altitudes ranging from a few thousand feet up to ten thousand feet, or a bit more—mostly depending on the weather. And the pilots flew straight and level at precise airspeeds so that the bombardiers could guide the aircraft to the exact point in three dimensions at which the bombs had to be dropped to achieve the most accurate hits.

Such tactics demanded precision airmanship and were accountable to the cruel mistress of physics; a bomb released only slightly out of parameters could not hit the intended target. For instance, bombs dropped from too high landed long, as did bombs dropped too late. Conversely, bombs dropped from altitudes lower than planned fell short, as did those dropped too early. Release airspeeds that were too fast sent the bombs long, whereas airspeeds that were too slow caused them to fall short. And, of course, heading errors—and aircraft not in balanced flight—caused bombs to fall left or right of the target. Combinations of errors could cancel or compound each other, and winds could also blow the bombs off course. All these factors made conventional aerial bombing a maddening science.

But so long as the target was large enough that it could be readily spotted in time to fly the aircraft into position for a good bomb run, the medium-altitude attacks—for which the B-25 was especially designed—produced satisfactory results. For instance, airfields, harbor facilities, and warehouse complexes were readily struck from medium altitude. But even then, good results were not always achieved. During the group's July 10, 1943, attack on the Logui #2 airstrip near Salamaua, the 501st Bomb Squadron's results were underwhelming, as more than half its bombs—dropped from eight thousand feet—missed the target. These results were not atypical.

Although medium-altitude tactics were reasonably effective against larger targets, they were much less so against small moving targets such as ships. And the missions were not even worth flying if whatever needed to be bombed was hidden in the jungle or brush. Indeed, it was almost impossible to hit enemy troop concentrations unless their positions were somehow marked, usually by white phosphorous smoke rounds fired by friendly artillery units.

In fact, on July 22, 1943, three of the group's squadrons were charged with bombing "the [Japanese] camp area on the ridge just north of Komiatum," located south of Salamaua. The measures taken to ensure the best possible results and to avoid bombing nearby friendly troops were very unusual and only possible because the Japanese air defenses in the area were so thin. "A practice run was made on target," recorded the 498th, "heading approximately 360 degrees, altitude 6,000 feet, in order that the target might be definitely recognized and not endanger our ground forces. A trail formation was used." In other words, the 345th's aircraft overflew the target before reversing course, separating, and then attacking one by one. Training exercises back in the States had been more complex. On that day, although most of the bombs fell in the target area, it was impossible to assess the results through the thick foliage.

The reality was that, out of their garrisons, Japanese troops were rarely able to defend against air attacks. It was simply too difficult to move antiaircraft guns and ammunition over the poorly developed trails that snaked through the jungle. But aircraft were not constrained by terrain, and Japanese fighters were occasionally spotted in the skies around Salamaua. That said, their performance was underwhelming, and they generally failed to engage the 345th with any enthusiasm during the first few weeks of its combat operations.

Although one of the group's B-25s was badly shot up during this period, the Japanese fighter pilots were remarkable only for their apparent disinterest or timidity. The 501st Bomb Squadron on a mission to the Salamaua area on July 5, 1943, described an example of their lack of aggressiveness: "8-10 radial engine A/C [aircraft] believed 'Zeke' [Mitsubishi A6M Type 0, or 'Zero' fighters] performing acrobatics below our bombers. Made no attempt at interception."

Buck Fowler, a gunner with the 500th, wrote of these missions in a letter to his sister Edna. "We raided the Japs a number of times since I last wrote to you. I'd like to tell you all about the actions but I can't. You wouldn't believe what I'd write anyway. It's too much like a dime novel. However, I will say this: It's great to be on the winning side."

His letter also indicated that the men did have opportunities for recreation. "I went swimming a few days ago and I fell off a pier. I had scratches all over myself. The Jap bullets aren't killing me, but I'm killing myself."[26]

The 345th flew more than a dozen missions to Salamaua and the surrounding area during the month of July 1943; it was the group's main focus of effort during the month. And there is no question that the 345th contributed materially to the reduction of the Japanese forces there. In so doing, the men proved their worth in combat and validated the investment in time and material that had been put into them. Ultimately, supported by units from the Fifth Air Force and the Royal Australian Air Force, Allied troops took Salamaua on September 11, 1943.

But the 345th had been essentially taken out of the fight during the previous month, August. Although the B-25 was an effective medium bomber, pioneering efforts by other units earlier that year proved that— modified to carry batteries of forward-firing .50-caliber machine guns— the aircraft could be operated against the Japanese much more effectively as a low-altitude bomber and strafer. Accordingly, the 345th's aircraft were flown to Australia to be similarly configured.

CHAPTER TWO

"That Made Him Very Happy"

IN FACT, IT WAS VIA THIS REMARKABLE INNOVATION—THE TRANSFOR-
mation of the B-25 into a low-altitude bomber and gunship—that the
345th distinguished itself throughout the rest of the war. The man behind
it was Paul "Pappy" Gunn. Part myth and part real-life hero, Gunn was
born in 1899 in Quitman, Arkansas. The schooling he received was
unequal to his considerable talents, and when he enlisted in the Navy
in 1917, his limited education stymied his dream of becoming a pilot.
Instead, he was made an aircraft mechanic. Although the assignment was
initially a disappointment, he grew to enjoy it, and the skills he learned
served him—and the nation—very well in later years.

Gunn was a young man who found ways to get things done. He saved
his pay and not only took flying lessons but also bought a surplus flying
boat, which he made serviceable again on his own time. Gunn reenlisted
in 1924 at the same time that the Navy started training enlisted men as
pilots. He completed flight training and subsequently excelled during a
career that included service as a fighter pilot, a flight instructor, and a
VIP transport pilot.

Joseph "Jocko" Clark, who later became a notable rear admiral and
task force commander, said that Gunn "was an excellent aerial gunner,
and at air combat, which was our main mission, he was rated as one of
the very best in the squadron [VF-2]." He also remembered that Gunn
"had a cheerful and inspiring personality, and a high sense of duty."[1] Others remembered him as a lovable teller of tall tales, a hard drinker, and a
master of bluff and bluster who did not suffer fools gladly.

When Gunn retired from the Navy in 1937, he worked for an airline in Hawaii and was later joined by his family in the Philippines, where he managed Philippine Air Lines. He and his wife and four children were living near Nichols Field on the outskirts of Manila when the Japanese bombed the Philippines after their sneak attack on Pearl Harbor. Gunn was commissioned into the United States Army Air Forces (USAAF) as a captain, and the handful of aircraft that made up Philippine Air Lines was impressed into American service under his command.

Gunn flew these and other aircraft continuously as he moved people and material around the islands and as far away as Australia. He was attacked in the air multiple times and shot down at least once. And when he wasn't flying, he shared his mechanical genius with his USAAF counterparts to put seemingly unflyable aircraft of all types back into service. Everyone agreed that he possessed a degree of energy and stamina unequalled by the much younger men with whom he worked.

Gunn was flying diplomats to Australia when Manila fell to the Japanese on January 2, 1942. Chagrined at having waited too long to spirit his family to safety, he put together a rescue plan and landed a Beechcraft on Manila's Quezon Boulevard in the middle of the night. His wife and children, who had never gotten word of the scheme, failed to show, and he was forced to take off without them. The Japanese subsequently interned his family at the Santo Tomas prison camp.

Unable to do anything for his loved ones, Gunn directed his considerable energy and talents—and a great visceral hatred—toward fighting the Japanese. On February 4, 1942, he was put in charge of a newly formed air transport command made up of a hodgepodge of aircraft.[2] But he also flew fighters and bombers whenever he could. Notably, he made many extremely risky supply and evacuation flights from Australia into the Philippines, for which he was twice awarded the Distinguished Flying Cross.

Other exploits were so extraordinary as to strain credulity. On January 26, 1942, after flying a B-17 to Surabaya, Java, to deliver supplies, he flew seven bombing missions against a Japanese convoy in the Makassar Strait. He scored two confirmed hits even though he had first touched the controls of a B-17 only the previous day. He additionally played a major role in a daring set of bombing raids—the Royce mission—staged from Australia and flown from an outlying airfield in the Philippines. Gunn also extracted clandestine operators from the Philippines as the Japanese tightened their noose around the archipelago during early 1942. And famously, through bluster and out-and-out chicanery, he "redirected" twenty-four idle Dutch B-25s into American hands. In truth, they were simply stolen.

But beyond Gunn's considerable achievements as a flyer—which, in addition to the two Distinguished Flying Crosses, also earned him the Silver Star—his greatest contribution to the war effort was his notion of converting the Douglas A-20 and the North American B-25 into low-level strafing aircraft. Based on his personal experience, he understood that both aircraft types, stuffed with as many forward-firing guns as possible and using low-level bombing tactics, would be more effective as close-in attack aircraft. He accordingly tinkered with various installation concepts and designed and fabricated many of the necessary components himself. And he salvaged the guns he needed from wrecked aircraft.

Notwithstanding his seemingly innate mechanical genius, the modifications Gunn made were necessarily makeshift—limited by a paucity of formal engineering and manufacturing resources. Still, he proved his concept for putting four .50-caliber machine guns into the nose of the A-20, together with long-range fuel tanks. Reconfigured examples began flying operational missions during the late summer of 1942.

Modifying the B-25 proved more problematic. The weight of the guns and their ammunition made the aircraft nose-heavy, which necessitated the installation of lead ballast in the aft section of the aircraft. The added weight of the guns, the ammunition, and the ballast had a negative effect on the aircraft's speed and range, which was obviated to a degree by removing the ventral, or lower, turret and tail guns. Another problem was the vibration and muzzle blast caused by so many guns firing at once, which caused rivets in the forward fuselage to break loose and the skin to warp and crack. This was mitigated by scabbing, or overlaying, metal panels and a thin layer of shock-absorbing material on the weakest sections and by installing blast tubes on some of the guns.

Gunn made friends with Jack Fox during this time. Fox was North American Aviation's technical representative in the area. The pair worked well together, and Fox's knowledge, together with his access to North American's engineering expertise, was no doubt useful to the effort. For his part, Gunn insisted on testing the modified aircraft himself as they often presented dangerous and unpredictable flying characteristics.

In due course, and through the contributions of others aside from Gunn and Fox, the experiment advanced through trial and error into a real capability. The first batch of modified aircraft carried four .50-caliber machine guns in the nose and two additional machine guns installed on each side of the nose below the cockpit, for a total of eight fixed, forward-firing guns.

George Kenney, who had been so impressed by Gunn that he had made him his chief "innovator," was especially keen on the B-25 as a strafer. "I figured I'd have a skip-bomber that could overwhelm the deck defenses of a Jap vessel as the plane came in for the kill with its bombs," he said. "With a commerce destroyer as effective as I believed this would be, I'd be able to maintain an air blockade on the Japs anywhere within the radius of action of the airplane."[3]

The type's big debut occurred early in 1943. On February 28, as the 345th's training was nearing completion in South Carolina, the Japanese sortied eight destroyers and eight troop transports from their fortress at Rabaul, on New Britain Island. The convoy was ostensibly protected by nearly one hundred aircraft, and its destination was Lae, New Guinea, about fifteen miles north of Salamaua. The Japanese desperately needed the troops and material to maintain their positions in New Guinea.

Notwithstanding the defensive air umbrella that the Japanese fighters were tasked with providing, the Allies—primarily Kenney's Fifth Air Force—savaged the convoy over a three-day period beginning on March 2. Ultimately, with the loss of only six aircraft and thirteen airmen, the Allies sank all eight transports and four of the destroyers. It was a remarkable victory that made banner headlines back in the States.

The multiday fight was noteworthy for its viciousness. When the crewmen of a B-17 bailed out of their stricken bomber, Japanese fighters shot them dead in their parachutes. The word spread quickly, and when there remained no more Japanese ships to sink, many of the Allied aircrews dropped to wave-top level and gunned the hapless survivors to bits. "What we didn't get, the sharks got," recorded one airman.[4] Nearly three thousand of the seven thousand Japanese troops destined for New Guinea were killed or drowned during the Battle of the Bismarck Sea.

The 3rd Attack Group's 90th Bomb Squadron participated in the action with twelve B-25s modified as strafers. Garrett Middlebrook, a B-25 pilot with the 38th Bomb Group, offered an eyewitness account: "I watched one of the strafers open fire on one of the moving ships. Long before he dropped his bomb, debris from the ship flew all over the water. I wondered what all the pieces of debris were and squinted harder. My God, they were human bodies!"[5]

Middlebrook made his first strafing attack a couple of months later. His experience underscored the effectiveness of the guns against land targets. On May 9, 1943, he led a flight against the Japanese airfield at Gasmata, on New Ireland. He opened his attack with a fusillade against a machine-gun position. "Good God, it was mindless cruelty what I did to those machine gunners. Two rolled all the way over the top of the embankment and fell as lifeless chunks of human flesh to the ground on the other side. Two others seemed to be impaled on the tripod of their gun while my firepower tore their bodies to shreds. The others were ripped and torn to bloody flesh and broken bones."[6]

In early August 1943, the 345th's crews flew their aircraft from Port Moresby to Garbutt Airfield near Townsville, Australia. There, at Depot #2, Gunn's experimental design and engineering work had matured into a formal modification line capable of converting the 345th's sixty-plus B-25s into strafers. Work started immediately.

While that work was being performed, the group's aircrews had little to do. A few had remained at Port Moresby, where they flew an occasional mission—usually single-ship weather-reconnaissance sorties. But at Townsville, arrangements were made for a C-47 to take a load of men to Sydney for a furlough on a first-come, first-served basis. "My buddy Mike Korczynski and I were among the first to sign up," said Tal Epps. "The list was filled very quickly. No one had had any time off, so a week in Sydney was a dream come true. And the fact that we had received several months of back pay that afternoon added to the excitement. I had a small fortune—more than seventeen hundred American dollars. I felt like a millionaire!"

Epps and Korczynski decided on a quiet night out before the C-47 departed early the next morning, August 7, 1943. "We made plans to shave and shower, and then go into town for dinner and a movie," Epps said. The two men meant to get to bed early so as to be well rested for a predawn wakeup call.

"As we left our barracks to board the bus to town, we got involved in a big dice game in the latrine," Epps said. By the end of the night, both Epps and Korczynski were still in the latrine, nearly penniless. They were not on speaking terms when they finally went to bed. "When the charge of quarters came by to wake us," said Epps, "I was undecided as to whether I still wanted to go to Sydney so I called over to Mike to see if he was still going." Korczynski brusquely directed Epps to perform an impossible sexual act on himself.

Epps was approached by Charles Zahora shortly afterward. Zahora had been a big winner at the dice game and wanted to buy Epps's seat to Sydney. "I told him that I wasn't going and that he could take my place—he didn't have to pay me," Epps said. "That made him very happy."

Epps and Korczynski were asleep again when the *Eager Beaver*, a C-47 of the 40th Troop Carrier Squadron, got airborne at 0500. Once aloft it turned south and climbed into the still-dark sky. Only twenty minutes later it crashed into Cleveland Bay, killing everyone aboard. Of the twenty-seven men who were killed, twenty were from the 345th's 500th Bomb Squadron, including Charles Zahora. Also among the 500th's dead was Buck Fowler, who had been such a dutiful correspondent with his sister Edna and who had been so tickled with the names of the *Boom-Boom*, *Dittum Dattum*, and *Wattum Chew*.

Epps and Korczynski patched up their differences that morning before they or anyone else knew of the crash. They borrowed some money and spent a few days sightseeing in a nearby town. "We enjoyed good food and plenty of sleep for about three days," Epps said, "then headed back to Townsville. When we passed through the gate at Garbutt a couple of our ground men expressed surprise and delight to see us alive and well. They informed us that the plane we should have been aboard had crashed and that there were no survivors." Epps, who had not been aboard Lee Ow's aircraft when it had smashed into the mountains around Salamaua, had cheated death once more.

The 500th Bomb Squadron needed to replace the men lost in the crash of the *Eager Beaver*. Aircrew replacements weren't readily available at that point, and Epps recalled that the squadron turned inward to make up the shortfall. "All had to be volunteers—no one could be ordered to fly in combat. Then they must be trained from scratch to fill positions completely foreign to any training they ever received. We had personnel from the motor pool, the dispensary, the kitchen, the armament section, etc." Ultimately, the makeshift staffing and training effort was successful enough that the 500th was able to meet its operational obligations.

Many of the 345th's men left behind wives and lovers. One of these was James R. Jones, or "J. R.," an Indiana farm boy who had studied at the University of Kansas on a track scholarship. Though not tall, he had been a broad jump champion. Intelligent and sensitive, he met the love of his life in Houston, Texas, in August 1941 while traveling with fraternity brothers.

J. R. was nervous about his blind date with red-headed Houston socialite Elnora Bartlett. His experience to that point led him to believe that redheads were either "extremely good looking, or extremely *good God*."[7] As it developed, Elnora was a stunner. Lively green eyes complemented her vivid red hair and pretty, heart-shaped face. She had a trim yet fully equipped figure and a smile that could render a man dumb. Best of all, she was spirited and witty and as smart as—or more so than—Jones.

It was love at first sight. Their personalities were different but harmonized, and they shared a love of music and dancing. Although he was twenty-two and she nineteen, neither had ever been so affected by another. The first date was magical, and the second ended too soon. After only two days, both were excited by the notion of a traditional, if long distance, courtship.

That notion was complicated when Jones received his draft notice later that month and was inducted into the Army in September 1941, just as he started his senior year at Kansas. However, he was soon selected for training as an aviation cadet. Before he left for that training, he arranged a second meeting with Elnora for two days at Christmas.

That the mutual attraction they had developed only a few months earlier was as strong as ever was indicated in the letter that Elnora wrote soon afterward: "Oh, but I miss your slaphappy wit and your kisses, and I know I'll miss you more than I will ever know, and more than you can imagine before I see you again. I can hardly wait for your next letters, for the last was so wonderful. If I read it once, I know I have read it ten times."[8]

Much later, as the 345th started for the Pacific in the spring of 1943, J. R. Jones finished his training as a B-25 pilot at Greenville Army Air Base. Although he and Elnora had kept up a stream of correspondence, they had not put eyes on each other since Christmas 1941. Finally, nearing the end of May 1943, he wangled a training mission to Houston. On May 22, after dodging a string of rainstorms, he set his aircraft down, parked it, and helped the rest of his crew button it up for an overnight stay.

Elnora and a family friend met Jones and his crew at Ellington. "As a pilot would say," he later wrote, "when I first saw you again—*I spun in*."[9] Jones proposed to Elnora that night in front of his crew. Since meeting, they had seen each other on only six different days. She accepted. Sadly, he had to return to Greenville the following day.

While the 345th was finding its footing on the other side of the world, Jones continued to woo Elnora. When he had proposed to her a couple of weeks earlier, he had no ring to put on her finger. During early June, he suggested that she take a train from Houston to Montgomery, Alabama, where he had earlier gone through flight training. He would travel to Montgomery from Greenville. Once together he planned to seal their engagement with a ring.

Elnora had a job but contrived a case of measles and made the trip. From June 9, for a couple of days, they immersed themselves in each other's company. Jones later wrote of it to Elnora: "Ah, so you like to remember our last night in Montgomery—frankly, so do I. Those days were a short frantic grab for happiness, but we made it. I've never been more content in all my life. Odd how one can be so completely happy just wandering around aimlessly as we did."[10]

Only two weeks after their Montgomery tryst, Jones received orders overseas. "I stare at these beautiful pictures of you and these snapshots of us by the hour," he wrote. "Heaven knows what it will be like over there. Knowing that you love me, though, and that you are more lovely than a picture can ever be, is one dream I've had come true."[11]

J. R. arrived in Australia in August 1943, while the 345th's aircraft were being modified as strafers. He was not initially impressed and wrote Elnora on August 21, the day he joined the 345th's 501st Bomb Squadron, "All the homes and places of business are very dirty and unkempt. It's really not a very pleasant effect. Everything looks as if it could use a good bath." He additionally observed, "The people are fairly friendly, but I don't believe the Australian soldiers care too much for us. They are really a wild lot and aren't too particular who they fight. For lack of anything else to do, they will fight each other."

But there was one aspect about the Australians that impressed Jones. "I haven't any idea how big the Royal Australian Air Force is, but they have the prettiest uniform of anyone. It's about the bluest blue I ever saw. I hope they have some airplanes to go with the uniform."[12]

The 345th began flying its newly modified B-25Ds back to Port Moresby during mid-August 1943. Aside from the four .50-caliber machine guns in a newly installed, solid nose, two more .50-caliber machine guns were added to each side of the forward fuselage below the cockpit. The two .30-caliber machine guns, one on each side of the rear fuselage, were retained, but, as with Pappy Gunn's original effort, the bottom turret was removed. An automatic camera was also installed on the bottom of the fuselage behind the bomb bay. Pointed down and to the rear, it captured images that proved invaluable in evaluating the effectiveness of bombing raids.

The 501st Bomb Squadron flew the 345th's first strafer sorties on August 23, 1943. The four aircraft that made up the raid dropped incendiaries on indiscriminate targets in the Markham Valley before shooting up some native huts and nondescript buildings. The damage done was trifling, and "inauspicious" was too lofty a word to describe the mission's results. The 500th Bomb Squadron flew its first strafer sorties two days later, on August 25. The eight aircraft made a low-level attack against gun emplacements in the Hansa Bay area. They dropped strings of parachute fragmentation, or "parafrag," bombs, as well as more traditional three-hundred-pound demolition bombs. At the same time, they strafed whatever targets presented themselves. The squadron sustained no damage or injuries and the results were satisfactory, if not remarkable.

Other missions were flown to Nadzab and Alexishafen. A raid on September 1 included three of the group's four squadrons, the 498th, the 500th, and the 501st, as well as squadrons from other bomb groups. The target was a heavy concentration of barge traffic in the Alexishafen area. This effort exposed the fact that the unit—still relatively new to combat—was occasionally prone to miscues in flying and judgment, as indicated by the 498th Bomb Squadron's report: "Our flight leader reported that the entire formation was very unstable and that it was not possible to form on the flight that this squadron was to follow in the attack. The conditions did not improve and Captain Giffin considered it unwise to attack and have our aircraft in the line of fire of the other squadrons. Therefore, this squadron turned off ten miles short of the target and returned to base." In other words, someone's inability to fly stable formation caused an entire squadron to turn back to base without dropping a single bomb. It was a waste.

The 500th and the 501st pressed on to Alexishafen but discovered, much to their disappointment, that most of the barges had already moved on. They assuaged that disappointment by attacking the remaining barges and whatever else needed it. Robert Larsen's actions were representative. The 501st Bomb Squadron's mission summary report described how he "made a minimum altitude run along the southeast edge of the runway, strafing this area. His flight path continued down the roadway through Mission Village where 8 bombs were released with unobserved results. This area was also well strafed. Swinging back to the right," the report continued, "short of Sek Island, Lieutenant Larsen then strafed the shoreline and small islands from Kananam Point to the Amron Mission area."

September 5, 1943, marked the first strafing mission in which all four of the 345th's squadrons participated. The group was at the vanguard of an air assault on the Markham Valley—the first large-scale operation to involve American paratroopers in the Pacific. Together with a coordinated ground attack and the imminent capture of Salamaua and Lae, it was one more step in Douglas MacArthur's deliberate march across the top of New Guinea. Specifically, it was intended to capture the disused airfield at Nadzab and turn it into a major airbase complex.

The highly choreographed affair tasked the B-25s of the 345th and 38th Bomb Groups to lead the way in a low-level bombing and strafing attack. They were to be followed by A-20 light attack bombers equipped with smoke canisters. The smoke was intended to blind Japanese defenders to the nearly two thousand American and Australian paratroopers embarked aboard ninety-six C-47s. The entire effort—to include Generals Kenney and MacArthur observing from separate B-17s orbiting overhead—was to be protected by 146 fighters.

The 345th's bomb run went well, although most crews were unable to perform follow-up strafing runs because of the fast-approaching C-47s. Douglas Busath, a navigator with the 499th Bomb Squadron, was aboard one of the few aircraft that was able to strafe. It was his first combat mission, and he naturally harbored fears about the perils he might face. "We came out of the first strafing run," said Busath, "and my pilot and copilot were laughing so hard they could hardly talk. I asked what was so funny and they said, 'You! You yelled all the way down that entire strafing run and we don't know where you got all the wind—you never took a breath!'"[13]

Busath was surprised and asked the two men if they hadn't seen the flashes of enemy gunfire on the ground. "And they said that no one was shooting at us. That was our bullets hitting the rocks and making sparks." Busath felt sheepish but noted that after having been "blooded" on that first combat flight, he never again suffered from a similar set of nerves.

As Busath's pilots noted, Japanese resistance to the air assault was almost nil. Enemy fighters failed to make an appearance, and only scattered pockets of Japanese troops were encountered on the ground. Notwithstanding the fact that his aircraft and crews were essentially unopposed, Kenney was justifiably proud of how his different units came together to make the effort a success. He boasted to his boss, Henry Arnold,

I truly don't believe that another air force in the world today could have put this over as perfectly as the 5th Air Force did. Not a single squadron did any circling or stalling around but all slid into place like clockwork. . . . The strafers checked in on the target at exactly the time set, just prior to take off. They strafed and frag bombed the whole area in which the jumps were to be made and then as the last bombs exploded the smoke layers went to work. As the streams of smoke were built up, the three columns of transports slid into place and in one minute and ten seconds from the time the first parachute opened the last of 1,700 paratroopers had dropped.[14]

Ultimately, the operation proved to be a splendid demonstration of the Fifth Air Force's capacity to support MacArthur's New Guinea offensive and, as such, proof of all that Kenney had done to create that capacity.

During this time, the Japanese fighter pilots that the 345th encountered continued to exhibit a curious lack of aggressiveness. This was highlighted on September 17, 1943, ten days after the Nadzab operation, when Charles Howard and his crew were sent to drop propaganda leaflets over Japanese-held Finschafen. The 500th Bomb Squadron crew was eastbound, approaching the Markham River, when "we were intercepted by six-to-eight enemy SSF [single-seat fighters] which we believe were Zekes." Charles Brown, in the top turret, let Howard know that four of the enemy aircraft were "on our tail."

Howard put the B-25 into a dive as a different Zero fighter—codenamed "Zeke"—attacked from ahead and out of the sun. Brown fired his guns and "saw his tracers enter the Zeke, pieces of the cowling fly off, and the Zeke fall off on one wing, smoking badly." Almost immediately, the B-25 was hit from the front again by another Zero. This attack blasted away the top turret's Plexiglas dome. Brown was hit in the head and started bleeding profusely. The radio man, Robert Walker, rendered first aid.

Fred Ellard, the waist gunner, left his position and stood ready at the still-functioning guns of the top turret. He needn't have bothered as, inexplicably, the enemy fighters motored away. Why the Japanese pilots failed to press their advantage is unknown, but Howard nursed the aircraft into Dobodura, where Brown received medical treatment and ultimately survived.

—⁓—

When the 345th arrived in theater in May 1943, George Kenney was impressed by its commander, Jarred Crabb. After meeting with Crabb on May 12, Kenney described him as an aggressive leader whom "I would bet on any time."[15] Kenney made a mental note to track Crabb's performance.

In fact, Kenney was impressed enough to pull Crabb from the 345th only just more than two months after it started combat operations. Kenney ordered him to duty as the Fifth Bomber Command's chief of staff. It was a position that perfectly suited Crabb's experience and leadership skills. Consequently, command of the 345th was passed to the executive officer, Clinton True, on September 19, 1943. Crabb's reputation as an accomplished flyer and leader was ultimately validated when he was made head of Fifth Bomber Command a few months later.

—⁓—

On September 25, 1943, two 345th squadrons, the 498th and 500th, were ordered to attack Japanese personnel in the vicinity of the Gusap River. The enemy was believed to be hiding in native villages and along the heavily jungled trails that connected them. Accordingly, each squadron made two bombing and strafing passes on a string of little settlements. Higher headquarters certainly must have directed the attack based on some sort of intelligence, but the mission summary reports offered no compelling evidence of a strong Japanese presence. A sole artillery piece—unattended—was the only indication that the enemy was, or had been, in the area.

The 498th reported that "6 bombs were released at Ragitsuma scoring direct hits on several huts and starting small fires. 2 bombs fell on huts at Maraisassa. 2 bombs were released on huts at Amari. 7 bombs were released at Boparinpum, destroying several huts. 8 bombs fell among huts in an unidentified village six miles northeast of Boparinpum.

8 bombs fell among huts at an unidentified village." This great holocaust of huts hardly seemed worth the resources the squadron expended to put twelve aircraft in the air that day.

For its part, the 500th reported that it also destroyed a great many huts. It additionally noted, "Several horses picketed along the creek bed directly south of Arifagan Creek, sighted by one crew making its first pass, were strafed by this crew on its second pass over the target." Neither squadron reported sighting enemy troops.

Although the targets hit by the 345th's squadrons on September 25 were not of obvious importance, such was not the case on September 27. On that day the group was tasked, together with the 38th Bomb Group and the 3rd Attack Group, to hit the Wewak airfield complex. It was a much different proposition than hitting undefended villages.

Anxious to shore up their positions in New Guinea, the Japanese had come ashore at Wewak, on New Guinea's northern coast, ten months earlier in December 1942. They subsequently established not only a naval headquarters but a complex of four airfields. There they fielded the Fourth Air Army. If they couldn't dislodge the Allies, the Japanese planned to keep them bottled up where they were.

In fact, Wewak grew to become Japan's largest airbase on New Guinea. Kenney was obviously concerned but felt powerless to do much as "recco [reconnaissance] photos showed too many fighters on the four airdromes, at But, Borum, Dagua, and Wewak itself, for us to expose our meager bomber strength in an unescorted raid, and our fighters based at Dobodura and Port Moresby didn't have the range to go to Wewak and return."[16]

The solution that Kenney and his staff developed during the early summer of 1943 was the clandestine construction of a new airfield at Tsili Tsili, only about fifty miles west of Salamaua and Lae, where ground battles were still ongoing. Fighter aircraft based at Tsili Tsili—which Kenney renamed Marilinan—could support the troops doing that fighting. They could also escort bombers to Wewak, three hundred miles to the northwest. While the airfield was being built, the Japanese were kept distracted by the purposely obvious construction of an emergency airfield at Garoka—in large part performed by the natives—and other construction activity at nearby Bena Bena.

The decoy activities paid off as the Japanese regularly bombed the ersatz airfield at Garoka, while the work at Marilinan went unnoticed. Kenney recalled, "The natives thought it was all a huge joke, and when the Japs put on an attack they would roll around on the ground with laughter and chatter away about how we were 'making fool of the Jap man.'"[17] The Japanese didn't discover Marilinan until the middle of August 1943. And although they bombed it, they were too late—Kenney's units were too well established.

At that time the 345th's aircraft were being modified as strafers. But Kenney still had other units available and sent four raids against the Wewak complex from August 17 to 21. The first mission was a resounding success as it caught a large Japanese force just as it was readying to take off for an attack against Marilinan. The Japanese were ill prepared and suffered devastating losses. Kenney wrote, "We found out afterward that the Japs referred to the attack as 'the Black Day of August 17th,' and that they had lost over 150 aircraft, with practically all the flight crews and around three hundred more ground personnel killed."[18] The subsequent raids effectively stamped out Japanese airpower at Wewak for a brief period. An enemy officer noted the hurt that was suffered: "At the time of the air attacks on Wewak on 17 and 18 August our defences were not alert. We lost 100 planes including light bombers, fighters and reconnaissance planes. It was a decisive Allied victory. We were planning to regain the balance of air power and were making plans to bomb Port Moresby and other areas. A few days before our projected plan was to materialise, we were bombed at Wewak and our air power was severely crippled."[19]

The Fifth Air Force, determined to keep Wewak beaten down, kept up the pressure with multiple raids. However, by late September the Japanese had recovered to a certain degree. Kenney remarked, "Our recco planes reported that the Nips seemed to be coming to life again in the Wewak area."

By that time the 345th had been back in action for more than a month, and on September 27, 1943, the group's four squadrons were tasked, together with the 38th Bomb Group, the 3rd Attack Group, and an escort of P-38s and P-40s, to hit Wewak and its airfield complex. The 345th's squadrons got airborne from their different airfields just before

0800 and rendezvoused soon after. The 498th Bomb Squadron led the formation with the group's new commander, Clinton True, at its head.

The 345th joined the other bomb groups and their fighter escorts over Bena Bena at nine thousand feet. From there, the 38th Bomb Group took the lead, with the 3rd Attack Group and the 345th following at two-minute intervals. There would be no element of surprise as a formation of B-24s shook the Japanese awake with a predawn raid. Approaching Wewak, the 345th's squadrons angled away from each other and toward their separate assignments.

The picture presented to the 345th's flyers was a burning, smoking confusion of targets, some of which had been wrecked during the previous month and some of which had just been blown apart minutes earlier. But there were also a great many untouched targets. It was a mixed milieu that included antiaircraft gun positions, aircraft, barracks, warehouses, supply dumps, and a handful of naval vessels. Punctuating the scene were streams of fire from light antiaircraft guns and ugly black pockmarks from heavier guns. The 499th noted, "Large balls of fire about six inches in diameter were shot at one of our airplanes while flying over Cape Wom."

The 345th added its bombs and machine-gun fire to the chaos. Each aircraft carried thirty-six twenty-three-pound parachute-retarded fragmentation bombs that were dropped in clusters of three. At the head of the group, Clinton True led the first flight of four aircraft from the 498th Bomb Squadron on a low-level run across Boram from west to east. "The strip was strafed," the squadron recorded, "and tracers were seen entering planes on the strip. Several planes were observed to break into flames." In all, including those destroyed by the preceding groups, the flight counted thirty flaming aircraft wrecks at Boram. Additional aircraft were shot up as the 498th continued east from Boram to the airfield at Wewak.

The 500th Bomb Squadron followed the 498th across Boram and Wewak, adding to the destruction. The 499th Bomb Squadron likewise hit antiaircraft positions, buildings, supply dumps, and aircraft on and around Wewak. "Oil drums and hut on Raiboin Island strafed, approximately fifteen camouflaged airplanes in dispersal area at the southeast end of the strip were bombed and strafed. Eight to ten fires were started in the dispersal area. Results were difficult to observe due to trees and camouflage."

The 501st had a heyday at Dagua, where the antiaircraft fire was light and targets were plentiful. Darwin Neuenschwander's run across the target, as described by the squadron's mission summary report, was typical: "His bombs were dropped in one trail straddling the runway. Several bombs were dropped in the south revetment area. Fires were started at the southwest end of the runway, bombs blowing up amidst airplanes."

Although there was little antiaircraft fire at Dagua, enemy fighters were active. A floatplane version of the Zero, code-named "Rufe," flew in front of the entire squadron, its pilot seemingly unaware of the B-25s about to run him down. Too late, he tried to turn away. For his trouble, his aircraft was holed by the nose guns of both James Clark and Henry Knoll. The enemy aircraft was last seen gliding toward the sea.

In the meantime, a Zero dropped behind Clark's aircraft. And trailing the Zero was the B-25 piloted by Orbry Moore, who "brought up the nose of his ship, and from a distance of 50 yards, effected a direct hit with his eight, forward-firing guns." A wheel dropped from the enemy fighter as it shed pieces and fell away, smoking.

The 345th had never encountered so many enemy fighters. Around and above the group, the six squadrons of escorting fighters tore into the Japanese defenders. The 499th reported, "One Zero shot down by a P-38 in water east of Wewak Point. One Zero shot down by a P-40, falling in flames near Muschu Island. . . . P-40 on fire and falling north of strip, altitude about 300 feet."

Still, as many as there were, the Japanese fighter pilots failed to make an impression. A Zero made a pass at a 498th aircraft "from above at 12 o'clock, chandelled, and left without firing." A Kawasaki Ki-61 single-engine fighter, code-named "Tony," also attacked a 498th ship "from 9 o'clock position and fired several rounds and swung off to the front and disappeared." Although the enemy pilot scored a few hits, the damage was minimal, and he failed to renew his attack. The 500th was attacked by six Japanese fighters. The squadron declared with a note of contempt, "No damage resulted from their feeble attempts."

The 345th completed its attack in less than ten minutes. No aircraft were lost, although two men in separate aircraft had been killed by enemy fire. Behind the group, as it winged southeast for Port Moresby, the air-field complex at Wewak was a flaming fiasco.

After the raid, however, photo analysts discovered extensive, well-camouflaged fuel and ammunition dumps that had gone unmolested. Kenney sent forty B-24s back to Wewak the next day. "The big ammunition dump exploded with so much force that it turned two of the B-24s on their backs, although they were flying at 12,000 feet," he said. "Black smoke from burning fuel billowed up higher than the bombers, followed by flames that were visible for fifty miles."[20] Although Wewak wasn't completely dead and would be bombed many more times until the end of the war, it never again posed a real threat to MacArthur's operations.

The 345th did virtually no combat flying during the next two weeks. The only mission flown during this period was a barge sweep on October 5, 1943, along New Guinea's northern coast by twelve aircraft from the group's 499th Bomb Squadron. The formation failed to rendezvous with its P-47 escort and grew smaller by two when one aircrew became lost in heavy weather and another turned back with a bad engine. The rest of the squadron bombed and strafed a grab bag of targets, including barges, villages, isolated buildings and outposts, and a single machine-gun nest.

The squadron ran into an antiaircraft ambush at Erima Plantation, where the Japanese threw up a curtain of antiaircraft fire set to burst at two hundred feet and below. "I was looking out the left side of the plane," said Frank Parker, "trying to locate the antiaircraft positions, when I saw Lieutenant [Chandler] Whipple's plane in flames. The cockpit and navigator's compartment was completely enveloped with fire. The plane continued on course with a slight increase to the dive into the ground."

Parker watched Whipple's aircraft slam into the earth. "As soon as it hit the ground, the gas tanks burst into flame, and the fire covered the whole area over which the wreckage was scattered. I think it impossible for any member to have been alive after the crash."[21]

—◆—

Port Moresby had evolved dramatically for the better since its early days. J. R. Jones wrote Elnora, only partly tongue in cheek, "I live in quite a state of luxury here. The food is good and much better than I had expected. A native boy makes our bed, cleans our tents, and does our laundry for a nominal fee. . . . Perhaps I should bring one home for a houseboy for us. It might, however, be a little difficult to get clothes on him."[22]

The food was better than Jones expected for a couple of reasons. First, when Kenney arrived a year earlier, he had been appalled at the food the men were being served. He immediately ordered improvements. What was done through army channels did make the eating experience better than it had been, but most men still found the menu uninspiring. They particularly hated the canned Australian bully beef, only half joking that it came from Texas longhorns that had been forced to swim to Australia.

Accordingly, many units organized a "fat cat" or "chow hound" system that operated outside officialdom. It was funded by an informal monthly tax of two or three dollars per man. So bankrolled, a small team flew an aircraft to Australia—usually Townsville—and purchased whatever diet-enhancing foodstuffs were available on the civilian market. The fat cat team returned a day or two later and gave whatever booty it had purchased to the cooks. The practice grew to be quite sophisticated with men eventually posted to Townsville on a semipermanent basis to identify, purchase, and stage food for shipment.

Melvin Best recalled one of the early trips during a period when the men had eaten Spam for forty-two consecutive days. "We had not had fresh food for three months when we flew two butchers from our squadron to a ranch near Woodstock Field, in Australia." As the butchers butchered, the rest of the crew went into Townsville and bought other provisions. The big prize was a hundred gallons of fresh milk.

"The trip back to Port Moresby was at 15,000 feet to chill the milk and preserve the freshness of the meat," said Best. "When we landed, the kitchen staff was waiting and began preparing the best meal we had had in months—fresh beef steaks, fresh vegetables, and cold, fresh milk! It was the first fresh milk we had had in four or five months. That night, we were the sickest four hundred men on the island!"[23]

CHAPTER THREE

"The Enemy Was Taken
Completely by Surprise"

DOUGLAS MACARTHUR'S STAFF ISSUED A DAILY SUMMARY ON OCTOBER 11, 1943, that noted an alarming buildup of Japanese aircraft in his area of responsibility: "The mounting air strength at Rabaul, to which attention previously has been called, reached culmination yesterday. Photographs taken at 0915L showed a count of 294 planes, or as large a concentration as ever photographed at that base."

———

Soon after seizing it from Australia during February 1942, the Japanese rapidly transformed Rabaul, located on the eastern tip of New Britain, into an air and naval bastion from which follow-on offensive operations could be launched and sustained. Rabaul's superb anchorage and its four surrounding airfields were ideally situated to support operations in New Guinea, the Solomon Islands, and elsewhere. The town itself was nearly destroyed by a volcanic eruption in 1937 but still offered warehousing, port facilities, and other infrastructure. Indeed, Japanese warships, readily fueled, fitted, and protected at Rabaul—together with army and navy air units—escorted the convoys that carried desperately needed troops and supplies to Japanese forces elsewhere in the region.

Those resupply efforts had grown ever more critical by the late summer and early fall of 1943. By that time Allied air forces in the theater had been buttressed by additional men, material, and aircraft—to include the 345th. Under constant attack from these increasingly powerful forces, the Japanese in New Guinea and other outposts were pushed onto the defensive. Only fresh troops and supplies staged through Rabaul kept them from utterly disintegrating in the steaming, stinking jungle.

As planners in Tokyo decided to reduce and consolidate the periphery of their South Pacific defenses toward the north and away from New Guinea, the situation for the Japanese troops fighting there grew more desperate. Even food was in short supply, as one despairing combatant, Kuroki Toshiro, recounted: "You will not find many smiling faces among the men in the ranks in New Guinea. They are always hungry; every other word has something to do with eating. At the sight of potatoes their eyes gleam and their mouths water. The divisional commander and the staff officers do not seem to realize that the only way the men can drag out their lives from day to day is by this endless hunt for potatoes. How can they complain about slackness and expect miracles when most of our effort goes into looking for something to eat!"[1]

The military complex at Rabaul was heavily defended against air and naval attack by more than three hundred antiaircraft guns, exclusive of those carried by whatever warships happened to be moored in the harbor—Simpson Harbor—on any given day. The complex was also well defended by aircraft, although their numbers fluctuated as units staged into or out of the area depending on the operational situation. However, the four airfields—Lakunai, Vunakanau, Rapopo, and Tobera—often hosted upward of three hundred bombers and fighters.

Control of these disparate air elements was aided by a net of radar stations that provided warning times of up to an hour depending on the route taken by attacking forces. The radar stations were backstopped by observation posts located along likely approach corridors. The entire network was linked by radio and telephone communications. A road system, greatly expanded since Rabaul's capture from the Australians, kept the installations that comprised the complex functioning efficiently.

To defend against an Allied invasion, the Japanese maintained a garrison of army and navy units—and civilian workers and engineers—that eventually exceeded one hundred thousand men. Equipped with more than a thousand artillery pieces of various sizes and entrenched within a lacework of nearly 350 miles of caves and tunnels, the garrison was exceptionally well prepared to meet an amphibious assault. On the other hand, such a force consumed prodigious quantities of material. So then, aside from provisioning outposts from Rabaul, Japanese strategists and logisticians were compelled to allocate enough resources to maintain and protect it. Failure to do so would make their positions in New Guinea and elsewhere in the South Pacific indefensible.

MacArthur had a plan to take Rabaul back from the Japanese. Operation CARTWHEEL had been underway since the middle of 1943 with the ultimate objective of seizing Rabaul once the Japanese bases that guarded its approaches had been neutralized or captured. His Southwest Pacific Area forces were tasked with dislodging the Japanese from their positions on the northeastern coast of New Guinea before establishing a base at Empress Augusta Bay on New Britain, at the far end of the island from Rabaul. Forces under Chester Nimitz, commander of the Pacific Fleet and the Pacific Oceans Area, were to proceed northwest up the Solomon Islands chain from Guadalcanal to seize Bougainville. Thus isolated, Rabaul would be ripe for an assault.

The Allied leadership met at the Quadrant Conference in Montreal during August 1943 and decided that isolating Rabaul—rather than seizing it—could achieve the desired effects. Capturing the enemy stronghold at a cost certain to include many lives—and much equipment and material—was not considered essential to the advance on Tokyo.

But Rabaul was hardly neutralized or isolated in October 1943. Accordingly, MacArthur tasked the Allied air forces with the job, and George Kenney's Fifth Air Force was given the lead. "My job," Kenney recounted, "was to pound away at the Rabaul area, beginning about the 12th of October, to get rid of the Jap air force there, destroy the supplies in the town, which were estimated at over 300,000 tons, and by sinking the shipping in the harbor, make the place untenable for Jap vessels."

In fact, Kenney's Fifth Air Force, together with a small Australian component, launched its largest attack to that point in the war on October 12, 1943. "Everything that I owned that was in commission and could fly that far was on the raid," Kenney said.[2] The 345th was owned by Kenney and had many aircraft "in commission" that "could fly that far." And it was most definitely included as part of the attack.

＊

It wasn't that Rabaul had not been hit prior to that day. To the contrary, since soon after the Japanese started operating there in February 1942, the Allies had mounted small harrying raids that achieved little. However, they did return with useful information about the disposition of Japanese forces that otherwise might not have been known.

The 345th had not been part of those raids, and most of its men didn't know or care about them as they readied for Kenney's big mission. It was to be the group's largest effort to date. Each of the four squadrons was tasked with putting up twelve aircraft, and the unit's ground crews worked into the early hours of October 11 to ensure they were available. In an all-out effort, the crew chiefs of the different aircraft traded muscle, expertise, and spare parts as they worked toward the goal. Jeeps raced across the different airstrips carrying whatever needed carrying, and clots of experienced mechanics formed under the wings of the balkiest aircraft. Those that were too far out of service were cannibalized to make others flyable.

At daylight on October 11, the designated aircraft from the 345th's four squadrons were ordered northeast from their airstrips at Port Moresby across the Owen Stanley Range to Dobodura, just inland from the northern coast of New Guinea. As at Port Moresby, a dozen or more airstrips comprised the airfield complex at Dobodura. Forward staging from there would save the 345th nearly two hundred miles of roundtrip distance to Rabaul, not to mention two fuel-sucking climbs back and forth across the cloud- and jungle-draped mountains.

This practice of moving aircraft to forward bases yielded obvious operational advantages as it allowed the 345th's aircraft to reach more-distant targets. The bases were sometimes already manned, provisioned, and equipped to support these sorts of operations, but often they were not. If such was the case, the logistical challenges were considerable. Aside from the aircraft and aircrews, mechanics and other support personnel also had to be brought forward, as did spare parts and material. Moreover, the personnel had to be sheltered and fed. These difficulties aside, the benefits outweighed the hardships, and the 345th was directed to move its aircraft to forward bases many more times through the end of the war.

Early during the morning of October 12, 1943, following their final briefings, the 345th's aircrews were trucked to their bombers, where the ground crews and armorers completed last-minute tasks. It was no secret that Rabaul was one of the most heavily defended Japanese bases in the Pacific, and most of the men were anxious. Phil Caputo of the 345th's 498th Bomb Squadron recalled, "It is so hard to explain war because it has its own rules, it's not like peace. There is no peacetime similarity to the type of feelings you confront in war. You're young. You were frightened—very frightened—but very excited at the same time. . . . You knew somebody was going to die. You *knew* it every time you went out. But you never believed it would be you. And everyone else thought the same thing."[3]

The 345th's specific target that day was the airfield at Vunakanau, ten miles south of Rabaul. It had been an Australian base prior to its capture, and the Japanese had made it their main airfield. Together with two squadrons of B-25s from the 38th Bomb Group, the group was ordered to hit Vunakanau in squadron waves of twelve aircraft each, separated by one-minute intervals. The 345th's 498th Bomb Squadron, with group commander Clinton True at the head, was to be first across the airfield, followed by the 501st, 500th, and 499th. The 38th Bomb Group's two squadrons were to bring up the rear.

True led the 498th airborne at 0731 and turned toward Oro Bay a dozen miles to the south. There he loitered for almost an hour while the rest of the group's squadrons and those from the 38th Bomb Group got airborne and joined him. John Bronson of the 498th recalled that the takeoff was anything but routine.

When the first B-25 roared down the runway, the massive power of two, big, radial engines caused a huge wall of coral dust. Each B-25, loaded down with ordnance and fuel, was to take off 10 seconds apart into zero/zero visibility [no forward visibility and clouds or obscuration all the way to the ground]. When it was my turn, I lined up on the runway center, at least what I thought was the center, set my gyrocompass to zero, and hit full throttle. The B-25 bucked and jerked as I fought to maintain runway heading, hoping and praying the guy in front of me got off okay. As forward speed increased and the controls felt lighter, I lifted her off at 145 m.p.h. and pulled back on the yoke. We broke out at 100 feet AGL [above ground level], and it was absolutely clear.[4]

Such a large number of aircraft had never been launched from Dobodura. The dust spun into the air created a veil so thick that the Royal Australian Air Force (RAAF) Beaufighters of 30 Squadron—whose target was the airfield at Tobera—had to delay their takeoff. Ultimately they got off the ground so late that they had no choice but to fly to Rabaul alone.

The other elements of the raid assembled and proceeded on course. In total, 349 aircraft were slated to participate. These included 84 B-24s, 114 B-25s, 12 RAAF Beaufighters, 125 P-38 escorts, and sundry weather and reconnaissance aircraft. The B-24s were directed to hit shipping in Simpson Harbor and Blanche Bay, while the B-25s and Beaufighters were charged with upending the airfields at Vunakanau, Rapopo, and Tobera. The P-38s—the only fighters with enough range to make the raid—were assigned as protective cover.

True rolled out of an easy turn and winged north out of Oro Bay at 0830 at the head of seventy-two B-25s. The six squadrons were arranged in diamond formations of twelve aircraft each—three aircraft flew in an inverted *V* at the head, three more flew to each side, and a final three-ship followed in trail. The 475th Fighter Group's three squadrons of P-38s rendezvoused with the bombers. The fighter pilots arranged themselves so that one squadron covered each flank of the B-25 formation, while a third crisscrossed overhead.

The straight-line distance to Rabaul from Oro Bay was approximately four hundred miles, but True was anxious to avoid tipping off the enemy and took a slightly longer route that added about fifty miles. Loping along at 220 miles per hour, he headed northeast across the Solomon Sea. Approaching New Britain he stayed over the water and angled northeast toward Warangoi Bay. En route, mechanical difficulties forced two aircraft from the 345th to turn back.

True navigated the overwater portions of the route at an altitude of about a thousand feet. The engines of the group's B-25s were equipped with special low-altitude carburetors that made flight at such altitudes more efficient than it otherwise would have been. However, it was still a comfortable height at which to fly formation—not so low that the pilots had to worry about flying into the water but low enough to stay below the scattered cumulous clouds that dotted the otherwise blue sky.

But the most important reason for flying so low was to avoid detection—the chances of success would be greatly increased if the Japanese were caught by surprise. So close to the water, the 345th's aircraft were shielded from enemy radars by the curvature of the earth. For instance, a radar installation at sea level could not detect a formation flying at a thousand feet until it came within approximately forty miles. The detection ranges decreased as the aircraft flew lower. So then, a formation flying at fifty feet was detectable by radar only when it approached within ten miles—almost too late to provide any useful warning at all. And radar was incapable of seeing through terrain. Consequently, aircraft could fly behind hills and ridges to screen their presence.

Nearing Warangoi Bay, True dropped the formation down to just a couple hundred feet above the water and turned west. Spotting the river of the same name, he crossed the coast at its mouth and followed it to the northwest. The squadrons behind him throttled back slightly to increase their separation from each other. It was imperative that they hit the airfield at Vunakanau in one-minute intervals.

Over land and with the target less than ten minutes away, the men donned flak vests and helmets. They checked and rechecked their guns and ammunition loads and squinted into the sky, looking for enemy aircraft. It was then, just before combat, that their anxiety peaked. Still, other than perform their duties, there was nothing they could do; at that point they were along for the ride whether they wanted to be or not.

Several crews spotted the airfield at Tobera less than two miles east of the 498th's course. There, parked wingtip-to-wingtip, were more than two dozen "black colored" enemy fighters. Tobera was the target assigned the RAAF Beaufighters that had been delayed at Dobodura. True could do nothing other than press ahead to his own target.

As the squadron completed its final turn toward Vunakanau, the pilots slid out of their four easily maneuvered flights of three aircraft each into an ungainly line abreast. Pilots could maintain such a formation only while flying a generally straight course; in a turn, the inside aircraft could not fly slow enough to maintain their positions without stalling, while the aircraft on the outside of the turn could not fly fast enough to keep the line from coming apart.

But ungainly or not, the broad, fast-flying front presented by the line of strafers was an almost irresistible force—a great aerial mowing machine—capable of shredding the sorts of targets that made an airfield capable of conducting operations. Among those were aircraft, supply depots, fuel dumps, motor transport, and personnel. In fact, each twelve-aircraft squadron of B-25s carried more .50-caliber machine guns than four American infantry regiments.

Once the formation was set for Vunakanau, the pilots maintained a rough separation from each other of one hundred feet, wingtip to wingtip. So arranged, the 498th crested the hills to the southeast of Vunakanau, and True, at the center, let his ship down to approximately one hundred feet. His pilots, careful not to sag into the jungle beneath them, referenced their positions relative to his aircraft. As they hurtled across the ground at more than four miles per minute, the enemy airfield quickly filled their windscreens.

Melvin Best of the 498th noted the difficulties that confronted the pilots. "The pilots saw less than anybody. If I took my eyes off, I put too many people in danger."[5] Indeed, the pilots not only had to keep an eye on the aircraft to either side of their own ships to avoid a collision but also had to avoid flying into the ground or trees or other obstructions. And most importantly—the entire reason they were flying such risky and costly missions—they had to spot and destroy worthwhile targets. An instant of inattention could make for a worthless mission, or worse, a mortal mishap.

This sort of line-abreast attack also demanded tremendous discipline. The crews had to accept whatever targets appeared generally in front of them rather than chasing after something more lucrative. A pilot flying over a taxiway devoid of any sort of meaningful target could only change the aircraft's course a degree or two to fire his guns at something else. And then, for only a couple of seconds. Deviating too far from his designated position and course risked a collision with a squadron mate. Nevertheless, parked aircraft were a particularly irresistible temptation, and pilots flitted toward them like moths to a flame.

"The enemy was taken completely by surprise as our squadron attacked at 1037 from minimum altitude," read the 498th's narrative report. "Troops were observed running for protection and A/A [anti-aircraft] guns were seen with the covers still on and pointing in the opposite direction." Indeed, the Japanese units at Vunakanau were hardly on an alert footing. Mechanics performed maintenance on a few of the sixty or more aircraft scattered around the airfield, and the low rumble of the engines they tested reverberated through the still morning air. Other aircraft, just landed or readying for takeoff, taxied to or from the runway, while still others flew in the traffic pattern or general vicinity. At the same time, various support personnel went about their regular duties, wholly unconcerned at the prospect of an air attack.

The 498th's crews could not have asked for an easier setup. True fired his guns at a Mitsubishi G4M twin-engine bomber flying low ahead of his ship. Given the Allied code name of "Betty," the Japanese aircraft was an approximate equivalent of the B-25. The unit's narrative report stated, "The plane was hit, but results were not observed." When he next fired his guns, there was no doubt as to the outcome. His rounds ripped into a Mitsubishi A6M Type 0 fighter, or Zero, code-named "Zeke," that had just lifted from the runway. "The plane was seen by other crews and is known to have been destroyed definitely."

As True pressed his attacks on the enemy aircraft, his copilot released clusters of parachute fragmentation bombs. Each aircraft carried seventy-two of them. "Frag clusters were dropped among other planes and six were believed destroyed." Toward the left side of the formation, Chester

AIR APACHES

Coltharp also fired at a Betty: "One airborne Betty was strafed and seen to crash later. Two medium bombers were destroyed on the ground."

Casey Dean, to True's immediate left, "definitely destroyed or damaged severely three airplanes. One inline engine fighter [Kawasaki Ki-61, code-named 'Tony'] taxiing on the strip was strafed, and tracers were seen to hit the fuselage from the tail up to the cockpit. This plane suddenly swerved to the side and stopped." Dean also hit a twin-engine aircraft identified as a Mitsubishi Ki-46, code-named "Dinah," as well as a Zeke. The right aileron of Dean's ship was hit by antiaircraft fire, rendering it useless, although the B-25 remained controllable.

Other 498th crews wrought similar destruction. Garvice McCall "strafed and bombed planes in the southeast dispersal area destroying or severely damaging 6 medium bombers definitely." Merton Kilgore's gunner "strafed a SSF [single-seat fighter] flying at low altitude at [the] north end of the strip." And Theodore O'Rear "strafed and bombed planes in the revetments, and personnel and installations east of the strip. One of the three Betty bombers that were airborne was definitely shot down by Lieutenant O'Rear."

Milford Magee, at the far left of the formation, drew a short straw: there were no attractive targets in his path. "Lieutenant Magee," the narrative report stated, "strafed and dropped bombs in the area west of the strip. Targets were indefinite and among trees, but area was covered [by his machine-gun fire and bombs]. No specific damage was observed." The weight and density of the gunfire was such that trees on and around the airfield were literally stripped of their leaves and branches.

The speed and ferocity of the attack stunned the Japanese. Most went to ground immediately, although some ran to the antiaircraft guns and a few pilots hurried to their aircraft, intent on either getting them airborne and safely out of the area or engaging the attacking Americans. All around the airfield and beyond, personnel, aircraft, buildings, and material were ripped apart by the overwhelming gunfire of the low-flying B-25s. And the 498th Bomb Squadron was only the first of the 345th's four squadrons to hit Vunakanau, not to mention the two additional squadrons from the 38th Bomb Group that were scheduled to follow.

54

Maintaining the planned one-minute interval between the squadrons was essential. Had they swept the airfield in close succession, the leading formations would have risked being hit by the gunfire of those that followed. And the trailing formations would have been in danger of overrunning the parachute fragmentation bombs dropped by those in front of them.

The 501st Bomb Squadron roared over the ridge to the southeast of Vunakanau just as the 498th was clearing the area to the northwest. But unlike the almost peaceable scene presented to the 498th, the airfield was chaotic—dotted with fires and explosions and shrouded with smoke. The squadron's narrative report qualified the damage the unit claimed: "Since the 498th Squadron passed the target one minute ahead and dropped their bombs in the same revetment areas, it is impossible to make complete claims." In other words, the 501st was wary of making claims against aircraft and other targets that might have already been hit by the 498th.

It was apparent that the Japanese were still confused as to what exactly was happening. Robert Larsen, a pilot with the 501st, recalled, "We had just come in over the water, popped up over this ridge, and then right in front of us was this airfield with aircraft all over. The guy in the [control] tower probably didn't know a B-25 from a locomotive. He gave us the green light to land. We didn't land. We blew him out of his tower."[6]

A particular curiosity is that at the height of the chaos a few Japanese aircraft attempted to land at Vunakanau rather than flee or recover at one of the other three nearby airfields. "At this time and locality," noted the 501st's narrative report, "a Jap transport and one SSF were seen trying to land on the airdrome." And most of the fighters that tried to get airborne were simply knocked down or shot apart. "One airplane, probably a SSF, was seen attempting to take off from the strip, then side-slipping off the strip due to a possible frag hit and strafing done by Lieutenant Sylvester Vogt. It was seen exploding."

George Cooper of the 499th Bomb Squadron—the third squadron across the airfield—was compelled to act fast. Incredibly, a Nakajima Ki-27, code-named "Nate," managed to take off without being hit. Once airborne it made a left turn across the 499th's line-abreast formation, and the pilots in the middle couldn't resist the temptation to give chase. "Near the end of the [air]drome," the narrative report stated, "Lieutenant Cooper and his flight had to turn left to avoid planes that were shooting at the Nate, taking off." Although five B-25s fired at the enemy aircraft, the results of their gunnery went "unobserved."

The 500th was the last 345th squadron across Vunakanau. Its post-mission summary indicated that the smoke, dust, and airborne debris created by the preceding three squadrons reduced visibility to a significant degree. "It is very likely that several more planes on the [air]drome were damaged by our bombs and strafing but it was impossible to observe results." Nevertheless, it is interesting to note that even at this point, Japanese aircraft were still moving about the airfield: "One Helen [Nakajima Ki-49] bomber with engines running was hit and left burning near the south end of the runway."

The effects of these successive attacks were overwhelming and additive. Waves of heavy machine-gun fire and cascades of parafrags were followed by more waves of heavy machine-gun fire and more cascades of parafrags. Ultimately, little was left intact that merited attention. Indeed, the 345th's airmen were so keen to do the Japanese harm that they even gunned and bombed a nearby garden plot.

The 345th and the two squadrons of the 38th left Vunakanau in a shambles. Aircraft, motor vehicles, buildings, and supply dumps blazed everywhere across the airfield. Burning ammunition cracked and popped. Wounded men screamed. Those who were uninjured crawled from their hiding places and exclaimed at the wreckage before them.

In the meantime, Clinton True and the rest of his force raced for home. True brought the 498th left to a heading of south, then turned left again to the east and crossed the coast without incident. The 501st and the 499th likewise egressed from the target unscathed. Along the way, one of the 501st crews made a report that confirmed the escorting P-38 pilots were hard at work. "Lieutenant Cather's gunner and radioman reported seeing an enemy SSF crash into the sea off the mouth of the Merai River. The pilot was seen to bail out and the parachute was noticed only partly opened when the pilot hit the water."

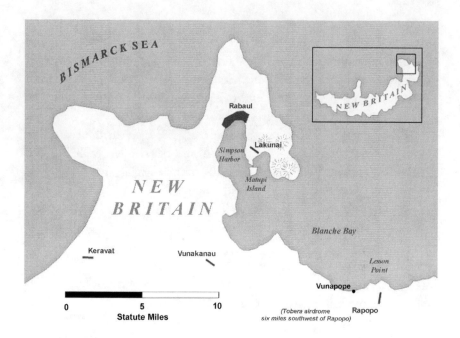

The Beaufighters of RAAF 30 Squadron were assigned to hit the airfield at Tobera simultaneously with the 345th's attack on Vunakanau. However, the dust created at Dobodura by the takeoff of so many preceding aircraft delayed their departure. Tobera was located to the southeast of Vunakanau, and several 345th crews reported a significant enemy fighter presence there as they flew past, just a short distance to the west. Pilot John Nusbaum's observation was typical: "Before reaching the target, 20–30 fighters were seen lined up wingtip-to-wingtip on the Tobera airdrome." The units there were obviously readying for action, as one of the 345th's trailing squadrons reported, "Five Zekes and one Val [Aichi Type 99] were observed taking off from Tobera Drome at 1035."

Tobera's fighters took off before the Beaufighters arrived. Once aloft they attacked the 345th's 500th Bomb Squadron as it made a left-hand turn following its run across Vunakanau. "Almost immediately after leaving the target we were intercepted by an estimated 6 Zekes and 6 Haps [code-name for a modified version of the Mitsubishi Type 0 fighter]— there may have been more."

The enemy fighter pilots dived continuously on the 500th Bomb Squadron's B-25s as they sped south and then east toward the sea in a fifteen-minute running fight. The squadron reported, "Approximately 24 passes were made, the majority of them from the 6 o'clock position [from the rear] just off the rudders." The B-25 crews were unimpressed by the Japanese pilots and called their attacks "weak and ineffective."

The Japanese pilots gave up just as the B-25s reached the coast. The 500th claimed, "Our gunners shot down one Hap and two Zekes; two additional Zekes are probably destroyed." Assuming that the claims were correct, the 500th bested the enemy fighter pilots, as the unit reported, "We suffered no casualties from the combat although one airplane had numerous holes received from the enemy fighters."

———

It is curious that the 500th's crews identified their attackers as both Zekes and Haps. Both aircraft were variants of the Mitsubishi A6M Zero and virtually indistinguishable from each other. The Hap differed from the Zeke primarily in having a different engine, a slightly shortened fuselage, and redesigned wings with squared tips. The engine and the modified fuselage would not have been noticeable to the crews, and in the heat of combat the squared wingtips would have been only barely evident. Whether or not both variants actually attacked the 500th is not clear.

Certainly aircraft identification during the raid was not perfect. For instance, the Nate was an older, nearly obsolete fighter with fixed landing gear. It had in fact been based at Rabaul during 1942 but was withdrawn from service there long before the 345th's attack on Vunakanau. However, it had similar lines to the Zeke, and the aircraft identified as Nates at Vunakanau were probably Zekes that had yet to raise their landing gear.

Misidentifications could have tragic consequences. As a pair of B-25 squadrons—unnamed but probably from the 345th—sped low over the water following their mission, they closed head-on with the "late to the party" Beaufighters of RAAF 30 Squadron. William Boulton was leading the Australians and recalled, "The leading B-25 squadron was at a height of approximately 80 feet and the second approximately 150 feet. The P-38 cover was at approximately 1,000 feet." When the B-25 pilots spotted the Beaufighters coming at them, the lower squadron spread out and opened fire without scoring. As the P-38s prepared to follow up the attack, Boulton managed to call them off over the radio. "The leaders of the B-25 squadrons both stated subsequently," Boulton said, "that they mistook the Beaufighters for Sallys [Mitsubishi Ki-21 medium bombers]."[7]

Although the American bombers were long gone, random explosions racked the airfield at Vunakanau every few minutes. A large number of the parafrags dropped by the B-25s had been snagged by trees or other obstructions before reaching the ground. When subsequently stirred by the wind or other forces, many of them slipped free, fell to earth, and detonated. Kiyoshi Yagita, a pilot at Vunakanau, recalled, "In the jungle belt on the south side of the airfield there were quite a few parafrags dropping from the disturbed trees, and occasionally, as the wind blew, they crashed to the ground and exploded."[8] Work parties were sent to recover them, but after several men were killed, the decision was taken to trigger the remaining bombs with machine-gun fire.

Aside from a few stragglers that landed at Kiriwina with mechanical issues, all of the 345th's aircraft recovered to Dobodura without incident. There were no casualties, and damage to the group's machines was light. The target had been hit hard, and the men were rightly pleased with their work that day. The 498th Bomb Squadron, which had led the attack, declared, "The mission was executed according to plan and was considered highly successful by all who participated in it. The enemy was completely surprised by the attack and the planes passing over twelve abreast covered the area well and gave him no opportunity to recover."

The 501st squadron concurred with that assessment but added a cautionary note: "The practice of flying abreast over the target was found to be very effective. It calls for a rigid adherence of each pilot to stay on his course and not to be tempted by changing same in order to improve his own effective machine-gun fire and bombing." Indeed, the only damage sustained by one of the squadrons—the 499th—was likely caused by another B-25. "Plane #591 received a .50-caliber slug in the main spar of the left wing which necessitates repair and probable replacement of the wing."

The damage wreaked by the 345th and the 38th at Vunakanau was real and extensive. Although a thorough on-the-spot assessment was obviously impossible, aircrew claims and photographs from the onboard cameras were carefully evaluated. Dozens of aircraft were destroyed and damaged, as was a great deal of support equipment and material. And not to be underestimated were the skilled and difficult-to-replace ground crewmen who were killed or badly injured. New aircraft could be built and delivered in a matter of weeks, but it took years to train and season a good mechanic.

Of course, the 345th's attack on Vunakanau was only one part of the air action that day. Although Tobera was missed, the airfield at Rapopo was hit hard by B-25s of the 38th Bomb Group. The "heavies"—the B-24s of the 43rd and 90th Bomb Groups—went after the dozens of warships and transports moored at Simpson Harbor and Blanche Bay. The majority of the Japanese fighters that had been able to get airborne directed their efforts against these formations. Consequently three B-24s were knocked down.

At his headquarters that day, MacArthur tracked the incoming reports. When it was clear that the massive raid had gone well, he declared, "It was a crushing and decisive defeat for the enemy at a most vital point. Once more, surprise was predominant. Rabaul has been the focus and very hub of the enemy's main advanced air effort. I think we have broken its back. Almighty God again blessed our arms."[9]

The actions of the B-25 groups merited special mention in American newspapers a few days later: "The vanguard of raiding Mitchell medium bombers flew in so daringly low, and in such tight formations that the enemy's antiaircraft defenses were overwhelmed, bewildered and, in some cases, abandoned. Such a demonstration of ability to dominate and demoralize Rabaul from the air very logically could hasten the end of the Solomons Campaign."[10]

Allied intelligence estimated the day's tally at 179 Japanese aircraft destroyed in the air and on the ground. This estimate was higher than actual losses, but the number of enemy aircraft put out of action was still significant. It was also determined that three destroyers were sunk, as were three large merchant vessels and upward of a hundred smaller barges and harbor craft. Valuable port facilities and warehouses were also put ablaze.

In reality, although several warships were damaged, none went under. Likewise, while many merchant and transport vessels were badly hit, the destruction was not as great as claimed.

Still, there was no denying the hurt that was done to the Japanese at Rabaul. The air component had taken a beating, and several ships were damaged enough that they were not immediately available for service. Importantly, the loss of skilled personnel could not be easily made up.

Curiously, Japanese claims against the Allied attackers were relatively muted rather than grossly inflated, as was usually the case. In radio broadcasts, the Japanese stated that their fighters and antiaircraft guns downed a combined total of fifteen Allied aircraft, which, surprisingly, was not an order-of-magnitude departure from the actual loss of five.

Based on their experiences that day, the 345th's crews were unimpressed with the defenses at Rabaul. The antiaircraft fire the men encountered was described as "light and ineffective" and "much less than anticipated." Moreover, the behavior of the Japanese fighter pilots seemed anything but aggressive. Rabaul hardly seemed the fearsomely defended bastion of Japanese power that had cost so many of the crews their sleep the previous night.

They would learn otherwise very soon.

Throughout the war, the 345th used a broad assortment of bombs to include 100-, 250-, 300-, 500-, and 1,000-pound general purpose, or demolition, bombs. Occasionally the bombs were wrapped in heavy-gauge wire to increase their lethality; when the bomb detonated, the wire was blasted into lengths that scythed through all but the toughest targets. George Kenney helped pioneer the notion in New Guinea. "To cut up aircraft on the ground, we had wrapped these bombs with heavy steel wire, and we dropped them with instantaneous fuzes on the end of a six-inch pipe extension in the nose." During a test, Kenney noted, "it cut limbs off trees a hundred feet away which were two inches thick. The noise was quite terrifying. The pieces of wire whirling through the air whistled and sang all the notes on the scale and screamed like a whole tribe of disconsolate banshees."[11]

The types and numbers of bombs carried on any given mission depended to a great degree on three factors: the sort of target being attacked, the range to the target, and the types of bombs readily available. For instance, if an attack was planned against barges, luggers, and other smaller vessels, bombs of lesser weight packed enough punch. And more could be carried so that more targets could be hit. On the other hand, five-hundred- and one-thousand-pound bombs were better suited for large ships, warehouses, or other substantial targets.

If a mission stretched the B-25's maximum range, the weight of the bomb load was sometimes reduced to keep fuel consumption low enough that the target could be reached. That being the case, careful consideration was given to the number of bombs carried. Large bombs caused more damage, but the odds of actually hitting the target with just one or two bombs were diminished. On the other hand, a greater number of smaller bombs increased the odds that the target—or targets—would be hit. But they did less damage.

Parademolition, or "parademo," bombs were usually 100- or 250-pound bombs fitted with a small parachute. The parachute opened once the bomb was clear of the aircraft and caused the bomb to stop its downrange travel and to descend more slowly and more generally straight down. These were particularly useful when making low-level attacks against targets on the ground as the aircraft was able to speed away as the bomb slowly descended. The fuzes were usually set to detonate instantaneously upon contact with the ground, but by that time the releasing aircraft was far away and out of danger.

On the other hand, it was critical that other aircraft not follow too closely behind. Otherwise they would fly directly into the descending bombs or overfly them as they made contact with the ground and detonated. No doubt several 345th aircraft were damaged or destroyed by this sort of mistake.

Parafragmentation bombs were especially effective against "soft" targets such as aircraft, vehicles, or personnel. These twenty-three-pound bombs were scored on the outside to more readily break into deadly fragments. Because the parafrags were so small, the B-25 could carry up to seventy-two of them in an arrangement of bomb-bay-mounted square racks. One drawback of these bombs was that the releasing aircraft was so far away by the time they exploded that it was often difficult to determine the exact damage caused.

Fuzing was critical not only to the effectiveness of the bombs but to the safety of the crews. For instance, once released, a conventional bomb "flew" with the aircraft for a while. Its forward velocity only gradually degraded as it fell toward the ground. If the aircraft was flying at very low altitude when it released the bomb, the bomb would still be almost underneath the aircraft when it finally hit the earth. If the fuze was set to detonate instantaneously upon making contact with the ground, there was a good chance the aircraft would be blown from the sky. Accordingly the fuzes for free-falling bombs were usually set for a delayed detonation—either four to five seconds or eight to eleven seconds after impact. As with parachute-retarded bombs, it was important that aircraft not follow others too closely as they might overfly the delayed-fuzed bombs just as they exploded.

A disadvantage of the delayed fuze was that the bombs often buried themselves on impact with the earth. Consequently, when the bombs exploded, the ground absorbed much of the energy and shrapnel. Interestingly, the 345th took advantage of this tendency of the bombs to disappear into the ground. A portion of the bombs were sometimes fitted with fuzes set to detonate several hours after impact. Unseen, these bombs exploded and killed—or at least rattled—Japanese personnel as they scrambled to recover from a raid.

The delayed fuzes were also crucial for shipping attacks. First, they helped ensure that the bombs penetrated to the interior of the ship before detonating. Second, as with low-flying attacks against land targets, the delayed fuzes prevented the bombs from exploding immediately upon making contact with the water or the ship. This was critical to keeping an aircraft from being blown out of the sky by its own bomb.

It must be considered that the 345th existed to put bombs on Japanese targets. Every person in the group—aircrew, cooks, mechanics, clerks, supply personnel, and so forth—was responsible at least in part for making certain this happened. And unquestionably the ordnance men were as directly responsible as anyone. Aside from the danger of the work, and notwithstanding the backbreaking, finger-smashing, grunting, and sweating physicality that loading bombs aboard aircraft was, the job also demanded intelligence and attention to detail.

For instance, after the bombs were selected, loaded, and transported from the ammunition dump to the aircraft, the right fuzes had to be safely installed and set. The attachment shackles and hardware often differed from one bomb type to another, and these had to be carefully mounted and checked. And obviously the bombs had to be lifted into the aircraft—often by hand. Most frustrating of all were those occasions when the group's aircraft were loaded for a mission only to have the target changed. This often required a different bomb load, and so the exhausted ordnance men were required to download the bombs they had just lifted into the aircraft and repeat the process with a different load of bombs.

Because it was highly demanding and technical work performed in primitive conditions, and also because of equipment and material failures—and aircrew error—bomb malfunctions were not uncommon, particularly with the more complex parademolition bombs. Fairly representative was the experience of the 498th Bomb Squadron during the mission flown to Borgen Bay on December 20, 1943. "The bombing was excellent with 38 of the 38 bombs dropped falling in the target. Ten of the bombs were returned to base, although the racks functioned perfectly on the ground after the mission."

No doubt the 345th's aircraft could carry a broad variety of bombs, but they were also fitted with a diverse spectrum of factory and ad hoc fuel tank arrangements—both temporary and permanent. So many and varied were these configurations that a definitive summation is virtually impossible. Bernard Schriever, a veteran pilot then serving with the Fifth Air Force's service command, described a "homegrown" example that was put into the aircraft at the same time they were modified into strafers: "Then, we took the lower turret out. We put four angle irons in the back of that B-25 and slipped a square, 300-gallon welded steel tank . . . up into the bomb bay and mounted it on a bomb shackle. So, we got about two hours and twenty-five minutes more of fuel than we did in a normal B-25. We'd burn that off first, and then we'd drop the tank. We had spring-loaded doors with old screen door springs on them that closed when the tank dropped out."[12]

— —

But before hitting Rabaul again, the 345th went back to Wewak. Kenney was keen to ensure that the Japanese did not reconstitute the airfield complex there while the greater part of his attention and resources were directed against Rabaul. It was better to kick Wewak while it was down than to return after it had been reinforced.

Accordingly, the group launched thirty-eight aircraft at 0815 on October 16, 1943. Three squadrons of P-38s rendezvoused with the 345th over Mount Hagen and accompanied the B-25s all the way to the target. Along the way, the 345th's formation grew smaller as aircraft turned back with mechanical issues. One of those issues was particularly unusual, as described by the 500th's mission summary report: "After reaching Sepu on the upper Ramu Valley, the [top] turret on Lieutenant James's airplane broke and fell off."

The plan for the attack was simple and called for the squadrons to sweep from east to west across the airfield at Boram and then the town and airfield at Wewak. The 500th Bomb Squadron was to lead the mission, followed by the 501st, 499th, and 498th. The different flights in each squadron—carrying either twelve wire-wrapped, one-hundred-pound demolition bombs or racks of twenty-three-pound parafragmentation bombs in three-bomb clusters—were to fly in a line abreast to ensure the broadest coverage possible.

"The enemy defenses were apparently waiting for the attack," noted the 500th's mission summary report, "A/A [antiaircraft fire] was encountered immediately [as] the formation came in range. However, the warning had not been sufficiently in advance of our arrival for all fighters to become airborne." In fact, although not every enemy fighter had taken off, about twenty were already aloft, and more were getting airborne. Indeed, "seven to ten single seat fighters were observed to take off from Boram strip, west to east, as the attacking force approached."

65

The group's attack and its results were similar to the earlier mission against the Wewak complex and the raid made against Rabaul a few days earlier. Aircraft, vehicles, supply dumps, and buildings were all strafed and bombed. Japanese personnel rushed for cover, and antiaircraft fire tore at the low-flying B-25s. Burning aircraft and material sent flames and smoke high into the sky.

The defending fighters seemed more zealous than usual. "Interception was made by 15-to-20 Zekes and Tonys," reported the 500th, "at 1052 to 1102 over the target and offshore from the target at 100 to 200 feet. In a free-for-all fight, enemy passes were made from all directions." The 500th's men claimed six Zeroes and three Ki-61s definitely destroyed but were by and large impressed with the enemy pilots, noting, "Several attacks were made from above, the enemy fighters passing under our B-25s. The Japs in several instances broke off their attacks when fired upon, but the crews generally reported that they were aggressive and experienced pilots."

One incident recorded by the 500th was especially amazing. "Over Dalman Harbor, one Zeke dove at 2 airplanes leading our withdrawal on a swing to the right, hit the water, bounced up and continued in the fight." Considering the physics involved, such a thing is hardly believable, especially as the Zero was known to be a particularly delicate aircraft. Nevertheless, the event is described in the 500th's mission summary report—an official document.

The 501st Bomb Squadron likewise was harried by Japanese fighters. J. R. Jones wrote about the mission a few days later to his fiancée, Elnora. "Yours truly had a very close one not so long ago. If they never come any closer, I'll be quite satisfied. Somehow I just can't get used to the idea of those Zeroes taking pot shots at me. I guess I just ain't the daring kind. I honestly thought one of those devils was going to come right through the cockpit."[13]

But as aggressive as the Japanese fighters were, the protective cover of P-38s matched them and more. An account from the 501st was representative of several other observations. "Lieutenant [Robert] Larsen reported two passes were made at his airplane by five Jap fighters, possibly one Mike and four Zekes. The attempted interception was abandoned when the P-38s closed in on the Jap airplane." To be sure, no 345th aircraft were lost to enemy fighters.

In fact, the B-25 pilots did their best to use their own aircraft as fighters when opportunities were presented. The 499th Bomb Squadron recorded how, after Philip Gath dropped seven bombs, "this plane was attacked by one Zeke from the front and above. Lieutenant Gath pulled his plane up to meet the attack, turning loose with all nose guns. The Zeke just barely cleared this plane, stalled out, and crashed out to sea."

The 501st Bomb Squadron referred to a type of enemy fighter code-named "Mike." This was the result of considerable confusion. The Kawasaki Ki-61, code-named "Tony," resembled the German Messerschmitt Me-109 to a very great degree, and when they first encountered it, American fliers believed the Japanese were flying a license-built version of the German fighter. It was subsequently given the code name "Mike." However, Allied intelligence discovered that the Ki-61 was in fact an indigenous Japanese aircraft, and it was given the code name of "Tony." Accordingly, the "Mike" code name quickly—and properly—fell into disuse. Nevertheless, the fact that both code names were used in the same mission report on this day is interesting. It indicates that the unit knew of the Tony but still believed the Japanese were also operating license-built Me-109s.

The 345th lost one aircraft in the Wewak raid. It was from the 500th Bomb Squadron and piloted by Donald Stookey. Hit by an anti-aircraft battery, it was set afire. The fire spread, and Stookey had little choice but to make a water landing. Henry Knoll of the 501st Bomb Squadron spotted the aircraft in the water and estimated that it sank within ninety seconds.

However, the crew cleared the wreck. The squadron reported, "Four men were seen in a life raft. Two men were seen swimming toward a raft nearby. Captain Knoll dropped an extra raft and radioed its position. He stated that the probability of the men being captured seemed very likely, as they were only about three miles offshore." Not long afterward, Knoll headed for Port Moresby low on fuel.

Stookey and his men, safely aboard their rafts, watched Wewak burn.

⸺❦⸺

They were subsequently captured by the Japanese. A couple or more of them were later murdered in the Wewak area, while Stookey and one or two others were later slain at Rabaul. Such unlawful slaughter of Allied airmen was normal, and the 345th's men understood that they would likely suffer similar fates if they were ever shot down and captured. Indeed, Ralph "Peppy" Blount of the 501st Bomb Squadron declared that, in the event he was shot down, he would shoot himself rather than surrender. He was hardly alone.

The murders of Stookey and his crew were horrific acts. But they were typical of the sorts of atrocities committed by the monster state that was the Empire of Japan. During the period leading up to World War II and during the war itself, the Japanese brutalized virtually every population over whom they held sway, often slaughtering civilians on an industrial scale. The most infamous example was the "Rape of Nanking," during which an estimated three hundred thousand Chinese civilians—including women and children—were viciously slain, often with bayonets or swords. And throughout Asia, millions more were pitilessly butchered, worked to death, or starved.

It is one thing to declare that the Japanese did horrible things, but it is quite another to consider their own descriptions of those horrible things. For instance, an army unit seized a Chinese family. "We played with the daughter as we would a harlot," wrote one Japanese soldier. He then noted that the soldiers killed the child's parents when they tried to stop her rape. "We then played with the daughter again as before, until our unit marched on, when we killed her."[14]

That Japan abused its prisoners of war is well documented and undisputed outside Japan. Aside from beatings, tortures, and starvation, murder was commonplace. At Camp 10-A on Palawan Island, a group of 150 American prisoners was forced into dugouts. Then, in an effort to burn them alive, the Japanese doused the dugouts with gasoline and set them afire. Remarkably, many of the men escaped the flames, only to be cut down by Japanese guards. However, eleven of the prisoners fled to safety and survived. Glen McDole was among them. He recalled how the

Japanese murdered a comrade who had escaped the fires: "I could see the bayonets draw blood when they poked him. Another Jap came up with some gasoline and a torch, and I heard the American beg them to shoot him and not to burn him. The Jap threw some gasoline on his foot and lit it, and the other Japs laughed and poked him with their bayonets. Then they did the same thing to his other foot and to his hand. When the man collapsed, the Japs then threw the whole bucket of gasoline over him, and he burst into flames."[15]

The Japanese also cannibalized prisoners, sometimes cutting flesh from them while they were still alive. In fact, one Japanese unit codified the practice when it issued an instructional memorandum titled "Order Regarding Eating the Flesh of American Flyers." A captured soldier from the Indian army described how Japanese soldiers beheaded a downed American fighter pilot and subsequently ate him. "I saw this from behind a tree and watched some of the Japanese cut flesh from his arms, legs, hips and buttocks and carry it off to their quarters. . . . They cut it in small pieces and fried it."[16]

Moreover, the Japanese subjected prisoners to unthinkable medical tortures. At Unit 731 in northeast China, they conducted ghastly tests with biological pathogens and chemical gases. Prisoners were also dissected alive and subjected to other bizarre experiments, including exposure to extreme cold in order to study the effects of frostbite. As always, the Japanese methods were hideously inhuman. One seemingly routine account described how two practitioners met prior to a scheduled experiment. They were early and sought to amuse themselves.

So he and another unit member took the keys to the cells and opened one that housed a Chinese woman. One of the unit members raped her; the other member took the keys and opened another cell. There was a Chinese woman in there who had been used in a frostbite experiment. She had several fingers missing and her bones were black, with gangrene set in. He was about to rape her anyway, then he saw that her sex organ was festering, with pus oozing to the surface. He gave up the idea, left and locked the door, then later went on to his experimental work.[17]

69

It was against monsters such as these that the men of the 345th fought.

Apologists explain away or minimize these sorts of bestial acts. They declare that such actions were consistent with Japanese culture. They explain that Japan's military institutionalized cruelty and sanctioned—even encouraged—mistreatment of anyone who was not Japanese.

Such reasoning is not far off the mark inasmuch as the Japanese military was a reflection of Japanese society. Perhaps the most racist civilization in existence, the Japanese implicitly believed themselves a superior race and that all others were lacking or even subhuman. The Chinese in particular were considered little better than vermin.

This psyche of eminence evolved for many reasons. Among these was the fact that, as an island nation, the Japanese had lived most of their history in almost complete isolation. Therefore, everyone from outside Japan was peculiar. And, at least in the Japanese consciousness, peculiarity equated to inferiority. Consequently, other peoples were scorned and derided.

The Japanese also believed they were favored by the gods. This was evidenced to them during the thirteenth century when the hitherto undefeated Mongols were turned back twice. These victories were won not only by their own fighting men but by typhoons, or "divine winds," that scuttled great portions of the invading fleets.

Moreover, there was the fact that, upon being forced by the Americans to open their doors to trade during the nineteenth century, Japan quickly modernized to become an industrial and military equal of the most advanced nations. And during this same period the Japanese defeated the world's two largest nations—China and Russia—in separate wars. Additionally, they seized and brutally occupied Korea in 1910 and also sided with the victorious Allies during World War I, for which they were rewarded with German territories in the Pacific.

But the dual perversions of Bushido—the samurai warrior code—and the Shinto religion were most responsible for creating a society capable of grand-scale cruelties. As the twentieth century got underway, Japan's military leaders played a growing role in the governance of the nation. Anxious to reinforce and grow that role, they turned parts of

Bushido—which had elements common to Western chivalric codes—to their own purposes.

Chief among these was an entreaty for their men not just to fight to the utmost but to fight fanatically and, if necessary, to the death. Surrender, no matter the circumstances, greatly dishonored not just the individual but the individual's family, his community, and the nation. Enemies who had surrendered obviously did not adhere to the same values and were accordingly worth nothing but contempt.

Another precept of Bushido was unwavering loyalty to the feudal overlord. But there were no feudal overlords in modern Japan, and the population accordingly directed its fidelity to the emperor. Emperor Hirohito, who assumed the throne in 1926, was a commissioned officer in both the army and the navy and was largely sympathetic to—if not complicit with—Japan's military leadership. Consequently, the Japanese people in large part transferred to the military their allegiance to their emperor.

The Shinto faith, loosely associated with Buddhism but more vaguely defined and with an emphasis on myriad natural spirits and gods, was also twisted into a form that best suited the military leadership. It was invigorated and sanctioned as the true religion of Japan. And the emperor, represented for centuries as a direct descendant of the sun goddess Amaterasu, was its head. As such, he was venerated as a god. And as a god, he had the right to rule not only Japan but the entire world.

These corrupted forms of Bushido and Shinto were inculcated not just in the military but across the entire nation by way of the educational system. So then, over a period of just a few decades, Japan's military—in the name of the emperor—warped the very fabric of the Japanese spirit. The people were hard-line nationalists and blindly loyal to the emperor and the military. Their actions were underpinned by an unshakeable belief that they were a superior race, possessed of a godly mandate. Japan's military further grafted these racist perversions onto the minds of its fighting men and turned them into the sadists who murdered millions, who raped the young and helpless, who tortured in the name of science, and who cannibalized prisoners.

Rationalizations aside, Japan had no excuses. It was a modern nation exposed to modern sensibilities. The West was available to emulate, just as it had been emulated when Japan modernized its industry and military. Moreover, it was offered a code of conduct for warfare in the form of the Geneva Convention, more formally known as the Convention Relative to the Treatment of Prisoners of War. It was a code that Japan, led by Hirohito, willfully rejected.

Ultimately, the Japanese killed up to 10 million people during the years leading up to and including World War II.

Rather than raw hatred, many of the 345th's men had conflicted feelings about the Japanese. "When I was getting shot at, I sure didn't like them," said John Baeta, a pilot with the 499th Bomb Squadron.[18] "The Japanese I knew back home in Sacramento were fine people—very hard-working. They picked the strawberry fields in the area. Some of them didn't speak English, but I didn't either until I got into grade school. My people were Portuguese."

"I had a Japanese friend, who worked with me in the same office before the war," Baeta recalled. "He was a duck hunter, and when the government started rounding the Japanese up to put them into internment camps after the attack on Pearl Harbor, he asked me if I would hold his shotgun until the war was over. They weren't allowed to have firearms. So, of course I said yes."

"I never heard from him again," Baeta said. "I don't know if he went into the Army and was killed, or what. I called all over after the war but was never able to locate him. His shotgun is still sitting in my garage waiting for him—after all this time."

CHAPTER FOUR

"The Squadron Was Attacked"

ANXIOUS TO ENSURE THAT THE JAPANESE AT RABAUL ENJOYED NO respite after the successful attacks of October 12, George Kenney's staff planned a number of follow-on missions. All were stymied by poor weather. Consequently, elements of the Fifth Air Force were not sent back to Rabaul until October 18. On that day, eight squadrons of B-24s, covered by P-40s, were scheduled to hit the airfields at Vunakanau and Lakunai. An hour later, two squadrons of B-25 strafers from the 38th Bomb Group were to hit the airfield at Tobera. At the same time, the 345th was to send its 498th, 499th, and 501st Bomb Squadrons, protected by a P-38 fighter group, against the Rapopo airfield.

With this plan, Kenney's staff hoped to set a trap whereby the enemy fighters sent from Vunakanau and Lakunai to oppose the high-flying B-24s would be compelled by the bombing to recover at Tobera and Rapopo just before the B-25s attacked. Packed onto the two airfields—and out of fuel and ammunition—the enemy fighters would be easy pickings. Almost as an afterthought, the 345th's last squadron, the 500th, was tasked with attacking the shipping in Blanche Bay moored between Vunapope and Lesson Point.

The 345th's four squadrons—with nine aircraft each—staged through Dobodura on the day prior to the mission. The next morning, October 18, 1943, the group rendezvoused at Oro Bay with its P-38 escort before passing by the Buna Wreck and collecting the two B-25 squadrons from the 38th Bomb Group. Soon after, the three-ship flight led by Charles Howard of the 500th Bomb Squadron aborted the mission when his

73

top turret failed. After nearly an hour, bad weather presented itself once more, and both the 345th and the 38th were battered with sheets of blinding rain as they descended to wedge themselves between the wind-whipped waves and a line of thunderstorms.

While the B-25s were thrashing through the vicious gale, the entire mission was recalled. Clinton True, the 345th's commander, was at the head of the formation once again. He either didn't hear the recall command or ignored it, but as he was nicknamed "Fearless," it was likely the latter. Regardless of what True heard or didn't, the B-25s penetrated through the foul weather toward Rabaul.

True brought the formation into the clear an hour later to find that the escorting group of P-38s was gone. The 501st's narrative report noted, "It is the understanding from interrogation of the combat crews that the fighters called in, notifying their decision to return to base." It is unclear if True knew this as the 498th's narrative report simply stated, "The flight leader [True], unaware that the fighters had turned back, continued to the target."

So then, rather than striking the airfield at Rapopo as the coup de grâce of a carefully orchestrated multigroup attack—protected by fighters—True and the B-25s were going it alone.

Approaching the coast of New Britain, the formation angled northward and stayed approximately twenty-five miles out to sea to lessen the odds of detection. Finally, True led the B-25s to the west toward Gazelle Point. Approaching landfall, the two squadrons of the 38th turned for the airfield at Tobera while True made for a point ten miles south of Rapopo to set up for a south-to-north attack. As Rapopo was located on Blanche Bay, this heading would put the 345th's B-25s safely over the water as they finished their firing runs. Meanwhile, the 500th separated to make its run against the shipping at Vunapope, while the 499th and 501st throttled back to ensure they hit Rapopo at half-minute intervals.

While the 345th's attack on Vunakanau on October 12 had gone nearly as perfectly to script as possible, the raid on Rapopo was not so well executed. True was able to make his attack with the 498th as planned, but the 501st cut the corner too close to Rapopo. "As a result, the 501st Squadron had difficulty in making a proper bombing and strafing run while still in their turn." In fact, some of the unit's pilots were unable to strafe during part of the run, and others were compelled to hit targets outside their assigned area of responsibility.

Orlen Loverin, leading the 499th, took the squadron through a full 360-degree circle just before hitting the airfield. This was a spacing maneuver intended to give the other two squadrons time to clear the target. Once out of the turn, he made a couple of quick adjustments before getting the 499th established on the proper heading.

The three squadrons that hit Rapopo did not use the broad line-abreast formation that had been so effective at Vunakanau a few days earlier but rather stayed in three flights of three aircraft each, arranged in an inverted *V* formation. This allowed the leaders to maneuver more aggressively. Once established on the final attack heading, the pilots spread out and presented a broader front. Just as during the attack at Vunakanau, many of the B-25s carried parachute-retarded fragmentation bombs. However, others carried payloads of twelve wire-wrapped one-hundred-pound demolition bombs.

Notwithstanding the fact that the 345th executed only a portion of the original mission—and not according to plan—the three squadrons that hit Rapopo did real damage. The 498th's mission narrative report noted a representative example: "Lieutenant McCall attacked the dispersal areas adjacent to the right side of the strip, destroying two Dinahs and one Zeke, and blowing the wing off one Betty." And "Lieutenant Magee bombed and strafed along the inside of the eastern edge of the dispersal area, destroying one Dinah and five Zekes. Destruction of these airplanes was positive." As the 498th's pilots completed their runs across the airfield and crossed the beach over Blanche Bay, virtually all of them strafed a corvette that was anchored in their path near Gredner Island.

The 501st was second across the target. Despite arriving overhead while still in a turn and out of position, the squadron made a number of claims, including the destruction of three Ki-49 bombers and one Ki-61 fighter. Among the claims made by the 499th, the last squadron to hit Rapopo, was the destruction of three Kawasaki Ki-48 light bombers, code-named "Lily," and one Mitsubishi Ki-57 transport, code-named "Topsy."

The experience of one of these 499th crews highlighted the importance of good maintenance and reliable components. "One plane of this flight experienced electrical trouble. Bombs failed to release and guns failed to fire." Essentially, every bit of effort to get that particular aircraft to Dobodura from Port Moresby and thence to Rabaul—at great risk—was wasted. However, notwithstanding the inability of this particular aircraft to contribute to the effort, intelligence assessments credited the 345th's squadrons with definitely destroying nineteen Japanese aircraft at Rapopo.

The fighting did not end with the attack on Rapopo. Although the group's B-25s were targeted by moderate volumes of poorly directed antiaircraft fire over the airfield, a greater danger awaited overhead in the form of dozens of Japanese fighters. The enemy pilots commenced their attacks as the 345th's B-25s sped north away from Rapopo, crossed the beach over Blanche Bay, and then turned southeast toward home. "Immediately after leaving the target," the 498th reported, "the squadron was intercepted by approximately 40 Zekes and Haps. The squadron got into close formation and flew close to the water to prevent attacks from below. In a running battle that lasted for 25 minutes, ten Zekes and Haps were definitely destroyed."

Incredibly, the Japanese fighters failed to do the 498th any harm whatever. "[Japanese] Pilots appeared experienced but did not press attacks, appearing reluctant to attack close formation. Our squadron suffered neither casualties to personnel nor planes." Inasmuch as it was the job of the enemy fighter pilots to knock down the American crews, they failed utterly.

The 501st cleared Rapopo shortly after the 498th. After making Blanche Bay, its aircraft were targeted by warships steaming out of Simpson Harbor. One pilot reported that the antiaircraft fire from the destroyers "was fired so as to hit the water under the B-25s and thus explode. Pilot states effect was very good and had B-25s been flying lower over the water, they would most likely have been hit by frags from these shells."

Just as the 498th was hit by enemy fighters over Blanche Bay, so was the 501st, as described in its report. "When still in their turn just past Gredner Island, the squadron was attacked by a large force of enemy fighters estimated at approximately sixty airplanes. Of this enemy force, it seems that approximately thirty airplanes stayed at altitudes of around 9,000 feet while the remainder made diving attacks on the squadron." As to why the entire force didn't fall on the fleeing B-25s, the 501st made a credible assumption: "It is the opinion that the enemy was expecting our fighter cover to be present above and for this reason did not apply their full force on the attack." The squadron also suggested that its crews absorbed the weight of the Japanese fighter attacks, as "it was noticed that the other squadrons were also attacked, but the main attack seemed to have taken place on the 501st Squadron."

The 501st described how, aside from returning defensive gunfire, its pilots responded to the enemy's attacks: "Our evasive action consisted of flying in a tight formation at minimum altitude. However, our airplanes were careful not to fly too low in order to deny the enemy [the ability] to adjust his aim by observing the bullet splashes in the water." The squadron's gunners claimed ten Zeroes shot down in aerial combat. And just as they had failed to inflict any real damage on the 498th, the Japanese fighter pilots did no harm to the 501st, although the squadron did note its good luck in a recap of the mission. "Air opposition was extremely heavy due to the lack of fighter cover, and it is considered extremely fortunate that all airplanes returned."

The 499th encountered a smaller group of fifteen enemy fighters. "A total of twenty passes were made [by the Japanese pilots], however most of these passes were made in a half-hearted manner and breaking off when fired upon at extreme range." Indeed, the squadron's crews had little regard for these particular enemy pilots, whom they described as "less experienced and much less aggressive than those encountered recently over Wewak." The squadron's gunners made claims for two Zeroes.

While the 345th's other three squadrons strafed and bombed Rapopo, the six remaining aircraft of the 500th swung further out to the west before racing north to strike shipping in Blanche Bay between Vunapope and Lesson Point. "As they swept toward the coast at tree-top level," recorded the squadron's narrative report, "the six strafers sprayed a hail of bullets from 48 forward-firing .50-caliber machine guns across camp and supply areas in their path. Breaking over the coast, they lined up in three-plane flights on a 5,000-ton freighter and a 6,000-ton freighter-transport lying at anchor."

Max Mortensen, at the head of the squadron and leading the first three-ship flight, together with Ray Geer attacked the five-thousand-ton freighter *Kinkasan Maru* with delayed-fused one-thousand-pound bombs. The ship was straddled by two of the bombs and "was seen to overturn." The squadron's report described how the flight pressed after other prey: "Still ruffling the water with their prop wash, the pilots headed for a corvette which was well under way and maneuvering to avoid attack. Two 1,000-pound bombs from Lieutenant [Thane] Hecox's airplane hit directly ahead of the warship, and the delay in explosions was just enough to catch the ship squarely, demolishing it."

Slightly behind and to the left of Mortensen, Lyle Anacker led his three-ship against the freighter-transport *Johore Maru*, "strafing all the way and setting the superstructure afire. One 1,000-pound bomb hit the deck and bounced off, but the other five exploded near or in the vessel, lifting it out of the water."

An estimated forty Zeroes dove on the six B-25s as they escaped eastward across Blanche Bay, low over the water. Although the enemy fighter pilots who had engaged the 345th's other three squadrons were unaggressive to the point of timidity, such wasn't the case with those who attacked the 500th. The gunners dueled with the Japanese fighters, but it wasn't long before Ralph Wallace's aircraft, *Tondelayo*, was hit in the right engine and began to slow. Both Harlan Peterson and Anacker dropped back to protect their stricken comrade. It was then that Peterson's aircraft, *Sorry Satchul*, was also hit by fire from the Zeroes.

Peterson's left engine "burst into flames," said Wallace, "and at the same moment the left landing gear dropped out of the engine nacelle. The bad engine was quickly feathered but still observed to be on fire." The three-ship of B-25s quickly turned into a two-ship as Peterson's aircraft was unable to keep pace with Anacker or with Wallace's damaged B-25. Even as their aircraft settled toward the water, Peterson's aircrew continued to fight and was observed to shoot down two Zeroes.

John Murphy, Wallace's gunner, kept an eye on *Sorry Satchul.* "Pieces started falling off the plane. Lieutenant Peterson made a smooth landing in the water about a mile off shore but was immediately strafed by seven or eight Zeroes." There is no further record of Peterson's crew. If any survived the water landing and subsequent strafing, they were likely captured by the Japanese and murdered. Among the crew was Mike Korczynski, Tal Epps's friend with whom he had cheated death aboard the ill-fated C-47 on August 7.

The two remaining B-25s of Anacker's flight continued southbound at minimum altitude while the Zeroes pressed their attacks. Howard Davis, Wallace's engineer, manned the top turret and shot a number of the enemy fighters into the sea. His counterpart in Anacker's ship, George Hardy, achieved similar successes. "I saw him knock down two of the attacking enemy," Davis said.

So low over the water, the two B-25s were difficult targets. Had the Japanese pilots also dropped to minimum altitude while attacking from anywhere but directly ahead or astern, not only would they have been presented with very fleeting and problematic deflection shots, but they would have had to devote considerable attention simply to keep from flying into the water. On the other hand, a level attack from dead astern would have offered the enemy fliers the surprisingly small and difficult-to-hit rear profile of the B-25s.

And a firing run from directly ahead would have put the enemy pilots at a firepower disadvantage, as the output of the B-25's forward-firing .50-caliber machine guns significantly outweighed what the Zero's two 20-millimeter cannons and two 7.7-millimeter machine guns produced. And finally, the B-25 pilots did not fly straight and level but worked to spoil the enemy's aim with abrupt turns and skids.

Consequently, the Japanese chose to make diving attacks. Doing so carried its own risks, as more than one Zero was observed to crash into the water. Mitsuyasu Yamakawa was part of a three-ship flight of Zeroes. He was so horrified to see his leader smash into the water that he flew directly into the resulting geyser. The shock to his aircraft was so great that Yamakawa believed for a moment that he had also flown into the sea.[1]

One Japanese fighter pilot likely misjudged his closing speed while making an attack and subsequently found himself boxed between Wallace and Anacker. "The Japs flew very close, showing their roundel on a gold background the edges of which had a fish scale appearance and a lightning bolt insignia. One nervy Jap eased into formation between the two B-25s and flew for more than a minute not more than 50 feet away from either Mitchell. The gunners did not dare to fire for fear of hitting their other plane. The Jap pilot was described by one gunner as a 'mean-looking bastard,' and not smiling as Hollywood shows them."

The Japanese pilot somehow slipped out from between the B-25s without being shot down, but the seemingly interminable running fight continued. "So numerous were the attacks," noted the narrative report, "that the gunners were kept busy firing short bursts at one enemy plane after another and declined to estimate any number of Jap planes probably shot down or damaged. Sergeant [John] Murphy, turret gunner on Lieutenant [Ralph] Wallace's ship, soon ran out of ammunition and called for more." The gunner and radioman teamed to relay more ammunition to Murphy. "These two men also were kept busy firing the waist guns, operating the radio to send out an SOS, and taking turns clamping their hands over a gasoline line which had been severed by a bullet and was flooding the plane with gasoline and fumes."

The two men also called out enemy fighters to Murphy in the top turret. They checked the position of his legs to see which way he was looking and alerted him over the interphone when the Zeros or Haps approached from his blind spots. This sort of ad hoc teamwork kept him rotating back and forth; the staccato boom of his guns vibrated through the already straining aircraft.

"All three men became groggy from the gas fumes," declared the squadron's narrative. "Sergeant [Burton] Eaton momentarily passed out while calling for a radio bearing and fell across the key, sending out a continuous signal. Reviving slightly, he grabbed his oxygen mask and sucked on the tube to get straightened out." Meanwhile, Murphy covered Anacker's aircraft, *Snafu*, when it was apparent that the turret gunner, George Hardy, was reloading or otherwise unable to fire.

And then the two B-25s parted company. "About fifteen minutes after Lieutenant Peterson's ship was seen to crash," said Murphy, "I saw ship 41-30054 [Anacker's aircraft] make a shallow bank to the right and leave the formation. He was headed towards the coast of New Britain. The last we saw of him was as he blended into the terrain over land. His turret guns were still firing as he was being chased by eight or ten Zeroes."

Wallace turned south toward Kiriwina while he and his men battled the enemy fighters. Wallace's copilot, Edward Hicko, felt he wasn't doing enough compared to the rest of the crew. He pulled his .45-caliber pistol from its holster, slid back his side window, and fired at the enemy fighters as they flashed by. For his trouble, he got shot in the guts and the hand. "It was while he was resting his pistol momentarily in his lap," the squadron narrative said, "that he was wounded, and the same bullet nearly severed his right thumb holding his pistol."

Wallace flogged *Tondelayo* further away from New Britain. "Some of the Japs appeared anxious to finish him off," noted the squadron's report, "and became daring in their maneuvers which resulted in four, and a possible fifth, crashing into the water as they wheeled low to attack Lieutenant Wallace who was flying at about 30 feet. Four of these are being claimed as definitely destroyed as a result of Lieutenant Wallace's wave-skipping strategy and superior flying."

The squadron report lauded Wallace's airmanship. "Despite having his ship crippled by the loss of one engine and by more than 41 gaping holes in it, he met head-on attacks four times by climbing into them, maneuvering, and then turning into his dead engine to get down to his former level." Finally, out of fuel, ammunition, or motivation, the enemy fighters gave up and winged away. "The remaining Zeke, apparently out of ammunition, did several slow rolls, finally waggled his wings [and] headed for home."

His ship shot up and low on fuel, Wallace nevertheless brought *Tondelayo* back to Dobodura. Both the pilot and the aircraft would return to service.

⌒⌒

Although Wallace's crew wasn't aware of it when they separated, Anacker's B-25, *Snafu*, was afire. A fuel leak in the radio compartment ignited and spread. The crew's flight engineer and top turret gunner, George Hardy, was shot in the head and shoulder. James Migliacci, the navigator, rendered first aid while he fought the fire. It quickly became apparent that the flames were going to burn the aircraft out of the sky. Migliacci had never flown with the crew and climbed over to Anacker's seat. "I informed him that we were burning terrifically and suggested that we attempt a ditching. He nodded his consent and I returned to helping Hardy."[2]

Anacker, with enemy fighters still making attacks, sped toward the area on the New Britain coast between Cape Ludtke and Cape Beeche. He hoped to ditch close to shore before his aircraft came apart. Somewhere along the way the Japanese pilots gave up their attacks and winged away.

There was no warning when the aircraft hit the water. "When I bobbed to the surface," said Migliacci, "I saw Sergeant Hardy who had been shot in the head and shoulder, floating about ten feet from me. He had no life vest so I grabbed him with the idea of getting him to shore." The coast was about a mile distant, and Migliacci struggled with the barely conscious Hardy. "While I was attempting to get him to shore, I noticed Captain Anacker. He was floating about fifty feet from us and was conscious as I noticed when he answered my request to help me with Sergeant Hardy. His face was completely covered with blood."

Migliacci never saw his pilot again. "I believe Anacker must have lost consciousness right after our brief talk and drifted seaward and eventually drowned or bled to death. I don't believe he ever got to shore because if he did within five miles of either side of the place I landed, there were friendly natives and they would have eventually taken him to our little party."

And try as he did to help George Hardy, the engineer, Migliacci could do no good. "While trying to get Sergeant Hardy to shore, he died—probably bled to death—so I let go of him and he sank beneath the water." Migliacci swam and rested in intervals until reaching the beach, where wreckage from their aircraft had already washed ashore. He pulled himself from the water, staggered upright, and stepped a short distance into the jungle.

There Migliacci rested in the cover of the thick foliage and watched the water for any sign of his fellow crewmen. At nightfall he forced himself on. After only a few steps through the jungle, he was surprised to find himself at the edge of a barely traveled road. Moving away from Rabaul, he traveled a short distance before stopping to spend a fitful, mosquito-filled night at the road's edge. The following morning he hiked until midday, when he came upon a village. Most of the inhabitants fled, but the chief, "Golpak," fed and watered him before backtracking him the way he had come—and further—to Cape Ormond, where he was delivered to an Australian Coastwatch team.

The following day Robert Henderson, Anacker's gunner, was also delivered by natives into the care of the Australians. He had been wounded in the wrist and arm during the air battle with Rabaul's fighters and was flung clear of *Snafu* after Anacker put the aircraft into the water. He thrashed his way through the waves to a life raft, only to find it badly burned. Clinging to various pieces of flotsam, he stripped naked except for his underwear and life vest and finally made it to shore. He stumbled upon friendly natives the next day.

Snafu's other crewmen, copilot David Koenig and radio operator Millard Svec, were never seen following the ditching. "I believe Svec was trapped in the plane after the crash into the ocean," said Migliacci, "or that he was killed at the time of the crash because there was no warning given and I am sure he was not prepared for the crash." It is likely that Koenig was also trapped or killed in the wreck.

———

The Australian Coastwatch outpost to which the natives took Migliacci and Henderson was headed by Peter Figgis. An intellectually quick and physically rugged man who was comfortable operating on both sea and land, Figgis was an intelligence officer with Australia's military forces at Rabaul when the Japanese struck during January 1942. After nearly three months on the run through the jungles of New Britain—with the Japanese continuously on his heels—he was finally evacuated to Australia.[3]

Safe at home, Figgis chose to go back into the fight. Australia's Naval Intelligence Division recruited him as part of a Coastwatch team. These small groups, equipped with radios and covertly supplied by air and sea, reported on Japanese naval, air, and land movements. Located deep within enemy territory, they were ruthlessly hunted by the Japanese, and dozens were captured and murdered. Nevertheless, the Coastwatch men continued their dangerous work, and the Allies—including Fifth Air Force units, the 345th among them—directly acted upon the intelligence they gathered.

Figgis was part of a team put ashore in New Britain in February 1943 by the American submarine USS *Greenling*.[4] That team was well established with virtually full cooperation from the natives by the time Migliacci and Henderson were saved from the Japanese eight months later. And as the raids on Rabaul intensified during the following months, Figgis collected a broad assortment of downed fliers not only from the United States Army Air Forces (USAAF) but from the Navy, the Marine Corps, and the Royal Australian Air Force. Ultimately, his team and the downed aviators—including Migliacci and Henderson—were extracted from New Britain by PT boats on March 25, 1944. For his work, Figgis was awarded the Military Cross.

<hr />

It is impossible to accurately tally the numbers of Japanese aircraft and vessels destroyed on the October 18, 1943, raid on Rabaul. The claims made by the 345th and the 38th at Tobera were totally inconsistent with Japanese admissions of losses. Even allowing for the fact that combat claims were quite often inflated or exaggerated by a factor of two, or even three or more, the dichotomy was still astounding.

The 345th alone claimed to have destroyed fifty-eight aircraft—thirty-nine in the air and nineteen on the ground. These figures do not include the aircraft counted as "probably" destroyed or damaged. The 38th Bomb Group claimed another twenty aircraft destroyed during its strike against the airfield at Tobera. For their part, the Japanese admitted to virtually no losses. A Radio Tokyo English-language broadcast described a raid of a hundred aircraft: "Japanese navy fighters rose to intercept, shooting down nine of the raiders. Heavy damage was done to another large bomber. Three Japanese planes were lost in this encounter, but no damage was done to the ground installations."

Notwithstanding the fact that the 345th's claims were likely exaggerated to some degree—*Tondelayo*'s crew alone claimed nine aircraft—the likelihood of a massive collusion by all the participating crews, the intelligence shops, and the command was slim. The debriefings were very thorough and detailed. For instance, for only the 498th, the following eyewitness reports were recorded:

> *One Zeke attacking from overhead from 3 o'clock position shot by gunner and seen to crash into sea; One Zeke attacking airplane 040 from above at 3 o'clock was hit by gunner and airplane was observed to crash into the sea; This plane hit the water at 7 o'clock and was definitely destroyed; Plane burst into flame and crashed into sea; Plane smoked badly and was seen to crash into the water; One Hap attacking from above at 7:30 o'clock was hit by tail gunner and plane burst into flame and crashed; Plane fell away on left wing and crashed into the sea; One Zeke or Hap attacking from above at 6 o'clock was hit by several bursts by turret gunner and crashed into the sea; Fighter continued right turn, lost altitude and crashed; and One Zeke attacking from above at 5 o'clock was hit by turret gunner as he broke off his attack. Plane nosed over and crashed into the sea.*

So then, eyewitnesses claimed to see nine separate enemy aircraft "crash into the sea" or into "the water." It is difficult to imagine that everyone involved was complicit in fabricating claims on such a grand scale. In all likelihood the 345th's claims were inflated to some degree due to a number of factors—chiefly, descriptions by several different crewmen of the destruction of the same enemy aircraft. However, the Japanese admission—or denial—of losses was propaganda, or more accurately, a lie. Of course, the Japanese were under no obligation to broadcast a precise compilation of losses. Unfortunately, too many records were destroyed during and after the war, and the question of losses will never be satisfactorily resolved.

One truth was that three B-25s had been shot down—two from the 345th and one from the 38th. And Clinton True was in trouble with George Kenney, the head of the Fifth Air Force. "I called him over to headquarters," Kenney said, "and bawled him out for disobeying our standing instructions that bombers were also to turn back if the fighters had to." Still, the attack and its results got good press. Newspaper articles lauded Kenney's audacious use of unescorted bombers to hit the toughest targets. He would have had a hard time censuring True even had he wanted to.

When Kenney pressed True as to whether he had heard the recall order, he later recounted, "The rascal looked me in the eye, grinned, and said, 'General, I didn't hear a word.' He was lying and he knew that I knew it but he was sticking to his story." Kenney admonished True not to commit the same offense again. "He said he wouldn't, saluted, and left. I had a suspicion he didn't have a single regret, in fact, was rather proud of himself. As a matter of fact, I was kind of proud of him, too."[5]

An extract from a group newsletter published the following month gave Clinton True's men more particulars about his prior life and service than they otherwise would have had.

Colonel True's boyhood days were spent in the colorful city of New Orleans. As he reached manhood, he moved north to the U.S. Military Academy at West Point where he gained fame as an All-American football and lacrosse player in 1937. Upon graduation, he entered the Army Air Corps where he took his training in such high-powered numbers as the P-6 and Keystone bomber. Following graduation from flying school, he transferred to Savannah where he flew A-20s, and then to Barksdale field where he piloted B-26s. A memorable moment in his life was his marriage to "Tinkie," an Army lass, and later the birth of his son, now aged 5.

The men now knew that "Fearless True," like them, had a real past with a real family.

J. R. Jones wrote Elnora after the October 18 mission to Rabaul and declared, "I've seen about everything now, and I didn't waste much time in doing it. I've really had my fingers crossed a couple of times. Every time it gets tough I take out that silver dollar you gave me and toss it for luck, saying to myself, come on, let's get back for Red [Elnora]."[6]

Censorship considerations precluded him from detailing anything specific about the Rabaul raids to Elnora. "I'm sorry I haven't written the past few days, but it has been rather impossible. I have been through a couple of hair-raising days, but I'll have to tell you about that some other time."[7] And he obviously expected more action: "I probably won't be able to write again for a few days, so there may be a short gap between letters. Not too long though, darling. It's rather hard to write when I have so much to tell and can say so little."[8] Still, although he didn't go into detail, he did characterize the nature of the low-level strafing for her. "The flying we do here is something that would curl your hair in a hurry. I know most of the other pilots don't envy us our jobs."[9]

Ralph Wallace's aircraft carried the unusual name *Tondelayo*. It was the name of Hedy Lamarr's character—a comely seductress—in the 1942 movie *White Cargo*. The 345th's crews, like virtually all USAAF crews, named their aircraft after many things and many people, including girlfriends, wives and other relatives, movie stars, race horses, places, and attributes. Among the many names carried by 345th aircraft during the war were *Sea Biscuit*, *Betty's Dream*, *Sag Harbor Express*, *Fatso*, *Lady Lil*, and *Wolf Pack*. It was quite common for art work—often very good—to complement the names. Perhaps most popular were paintings of naked or scantily clad women.

Vic Tatelman's aircraft was already called *Dirty Dora* when it reached the 345th's 499th Bomb Squadron as a hand-me-down from the 38th Bomb Group. Quite by chance, Tatelman met the original pilot, who told him how the B-25 got its name. While on furlough in Sydney, the 38th pilot met a girl, Dora Bennington, who spent the week with him. When making love, Dora, described as having a sensual temperament, lost any sense of restraint or decorum she might have possessed and let loose at high volume with profoundly profane words and phrases that struck the pilot as "poetry." He was so impressed by Dora's sexual appetite that he gave the aircraft her name.[10]

The 345th's squadrons also had nicknames. The 498th was known as the "Falcon" squadron, the 499th's men called themselves the "Bats Outta Hell," the 500th's fliers were the "Rough Raiders," and the 501st was the "Black Panther" squadron. Beginning generally after the aircraft had been converted into strafers, each squadron applied to its B-25s unique markings and paint schemes that evolved over time.

The 498th painted the noses of its aircraft with the head of a fierce bird of prey—green with a striking hooked, wide-open yellow beak. Other identification markings included yellow engine cowling rings and white vertical stabilizers. The noses of the 499th's aircraft were painted with blue bat wings arranged around a head with a set of teeth similar to those carried by the aircraft of the famed Flying Tigers. These aircraft were also painted with blue engine cowling rings, and the bottom one-third of each vertical stabilizer was painted white.

The 500th's B-25s were painted with a white vertical band around their fuselages, aft of the wing, and red engine cowling rings. Later its cowling rings were olive green to match the rest of the aircraft. The vertical stabilizers of the 500th's aircraft also carried a circular field of blue, edged in white, upon which was painted the head of a snorting white horse in profile. The 501st's squadron insignia was a black panther leaping in profile over a quarter moon. The vertical stabilizers of its aircraft were painted with a white horizontal stripe across the middle, and its engine cowlings were orange.

However, squadron markings weren't applied to every aircraft, as the operational tempo sometimes precluded it before the aircraft was shot down, wrecked, or transferred out of the unit. And the noses of many aircraft carried personalized artwork of their pilots' choosing rather than their squadron's markings. Moreover, some aircraft—received from other units—flew for a time with the previous organization's markings.

Chapter Five

"The Pilots Did Not Appear Eager"

George Kenney intended to keep pressure on Rabaul so long as the weather permitted. To that end, as part of a larger attack force, the 345th hit the airfield at Vunakanau again on October 24. This reprise was virtually identical to the attack of October 12 with the exception that the squadrons attacked in a different order and their B-25s carried one-hundred-pound demolition bombs rather than parafrags.

It also seemed to the 345th's aircrews on this second attack on Vunakanau that the Japanese air presence at Rabaul was growing a bit thin. They observed, "There were not as many planes on the ground as on the first mission, but the planes in the revetments seemed serviceable." And the fighters that did rise to meet them, described by the 498th as "20 Zekes painted black and red," were ineffective as "the pilots did not appear eager for the most part and did not press the attacks in general."

Another mission was launched on October 28 but was aborted when a line of thunderstorms was encountered partway to New Britain. Clinton "Fearless" True was not leading the group that day. Weather continued to stymie Kenney as his crews were readied for several missions during the next few days but were forced to stand down each time.

Douglas MacArthur was anxious for Kenney's men to hit the shipping crowded into Rabaul's Simpson Harbor and adjacent Blanche Bay. Staging from these anchorages, the Japanese were almost frantic in their efforts to block Allied advances up the Solomon island chain. In particular, they were determined to wreck the landing made the previous day by American Marines at Bougainville's Cape Torokina in Empress Augusta

Bay. During a fierce and confused night action, shortly after midnight on November 2, an Imperial Japanese Navy force of four cruisers and six destroyers—which had sortied from Japan via Rabaul—engaged Task Force 39, the roughly equivalent American naval element that protected the landing. The American task force sank a Japanese cruiser and a destroyer in what came to be called the Battle of Empress Augusta Bay. The defeated Japanese force limped back to Rabaul as Kenney's airmen waited for the weather to clear.

The elements continued their mercurial ways on November 2. A raid to Rabaul was launched but was recalled even before all the participants got airborne out of Dobodura. However, reconnaissance aircraft later reported clear skies over the target area, and the attack force was ordered to take off once more.

The 345th's ground crews finished topping the aircraft off with fuel, and the group was airborne again at 1045. After assembling at Oro Bay and then picking up the 3rd and 38th Bomb Groups at Cape Sudest, the formation winged northeast nearly four hundred miles before making a left turn northwest up the St. Georges Channel between New Britain and New Ireland. Past Kabakon Island at the mouth of Blanche Bay, the 345th's four squadrons arced northwest past Rabaul before sweeping left and back to the south, making landfall near Nodup.

Aside from a protective cover of P-38s, the mission was an all-B-25 show in which the 345th was to play a supporting but critical role. The plan was for the escorting P-38s to run interference ahead of the strikers by clearing out or otherwise distracting the enemy fighters. Immediately on the heels of the P-38s, the four squadrons of the 345th were to sweep down from the hills to the north of the town. Carrying a mix of parafrag and phosphorous bombs, the 345th's crews were charged with destroying or neutralizing the considerable antiaircraft defenses that ringed the harbor, as well as any worthwhile targets of opportunity.

Ideally, the 345th's strafing attacks—together with the parafrag bombs—would force the antiaircraft personnel who weren't killed outright to take cover. However, as insurance, the phosphorous bombs would blanket the defenders with a shroud of smoke so thick as to effectively screen from view the B-25s from the 3rd and 38th Bomb Groups as they attacked the shipping. Sinking as much of this shipping as possible—including warships—was the chief objective of the day's effort.

The raid was anything but a surprise. The 498th's narrative report described how two destroyers and a light cruiser "were passing out of Blanche Bay past Cape Gazelle and threw up a concentrated barrage of antiaircraft fire as planes passed over on way to target at 1332." Enemy fighters were also ready and airborne although they did not press their attacks at this point. "Three aerial burst bombs which exploded throwing long red streamers were dropped by enemy fighters," the 498th declared. "One bomb exploded on same level as bombers but one hundred yards in front. One hit the ground before exploding and one dropped from 1,500 feet burst 700 feet above bombers."

These aerial bombs, although somewhat unusual, were already well known to Allied intelligence, which had published a bulletin months before: "The Japanese bombs, appearing to weigh from 50 to 100 pounds, can be seen clearly from the time they leave the enemy plane. They explode about 5 to 10 seconds after leaving the plane, producing a vivid color, followed by white smoke streamers (which might indicate phosphorus) in a waterfall effect. One officer is of the opinion that if one of the larger bombs exploded inside a five-plane Vee it might set most of the planes on fire, because of its intense heat."[1] That officer's assessment was tempered by the acknowledgment that "to date there has been no report of substantial damage to our planes by Japanese bombs." In fact, although the Japanese used these weapons sporadically throughout the war, they were entirely ineffective.

Except for the aerial bombs, the 345th's squadrons went unmolested by enemy fighters as they continued toward Rabaul. Upon crossing the coast, the formations separated to hit their targets. The 498th, carrying parafrags, was assigned to hit the northern section of Rabaul. The 500th was to follow a short time later with its phosphorous bombs. Likewise, the 501st was to attack the eastern part of Rabaul with parafrags, followed by the 499th with phosphorous bombs.

The 498th sprayed Japanese antiaircraft positions with machine-gun fire as it crested the high ground north of the town. Once over the ridge, it descended the slopes toward the harbor, where it strafed and bombed the antiaircraft guns on the north side of Rabaul. The effects of Chester Coltharp's leading three-ship were typical as it attacked "at an altitude of 125 feet, strafed and bombed along the north shore of Simpson Harbor. Antiaircraft positions were silenced and stores, installations and numerous small boats were damaged. Lieutenant Magee strafed and released bombs on two freighters unloading at docks. Freighters were left smoking and reported by other squadrons passing over the target later to be burning." The 498th also made an observation that no doubt vexed the Fifth Air Force's planners, especially as so much effort had recently been directed against the harbor at Rabaul. "Docks appear in excellent condition with large storage dumps in the open, along the shore."

Enemy fighters then dived on the 498th while the 500th hit the same targets. The 500th was carrying phosphorous—or more accurately, white phosphorous—bombs. On that day, they were used for the smoke they generated, but they also created other, more terrible effects. White phosphorous was an incendiary chemical that burned at a very high temperature and consequently caused any reasonably flammable material to catch fire. It was not readily extinguished by water, and when it contacted skin, it stuck and continued to burn, causing deep, weeping lesions. And when it exploded, the blast resembled a multitentacled monster. Neither was white phosphorous particularly well loved by the bomb crews who had to load it aboard the aircraft, as it was fussy and more prone to accidents than more conventional explosives.

The 500th recorded that its crews "effectively blanketed the northwest shore area of Simpson Harbor with 9,200 pounds of white phosphorus bombs as they strafed and bombed from tree-top level. Photographs show an impressive display of fireworks as the bombs exploded in the assigned area."

More impressive and more tragic was the fate that overtook Alfred Kramiskas's crew. "Kramiskas was flying the number two position in the lead element of our formation," said Max Mortensen, who led the 500th that day. "Our formation was over the target flying at an altitude of 100 feet. Bomb bays were open in preparation of the bomb run."[2]

"The ground fire was pretty thick and fairly accurate," recalled Mortensen. "One ack-ack shell exploded directly beneath Lieutenant Kramiskas's ship, a fragment of which flew into the bomb bay, exploding his phosphorous bombs."

James Du Bose piloted the third ship in Mortensen's flight and said that Kramiskas's "cockpit filled with smoke as soon as the fire broke out." Max Mortensen described the doomed crew's last seconds: "He broke formation and tried to climb; the attempt was futile. The ship rolled and made a plunge to the ground, smoking and burning fiercely. Upon crashing, the gas tanks exploded with a resounding roar. A huge pillar of black smoke billowed up from the wreckage."

Mortensen's B-25 was also hit in the bomb bay, and his phosphorous bombs likewise caught fire. "Smoke poured throughout the plane and streamed from the right engine as though it were on fire," noted the 500th Bomb Squadron's narrative summary. "Captain Mortensen feathered the prop, dropped his bombs and cleared most of the smoke out of the plane. He kept up with the formation, soon noticing the right engine appeared to be undamaged and serviceable." Realizing that his right engine was operable, Mortensen restarted it and continued out of the target area with the rest of the squadron.

As did the other squadrons of the 345th, the 501st shot its way into Rabaul. "Only one run was made over the target," the squadron declared, "at an average of 100 feet altitude. Rabaul Township, Lakunai airdrome, and Matupi were thoroughly strafed. Our frag bombs were dropped in the Sulphur Creek area as scheduled, with excellent bombing results."

Those "excellent bombing results" came at a cost. "Immediately after dropping down onto the township area," said John Manders, the 501st's leader, "we started firing our guns and dropping bombs. After we'd gone about one quarter of the way down the run, laying just about broadside to us, at that point, was a cruiser which kept firing at us. It is my opinion that Lieutenant Orbry H. Moore was hit by this cruiser; at that time his right engine burst into flames."[3]

Manders called Moore and told him to take the lead position so that the squadron could protect him. "For a moment or so after that," Manders said, "it looked as though he had put the fire out with the use of his Lux System [fire extinguisher]."

But the engine started burning again a short time later. "This time," said Manders, "the fire had spread from the engine nacelle to approximately one third of the wing." The fire was so hot that the landing gear—which had self-extended from the right engine nacelle—became almost molten so that it twisted in the wind stream. At that point, Moore pulled up and turned west to put the aircraft into the water. Manders followed him for a short while before turning away, back on course. A P-38 pilot later reported seeing Moore's B-25 make a good water landing east of the airfield at Rapopo.

Even while they tried to shepherd Moore to safety, the 501st's crews continued to attack the enemy. "One four-engine float plane was strafed offshore at the mouth of Sulphur Creek. Some of our parafrag bombs were dropped on Lakunai just as Zeroes were taking off." Not satisfied with its work to that point, the squadron winged its way to the airfield at Rapopo "where one Betty bomber was destroyed by strafing. Three new twin-engine fighters on Rapopo strip were also strafed with unobserved results."

The 499th was tasked with following the 501st's initial attack and blanketing the survivors with smoke. As the squadron approached the rim of high ground that protected Rabaul from the north, it encountered heavy barrage fire, which it observed "was not fired directly at the formation, but rather in a pattern which was intended to catch our formation when it hedge-hopped over the ridge, since our squadron was below the altitude of the ridge." In effect, the Japanese were simply filling a piece of the sky—through which they anticipated the 499th would fly—with a heavy concentration of antiaircraft fire. The squadron answered with its machine guns "by thoroughly strafing these positions and then pulling up sharply." No aircraft were lost in this "barrage box."

Just then the 499th narrowly missed colliding with the 500th, which crossed in front of it from the left. Once clear of its sister squadron, the 499th dropped down the opposite slope and onto its targets.

"Looking out over my port-side .30-caliber machine gun, I only saw rows of buildings—huts and shacks, etc.," said Donald Hitchcock, the radio operator aboard William Cabell's aircraft.[4] "Everybody else was shooting at something, so I thought I should be doing the same. Besides, it made me feel better."

Hitchcock quickly shot up the gun's ammunition. "Unwrapping another belt," he said, "I reloaded the rack, charged the gun, and looked back out the window. Instead of crude huts and shacks, however, what I saw was a single-engine plane pointed right at me, with a row of red lights blinking along the leading edge of his wings." Hitchcock swung the barrel of his gun toward the enemy aircraft. "He was dead level with us and not very far out. I was sure I couldn't miss—he was that close."

Hitchcock squeezed the gun's trigger. "The gun fired one bullet and stopped! I quickly charged it again, but the plane was no longer in sight. The gun worked just fine after that, but I never had such a perfect set shot again."

Unlike the 500th, the 499th experienced no mishaps with its phosphorous bombs. Its nine aircraft, in flights of three, continued through the town and shot up whatever needed it. Once the planes were over the harbor, antiaircraft fire from merchant and combatant ships ripped through the formation. Geysers erupted from shells that hit the water. The pilots maneuvered aggressively—"bobbing and weaving"—to avoid being hit. "These tactics," observed the squadron, "no doubt are responsible for the lack of serious damage sustained."

All the squadrons were attacked by Japanese fighters as they cleared their targets. The 501st described how "the squadron was intercepted by a large flight of Zekes and Hamps [Mitsubishi A6M fighter—essentially the same aircraft as a Zero], estimated as being from 50–60 airplanes in all." In fact, the fighter force at Rabaul had recently been reinforced by Imperial Japanese Navy units—numbering more than two hundred aircraft—from Truk in the Caroline Islands. It seemed that these pilots had none of the reticence exhibited earlier, as "the enemy pressed their attack home very closely and displayed exceptional aggressiveness." The 498th declared that the escorting P-38s "were outnumbered and were unable to give the squadron protection immediately after leaving the target."

In the 499th's formation, the squadron reported that Jack George's aircraft "was hit by antiaircraft fire off Raluana Point, damaging the hydraulic system and spraying fluid on [the] windshield. At the same time this plane was attacked by an enemy airplane which inflicted leg wounds on the copilot and seriously wounded the radio operator and engineer." The copilot, Mack Simms, ignored his wounds and twice crawled over the bomb bay to the rear of the ship where he administered first aid to the other wounded men.

Still, the combination of the protecting P-38s—outnumbered or not—and the 345th's own defensive fire and low-flying formations was enough to keep the enemy fighters from scoring. Rather, as they had during their previous raids to Rabaul, the B-25 crews claimed multiple aerial victories. Typical was the report filed by the 498th.

One Zeke attacking airplane 176 from 5:30 o'clock was hit by tail gunner as he pressed the attack and was seen by three crew members to crash into the water. Attack took place at 1349/L. One Zeke attacking airplane 176 at 7:30 o'clock was hit by a long burst from the turret and started smoking badly and broke off the attack. Fighter was seen by other crews as it crashed. One Hamp attacking airplane 024 from 12 o'clock was hit by turret gunner as [it] pressed the attack to within 500 yards. Fighter burst into flames and went out of control at 100 feet altitude. He was observed to crash.

Although the 345th engaged enemy fighters in a running gun battle for half an hour, the action became a sideshow to the main event. That main event was underway over Simpson Harbor and Blanche Bay, where the B-25s of the 3rd and 38th Bomb Groups raced low over the water to attack merchant shipping as well as warships of the Imperial Japanese Navy. The skyline was pocked with black antiaircraft explosions, and geysers shot skyward as heavier shells punched into the water. The harbor's surface was further ripped by lines of machine-gun fire from both the attacking aircraft and the defending ships. More antiaircraft fire lashed down at the B-25s from the hills and ridges above the town; the 345th had suppressed many of the Japanese guns, but knocking them all out of action was not possible. The spectacle was made more confused as the phosphorous smoke from the 345th's bombs drifted in ghostly patches through the more than forty large ships sheltering in the harbor.

Dick Walker was a pilot with the 3rd Bomb Group. The leader of his squadron tried to make a turn while his crews were spread in a broad line-abreast formation. "Wheeling a line of eleven airplanes into a wide turn while flying line abreast puts a lot of pressure on the inside man," said Walker. "Carrying a heavy bomb load and making a tight turn without stalling out or getting ahead of the rest of the line is tricky, so just before we reached our designated turning point, together with my wingman, I initiated a turn."[5]

When Walker came out of that turn, he saw that his wingman had been hit and was hurtling down. The rest of the squadron was nowhere to be seen. "Our squadron commander, for some reason, never turned in to attack. Instead he circled the city [the town of Rabaul] and dropped his bombs somewhere other than against the shipping. The rest of the squadron followed him and none of them ever hit the target. By that time I was out in the harbor alone."

Walker—with no other good choices—set to his task. "I maneuvered among the ships flying as low as I could, concentrating on staying between the ships, and then lined up on a merchant vessel." He flew directly at the ship until it seemed to him that a collision was imminent. At that point he released his two one-thousand-pound bombs, hauled back on the controls, and arced skyward. Behind him, the bombs slammed into the ship and rocked it with a mighty blast. It settled then, dangerously down at the stern.

Raymond Wilkins led the 8th Bomb Squadron of the 3rd Bomb Group. The 3rd was the last group across the harbor, and Wilkins's squadron was the last in the group. Visibility by that point was greatly degraded, and Wilkins took his squadron across the harbor on a route different from that planned. His aircraft was hit almost immediately in the right wing; yet—still barely above the water—he pressed ahead and sprayed his machine guns at a handful of small craft before stuffing a one-thousand-pound bomb into the side of a destroyer.

The enemy warship erupted in flames as Wilkins raced away with a damaged left vertical stabilizer. Although his aircraft was increasingly difficult to control, Wilkins was relentless. A large transport vessel sat astride his flight path. He slammed his remaining one-thousand-pound bomb into its side, causing it to explode.

A cruiser blocked Wilkins's escape route. He mashed down on the firing button, stepped alternately on each rudder pedal, and whipsawed a violent hail of .50-caliber rounds back and forth across the big ship's deck. Still, as powerful as they were, they were no match for the cruiser's armor. He lifted the aircraft's nose and hauled it around in a turn to the left. As he did so, he was caught by the ship's antiaircraft fire. His left wing crumpled, and the mortally wounded B-25 smashed into the water.

Wilkins and his crew were dead. He was posthumously awarded the Medal of Honor for his actions that day.

The 345th lost one more aircraft. The B-25 of Bud McGowan, a pilot with the 501st, was badly shot up by antiaircraft fire over the target. Although he successfully nursed it back to Dobodura, the aircraft was wrecked when he landed and subsequently scavenged for parts and scrapped. His crew suffered no significant injuries.

Other than the report that the 501st's Orbry Moore had put his damaged ship down in the sea near Rapopo, nothing more was learned of him or his crew. It is virtually certain that they were pulled from the water by the Japanese and subsequently murdered on the spot or sometime later. However, no records have been discovered, and it is unlikely that their exact fates will ever be known.

Max Mortensen made it back to Dobodura with his crew; the effects of the phosphorous bombs that had briefly burned aboard his aircraft before he salvoed them were described: "The plane was still smouldering and glowing from the phosphorous, hours later." Notwithstanding the dangers associated with using the phosphorous bombs, Kenney gushed, "They were a distinct success, creating a thick wall of smoke, which blanketed practically all the shore antiaircraft gun stations, and in addition setting most of the town on fire."[6] Indeed, due to his enthusiasm these phosphorous bombs were dubbed "Kenney cocktails."

Kenney was ecstatic about what his men had achieved that day. "In the space of twelve minutes we had destroyed or damaged 114,000 tons of Japanese shipping, shot down or destroyed on the ground eighty-five Nip airplanes, and burned out half the town of Rabaul, with a loss of supplies to the enemy estimated at 300,000 tons."[7] Moreover, Fifth Air Force crews—both bombers and fighters—claimed sixty-seven Japanese aircraft knocked down in aerial combat.

Although the raid was a success, Kenney's excitement pushed him toward hyperbole when he declared, "Never in the long history of warfare had so much destruction been wrought upon the forces of a belligerent nation so swiftly and at such little cost to the victor."[8] Samuel Eliot Morison, who penned the official wartime history of the United States Navy, took a swipe at Kenney and the United States Army Air Forces in general. He later wrote, "Never, indeed, have such exorbitant claims been made with so little basis in fact—except by some of the Army Air Forces in Europe, and by the same Japanese air force which General Kenney believed he had wiped out. Even on that day the Japanese out-Kenneyed Kenney by claiming 22 B-25s, and 79 P-38s as 'sure kills.'"[9] Fifth Air Force losses were actually eight B-25s and nine P-38s.

Morison had a point. Although the blow Kenney's force had dealt was certainly hurtful, its results were overblown. The Japanese admitted only to losing a large tanker, three smaller freighters, a mine sweeper, and a handful of lesser boats. The Fifth Air Force's claims exceeded the Japanese admissions and included three destroyers and eight large freighters sunk, apart from damage to many more vessels, including two cruisers. It is difficult to reconcile the differences not only due to the chaos of the actual combat but also because vessels that were sunk or badly damaged could be—and often were—refloated or repaired and returned to service.

Further, the press apparently believed that American claims were often, for various reasons, purposely inflated. An authoritative Australian source noted, "Correspondents at MacArthur's headquarters resented being made tools for the dissemination of false claims but could do little about it. At press conferences the correspondents greeted the more glaring examples of exaggeration with guffaws and sardonic quips. However, under the rules of their accreditation they could not criticise communiques, although they could and sometimes did."[10]

———

A few days later, on November 5, 1943, the Navy launched an impressive carrier strike against Rabaul that was immediately followed by a high-altitude raid by Fifth Air Force B-24s. However, the 345th never returned to Rabaul. In fact, following a few more high-altitude B-24 raids—and a handful of small but audacious Royal Australian Air Force forays—the Fifth Air Force no longer played a major role in shutting down the once-mighty Japanese bastion. Responsibility for finishing the job was transitioned later in November to Admiral William "Bull" Halsey's Southern Pacific command. During the next several months, air actions by the Navy, the Army Air Forces, the Marine Corps, and Allied forces reduced Rabaul to the point that it could offer no meaningful air resistance and was in fact barely able keep its garrison from starving.

———

The 345th, through its entire combat career, lost many more aircraft to antiaircraft fire, weather, mechanical failures, and accidents than to enemy fighters. The reasons were manifold and included the fact that the group's crews were often given excellent protection by their fighter escorts. Moreover, Japanese fighters became fewer as the war progressed, and Japanese replacement pilots were less experienced and not as well trained as those who had started the war. Additionally, depending on the type, many of the Japanese fighters did not carry armament heavy enough to readily knock down the sturdy B-25 Mitchell.

But it was the 345th's very low formation flying that most vexed the Japanese fighter pilots. They typically preferred to make diving attacks from high above as they could fire their guns and subsequently escape in a high-speed plunge. But because the B-25 pilots flew at minimum altitude, the enemy pilots could not make those sorts of firing runs without flying into the ground or the water.

Consequently, the Japanese fighter pilots were left with few options—almost all of which forced them to expose themselves to the guns of the B-25s for too long. For instance, if an enemy pilot attacked from one side or another, he had to overfly the group's formation, which exposed him to point-blank gunfire, or he had to break off his attack and turn away too early to do much harm. And as he turned away, he presented the entire underside of his aircraft—wings and fuselage—as a large, vulnerable target.

Head-on and tail attacks were equally dangerous. Attacks from behind occurred at relatively slow closing rates, which gave the B-25 gunners plenty of time to adjust their aim and concentrate their fire. And again, the attacker could not simply dive away but had to either overfly the formation or turn away, consequently exposing himself to withering defensive fire. Conversely, attacks from in front of the formation happened at much greater speeds, which limited the tracking and firing time for both the fighters and the bombers. However, it is arguable that the bomber men had the advantage as the Japanese fighters were exposed to brutally powerful fusillades from the gun-packed noses of the B-25s as well as to fire from the top turret guns.

It is therefore understandable that Japanese pilots were often described as "not eager," or were criticized for breaking off their attacks at long distances, or were seen on several occasions to misjudge their flight paths and hit the water. Simply put, it was very difficult to make an effective firing pass at a group of low-flying B-25s. And it was dangerous.

Notwithstanding the fact that the enemy fighters were not especially effective against the B-25s, they still made an impression on the 345th's aircrews. Unlike the bunkered and camouflaged antiaircraft guns that lashed out from seemingly nowhere, fighters were a readily apparent manifestation of the enemy. At the controls of each Japanese aircraft was a pilot who wanted to shoot down and kill the 345th's men. The thoughts of J. R. Jones were representative as he wrote to his fiancée, Elnora, "It's no joke to have the enemy on your tail, and those red circles really show up on a Jap's plane."[11]

But tropical diseases afflicted more men than did Japanese fighters. In a letter to Elnora, Jones explained that he was hospitalized. "Don't get excited, it's nothing serious, nothing more than good old dysentery. I'm all right now, and the reason I'm here is because they have me on a diet. I'm getting swell food, and I'm not the least bit hungry. I did spend two very miserable days, and I hope I've seen the last of this business."[12]

He could not be blamed for hoping that he had "seen the last of this business." Dysentery, while not often fatal, was characterized by severe stomach cramps, fevers, and sudden and frequent bouts of watery, foul-smelling diarrhea. Victims also suffered dehydration and feelings of incomplete defecation. More severe cases were marked by bloody stools.

The disease came in three primary forms: bacterial, viral, and parasitic. Natives defecated directly onto the ground, and rain washed the waste into local rivers from which Allied units drew their drinking water. Improperly treated water sickened the men. Moreover, flying insects sampled the fecal matter and subsequently flew into the camps, where they landed on a variety of surfaces and materials that the men touched or ingested. In fact, few men who spent any length of time in New Guinea didn't exhibit symptoms of dysentery at one time or another. Most cases were not serious, and the majority of men, like J. R. Jones, returned to duty within days.

Aside from maladies that kept them from their duties, the men fought all manner of nondebilitating rashes, sores, and mild infections they had never encountered. "I have a recurrence of this blasted itch," Jones later wrote Elnora, "and it's about to drive me nuts. I have no idea what causes it, but it's a might uncomfortable."[13]

CHAPTER SIX

"I Turned Back to Pick Him Up"

FOLLOWING THE NOVEMBER 2 RAID ON RABAUL, THE 345TH WAS SENT against a number of different targets through the rest of the month. These included the airfield complexes at Wewak—Kenney was not about to lift his foot from the throat of the Japanese units there. Raids against Japanese resupply efforts, both ashore and at sea, also continued. Among those targets were the shipping, jetties, material dumps, and airfields at Hansa Bay on New Guinea's northern coast, approximately one hundred miles east of Wewak. It was a critical distribution point that served a number of enemy garrisons.

On November 20, 1943, the 345th's 498th and 500th Bomb Squadrons each put up nine aircraft to strike a convoy reported to be moored at Hansa Bay. The 500th led the two squadrons northwest on an overland course parallel to the coast and picked up an escort of four squadrons of P-47s along the way. Once past the objective, the formation wheeled around in a wide right-hand turn back to the southeast and directly at Hansa Bay.

It quickly became apparent that the convoy was gone. Accordingly, the crews switched to alternate targets and attacked barges, luggers, antiaircraft positions, and whatever else merited their attention. The 500th's attack was similar to that of the 498th: "Five barges, a lugger and a jetty were destroyed, and other small craft were possibly damaged by near misses."

Once clear of Hansa Bay, the formation simply continued southeast down the coast and hit targets of opportunity. "Continuing toward Alexishafen," the squadrons declared, "the airplanes destroyed several huts in the Hatzfeldt Harbor area and dropped bombs among houses at Basip near Cape Gourdon and among modern type buildings in the vicinity of Nake and Mt. Kegel, west of Alexishafen. One bomb caused a landslide on a good dirt coastal road below Uligan Harbor, and a village at Belan, west of Madang, was bombed."

The P-47 escort had no trade as Japanese fighters declined to intercept the B-25s. However, the antiaircraft fire was effective and caught the left side the 500th Bomb Squadron aircraft flown by Frank Gullette. His left wing was holed, and the engine was damaged. "When out over the water in Hansa Bay immediately after passing over the target," said Robert Long, "we noticed Lieutenant Gullette's left engine smoking quite badly and oil running from the underside of the nacelle. Lieutenant [Robert] Van Ausdell immediately started to slow down while we tried to attract Lieutenant Gullette's attention to the motor. He nodded and made motions indicating that he was fully aware of the trouble."[1]

Van Ausdell was the leader of the three-aircraft flight of which Gullette was part, and Long was his copilot. The other wingman was Raymond Geer, who recalled, "At first it seemed that he would be okay for he pulled up even with the lead ship and motioned [that he was] okay. The flight flew down the coast approximately 40 miles."

"Here," said Long, "Lieutenant Van Ausdell decided we had better continue along the coast to Lae or Dobodura to give Lieutenant Gullette a better chance." Nearing Uligan Harbor—which was held by the Japanese—the crews spied four boats. Van Ausdell and Geer bombed and strafed the vessels and rejoined Gullette.

However, Gullette's aircraft was failing. Engines straining, it slowly dropped toward the water and fell behind Van Ausdell and Geer. "I turned back to pick him up," said Geer, "and saw him just above the water. While I was still in my turn, the airplane hit the water in a perfect water landing, completely under control."

Notwithstanding the apparently flawless ditching, it was obvious to their comrades circling overhead that Gullette's men were having trouble. "There was no evidence that they were able to get their own life raft or any emergency equipment from the ship," said Long. "Only five men could be seen in the water by our crew, although it is possible that a sixth person was there—there was a great deal of debris in the water."

Both Van Ausdell and Geer dropped multiple life rafts to Gullette's crew. "Then my lower hatch jammed," said Geer, "and I was unable to reopen it. I circled 5 or 6 times and watched [Van Ausdell] drop food and rafts." Low on fuel, Van Ausdell and Geer finally joined and winged for home. Long noted, "There were signs of Jap activity among houses along the road which runs along the shoreline from Hansa Bay to Madang."

Max Mortensen had led the 500th over Hansa Bay that day. "Upon our arrival at Jackson airdrome, I made every effort to secure a Navy PBY flying boat for the search." Mortensen was told that none were available until midnight. "We offered the services of a pilot as we were of the opinion that an immediate search would bring results."

Mortensen, together with Van Ausdell and another 345th pilot, got airborne as passengers aboard a PBY just before midnight. "We flew along the coast to Milne Bay, from there to the scene of the crash, arriving at 0815 Sunday morning," said Mortensen. "The area was covered for a radius of 100 miles." Approaching noon, the PBY landed at Oro Bay to take on fuel and food. Airborne once again, the men aboard the PBY searched until nightfall. It was no good. No trace of Gullette and his crew was spotted.

In fact, they had already been captured by the Japanese and were later murdered.

In his report, Max Mortensen declared, "The squadron has lost crews and airplanes which might have been saved if radio contact could have been made with PBYs or ground stations, informing them of the location and details of the crashed airplane."[2] In reality, air-sea rescue operations in the area had only recently received much priority, but those operations were obviously not enough to save Gullette and his crew.

Indeed, when the Fifth Air Force rescue service was formed during January 1943, it was staffed by only a single officer, John Small, who was assisted by one enlisted man.[3] To his credit, Small worked tirelessly to coordinate and improve air-sea rescue efforts across the Fifth Air Force, the Navy, and the Royal Australian Air Force. The Navy's PBYs—amphibious flying boats—carried much of the load. However, the rescue of downed aircrews was only one of many missions for which the PBY crews were responsible. They also flew antisubmarine sorties, maritime patrols, antishipping strikes, and various and sundry transport missions. In short, although they stretched themselves to the maximum, they couldn't meet all the Fifth Air Force's needs.

Still, the Navy crews expended a great many resources to help their USAAF cousins. This was evidenced by their efforts to recover the 345th's William Kizzire and his crew when they were shot down during an attack on Boram Airfield on November 27, 1943. Kizzire's aircraft, at the head of the 498th Bomb Squadron, was hit in the right engine by antiaircraft fire from a cargo ship. It appeared that the engine's propeller blades failed to feather. "Captain Kizzire," reported the 498th, "was seen to continue on the heading he was flying of 35 degrees after being hit, and then circling to the right and proceeding down the coast, losing altitude and airspeed, and crash landing at Marik." His squadron mates spotted six men standing on the wing of the downed B-25, which did not sink but rested on the bottom of Karau Lagoon. After dropping rafts and supplies, they turned for home.

The following morning, November 28, Ralph Robinette and his crew took off in a B-25 to look for Kizzire and his crew. They spotted two of the men southwest of Karau Lagoon and dropped more supplies as well as charts plotted with escape routes. It appeared to Robinette and his crew that the two men recovered the material that was dropped.[4]

Late that night, Robinette was aboard a PBY of VP-11 as it took off from Port Moresby. The slow-flying aircraft arrived at Karau Lagoon at first light on the morning of November 29. After a couple of hours, burning flares were spotted three miles west of the lagoon. At the same time, a Japanese Betty bomber flew past only a short distance away. The Navy crew turned for Port Moresby, justifiably concerned that the bomber crew would tip enemy fighters to the PBY's presence. Although a sturdy aircraft, the PBY stood little chance of surviving alone against determined fighter attacks.

Robinette stuck with the PBY crew, which gamely took off again late that same night. Another PBY followed shortly afterward and picked up a fighter escort of nine P-47s and two P-40s. Arriving at dawn on

November 30, both crews scoured the area for a total of about three hours. They found no sign of Kizzire's crew, and the PBYs returned to Port Moresby.

The men of VP-11 made one more attempt to find the downed aircrew on the afternoon of December 1. The PBY picked up an escort of twelve P-40s, which, for reasons not stated in the record, refused to continue all the way to the search area. The Navy airmen were leery of being caught alone by enemy fighters in broad daylight. Although their decision to turn back was not a popular one with the 345th's men, it was a reasonable one.

As it developed, some or all of Kizzire's men were captured and slain. The Japanese made curious radio broadcasts a few months later, no doubt for propaganda purposes. On March 6, 1944, a radio broadcast received in the United States mentioned Kizzire's radio-gunner. "The name is Roy Showers, Box 1297, Tampa, Texas, and here's his mother's name too, Mrs. Roy L. Showers, same address. That's swell. Probably the Red Cross will have someone notify her that he is all right."[5]

A similar message was received on March 17, 1944. "Just make a brief note of new missing men. . . . Now if there is a post card handy, please address it to Wilford Joseph Paquette of 117 Franklin Street, North Hampton, Massachusetts. Notify Mr. Joseph Paquette of the same address that his son is alive and well, a prisoner of war in Wewak, New Guinea." Joseph Pacquette had been Kizzire's engineer-gunner.[6]

A final message was intercepted on March 22, 1944. It concerned Kizzire's gunner. "Send a short note to Edna Irene Nightwine of Water Street, Slippery Rock, Pennsylvania, and tell her that Ted John Nightwine is now a prisoner of war of the Imperial Japanese Army in Wewak, New Guinea. He has participated in a raid on Japanese positions in the vicinity of Madang. . . . Just let Mrs. Nightwine know that she need not fear for the safety of her son who is now a prisoner of war and no longer an active participant in frontline combat in the South Pacific."[7]

Whether the men named in the broadcasts were actually alive at the time is not known. However, they did not survive the war.

The air-sea rescue coordination between the Fifth Air Force and the Navy gradually improved, and so did the assistance the Navy provided. The recovery of downed aircrews was significantly enhanced when PBYs, usually covered by a protective screen of Fifth Air Force fighters, orbited a safe distance from the target during particularly heavy strikes. So positioned, they were able to quickly sweep in and pluck downed aircrews out of the water. It was dangerous work, but few missions were more appreciated.

Later, as more experience was gained and more resources were available, the assets arrayed to cover strikes included multiple aircraft, ships, and submarines. Reluctant, or perhaps embarrassed, to be totally reliant on the Navy, the USAAF finally fielded its own rescue units that operated a variety of aircraft. Chief among them was the OA-10, the USAAF's designation for the venerable PBY.

—⁓—

J. R. Jones had earlier been unimpressed by the frontier towns of Australia's outback, but his assessment of the Land Down Under was considerably improved on his first rest trip to Sydney. "Really, my dear," he wrote Elnora, "you have never seen a place like this. It would quite startle you. I know I never suspected Australia of possessing such an amazing place. It is a large city and spreads for miles around the harbor and hills. San Francisco is the only place I can think of that resembles it."

"The squadron rents a house there," he continued, "and the boys live there while on leave. It is situated on top of a hill and from the front porch you can see a great portion of the city. It certainly is a romantic sight at night, looking down over the bay." And about the women, he wrote, "The Australian girls really go for the Americans in a big way. I don't know what it is, but I think they would all marry Americans if they could. Maybe it's because most of the Australian men are in the army, but I think it is a little more than that. They really go for our cigarettes, and your life isn't safe if you pull out a package in public."

Dining out was an interesting experience. "It's rather hard to eat too much in a restaurant as they have a price limit on meals and if you have an expensive entrée, that's about all you can get. Those girls can really eat, too. I've never seen anything like it. Oddly enough, they don't seem to suffer too much for it."[8]

Jones perfectly captured the action at the iconic Australia Hotel, which he described as "the nicest one in town." It reminded him of an officers' club, and he was impressed by its seemingly innumerable dining rooms. "In the bar, the boys all throw Australian pennies up into the chandeliers. The pennies are about the size of a fifty-cent piece, and no one likes to carry them. You should hear the noise when the place is crowded. Everyone talking at the top of his voice, and those damned pennies flying all over the place and landing on the marble floor."[9]

About the Australian servicemen, Jones's attitude had changed a bit as well. "Those Aussie Diggers can let loose like no one I've ever heard. After what some of them have been through, I can't blame them. They are terrific soldiers and the job they do is amazing."[10]

The 345th's contemporaneous history described the rest trips to Sydney with folksy patter that no doubt sought to emulate the clever, corny style of the narrated short subject films that were so popular at the time.

> No time lost calling the old gals or chasing down some new ones— meet me at the Australia—or I'll be around to get you at so-and-so. Did any city ever have gals like Sydney? Well, we take off for Prince's or Romano's or the all-Yank Roosevelt in King's Cross. They say some of the boys even went to the Gilbert and Sullivan shows but we can't prove it. Favorite pastime: The steak and salad dinner the gals would cook in your flat, with the culinary extras and otherwise. Always those fun-loving Rovers and their Sydney gals—the Battle is on! Black market chicken, or steak, or grog to make that "rest leave" really restful. And those Sydney gals!

Tal Epps met "and lost my heart to a lovely young girl" in Sydney during December 1943. They enjoyed chatting at a "milk bar," or soda fountain, on the night they met and walked across the Sydney Harbor Bridge to Luna Park—a popular amusement park—on their first official date. Her name was Ruth Pearson, and she worked in a tobacco factory. She was lively, quick-witted, and beautiful. And Epps fell head over heels in love.

But quite frankly, most of the men were not interested in romantic relationships. They were young, and many of them were keen—as young men always had been—on physical contact with the opposite sex. Some among Australia's young women were similarly intent, especially as so many of the nation's men were overseas in military service. A story carried in the 501st's newsletter late in 1943 was instructive: "One of our boys was down [in Sydney] on the first day of his furlough. He met a girl in a hotel lounge and was pouring her a drink. 'Say when,' he said, tilting the bottle. She replied, 'After the first drink.' Yep. It's a great place for a rest."

Although the group was a combat unit, it still conducted training flights. Low-level bombing attacks at sea were drilled especially vigorously. The "Moresby Wreck," upon which the 345th's crews and those of so many other units practiced their strafing and bombing, had once been the 4,698-ton SS *Pruth*. She became stuck on a poorly charted hazard, the Nateara Reef, on December 31, 1923, while inbound to Port Moresby to pick up a cargo of copra. Resisting all efforts to recover her, the freighter was unloaded and remained atop the reef—mostly unmolested—until the onset of the war. Her proximity to Moresby and the fact that she was similar to many of the freighters used by the Japanese made her an excellent practice target. Moreover, the 345th's men were especially delighted when Japanese heckler aircraft occasionally wasted bombs on her, mistaking her for a viable Allied ship.

But the Moresby Wreck and Port Moresby itself were left behind at the end of 1943 when the 345th made the first of its many moves while flying combat. Although the various airstrips at Port Moresby had grown and evolved out of their early primitive states—and were more secure than ever from Japanese attacks—they were increasingly too far from the action. This was evidenced during the October and November raids on Rabaul for which the 345th was compelled to stage its aircraft across the Owen Stanley Range to the base at Dobodura, which was situated about fifteen miles inland from New Guinea's northeastern coast. Doing so took time and men and consumed valuable fuel and parts, not to mention the extra wear and tear it forced on the aircraft.

Although the men grew quite practiced at them, such staging operations were costly and inefficient.

Accordingly, the aircraft were permanently flown from Port Moresby to Dobodura on December 23, 1943. Moving aircraft was one thing, but moving the men, material, and special equipment was quite another—especially as there was no overland route. Equipment too big to fit inside an aircraft was sent by sea, while everything else was moved inside the B-25s or via C-47 transport aircraft. In fact, the move required more than three hundred C-47 sorties, for which the 345th was especially appreciative. "To the C-47 pilots, the unsung moving men of the New Guinea campaign, go our thanks. They flew a difficult and dangerous route, often overloaded, and all of them got there."

<hr />

Air strikes such as those the 345th had flown during October and November were a good start in isolating and choking Rabaul. But the choking could only be completed once the system of bases that supported and protected Rabaul was also neutralized or captured. To that end, Douglas MacArthur ordered the seizure of Japanese encampments and bases at Cape Gloucester, in particular the two airfields. Those bases, like Rabaul, were on the island of New Britain, but they were situated at the opposite end, 275 miles to the west. Securing the area would also make operations in and through the Vitiaz Strait, which ran between New Britain and New Guinea, less dangerous.

In preparation for the assault, intensive air strikes were made against Japanese positions in the area. The 345th made its first raid there on December 2 and followed it up with several more missions during the next few weeks. Additionally, the Army seized Arawe, on the southwest coast of New Britain, on December 15. This was in part a diversionary effort intended to focus Japanese attention away from Cape Gloucester. Arawe was also ideally positioned to block Japanese efforts to resupply western New Britain from the east.

Coordination between American air, naval, and ground units had grown more sophisticated since the early days of the war. The assault on Cape Gloucester was planned to leverage the goodness that such coordination provided. Basically, the scheme tasked Navy warships with bombarding Japanese defensive positions. Then, as landing barges motored toward the beach, the naval bombardment was to be lifted as air elements, including the 345th, dropped bombs and ripped the landing area with gunfire. The air attacks were to cease just as Marines from the 1st Marine Division, veterans of the bloody fighting at Guadalcanal, made landfall. Ideally, the Japanese defenders would have little time to recover before the Marines hit the beach.

The tempo of operations during this period was high, and its effects on the aircrews showed. John Bronson, a pilot with the 498th recalled how the unit's flight surgeon assessed the flyers.

During the morning briefings for our missions, the pilots would all gather in the briefing tent, and before we took our seats, we filled our coffee cups from a coffee urn located in the corner. With our hands shaking, knowing what lie[s] ahead in the next few hours, we walked to our seats. Capt. Blumenthal sat in the back of the room and watched us. If you made it to your seat with at least a half a cup of coffee, you were fit and able to fly. If not, and your shaken cup were empty, you would be pulled off flight status. "Nervous in the service" is what he called it![11]

Early on the morning of the actual assault, December 26, 1943, warships from two task forces ripped the landing areas at Cape Gloucester with naval artillery. Nearby, approximately eighty transport ships of various types readied to put more than twelve thousand Marines and nearly eight thousand tons of equipment and material ashore. It was a massive effort that marked the start of a months-long campaign.

Clinton "Fearless" True, flying with the 500th Bomb Squadron, led thirty-nine aircraft from the 345th out of Dobodura at 0530 that same morning. Flying north to Finschafen, across the Vitiaz Strait and through Dampier Strait, he circled Sakar Island, only about twenty miles west of Cape Gloucester. He flashed his landing light periodically as the other squadrons, the 499th, 498th, and 501st, in that order, flew through the predawn inkiness and found their positions in the formation.

After dawn, and with the group gathered behind him, True departed Sakar Island and headed east at 0715, as described by the mission summary report. "Skirting the line of warships which were shelling the north coast of New Britain," the report observed, "our planes flew around the most easterly ship in line and went in for the attack. The plan called for radio communication between our lead plane [True] and the Navy to inform them we were ready for the attack, but contact was not made. However, the naval fire stopped as our planes came round the last ship and headed for the target."

Taking an easterly heading, True edged just to the north and east of Cape Gloucester and pointed the 345th southeast toward the landing area—Yellow Beach—at the western side of Borgen Bay. It was an area the group had attacked many times before, including twice during the previous day—Christmas. First across the target, the 500th's aircraft were each loaded with twelve one-hundred-pound phosphorous bombs. These were intended to mark the target area and the small rise, "Target Hill," that backstopped it. The choking smoke would also make it nearly impossible for the defending Japanese to target not only the aircraft that followed the 500th but also the landing craft bringing the Marines to the beach.

The 500th's pass went flawlessly, and "the resultant smoke completely blanketed the area." Following the 500th, the 499th's aircraft each carried twenty-two one-hundred-pound demolition bombs. Flying in flights of three, at thirty-second intervals, the nine 499th aircraft dropped down to one hundred feet and put their bombs into the target area, strafing as they did so. Off the target, the 499th followed the 500th in a left-hand turn over Borgen Bay. The 498th and 501st likewise laid their bombs into the target area as they strafed. Once through the target, they also turned left.

As the last element of the 501st finished its initial run across the target and turned left across Borgen Bay, True and his two wingmen had already circled back and begun a strafing run. The 345th was essentially arranged in a huge wheeling formation of three-aircraft elements. As they ripped the target area at thirty-second intervals with thousands of rounds of machine-gun fire, the defending Japanese had no choice but to keep their heads down.

True turned hard across Borgen Bay after his third pass across the target, then reversed course to the south to cut across New Britain. He watched as the rest of the group's crews finished their strafing runs and turned to follow him. The time was 0740, and the first landing craft were only yards away from the beach.

The mission was performed about as perfectly as possible. Shrapnel from their own bombs had holed two aircraft but did no serious damage. If the mission had a downside, it was that the jungle foliage and the phosphorous smoke from the 500th's bombs combined to make it virtually impossible not only to find specific targets but to determine the effects of their attacks. Regardless, Yellow Beach had been well and truly saturated with bombs and gunfire.

When elements of the 1st Marine Division waded ashore through the choppy surf, they encountered little resistance, in large part due to the 345th's B-25s, which were just disappearing over the southern horizon. Indeed, the Marines made good progress toward their main objective— the two Japanese airfields at Cape Gloucester. In truth, the Japanese troops who opposed them were outnumbered and outgunned and consequently put up little fight. Nevertheless, the assault was still strongly contested from the air. Japanese army and navy air elements made several attacks during the day, and those attacks were still underway when the 345th returned that afternoon.

The tasking for the group's second mission was much the same as it had been that morning, as described by the 500th Bomb Squadron's mission summary report: "The second part of a double-header strike to cover our troops invading the northwest coast of New Britain." Specifically, the unit was to hit Japanese defensive positions at Natamo Point, a small spur that jutted north from the southern coast of Borgen Bay. Each of the four squadrons put up six aircraft beginning at 1300. The route was essentially the same as that flown during the morning, although "aerial combat over Sakar Island prevented the planes from flying to this point and the formation followed up the Dampier Strait and turned right to approach the target."

Earl Giffin of the 498th led the group, followed in order by the 499th, the 500th, and the 501st. Clinton True chose to fly back in the pack with the 500th—likely to have a better view of the entire formation and possibly to give Giffin more experience at leading a large formation. At any rate, Giffin wisely avoided the air combat over Sakar Island and turned the group east toward Cape Gloucester. There, the 345th flew into a maelstrom, as observed by the 500th: "The scene over the target was a mass of action of airplanes chasing each other through the sky, some crashing in flames, dive bombers attacking naval vessels and every vessel in the area spewing skyward all the ack-ack they could muster."

After passing Cape Gloucester, Giffin rounded Silimati Point at the western mouth of Borgen Bay and turned southeast toward Natamo Point. As they readied to drop their four five-hundred-pound bombs, the aircrews took in the fracas around them. "Japanese planes were observed to score a hit on a large barge, leaving it burning. One bomb burst was seen on Silimati Point as planes left the target. One plane was seen to crash into water 2,000 feet east of Silimati Point. One B-25 was seen to circle East of Borgen Bay and disappear. One unidentified plane was seen to crash 10,000 feet southeast of Natamo Point. One large fire was seen one-half mile east of the north end of Gloucester strip #1."

Notwithstanding the mesmerizing action, the 498th's men pressed on to Natamo Point in two flights of three and released their bombs. "Bombing was excellent and the bombs were concentrated on the small targets. The target was strafed in the single pass."

Despite some jockeying to get lined up on the target—during which one of the gunners knocked down an Aichi Type 99 "Val" dive bomber—the 499th's attack was similarly successful. Although a few bombs fell short of the target and into the bay, most of them cut across the center of Natamo Point.

Whereas the morning mission in support of the Cape Gloucester operation had been a model of interservice cooperation, the afternoon mission was not—particularly in terms of aircraft recognition. This became apparent as the 500th set up for its attack. Below the squadron's B-25s, landing craft were loaded and unloaded, and Marines pushed inland toward their objectives.

And then an enemy aircraft, another Val, flew in front of the squadron and headed toward the shoreline. "Some of our planes opened fire on it," noted the unit's mission summary report, "causing no damage to the Val. It is not known definitely whether or not our fire went past the Val and into the Allied positions or beyond. In any case, however, intense and accurate antiaircraft fire of medium and light calibers was received immediately from these positions and all but two of our planes were riddled."

The misguided marksmanship of the American gunners was good, and William Kyser's aircraft, on the left side of the leading three-aircraft formation, was hit. New copilot Richard Whitman flew with Kyser. Ripped with friendly gunfire, the B-25 immediately rolled left and down and a few seconds later smashed into Borgen Bay "leaving a burning mass on the surface." It was a violent end, and "crews who saw the crash agree that there could have been no survivors."

The following element of three aircraft "caught hell" as the American gunners, mistakenly identifying the B-25s as Japanese, continued their deadly fire. Clinton True's ship "was set on fire around the bomb bay and right engine and immediately began to lose speed. It continued toward the target, but before reaching Natamo Point it veered to the left as its wheels dropped down and battery and oxygen tank fell out." True, his aircraft afire and losing altitude, motored away from the beach to the east.

True's wingman, Frank Latawiec, was also hit in the right engine. However, it did not catch fire, and he continued to the target and dropped his bombs. The squadron reported that the American guns absolutely sieved George Mitchell's ship, "riddling it with an estimated 100 holes of various sizes. Lieutenant Mitchell continued and dropped four bombs on the target. The radioman in this plane was wounded, not seriously, in the right leg." Both Latawiec and Mitchell coaxed their planes to safety.

The 501st was the last of the 345th's squadrons across the target. Its crews saw Clinton True "go down in Borgen Bay, making a good crash landing about 400 yards offshore at point 804887." They also spotted a destroyer "blown up by a direct hit by a dive bomber. This DD [destroyer] was leading a column of five DDs out to sea at the time it was hit." The destroyer was the USS *Brownson*, which went down with 108 dead.

The squadron reported, "Vals were in the area and were attacking our ground forces at Yellow Beach." Multiple B-25s fired on one enemy aircraft

Lyle Anacker and his crew were shot down in a bloody low-level gunfight with Japanese fighters during the raid to Rabaul on October 18, 1943. USAAF

Thane Hecox was an early stalwart of the 345th's 500th Bomb Squadron. He and his crew went down in flames over Kavieng on February 15, 1944. USAAF

B-25s parked at one of Dobodura's many runway complexes. USAAF

Like Lyle Anacker, Harlan Peterson and his crew were shot down during the mission to Rabaul on October 18, 1943, after a fierce gun battle with Japanese fighters. USAAF

Major General Richard Sutherland looks over a crash-landed B-25 of the 345th's 498th Bomb Squadron. Note the open escape hatch just behind the wing and the airborne C-47 in the background. USAAF

Twenty-three-pound parafragmentation bombs descend on Japanese aircraft at Vunakanau from a 500th Bomb Squadron aircraft during the 345th's first raid on Rabaul on October 12, 1943. USAAF

Dirty Dora flew combat with the 38th Bomb Group before being assigned to the 345th's 499th Bomb Squadron. This photograph shows it supporting the Cape Gloucester landings on December 26, 1943—the same day that William Kyser was killed. USAAF

The United States Army Air Forces struggled in New Guinea and elsewhere in the region until General George Kenney arrived and took charge during the latter part of 1942. USAAF

B-25s of the 345th's 501st Bomb Squadron race over a Japanese airfield at Cape Gloucester during December 1943. The near aircraft, Quitch, suffered a mid-air collision over Ternate on August 15, 1944, and was ditched at Noemfoor with all crew surviving. USAAF

Red Wrath of the 345th's 498th Squadron, flown by R. W. Judd, overflies antiaircraft guns at Boram on October 16, 1943. Japanese gunners are crouching for cover. USAAF

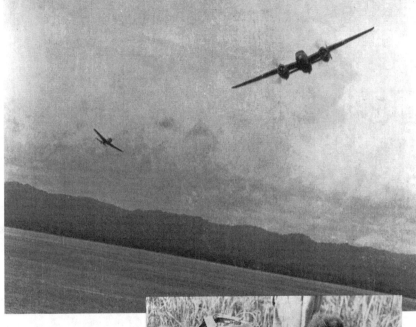

A Japanese Ki-43 "Oscar" attacking a B-25. USAAF

A New Guinea native, or "fuzzy wuzzy," poses with a wrecked turret gun. USAAF

Unrelenting Allied air attacks turned the Japanese airfield complex at Wewak into an aircraft graveyard by early 1944. USAAF

Japanese phosphorous antiaircraft aerial bombs were attention-grabbing but almost entirely ineffective. USAAF

The 345th supported the air assault on the Markham Valley in New Guinea on September 5, 1943. Here, Allied troops jump from C-47s. USAAF

Parafragmentation bombs are dropped on Japanese G4M "Betty" bombers at Vunakanau on October 12, 1943. USAAF

The crash of William Kyser's B-25 as seen from an LST at Cape Gloucester on December 26, 1943. USAAF

B-25s of the 345th's 500th Bomb Squadron attack the airfield at Boram, near Wewak, on October 16, 1943. USAAF

In New Guinea, the 345th and other Allied units sometimes targeted featureless, unremarkable native villages such as this, believing them to shelter enemy soldiers or supplies. USAAF

The 345th hits the airfield at Dagua, near Wewak. Note the three Ki-61 "Tony" fighters in the foreground. USAAF

The B-25 *Here's Howe* was assigned to the 38th Bomb Group when it flew against Japanese shipping at Rabaul on November 2, 1943. It was shortly thereafter transferred to the 345th and shot down at Cape Gloucester with William Kyser's crew on December 26, 1943. USAAF

On the November 2, 1943, mission to Rabaul, two 345th squadrons dropped phosphorous smoke bombs to cover the attacks against shipping in Simpson Harbor. USAAF

Elnora Bartlett and James "J. R." Jones were engaged before he went overseas. SUZANNE JONES NEFF

345th B-25s visit the Japanese at Dagua with parafragmentation bombs. USAAF

Ralph Wallace of the 501st Bomb Squadron points at the image of *Tondelayo*. The panel painted with the lower part of the image has been replaced. Wallace and his crew barely survived a running low-level gun battle against Rabaul-based Japanese fighters on October 18, 1943. USAAF VIA BYNUM COLLECTION

Clinton "Fearless" True led the all-B-25 strike against Rabaul on October 18, 1943, without fighter protection. A tough, no-nonsense leader, he later took command of the 345th from Jarred Crabb. USAAF VIA BYNUM COLLECTION

Photographed here after being promoted to brigadier general, Colonel Jarred Crabb stood up the 345th Bomb Group in the United States and oversaw its training and introduction to combat. Much of the success the group enjoyed was due to the foundation Crabb put in place. USAAF VIA BYNUM COLLECTION

A 345th B-25 takes off from a Port Moresby airstrip early during the group's combat career. This aircraft has not yet been converted to the strafe configuration. USAAF VIA BYNUM COLLECTION

345th B-25s dump parafragmentation bombs on Japanese aircraft at Dagua, near Wewak, New Guinea. USAAF

The smoke screen in the background was laid by 345th B-25s to protect the aircraft attacking the shipping at Rabaul from enemy shore batteries on November 2, 1945. USAAF

Administrative and logistics personnel were vital to the functioning of the 345th. The calendar at the far left is turned to October 1943, which means that this photo was taken somewhere at the Port Moresby complex, probably Jackson Airfield. Several "girlie" posters adorn the walls. USAAF VIA 345TH BOMB GROUP ASSOCIATION

The group's teletype kept the unit connected to higher headquarters. Orders were received and reports were sent via this gear. USAAF VIA 345TH BOMB GROUP ASSOCIATION

The 345th's 501st Bomb Squadron reported strafing the Japanese flying boat in the center of the photo at Rabaul on November 2, 1943. USAAF

Ralph Wallace, left, the pilot of *Tondelayo* on the October 18, 1943, mission to Rabaul, poses with crew members Weldon Isler, Burton Eaton, and John Murphy. Copilot Edward Hicko had been shot up during the mission and was recovering in the hospital. USAAF VIA BYNUM COLLECTION

The chow line was not just about nutrition; it was also a social event. Note that the 345th's men maintained their own mess kits.
USAAF VIA 345TH BOMB GROUP ASSOCIATION

A 500th Bomb Squadron aircraft flies low over the Wewak area. USAAF

A B-25 from the 501st Bomb Squadron drops parafragmentation bombs and fires its guns at a target near Madang, New Guinea. USAAF VIA JOHN RAUZON COLLECTION

An early 345th training flight over South Carolina. USAAF VIA JOHN RAUZON COLLECTION

Sam Vojnovich was the gunner aboard William Kyser's aircraft on December 26, 1943. He was killed together with the rest of the crew. PERRY HURT COLLECTION

This sign was strung across a main road at Port Moresby. The reverse side read, "I told you so!" USAAF VIA 345TH BOMB GROUP ASSOCIATION

Parafragmentation bombs fall on a Japanese fighter at Wewak. USAAF VIA 345TH BOMB GROUP ASSOCIATION

Rabaul-based Mitsubishi A6M "Zero" fighters. The 345th encountered this enemy aircraft throughout the war. NATIONAL ARCHIVES

The Air Apaches frequently encountered the Ki-61, which was code-named "Tony." Its resemblance to the German Me-109 led many to believe that it was a license-built version of that fighter. USAAF

Melvin Pollock's letters to his father painted an invaluable frank, contemporary picture of training and combat. MARCIA POLLOCK WYSOCKY

The distinctive falcon head nose art of the 345th's 498th Bomb Squadron was sometimes mistaken for a parrot. SAN DIEGO AIR & SPACE MUSEUM

The hard-worn B-25D Jayhawk of the 345th's 499th Bomb Squadron. It survived long enough to be declared war weary and was transferred out of the group during the fall of 1944. USAAF

The 345th's 501st Bomb Squadron leaves Japanese aircraft afire at Hollandia. USAAF

Max Mortensen of the 345th's 500th Bomb Squadron was one of the group's old hands. He flew combat with the Air Apaches from beginning to end. USAAF

A B-25 of the 345th's 500th Bomb Squadron flies over Wakde Island, near Biak, on May 11, 1944. The 500th's snorting horse head insignia is barely visible on the vertical stabilizer. USAAF that was observed to be hit. Nevertheless, as it "was not seen to definitely crash or disintegrate," the crews claimed it as only "probably destroyed."

As with the 500th, the American gunners mistakenly fired upon the 501st. The aircraft commanded by Henry Kortemeyer was hard hit, and Henry Cohron, the engineer, was killed. J. R. Jones, who normally piloted his own aircraft, flew in place of Kortemeyer's sick copilot. Censorship constraints precluded him from writing about his missions, and none of the hundreds of pages he wrote to Elnora included such details. Consequently, the statement he provided for the 501st's mission summary report is the only known description of his personal combat experiences.

"When coming into Yellow Beach," he said, "we saw gunfire coming at us from the barges [landing craft] and from the woods behind the barges. This was machine-gun fire, and it was very intense. There was also 20-millimeter fire coming at us."

The friendly fire was precise, and Jones said that "a 20-millimeter shell hit the nose of our plane right below my feet." Jones was wounded. Rocked by gunfire, he and Kortemeyer had difficulty controlling the aircraft. "A few seconds later, a bomb burst in the ground in front of us," Jones said, "throwing mud in the air which splattered all over our windshield, completely blocking our visibility."[12] Kortemeyer simply reached through the sliding window on his left, leaned forward, and wiped the mud from the windshield.

"We immediately salvoed all of our bombs," said Jones. "The right engine quit, and by the time we got the prop feathered, we were just about over our assigned target." Free of the bombs, and with the right engine shut down and its propeller feathered, Kortemeyer cajoled the damaged aircraft into a gentle climb.

"Lieutenant [Sylvester] Vogt, flying plane 082, saw we were in trouble, and even though there were enemy fighters in the immediate area—Zekes [Zero fighters] were directly ahead of us in our path of flight—circled back and gave us immediate cover. It was a good thing he did," said Jones, "because we learned later our gunners were injured, and could not have fought off an attack by themselves." The two B-25s flew on, unmolested by the enemy pilots.

"At this time," Jones said, "I noticed that Lieutenant Kortemeyer had been hit in the elbow and was bleeding visibly. He kept right on flying the plane and was doing a marvelous job of it." With Vogt and his crew as an escort, Kortemeyer and Jones flew their B-25 low across New Britain while the rest of the crew gave each other first aid. "When we reached the south coast of New Britain, the squadron had turned back for us, and formed around us."

Anxious to stay out of the shark-infested Vitiaz Strait, Kortemeyer's crew threw overboard everything that could be lifted. In the cockpit, Kortemeyer fired the nose guns until all the ammunition was expended. This further lightened the aircraft. The crew's efforts paid off, and the aircraft had put a thousand feet between it and the sea by the time the crew reached Finschafen, on New Guinea's northeastern coast. However, even though his aircraft was shot up, and despite the fact that he and the rest of his crew were wounded, Kortemeyer had second thoughts about landing on Finschafen's pierced-steel-plank runway. If the landing went badly, he worried, sparks caused by the metal aircraft scraping along the metal runway might ignite a fire.

Instead, he flew fifty miles further west to Lae, where he found a string of transport aircraft taking off. "We had to make two circles," said Jones, "while the rest of our squadron's planes buzzed the field to warn them that we had to make a crash landing. On our second circle around the strip, we tried to lower our wheels, but the hydraulic system was out, and our right wheel and nose wheel went down part way, and our left wheel wouldn't go down at all."

The partially extended landing gear created drag, and the B-25 lost altitude immediately. Moreover, the flaps would not extend. Gravity worked its awful magic, and the earth rose to meet the shot-up aircraft. Kortemeyer and Jones had little choice but to wrestle it around for a downwind landing that promised to be dangerously fast. "The transports on the field just barely got out of the way in time for us to come in," said Jones.

"We hit on the left side of the runway, and slid along the ground for about 200 yards, and then the plane spun violently to the right." The B-25 finally scraped to a stop, and Kortemeyer, Jones, the radioman, and a cameraman aboard especially to film the mission scrambled out of the aircraft and onto the runway. The fire they feared did not come. "The crash truck was right there," said Jones, "and we had to chop out the tail to get the other two men out of the rear of our plane."

"It was after everybody was out of the plane that I first learned that Lieutenant Kortemeyer had been hit in the back by shrapnel when our plane was under ack-ack fire," Jones said. Kortemeyer's wounds were treated on the spot. "I can truthfully say that all of us in that plane owe our lives to Lieutenant Kortemeyer for the skillful way in which he kept control of himself and his plane."

After being shot up by his own countrymen, Clinton True ditched his aircraft on the eastern side of Borgen Bay. Between the gunfire and the water landing, everyone on the crew was injured—two of them seriously. Still, True got them aboard one of the aircraft's life rafts, which proved to be too small for the entire crew. Knowing they risked being savaged by sharks, he and another man stayed in the water for hours until dusk turned to night.

The drifting crew was in a situation where capture was as likely as rescue. Regardless, True fired several flares into the dark. There was no response. Finally, after midnight, the wounded men paddled to shore and sneaked into the jungle scrub that ran up to the beach. There, they stumbled into a Marine patrol. The blackness of the night made for a tense situation, especially as the Marines demanded the day's password. True didn't know it; however, his especially colorful and profane commentary left little doubt that he was very much an American. Later the next day, the Marines evacuated True and his men to a ship aboard which they received medical care.

J. R. Jones did not want Elnora to know how close a thing the mission to Cape Gloucester had been. In his letter to her the following day, he referenced his combat action in vague terms: "We have been busier the past days than any since I have been up here. You probably can guess why when you read the news. Just mark Sunday [December 26, 1943] in your calendar, and I'll tell you about it, someday. Suffice it to say it was the roughest day in my life."

And in answer to an earlier query about whether a silver dollar she had given him had brought him any luck, he replied, "Darling, you'll never know how much. I have never been without it since you gave it to me. That's one piece of money I'll never spend."

Nevertheless, he had been wounded and was anxious to keep that fact from his fiancée. After receiving a telegram from the War Department informing her of his injury, however, Jones's mother informed Elnora. When he learned that she knew, Jones was unhappy but provided more details. "You've heard that song, *Comin' In on a Wing and a Prayer*? Well that's me, and oh how I prayed." He soft-soaped the extent of his injuries. "We really had it bad, but I was extremely fortunate and only got a few small scratches on the back of my legs. Some weren't so fortunate. We crash-landed and [had] some fun. Oh, well, I'm all right."[13]

He wrote Elnora a week later and discussed the mission further. "I was the luckiest on the plane. Guy next to me [Kortemeyer] got some pretty big pieces. One was killed [Henry Cohron], one badly injured. We got home on one engine and crash-landed because the hydraulic system was shot out. I guess strain was the worst effect on me as they shipped me off on leave immediately. I'm flying again, so you know I'm quite all right, and you shouldn't have heard anything about it in the first place."[14] Jones was still upset that his mother had told Elnora of his injuries.

Jones and Elnora were inveterate letter writers, as were many of their contemporaries. It was the only way the men serving overseas could communicate, and they expended much effort and resources to ensure they stayed connected. Jones's morale rose and fell on mail deliveries—he wrote ceaselessly about it, and his appetite for news from Elnora was seemingly insatiable. But he was a good correspondent and wrote not only to her but to various family and friends. Still, he would have preferred not to have been so dependent on writing. "The mail has given up again for the past few days," he wrote during one of the many periods when deliveries trickled down to nothing. "I'll really be a happy man when my letter writing days are over. I don't want to write any more letters to you. I want to do my talking and wooing in person. It's much better that way, I'm told."[15]

In truth, getting the mail back and forth between the States and the combat theaters was problematic. First, the volume was huge—it took up space and weight that would otherwise be valuable for war material and equipment. And a system capable of handling millions of items across an area as broad as the Pacific required thousands of postal specialists to get it sorted and delivered.

Victory Mail, or "V-Mail" did save some weight and volume. It was a process that transferred letters written on specialized form to small rolls of microfilm. Upon reaching their destinations, the letters were printed from the film onto small sheets before being delivered. The weight of 150,000 single-page letters was reduced from more than 2,500 pounds to 45 pounds. But still, the process did require special equipment, material, and trained personnel.

Moreover, the vagaries of war worked against a smooth-running mail service. Mail got lost when the ships or aircraft carrying it were destroyed or damaged in combat. Also, units moved frequently, and mail often took weeks or months to catch up. More difficult was getting it to individuals who bounced from one location to another—and then several more—before being permanently assigned to a unit. It was not unusual for a man to go weeks without receiving anything, only to be handed dozens of letters on a single day.

Lincoln Grush and his fiancée, Gloria, wrote each other daily. "We used to number the letters," said Grush, a pilot with the 500th Bomb Squadron. "We were island hopping, and we'd get a thick packet of letters that were a month-and-a-half old. So we'd number them so that when we received them we could put them in order."[16]

The letters the 345th's men sent home were censored to ensure they included no information that, in the wrong hands, could endanger the war effort. The officers performed the censoring, and they hated it. Every letter from every man had to be read. Most of them were mind-numbingly mundane and included nothing of interest to anyone outside the sender and recipient. When potentially sensitive information was noted, the censor was compelled to cut or black it out.

J. R. Jones loathed the task. "I'm O.D. [officer of the day] and that means censoring the mail again," he wrote Elnora. "That's one of the roughest jobs I've seen." He wrote that he became "more discouraged every time I get that job" and that "most of [the writers] are pretty cheerful, but you must have the usual percentage of bellyachers."[17] After one stint he observed, "It was the most I've ever seen, and I was heartily sick of letters by the time I had finished. You have no idea what a dull job that is. Most of them sound alike, and if I thought I sounded like that, I'd quit here and now. . . . It's a good thing that job doesn't come around too often, or I'd be a roaring maniac."[18]

Jones's own writing was more polished than most, but he was besotted with love, and his letters showed it. Still, he could be clever: "You know, Elnora, the more I look at your pictures, the lovelier you get. If I didn't know I were engaged to you, I'd be nuts by now. That close-up snapshot you sent me nearly finished the job. I know only too well you can smile that way. Please be careful who you aim it at. It's a mighty dangerous thing coupled with that red hair—I ought to know."[19]

The least welcome letters were those from girlfriends, fiancées, or wives who no longer wanted to be girlfriends, fiancées, or wives. One man described how some of the men exacted a small measure of revenge after being dropped by their true loves. "Our privy was an open, many-holed thing, exposed to the sunshine and available for all to use or observe. It became somewhat of a meeting place where troops met to discuss the cares of the day, the weather and news of home. In it, too, men hung photos of their girlfriends who had sent them 'Dear Johns.'"[20]

Toward the end of January 1944, the 345th was fully operational at Dobodura. The airfield featured two connected airstrips, and the 345th operated two squadrons from each. The men were billeted in two separate camps miles from each other and a good truck ride from where the aircraft were parked. It wasn't an ideal arrangement, but it was good enough. And it was closer to Japanese bases.

J. R. Jones was pleased enough with the move. He wrote to Elnora, "I really like our new home. It's much cooler and not so many mosquitoes. Our new club is right on the edge of a river, and it is rather a pretty sight. We do most of our bathing in the river these days. All in all, it could be worse."[21]

CHAPTER SEVEN

"We Think We Destroyed the Mission"

THE GROUP REGULARLY FLEW BARGE SWEEPS ALONG THE NORTHERN coast of New Guinea during this period. These missions were intended to interdict Japanese resupply efforts. Rather than concentrate on one specific point where enemy shipping might or might not be located, the B-25s swept along the coast and attacked whatever vessels they encountered.

The men also pounced on other targets of opportunity. Quite often these were obviously military targets, such as enemy vehicles or personnel. But the crews bombed and shot up seemingly anything and everything, including native villages, missionary compounds, and even small, canoe-like craft. They reasoned that any habitation or infrastructure behind enemy lines was useful to the Japanese. The 500th Bomb Squadron's mission summary report for January 22, 1944, offered an example. During this particular effort, the squadron's aircraft swept the northern New Guinea coast from Cape Gourdon to Cape Croisilles, a distance of about fifty miles.

The bridge at Kronprinz Harbor was partially destroyed, and native buildings along the harbor perimeter were bombed. At Magnus Point and Tete Village native buildings were bombed. . . . The mission buildings at Korak were bombed; we think we destroyed the mission. We destroyed a house at Bunabun Village by bombing, but missed a supply shed at Dove Point. We dropped eight bombs on the mission at Malas and probably destroyed it. . . . Four of our bombs

landed amongst the huts in Dylup, and at Biranik Village, our final
stop on the way down the coast, we dropped our last two bombs,
destroying a house.

Certainly, many of these were legitimate targets used by the Japanese. And just as certainly, the natives had already fled some of these habitations. But there can be little doubt that some of what the 500th destroyed that day was not used by the Japanese, and the attacks quite possibly wrecked native property and took native lives. How many native deaths can be attributed to this sort of bombing and strafing cannot be determined, but it must have caused some degree of ill will among those who were wrongly targeted.

Although the Japanese were increasingly beleaguered during this period, the missions were still not cakewalks. A couple of days later, on January 25, 1944, the 345th led elements of the 38th Bomb Group to hit targets on Manus Island, two hundred miles north of New Guinea. The assigned targets were the airfields at Momote and Lorengau as well as "shipping, barges, supply areas and facilities."

The 345th's 500th Bomb Squadron led the attack. John McLean led the squadron's third flight of three aircraft and was caught by antiaircraft fire. George Hurt, a bombardier flying in the first flight, recalled that McLean's "left engine and bomb bay caught fire. He tried to land in the water, but the ship got away from him. Exploded on impact. Evidently the gas line and control cables were hit."[1] No one survived the crash.

The 499th Bomb Squadron followed the 500th, and Jim Mahaffey was the navigator aboard Kenneth McClure's aircraft. "Everyone had a job to do," he said. "Mine was to keep track of time and place, and to hold on to Flight Officer Flaps, our poodle mascot, given to McClure by General Wilson of MacArthur's staff in Brisbane. He was a friend of Mac's mother, back in Ohio."[2] Although it wasn't typical, the crews did sometimes take unauthorized "passengers" with them on combat missions.

McClure and his crew hit targets of opportunity along the coast, as did the rest of the formation. Approaching Papitalai Harbor, they saw John McLean's B-25 crash and explode at the east end of the harbor. The explosion was violent, and the 500th's report declared, "All six of the crew must be considered lost." Mahaffey recalled that McLean was a friend of McClure's and that McClure turned his aircraft hard toward the crash site to "avenge" his comrade.

The 499th described how McClure's ship was hit: "Here, he was at very low altitude and just as he topped a small ridge, he saw heavy anti-aircraft bursts just in front. He banked sharply to the right but just as he did so, he felt a burst hit his airplane. The crew described it as sounding like a lot of stones hitting the plane."

"It went right through the left oil cooler and out the top of the wing," Mahaffey recalled. "It was an unreal feeling knowing you were hit and in trouble and almost helpless. It looked like someone had poked a post right through the wing and burning oil was running everywhere."

Despite his aircraft being hit, McClure made another full circle and bombed the area from which he believed the antiaircraft fire had originated. After making that final run, McClure hauled the aircraft toward the open sea and started to climb. "Mac headed for some clouds," said Mahaffey, "thinking he could put out the fire."

But the clouds had no effect on the flames that enveloped his left engine. Nor was the engine equipped with a fire extinguisher. And because the engine had lost most of its oil, the propeller would not feather. A B-25 from the 38th Bomb Group joined on his wing; McClure pointed out the bad engine to the other crew and signaled that he didn't think his aircraft would stay aloft much longer.

The other aircraft left after a short time, and then the engine quit. The windmilling propeller, together with vibrations from the right engine, which was running at full power, shook the stricken aircraft. Notwithstanding McClure's best efforts, it slowly descended toward the sea. He notified the formation leader that he was ditching and then, low over the wave tops, extended the flaps to slow his speed further. The airplane smacked the waves violently, bounced, and hit the water hard again.

"I was in the navigation compartment," Mahaffey recalled, "and did not have a seat or a seat belt and was holding Flaps. Hitting the water at 120 miles per hour is like hitting a brick wall at 80 miles per hour. I slid forward and hit the bulkhead knocking Flaps out of my hands. Water was coming in so I decided I should get out."

The dog was nowhere to be seen. The men in the front soon gave up looking and squirmed out of the aircraft through the escape hatch above the cockpit. "We were all soon out on the wings," said Mahaffey, "and Mac [McClure] wanted to go back to look for the dog but we talked him out of it." The men climbed into two life rafts as the aircraft slipped below the waves with the dog still somewhere inside.

The rafts were spotted by several crews of the 501st Bomb Squadron, who circled overhead for a time and dropped survival packages of various sorts. Most of these broke apart on impact with the water and proved of little use. Once the B-25s set course back to Dobodura, the men collected what items they could, assessed their situation, and then started paddling south, away from the Japanese-held island. The squadron recorded, "They noticed many sharks around them all the time. Consequently, firearms were made ready to fire in case of attacks on the boats."

The sharks did not molest the rafts, and the men soon realized that the winds and currents were moving them south faster than they could paddle. Accordingly, they drifted to save their energy. Mahaffey remembered that their odds "did not seem good when all the other planes had gone back to base and we had hours to wonder. After about six hours of drifting and worrying we heard a sound to the north, and we saw airplane activity toward the island. They appeared to be Zekes [Japanese Zero fighters] but as they came closer we saw they were P-47s. We fired a Very pistol flare to make sure they saw us."

"Someone had told them we were nearer to Manus Island," said Mahaffey, "so the Catalina [PBY rescue aircraft] had given up and was headed south for home when the P-47s found us." The friendly fighter pilots contacted the PBY pilot, Herbert McPike of VP-52. A short time later, McPike put his aircraft down, and his crew pulled McClure and his men from the water. They spent the night at Finschafen before returning to Dobodura the following day.

Admiral William "Bull" Halsey's Southern Pacific command had been steadily grinding away at Rabaul ever since the 345th flew its last mission there on November 2, 1943. That task was proceeding apace but was not yet complete as a handful of supporting bases were still quite active. The Japanese airfield and port at Kavieng—150 miles northwest of Rabaul on the island of New Ireland—was one of these. MacArthur wanted to neutralize and capture it.

Seized by the Japanese during January 1942, Kavieng was transformed into a key air and naval base. As such, like all the Japanese garrisons that guarded Rabaul, it was targeted by Allied air strikes. During February 1944, in preparation for an invasion that would remove it as a threat once and for all, George Kenney's Fifth Air Force launched a series of raids. The culminating blow, a low-level B-25 strike, was scheduled for February 15.

On that day, A-20s of the 3rd Bomb Group were to attack shipping in Kavieng Harbor, followed an hour later by B-24s tasked with cratering the airfield east of Chinatown, the waterside community that linked the harbor with the island's interior. The low-level B-25 attack was to follow the B-24s fifteen minutes later. The B-25 crews were directed to hit supply dumps, warehousing, personnel, antiaircraft guns, and anything else of value.

The 345th started launching its aircraft just before 0800 that morning. The evolution went without incident until nearly all the bombers were airborne. Then, as John Wilson of the 499th Bomb Squadron lifted his B-25 from the runway, he experienced an engine failure.

The 345th operated field-modified aircraft with weapons and payloads never envisioned by North American Aviation's designers. They were very heavy, and single-engine flight immediately after takeoff was, if not impossible, almost so. Wilson and his copilot, Joseph Koch, struggled with the aircraft.

They lost that struggle. The B-25 fell into the jungle and exploded in a blinding flash. The entire crew perished. Nothing could be done, and aircraft continued to take off, altering course slightly so as not to overfly their immolated comrades.

The other forty-seven aircraft making up the group's effort that morning—each carrying five five-hundred-pound bombs—fell into formation behind the 38th Bomb Group. The 345th's four squadrons were to trail the three squadrons of the 38th. The B-25s met an escort of P-38s over Sand Island before proceeding northeast to Kavieng. Their route took them "to Danu on the south side of New Ireland and thence up along the south coast of New Ireland to a point directly south of Kavieng Township." From there, the B-25s were to jump the hills and attack their targets on a northerly heading.

The 38th Bomb Group struck first, and consequently Kavieng was already afire as the 345th's first squadron, the 500th, approached from the south. "Much smoke and flames were already visible from bombing by other units before our attack," observed the squadron. Still, the entire area was a smorgasbord of targets that included aircraft, ships, supply dumps, buildings, antiaircraft positions, personnel, and more. The B-25 pilots dropped their bombs and fired their guns at an almost frantic tempo as choice targets slid by in the smoke, dust, and flames that veiled the wharf, the town, and the airfield. So violent were some of the explosions that Max Mortensen, leading the 500th, "reported seeing a gasoline drum being blown up alongside of his plane."

During the briefing earlier that morning, the 345th's intelligence officer apologized that he didn't "know the location of the light flak and machine-gun emplacements. All the pictures we have of this target were taken by the Thirteenth Air Force from 17,000 feet."[3] Now, as the 345th's crews raced over Kavieng at a hundred feet or less, the locations of those guns were readily apparent. Streams of antiaircraft rounds lashed at the low-flying bombers. "Captain [Michael] Hochella's plane became damaged while on its run," the 500th recorded, "and after breaking away from the target was last seen two or three feet above the water traveling at an estimated 125 miles per hour, heading southeasterly toward Edmago Island with one prop windmilling. Although no one saw him actually crash, no further word has been received from him or his crew; they are listed as missing."

Another of the 500th's ships was struck. "While approaching Chinatown, Lieutenant [Thane] Hecox's plane was hit and started to burn. Before it crashed and exploded in the plantation immediately northwest of Chinatown, however, Lieutenant Hecox had dropped his bombs in the target." George Hurt, a bombardier aboard William Ames's aircraft, recalled, "Lieutenant Hecox evidently was over a fuel dump when it exploded. Blew both wings off."[4]

The 500th continued to take a beating. "Captain [William] Cavoli's element, close on Lieutenant Hecox's wing, dropped all but three of its bombs through the target. Lieutenant [Francis] Doman's plane was hit while on its run, and as the pilot was fighting to keep his plane in the air, he was forced to salvo three of his bombs in the water after breaking away from the target."

Doman was able to keep his ship airborne. Cavoli was not so lucky. After dropping two bombs into a supply dump, his crew spotted Hecox going down, afire. Cavoli's copilot, George Braun, recorded the action for the squadron's mission summary report: "We then flew into a column of smoke and saw Lieutenant [Arthur] Frey, who was on Lieutenant Hecox's right wing, skid under us. I couldn't drop our bombs for fear of hitting Lieutenant Frey. Our right engine was hit then, and as Lieutenant Frey skidded out to our left again, I toggled out the remaining bombs in the Chinatown area."

The smoke was so thick that Cavoli was forced to fly on his instruments. Copilot Braun reached to activate the fire extinguisher on the burning engine but found that "it had been removed. As soon as we left the shore our right wheel fell out of the nacelle and the rear end of the nacelle burned off."

Cavoli coaxed his aircraft west over the water as noted by the squadron's mission summary report: "I immediately tried to feather the right prop[eller], and when it was almost feathered, it started up all over again. I gave the good engine full power." The drag created by the propeller of the burning engine—not to mention the spreading fire—doomed Cavoli's B-25. He stomped on one rudder pedal and turned his control yoke in the opposite direction. The aircraft yawed almost sideways and fell further. "Slipping the plane in a vain attempt to put out the terrific fire that had started, I again attempted to feather the prop, but to no avail."

Cavoli committed to a ditching. "We hit the water," Braun said, "with the bomb bay open and no flaps due to hydraulic failure when fire burned the nacelle and the wheel fell out. If we had used flaps, the right wing was so badly burned that the flap probably would have failed, causing a spin."

The aircraft skipped twice and twisted itself apart as the nose plunged under the waves. The engineer, Weldon Isler, popped open the escape hatch above the pilots, and Braun was first out, followed by Cavoli. Isler stayed put until Robert Lewis, the navigator, lifted himself clear, at which time he also crawled out of the aircraft. "Sergeant [John] Murphy," Braun said, "was in the turret when we hit the water. The turret went out the bottom of the ship with Murphy in it.

"I stayed in the turret figuring we would blow up before we hit the water," said Murphy. "I wound up going through the bottom of the plane, still hooked up to the turret. After about twenty feet under water, I finally got loose."[5] Braun recalled that while Murphy fought himself free of the turret, "Isler assisted Captain Cavoli to release Sergeant [Thomas] Freeman who was trapped in the radio compartment."

The bomber stayed afloat for almost five minutes before slipping under the surface. Cavoli got his men into a raft and, despite their injuries, started them paddling north, away from Kavieng. There, the sky was black with smoke and fire, and the sound of the burning vortex that the target had become was clearly audible.

The escorting P-38 pilots looked down into the hellish, otherworldly maelstrom as they weaved a couple of thousand feet above the target area. Large antiaircraft rounds spattered the sky around the B-25s with bursts of white-hot shrapnel, while tracers from smaller guns streaked after the attacking flights in bright, curving arcs. The guns of the bombers spat back, and bright orange flashes marked their muzzles. Lines of gray gun smoke ripped down their sides with each burst. Bombs exploded and lifted dirt, debris, and sundered material and equipment high into the sky, where it paused for just an instant before gravity pulled it, smoking and flaming, back to the ground.

Carroll Anderson, one of the P-38 pilots, watched the olive drab bombers hurtle through the deadly chaos, only dozens of feet above the ground. He winced involuntarily each time one of them was hit by the defending gunners. Aircraft that initially trailed only thin streams of raw fuel quickly ignited into flying fireballs. "It seemed as if the strafers would never stop crashing," he recalled.[6]

The 501st followed the 500th over Kavieng. Its crews added their bombs to the havoc and hosed the area with their .50-caliber machine guns. With two squadrons still to follow, the area was already totally afire. "All crews reported it was the most complete destruction they had ever seen," the squadron reported. "The entire area was a mass of wreckage, flames and heavy smoke." The 498th's crews, close in trail of the 501st's, made almost the exact same observation: "It was the opinion of all combat personnel participating in this attack that more damage was done to this target than any other target they had ever attacked."

Damage was also done to the 498th. Ed Cavin, pilot of *Gremlin's Holiday*, hauled back on the aircraft's yoke to clear a boiling mass of smoke, flame, and flying fuel drums. One of the preceding groups had set a fuel dump afire. Cavin cleared the fiery cyclone, but his aircraft was a perfectly silhouetted target for Kavieng's antiaircraft gunners.

They did their job. Fred Arnett, the crew's radioman, was firing his machine gun "when I heard an explosion."[7] He turned to see David MacCready, the turret gunner, stumble back toward him clutching his parachute. MacCready was badly burned. "The [radio] compartment was a raging inferno," Arnett said. "We caught incendiary bullets in the 150-gallon tank mounted in the radio compartment. About the same time, we caught incendiary bullets in the right wing tank."

Arnett had stored his parachute atop the fuel tank in the radio compartment. At that point it existed as little more than a memory. "I told Mac," he said, "that I didn't think we would ever get high enough to use the chute, but if we did, he was going to have a passenger on the way down."

The right engine was afire, and Cavin and his copilot, Elmer Kirkland, shut it down and feathered the propeller. At the same time they rolled the aircraft to the left and over the water—away from Kavieng. The rest of the crew fought the fire inside the aircraft but had little success. The flight engineer, Lawrence Herbst, crawled with a fire extinguisher toward the heart of the flames but was immediately overcome by the fierce heat. He retreated to the cockpit where he calmly advised Cavin to put the aircraft down. "I had no idea where," he later said, "but I was afraid the plane would start to disintegrate because we had a real good fire going."[8]

Kirkland left his seat to investigate and confirmed Herbst's declaration that the fire was out of control. "I told Lieutenant Cavin three or four times to put down," said Herbst, "but he was trying to put as much distance as possible between us and the Japanese. I didn't know whether the plane would hold together or not."

Robert Huff, the squadron's adjutant, was not supposed to be aboard *Gremlin's Holiday*. He was not a flyer but wanted a taste of combat and had prevailed on Cavin to let him come along that day despite the fact that doing so was very much against regulations. At that moment, from where he stood underneath the navigator's astrodome, he watched the fire eat away at the aircraft's right wing. No doubt Huff questioned the wisdom of his decision.

Finally, having nursed *Gremlin's Holiday* about three miles from Kavieng, Cavin let the aircraft down into the water. The stricken bomber kissed the waves once, bounced airborne briefly, and then dropped back hard. The fire was doused, but the impact smashed the crew against hard and sharp things. Both Cavin's and Kirkland's seats were ripped from the floor of the cockpit, and Cavin was trapped in a tangle of torn metal. MacCready, already badly burned before the crash, sustained a broken ankle and was nearly drowned when his pistol belt caught on the torn opening in the fuselage through which he tried to swim. Arnett was knocked unconscious. His head was sliced open, his eyes were blackened and swelled up, and his back was badly lacerated.

Huff, who should never have been there, was also snared by the wreckage as it started to sink. It was only with the help of the others that he wriggled clear. Still, his back was seriously injured, and one leg had sustained a jagged cut. Moreover, he had lost his trousers and shoes.

Cavin extricated himself from the twisted wreck that had been the cockpit and escaped the sinking aircraft, as did the rest of his crew. They rallied on a wing while a pair of B-25s circled overhead. As *Gremlin's Holiday* started to slip out from underneath them, Cavin ordered the men to swim clear. "We all started swimming," said Huff, "and the next time I looked back, the plane was gone. The other planes of the 498th were immediately aware of our plight. They each flew over our group and dropped various equipment to us since we were unable to salvage any emergency equipment from our own plane. They dropped a six-man life raft and a two-man raft along with emergency rations, medical kits, radio, etc."

Cavin and his crew splashed through the water, hauled themselves aboard the rafts, and collected the rest of the air-dropped booty. Cavin, likely suffering from shock and certainly near total exhaustion, turned to his "guest crewman," Robert Huff. "Damn it, Huff! If I had known this was going to happen, I wouldn't have invited you along today!"[9] Huff's spirited reply that he felt similarly probably wasn't necessary.

One of the B-25s orbiting the crew of *Gremlin's Holiday* was captained by Tony Chiappe, the 498th's operations officer. He tried to contact the PBY Catalina rescue aircraft that was supporting the raid but was unsuccessful. "So I decided to fly where they were supposed to be located and bring them to the scene of the crash."[10] It took Chiappe, accompanied by Joe Armijo and his crew, half an hour to reach the point where the PBY was loitering a hundred miles out. Again Chiappe could not raise the Navy crew on the radio. "I buzzed them, and then started towards Kavieng, hoping they would follow me. They did not, so I returned and flew alongside of them and motioned for them to follow me." The PBY crew, of VPB-34, finally understood Chiappe, and pilot Nathan Gordon turned north for Kavieng.

Meanwhile, William Cavoli's men paddled their raft away from the Japanese base as quickly as they could. "Captain Cavoli remained calm, cheerful and alert to the welfare of his crew," recalled copilot George Braun. "He gave them encouragement, administered first aid and comfort—there was no morphine—to his men. Only about a half mile from shore, well within sight of the enemy, who started to fire at us in the raft with their coastal guns, we rowed about three-quarters of a mile further from shore."[11]

Likewise, the six men of Ed Cavin's crew, a couple of miles further out to sea, paddled seaward. This they did in spite of their injuries. If they drifted out to the broader ocean, they might or might not survive. But captured by the Japanese, they would almost certainly be slain.

Meanwhile, most of the 345th's crews winged for home. The smoke that had choked the target area adhered to their aircraft. "Windshields and leading edges of several of the planes were blackened with dense smoke," noted the 500th, "and the pilots deliberately flew into a rainstorm on their return to wash them down." The heavy tropical raindrops washed the soot of Kavieng away, and clean, unfiltered light streamed into the aircraft. But it took more than rain showers to dissipate the terror of the just-finished mission.

❧

Escorted by Chiappe and four P-47s that had been assigned to cover him, PBY pilot Nathan Gordon was impressed by the burning, smoking wreck into which Kavieng had been transformed. Only one B-25 remained over the area in which the 345th's downed crews floated. It was Chester Coltharp, the 498th's commanding officer.

Gordon's crew spotted a yellow-green plume of dye marker in the middle of which floated a couple of life rafts. They drifted only about a mile from the shore and appeared to be abandoned. Gordon knew that it was "extremely difficult to locate objects in the sea. But we knew someone had been shot down at this spot because of the dye marker and rafts. Since landing and taking off from the open sea under the best of conditions is hazardous, we were reluctant to land unnecessarily."[12]

These were not "the best of conditions." The swells that day were dangerously large, and the Japanese still had aircraft and boats that might intercept them. Still, there was a possibility that someone was in the water, and Gordon was loathe to leave anyone behind. He overflew the rafts in his PBY—nicknamed *Arkansas Traveler* in commemoration of his home state—and dropped two smoke markers on the water.

Using the markers to judge the wind, Gordon made his approach, intent on making a full-stall landing. The heavy seas made it difficult to judge the touchdown, and the ungainly aircraft smacked hard into an enormous swell. Spray flew over the PBY's wings, and water rushed into gaps in the hull where a number of rivets gave way.

And it was for naught—no one was with the rafts. Gordon swung *Arkansas Traveler* into the wind and advanced the throttles. The aircraft slogged through the heavy sea and accelerated slowly. The hull banged and banged and banged against the waves in steadily decreasing intervals, and water splashed hard against Gordon's windscreen. Finally he lifted the plane clear of the punishing swells and into the smoothness of the sky. Water poured from the open seams in the aircraft's hull as he banked toward where he spotted a downed crew bobbing in the water.

That crew was Ed Cavin's. He and the rest of the men of *Gremlin's Holiday* had watched Gordon's first landing and cringed at its violence, hoping that the rescue craft—their sole hope—was not damaged. As the swells lifted and dropped them, they watched his search as best they could. When the PBY got airborne again, they were terrified that it might turn away and leave them behind. The joy the crew felt when it banked directly toward them was physical.

Gordon smashed his aircraft onto the water once more. Japanese shore guns immediately fired, and shells dropped nearby. Worse, a Japanese patrol boat that had somehow survived the just-finished strike motored directly at them. The escorting P-47s dived and fired on the boat, compelling it to turn away. Still, there was no time to waste. Gordon's crew tossed the men in the raft a line, which MacCready—with his badly burned hands—caught and held with an unyielding grip.

But the tug of the PBY's idling motors and the rough sea were too much. As desperate as he was, the line slipped through MacCready's blistered hands. "I finally realized," Gordon said, "that if we were going to get the men out, I would have to cut my engines. That of course, entailed some risks because sometimes the engines, under such conditions, simply wouldn't restart. Before making a final decision, I called my plane captain and said, 'Wiley, if we've got to stop the engines, can we get them started again?' He said he was pretty sure we could."

"Pretty sure" was good enough for Gordon. He cut power to the two engines. The comparative quiet was unnerving. There was little for Gordon and his copilot to do except listen to the waves slap against the hull and hope that the aim of the Japanese gunners did not improve. His men pulled Cavin's crew from the water and into the rear of the aircraft.

David MacCready recalled, "The sailor in the blister [opening on the side of the aircraft] was a big, young kid. When we were alongside the aircraft, he just reached down and grabbed me by the hair on my head and thrust me into the aircraft."

Gordon and his copilot went through their engine-start checklist as Cavin's crew was settled into the back of the PBY. The starter of the first engine whined and ticked and spun the propeller faster and faster until the engine caught with a comforting, smoking roar. Likewise, the second engine also growled back to life. Excited smiles marked the faces of everyone aboard the aircraft.

Gordon bashed his aircraft through the water and heaved it airborne once more. Immediately he was called to turn and pick up another crew, this one from the 38th Bomb Group. "We were getting considerably more enemy fire," Gordon said, "but somehow it didn't worry me. I had too many other things to think about." The second rescue was nearly identical to the recovery of Cavin's crew except that there were only three survivors to be saved. Once they were aboard, Gordon flogged *Arkansas Traveler* airborne again and climbed for VPB-34's base at Finschafen.

William Cavoli's crew was crestfallen as they watched the PBY disappear. Yet, as the 498th noted, Chester Coltharp, who had circled overhead the entire time, was not about to let them be left behind. "Before picking up the third and last crew, the Catalina left the area since it thought it had picked up all the crews which had crashed into the sea. Major Coltharp located the third crew that went down and immediately took chase of the Catalina which was proceeding to Finschafen since radio contact could not be made. Major Coltharp eventually brought back the Catalina where the third crew had crashed."

Cavoli's men, despite their efforts to do otherwise, had drifted within half a mile of the enemy shoreline. Moreover, the prevailing wind was such that Gordon would have to bring his slow-flying PBY over the still-burning target area in order to land close enough to effect a rescue. Worse, he would have no escort as the P-47s had headed back to their base, low on fuel. Essentially, Gordon risked undoing that day's extraordinary rescue efforts by making one more implausible attempt.

He swung the slow-moving PBY inland and across the blazing ruin that was Kavieng before banking back over the water in a descending turn. Tal Epps, aboard Coltharp's aircraft, recalled that Gordon and his crew flew "only a few feet above the heads and guns of the shore battery. I couldn't believe what I was seeing." At the same time, an enemy boat emerged from the smoke that blanketed the coast and headed for the downed crewmen. "Major Coltharp quickly annihilated it," said Epps.[13]

Remarkably, the PBY was not hit by the considerable volume of antiaircraft fire. The water landing was just as violent as the others, but the stoutly built aircraft held together. The engines were shut down a final time as Cavoli's men were pulled aboard and, just as before, started again without incident. Gordon whipped *Arkansas Traveler* into the air one final time and turned for home with a planeload of grateful airmen. "It was one of the most beautiful sights I have ever witnessed," said Epps.

"Lieutenant Gordon came back and checked the welfare of his passengers," Cavoli said, "and I was delighted when ham sandwiches, oranges and ice water were passed to us—things we had not had since coming to New Guinea. God bless the Navy! This proved to me once and for all that the U.S. Navy goes only one way—first class!"

Chester Coltharp made for the airfield at Cape Gloucester on the tip of New Britain knowing there was a good chance that he would not have enough fuel to make it. Yet he did, with an estimated ten gallons of gas remaining. For his actions that day, Coltharp was awarded the Distinguished Service Cross, second only to the Medal of Honor.

PBY pilot Nathan Gordon was justifiably awarded the Medal of Honor. It was well earned as there is little doubt that the men he rescued would otherwise not have survived the war. His crewmen, who had shared the risk and performed superbly under fire, each received the Silver Star.

For his part, J. R. Jones was exhausted after the Kavieng mission. "I am plenty pooped tonight," he wrote Elnora. "It's getting so I can hardly stay awake long enough to even go to the show. I'm really shot at this moment, and I feel so dull I can't think straight."[14] Jones was a collegiate athlete. The fact that he was so exhausted made apparent the toll that continuous flight operations in primitive conditions took on the men.

The 499th's narrative summary acknowledged that morning's loss of John Wilson and his crew with one soulless line: "1st. Lt. J.D. Wilson crashed shortly after takeoff."

In contrast, in a letter to the fiancée of Thane Hecox's copilot, James Webb DuBose, a friend did his best to console her while at the same time giving a true account of what happened. It was against censor guidelines.

> *The target was blanketed with black smoke and flames; the antiaircraft fire was terrific. Jim was seen going down over land by Captain Cavoli and his copilot, Lieutenant Braun. His right engine was out and they waved to him. He waved back and then "went in."*
>
> *That is as much as anybody can tell you. I held out a hope that perhaps he was a prisoner of war, but I have been assured by those who flew on his wing that he is dead. You can be certain that he swept out of this world in a storm of fury. He loved to fly and, believe me, he was at all times as you picture him—noble, honorable and courageous.*[15]

Du Bose, whom the letter had described as "noble, honorable and courageous," had also been a sentimentalist. His brother remembered, "When the time approached for him to graduate from advanced training, Webb asked mother to send him one of the large sterling silver spoons from her flatware. He used to eat his cereal with one of these while he was growing up. He wanted the spoon to remind him of home and his family. He had a silversmith melt down the spoon and cast it into his wings for his uniform."[16]

On the day following the attack on Kavieng, February 16, 1944, the 345th was sent, along with the 38th Bomb Group, to the island of New Hanover, which was situated only about twenty miles west of Kavieng. A Japanese convoy of more than a dozen ships was reported to be in the area; destroying it was imperative. The 500th Bomb Squadron swung around the eastern end of New Hanover, while the rest of the 345th, together with the 38th, navigated around the western edge of the island.

The 500th's crews spotted a tanker and a corvette, which they aggressively engaged with both bombs and machine-gun fire. The tanker was anchored and presented an easy target, but the corvette, as noted by the mission summary report, "was maneuvering wildly to escape the blistering strafing and skip bombing assault. The attack brought the Mitchells so close that one pilot reported seeing his tracers knock a white-uniformed man from one side of the corvette across the deck to the other. As our planes withdrew, the tanker was burning fiercely and was being rocked by internal explosions."

It is interesting—and indicative of how combat distorted and skewed what men saw and recalled—that no one noted the enemy submarine that was surfaced near the burning tanker. Later analysis of strike photos, as recorded by the 500th, showed "a submarine off the starboard quarter of the tanker which bomb bursts, near misses on the tanker, must certainly have destroyed." Despite the 500th's declaration, it is uncertain whether the submarine was actually sunk.

The 499th's crews also went after the beleaguered enemy corvette. Carl Conant led the squadron that day, and he put two more bombs into it while also strafing the Japanese sailors who had already abandoned the ship and were paddling for shore. Other crews also attacked the doomed vessel.

Among them was Carl Cessna, who dropped three bombs, one of which struck the corvette squarely and caused a massive explosion. Chunks of the Japanese ship smashed into the underside of Cessna's B-25 and set several boxes of ammunition afire. While Cessna hauled the aircraft around for another bombing run, his crew threw one of the burning boxes overboard and smothered the flames coming from the others.

Following his second bomb run, Cessna turned his guns against the Japanese in the water. The squadron recorded the effects of his grisly work: "He expended almost all of his ammunition in this strafing and reported that practically all of the Japs were killed. Very few reached shore and those that did seemed barely able to walk." The report additionally noted, "When he and the others first started strafing, many of the Nips were seen thrashing about in the water with their arms and legs, but after they finished, all remaining were motionless and the sea was colored with blood."

It was additionally observed that "life vests prevented [the Japanese] bodies from sinking." The scene the 345th's crews left behind was a grim one. A great raft of enemy bodies—and pieces of enemy bodies—rose and fell on the same blood-red swells that lifted and dropped the burning corvette they had so recently crewed. The scene was backdropped by the smoke and fire of the burning tanker the corvette had escorted.

Meanwhile, the 500th Bomb Squadron's crews dropped their remaining bombs on nearby targets. During this time, while flying past Selapiu Island, "Captain [John] Dougherty flew low over the north shore of the island to investigate what he thought was a life raft which might contain a crew of this squadron lost on the previous day's mission." Dougherty spotted two men on the beach, who waved at him with great fervor. They ran to the raft and pushed out into the water so that they could be better seen, "then returned to shore to get at least three other men, and the five paddled out."

George Hurt was the bombardier aboard Dougherty's aircraft. He recorded that the crew "dropped emergency rations and circled for an hour trying to call rescue service. Had to leave due to low fuel and landed at Finschafen to refuel and see rescue squadron. They radioed immediately to a ship [rescue aircraft] already in the area." Hurt and the rest of Dougherty's crew were hosted by a seaplane tender and appreciated the amenities their Navy hosts provided: ."Spent the afternoon drinking ice water and eating donuts."

The men in the raft were from Mike Hochella's crew, who had been shot down the previous day. Although they had been reported low over the water headed southeast from Kavieng, they were in fact on Selapiu, southwest of Kavieng. The engine, which had been shot up over Kavieng, eventually caught fire. When the aircraft went into the water, it rotated half a turn, and the nose was torn away. Hochella, still strapped in his seat, was thrown into the water. Still, he and the rest of his crew—except navigator Jack Howard, who was never seen again—climbed into the life raft and paddled to shore.

John Dougherty joined a PBY crew from VP-34 the following morning. The PBY, captained by Orazio Simonelli, was escorted by a flight of P-47s because the airfield at Kavieng, although battered, was not out of commission. Ultimately, the fighters ran short of fuel and turned for home, short of Selapiu.

Simonelli was left with a terrible decision. If he continued, there was a good chance that enemy fighters would discover his lumbering and lightly defended ship. Were that to happen, he and his crew—and John Dougherty—would likely be shot down and possibly killed. On the other hand, if he turned back, Mike Hochella and his crew would have to spend at least another day in enemy-held territory. If captured they would almost certainly be tortured and killed. As it was, they had already spent two nights on the island.

Simonelli pressed ahead; it was akin to sneaking into the devil's house. Luck was with him and his crew as the Japanese did not contest his approach or landing. He coasted to the beach where Hochella and his four fellow crewmen—two of them badly injured—were hauled aboard. Wasting little time, he powered the PBY off the water and turned for home. For his valor that day he was awarded the Navy Cross. The narrative to his citation read, in part, "Although your fighter escort was forced to abandon you before you reached your objective, you completed your mission, rescuing five airmen who had been shot down by enemy gunfire two days before, some of whom were badly injured, and all of whom faced capture or death at the hands of the enemy."

Chapter Eight

"Many Strange Faces"

THE 345TH WAS WELL BLOODED BY THE END OF FEBRUARY 1944, WHEN the first of its fliers, having completed their combat obligations, were being rotated back to the States, as described by the group's monthly narrative report. "The first '50-mission men' began to return to the United States during February. Pilots originally assigned as replacements were becoming first pilots and flight leaders, and proving as capable as the original members of the group who had been their mentors."

In terms of numbers, a steady flow of replacements enabled the 345th to maintain its strength at close to 1,600 personnel. The group carried on its roster 161 pilots and copilots, 35 bombardiers, and 19 navigators; the bombardiers performed navigation duties primarily. There were also 285 enlisted fliers. Nonflying personnel included 76 officers and 987 enlisted men. Together, they operated 58 B-25s, 10 fewer than at the start of the month.

By this time, new aircrews were being checked out and introduced to operations in the Southwest Pacific by a Fifth Air Force–operated replacement training unit. There, they received indoctrination flights and jungle survival training, as well as lessons on other topics unique to the area. After completing the various courses, the men were parceled out to combat units, including the 345th.

Upon reaching the 345th, the monthly narrative observed, "each pilot flies first in combat as a copilot, learning constantly from his experienced first pilot. Later, after demonstrating proficiency in day, formation, and instrument flying under the direction of his first pilot, he may himself be assigned a plane." Additionally, when not flying combat, the 345th's squadrons also flew training missions not only to teach more advanced skills but to ensure the group's fliers stayed current and sharp.

Of the newcomers, the group's monthly narrative noted, "Many strange faces in the mess halls. Those of us still here are trying to give them something of the tradition of the 345th, and we hope to imbue them with the fine 'esprit de corps' that has distinguished this unit ever since training days. We expect a lot of them, as our older boys were 'tops,' but they all come through when their time comes, no doubt about it."

Robert "Bear" Britt, one of those "strange faces," was assigned to the 500th Bomb Squadron. "Herman Reheis was the squadron operations officer and took all the new pilots on an orientation flight and briefed us on how he wanted us to fly formation, land, take off, etc." Britt recalled the very basic wisdom that Reheis gave him afterward. "Herm put his hand on my shoulder and told me that the food wasn't worth a damn, the bed was a cot without a mattress and a tent was my only shelter. His advice was to stay out of the tent and do something to get hungry. In that way, the bed would feel comfortable and the food would taste good and the tent would be a comfort to me."[1]

J. R. Jones envied his worn-out comrades who were headed back to the States. "I know how happy they must feel," he wrote to Elnora. "I know how I would feel in their shoes. The word *home* certainly covers a lot of territory now. Any place in the U.S. would be home now. It would be waking up in the morning without wondering if you're going to see the end of another day."[2]

Conversely, although Tal Epps was also in love, he did not want to go back to the States. "To go home was the goal, the hope and the dream of just about everyone," he said. He was among the 345th's original fliers and by that time had flown more than enough combat missions to leave the unit. But he had met and fallen for an Australian girl, Ruth Pearson, at the end of 1943. Hopelessly smitten, he developed "a desire to spend the rest of my life with her beside me."

Certainly Epps could have returned to the States and waited for the war to end before reuniting with Ruth. But no one knew when that would be. Or he could have stopped flying and taken a ground job, but ground personnel went to Sydney much less often—if at all. It was a devilish dilemma.

So then, fully aware of the risks, Epps opted to continue flying combat. The choice to do so when the majority of the experienced crews were leaving was a difficult one. The replacement men lacked experience and had to learn in a hurry. And learning in a hurry was a good way to die in a hurry. Nevertheless, Epps committed himself to flying with them.

Regardless of their desire to go home to the States or not, Epps and Jones and the rest of the 345th moved to a totally new home at the end of February 1944. As Douglas MacArthur's plans bore fruit and the Japanese were pushed further northwest up the coast of New Guinea, the Allies needed airbases close enough from which to chase them. Accordingly the 345th was sent to Nadzab, which had been developed into a large airbase complex.

Nadzab's topography was more savannah than jungle, and consequently it was almost temperate as compared to Port Moresby and Dobodura. And it was more thoughtfully organized. "Here at Nadzab in the beautiful Markham Valley, we have a really fine arrangement," said Aldridge Nichols of the group's headquarters. "For the first time since landing overseas, our four squadrons and group headquarters are together. The area is compact and everyone likes the layout with two squadrons on either side of a main roadway."

The living arrangements were also more comfortable. The enlisted men were billeted far enough from the road so as not to be bothered by dust and noise, while the officers moved into tents located on rising terrain that caught the breezes and offered expansive views of the valley. Aldridge waxed almost poetic: "The magnificent view across the floor of the Markham Valley, its airstrips and roads buzzing with activity, the sunsets over the distant hills, all combine to give adequate compensation. The view at night is inspiring; a miniature city lies at our feet. . . . [F]ew will ever forget Nadzab and this."

J. R. Jones was equally enchanted by the group's new base. He wrote to Elnora, "Well, here I am again writing from my new home. It's funny, but when I first arrived in New Guinea, the Japs owned this place. I must say, they didn't do a great deal toward improving it."[3]

Still, he liked the new arrangement. "We are moved now and what a joint this is. We live on top of a mountain that overlooks a plain. It's quite a sight at night—you might think you're on Knob Hill in San Francisco, but the illusion doesn't last long." Jones observed, "One nice thing about this place is that there is a constant breeze, and we are up high enough to keep from burning up during the day. There are very few mosquitoes, but we have grasshoppers big as frogs. They are really fierce."

His letter also underscored the point that the men were largely responsible for erecting and improving their own tents. "We haven't had time to put up our permanent home. I have blisters all over my hands now from sawing lumber to build this place." In fact, Jones had lumber to saw because the group had rigged itself a primitive sawmill using a blade that Clinton True brought back from Melbourne, Australia. Tents with wood floors and sides were a luxury that many of the group's men enjoyed at Nadzab.

Replacements continued to join the 345th at Nadzab. Many of them had gone through the formal training syllabus in the States and arrived as fully qualified B-25 crews. Conversely, some had never seen a B-25. Indeed, James Baross, among others, had almost no experience with aircraft whatsoever. Trained as a radio operator, he boarded a C-87 at Hamilton Field, California, bound for New Guinea on February 14, 1944. "It was only my fifth time in an airplane, having flown once [upon] returning to college in 1940, once at radio school, twice in gunnery school, and here I was going to fight a war in an airplane, the inside of which I had never seen."[4]

Notwithstanding these sorts of administrative inefficiencies, the nation still mobilized both its industry and its military on a scale never seen before or since. But in this time before computers, men were often simply lost, misplaced, or forgotten. In such an environment, enterprising—or anxious and frustrated—personnel could make things happen on their own.

James Baross offered an example. After arriving in New Guinea, he and his comrades whiled away their time at Port Moresby doing various odd jobs that had little or nothing whatever to do with their specialties. One of them worked with a communications unit and intercepted a teletype from a Nadzab-based B-25 unit requesting a dozen radio operators as replacements. Baross recalled that his friend "knew more about airplanes than I did and told me that he thought they were pretty good planes and that he was going to go to Nadzab. I told him I would go too. He told the others of our original bunch of twenty, and twelve of us said we'd go."

The men did not forward the request through the proper administrative channels. "We simply filled the order in a somewhat more informal manner." Baross and his comrades were ready and waiting when a B-25 from the 345th arrived the next morning. "Not a bad-looking plane, I thought, but I didn't really know anything about them, or any others for that matter."[5] Upon arriving at Nadzab, Baross was assigned to the 501st Bomb Squadron.

Baross was scheduled for a check ride a few days later to verify that he knew how to operate an airborne radio set. He met with the pilot and copilot and rode on a truck from the billeting area to the airfield. He watched the other two men climb into the cockpit at the front of the aircraft and then looked for a way into the rear. "I looked around for a handle, or a hook, or a knob, or a wire, or a hole or something—anything—that would let me into that plane."

He had no success and, mortally embarrassed, went forward and banged on the nose of the aircraft. "Disgust, total disgust was on the copilot's face as he climbed down and very slowly explained that if I pushed on this gadget, the rear hatch would open. What could I do? I thanked him and climbed aboard."[6] Once inside, Baross performed his radioman duties well and was soon flying combat missions.

Regardless of the airfield from which the 345th operated, the aircrews were usually billeted so far away that they were trucked to their aircraft before each mission. There, the maintenance men finished readying the aircraft. "The man in charge of the plane on the ground, the crew chief," recalled James Baross, "had on his staff a radio mechanic, an engine mechanic, and an armorer who serviced the plane and made it ready for flying a mission." Baross noted, "The crew chief was responsible to the line chief who was responsible for all the planes in the squadron."

Although many of the individual aircraft nominally "belonged" to a particular crew—and sported that crew's nose art—Baross dispelled the notion that they were flown by only one crew. "We did not fly the same plane, mission-after-mission. Planes were often laid up for repairs so there had to be spares." Moreover, aircraft were lost to mechanical failure, pilot error, or enemy action. And aircrews were often shuffled around—even between squadrons—when other aircrews were not available due to sickness or other causes. Practically every aircraft in a squadron that survived any length of time was flown by every aircrew at one point or another.

"Arriving at the plane before a mission," said Baross, "we would stow our gear and then walk around the plane, checking whatever fell into our specialty. Engineers checked engines, armorers checked guns and bombs, and radiomen checked antennas. We would tell the pilot if anything appeared questionable."

The aircrews often helped the maintenance men pull the engine propellers through a revolution or two. When a radial engine was shut down and left idle for more than a few hours, oil often pooled in the lower cylinders. Too much oil in those cylinders would create too much pressure and cause damage when the engine was started. However, rotating the propellers by hand redistributed the pooled oil and lessened the chances of harm to the engine. "It usually took three men to do it," said Baross, "but four made it a lot easier. Props knew no rank. Whoever was there did the work."

It was generally just muscle work, but the men still found all manner of ways to hurt themselves. Baross did so as he joined his comrades in pulling a propeller. "One morning as I reached up, the lighted tip of the cigarette I had in my mouth came into contact with my arm and smashed there. It burned right in. I still have the scar."

Baross remembered that the engine weatherheads were also checked and drained to ensure that the carburetors were not flooded with water from rain or condensation. "A plate on the engine cowling was removed and a small quantity of gasoline was drained out, giving us an opportunity to fill our Zippo lighters. One hundred octane gasoline burned well, but if we overfilled our lighters, the seepage caused raw, red blotches on our skin."

Most of the 345th's men were smokers, and there were few places they didn't light up. "We smoked during flights, but never during takeoff," said Baross. "On the ground, the vapors of gasoline were pretty strong. Once airborne, the air drifted through the plane and no gasoline could be smelled. It was perfectly okay to smoke during flights."[7]

He recalled that he and his comrades "didn't give much thought to what the tobacco companies were doing to encourage use of their products." That encouragement was considerable. "Every person in the area was issued one carton of cigarettes, six cigars and one plug of chewing tobacco, every week, rain or shine." And the men got the best: "We had no choice as to brand, but only the leading brands reached us. The second- and third-rated brands were not sent to us. Wings, and Fatimas, and Fleetwoods and Spuds were sold back in the States."

Baross confirmed that the tactics used by the tobacco companies were effective. "Those who did not smoke received the same ration as those who did. Most eventually began smoking."[8]

The 345th was sent to support troops seizing Los Negros Island on March 5, 1944. It was one of the Admiralty Islands west of the Bismarck Archipelago. Its capture would further isolate Rabaul and offer the Allies a base from which to conduct both air and naval operations. Operating under the close control of an air liaison party, the group's aircraft plastered the area around Momote.

The results were fair, and the mission was unremarkable, although the 500th Bomb Squadron's George Mitchell and his crew endured a series of setbacks as recorded by George Hurt, Mitchell's bombardier, in his diary: "Enroute to target, front escape hatch fell out, leaving a gaping hole in nav[igation] compartment. Second pass over target, the hydraulic system was shot out. The plane was immediately covered inside with hyd[raulic] fluid. Had to straddle the hole to crank bomb bay doors shut. Got soaked with fluid. At the field, I cranked the nose wheel down. The radio man tried to crank down main gear. Wouldn't quite latch. Tried everything. Even tried bouncing the nose wheel off of the ground."[9] Ultimately, low on fuel, Mitchell set up for a long, slow, straight-in approach while the radio operator cranked the flaps down by hand. After touching down, the aircraft rolled for several hundred feet before the landing gear collapsed. Skidding on its belly, the B-25 finally scraped to a halt, and its crew escaped without injury.

On this mission, as with every mission, a preliminary report was sent to Fifth Air Force headquarters as the aircraft cleared the target area. The Fifth's staff was understandably anxious to know the results of the missions it sent out. The earlier that information became available, the more time there was to plan subsequent missions.

Typically, after canvassing the other pilots via the relatively short-ranged VHF voice radios, the lead pilot queried his own crew about their assessments of the strike's effectiveness, then gave his radio operator, as recalled by James Baross, "his estimate as to the damage done, the percentage of bombs that hit the intended target, weather conditions, type of antiaircraft activity—anything of interest to intelligence."[10]

The radio operator drafted the message—in encrypted Morse code—and tapped it out in four-letter groups. "Each four-letter group was sent twice," said Baross. "If the ground station needed anything repeated after they received the message, they sent [via Morse code], 'dit-dit-dah-dah-dit-dit,' which meant, 'repeat.' We referred to that as 'ditty-dum-dum-ditty.'"

Japanese radio jamming often stymied the effort. "They attempted to keep us from getting any message back to our headquarters," said Baross. "It was frustrating to get an acknowledgement from AR1 [headquarters] that they were standing by, and to try to get the message sent, all the while getting jammed by the Japanese."

Transmitting in Morse code was labor-intensive and time-consuming and was made more difficult by the excitement that typically followed a particularly tough mission, or by turbulence, or by the distraction caused by battle damage or mechanical difficulties. To ease the effort, a series of "Q codes," developed early in the century by radiotelegraph communicators, was adopted.

James Baross offered examples of these Q codes. "To ask our signal strength, we sent INT QSA [which was] 'What is my signal strength?' Readability was QRK. To ask our readability, we sent INT QRK, 'What is my signal strength?' To send a strike message, we would send to the ground station, AR1 QMM OP INT QRK INT QSA K. That meant,

'AR1, I have an operational priority message for you. What is my readability and what is my signal strength?'"

"There were Q codes for just about anything that could occur," said Baross. "Those we used frequently were not hard to remember, but some that were used infrequently were devilish to remember." Regardless, they were effective and readily used.

Aside from his duties as a radio operator, Baross frequently fired the .30-caliber waist guns carried by the group's B-25Ds. He observed that the gun mounts were "not very secure" and recorded how on one mission he manned the right waist gun, which "was chattering along quite nicely when it jumped out of its socket. I tried to hold it away from me but the trigger, actuated by the thumb, could not release as my thumb was on it. The gun kept creeping back and firing madly, recoiling on the point of my chin. I was able finally to get the trigger released and replace the gun into its socket, but my chin was a mess."[11]

Most of the USAAF's organizations had nicknames, but the 345th went without until early March 1944. A contest was held, and the 501st Bomb Squadron's log for March 7, 1944, described the outcome. "Technical Sergeant H.R. Bartlett, a radio-gunner of this squadron, gave the group its new name, 'The Tree Top Terrors,' and was rewarded with a quart of gin by Colonel True, the commanding officer of the 345th group, at the G.I. movies last night. We were told that it's permissible to refer now to our group in letters back home as 'The Tree Top Terrors.'"

The nickname referred to the low-level nature of the group's strafing and bombing attacks. Indeed, the men sometimes flew so low that they had to pull branches and leaves from their aircraft after landing. That they struck terror in the hearts of the Japanese was certain.

But that terror striking was not one-sided, and the terror that the Japanese dealt to the 345th took its toll. This was highlighted during a mission to the Wewak area on March 17, 1944, when the group was part of a large strike against various targets. Unusually, three of the 345th's squadrons were tasked with hitting a gun position from medium altitude, while the 500th was to make a low-level attack across the peninsula.

The takeoff was normal, as was the leg to Gusap, where the group was to meet up with its fighter escort. Approaching Gusap, Arthur Frey turned back for Nadzab when, as the 500th's mission summary report observed, his copilot, William Siegrist, "suddenly went insane." The report declared, "Lieutenant Frey had been forced to draw his pistol on Lieutenant Siegrist when he grabbed the controls and nearly caused a collision with another plane in the formation."

Frey waved Siegrist back, and the addled copilot released the controls and crawled back to the navigator's compartment. The squadron reported, "Lieutenant Siegrist's gun was taken from him, and soon afterwards, fisticuffs resulted when Lieutenant Siegrist suddenly slugged Lieutenant [James] Quinn, the navigator."

Siegrist continued to beat on Quinn until overpowered. At that point, Frey handed control of the aircraft to Daniel Brick, the engineer. "Lieutenant Frey," the report noted, "fearing that Lieutenant Siegrist might have to be shot, and not wanting an enlisted man to shoulder the responsibility, kept his pistol on Lieutenant Siegrist until they were ready to land."

Upon reaching Nadzab, Frey took control of the aircraft from Brick and landed the aircraft. Both Siegrist and Quinn were taken to the hospital. Quinn suffered little more than bruises. Siegrist was diagnosed with "acute psychosis, manic phase."

George Hurt, a bombardier with the 500th, offered insight as to what might have caused Siegrist to have, as he said, "slipped his blocks." Siegrist had recently come to the 345th as part of a replacement crew. When Thomas Flannigan crashed on a training flight on March 13, two men from Siegrist's original crew were killed.

"He saw the crashed plane," wrote Hurt in his diary. "Guess the sight of it, loss of his crew members, and strain of combat were too much for him."[12]

—◦—

Both J. R. Jones and his fiancée, Elnora, loved music, books, and films, and they often wrote to each other about what they had read, listened to, or seen. Movies, some new, some not, were shown almost nightly at the

345th, usually outside. "I really saw a good show last night," he wrote. "It was Fred Astaire in *The Sky's the Limit*. We must get the films pretty quickly over here. The music wasn't as good as it usually is in his pictures, but the dances were better than ever."[13] He was an honest critic and most often characterized films he didn't like as "stinkers."

The couple appreciated popular music but also listened to the classics and orchestral works. "You said you had *Rhapsody in Blue* and *Love Walked In* by Kostelanetz," he wrote. "So have we, and you have nothing on us even in the sticks. You love your music, don't you, darling?" Among the contemporary artists, it seemed that J. R. appreciated Frank Sinatra's talent but possibly not his behavior. "I can't see anything wrong with him. Just too much publicity and some of it bad. Anyone who can make a pile of money, I say go for it."[14]

And he was constantly reading or looking for something to read. "I finally dug up another book to read," he wrote. "It is *Quietly My Captain Waits*. It's a novel about early French America. It's supposedly pretty good, but I'll read it whether it's good or not." He failed to mention whether or not he liked that particular novel, but he was very taken with another book. "It is *The Robe* by Lloyd C. Douglas. I highly advise that you read it, darling, if you haven't already. You'll like it as no book you've ever read before."[15]

As to when he would see his fiancée again, Jones had no idea. There had been pushback from various quarters that fifty missions no longer constituted a complete combat tour. The result was considerable confusion as evidenced in Jones's letter of April 7, 1944. "Well, here I am again and with none too cheerful news. It seems I made a slight error in my estimate of coming home. Yep, they changed the rules, and as usual I got caught in the midst of it. Now, we must spend a year in this theater before we get a break." His next sentence made clear that the average flyer was utterly in the dark about the requirements for rotating back to the States: "Missions and hours don't mean a thing, and Lord how we'll stack them up."[16]

MacArthur's campaign to isolate Rabaul and its surrounding bases, Operation CARTWHEEL, was essentially completed during the spring of 1944. As with Rabaul, the decision was also made to bypass Kavieng. In fact, the last opposed assault—the seizure of the Admiralty Islands—was launched during February. The archipelago was declared secure in May. Moreover, sustained Allied air, ground, and naval operations in and around New Guinea were proving effective. In particular, the Japanese 18th Army was increasingly hard-pressed not just to maintain its military capabilities but simply to keep from disintegrating.

The initial Allied plans for defeating the Japanese in New Guinea considered a northwestward advance along the northern coast that included the lockstep capture of each major Japanese stronghold along the way. However, following the hard-fought Allied victories at Lae and Finschafen, MacArthur and his staff revisited the need to take the heavily garrisoned Japanese bases at Hansa Bay and Wewak before moving against the airfield and port complexes further up the coast at Hollandia. Considerable and sustained air attacks against both strongholds had reduced their capacity for offensive operations. And it seemed that continued air operations at a reduced tempo would be sufficient to keep both bases tamped down.

Accordingly, MacArthur proposed to penetrate well up the coast to Hollandia. Such a move would negate the need for two major assaults—guaranteed to be meat grinders—and would consequently save considerable material, equipment, and men. Moreover, the seizure of Hollandia would provide an airbase complex much better situated for follow-on operations directed at the Philippines or Formosa. And adjacent Humboldt Bay—the best anchorage on New Guinea's northern coast—could handle the shipping necessary to support future offensive plans. The bold move was given a fitting code name: Operation RECKLESS.

If this bypassing of Japanese forces in New Guinea was a bit untidy and an affront to the sorts of military traditionalists who decried the presence of enemy forces to the rear, it was nevertheless a logical and effective strategy. Capturing every enemy base—and chasing the starving specters of once-proud Japanese army units through nearly impenetrable jungle—would have consumed men, material, and time to no good purpose. Those resources could be better used in a more direct and urgent push toward the Philippines or Formosa and, ultimately, Japan.

And the isolated Japanese units—specifically the 18th Army—were for all practical purposes already imprisoned. Allied air and naval operations generally kept them from being resupplied, reinforced, or evacuated by sea. And overland travel was brutally difficult. Swampy terrain in the lowlands and nearly impassable ground in the mountains aside, heavy jungle canopies made simply moving in the right direction a challenge. One Japanese officer noted, "One advances as in the dark. No matter to what place one climbs, the eye can penetrate only a short distance, and since one cannot depend on this to see the form of the mountains in the vicinity, it is difficult to orient the actual terrain with maps."[17]

To be sure, large-scale troop movements in New Guinea could be made only with great difficulty and at little more than a snail's pace. Losses to disease and starvation—not to mention substantial degradations to combat efficiency and morale—were a certainty. In fact, the island's very nature made it an excellent prison that required little more of the Allies than keeping the ocean approaches clear of Japanese relief vessels. The 18th Army would later attempt only one real offensive operation, which, as could only be expected, was duly broken up and defeated.

The Fifth Air Force opened preinvasion operations against Hollandia with a B-24 strike on March 30, 1944. Two additional raids followed on March 31 and April 1. The 345th and the other Fifth Air Force B-25 and A-20 groups were scheduled to fly their first missions to the Japanese stronghold on April 3. There was a great deal of anticipation, as Hollandia was expected to be as tough—and lucrative—a target as Rabaul had been during the "old days" of just a few months earlier. The 345th's monthly narrative captured the group's enthusiasm at the prospect of this "long awaited strafer strike."

From Colonel True and every combat crewmember down to the lowliest KP [Kitchen Patrol], the 345th had been looking ahead to this day. Hollandia! The name conjured up pictures of great Jap aerial strength; a large, important enemy base; a stronghold in his outer defense line now that the Wewak area [air]dromes had been denied to him; a well defended and strategically located target. Hard to hit, it would be costly we said, but all agreed it would be worth it. The Jap thought he was beyond practical strafer range, certainly beyond range of fighter escort for our bombers.

The Japanese were mistaken and in fact were startled when the Fifth's B-24s appeared over Hollandia with P-38 escorts. After all, the P-38s were based with the 345th and other major units at Nadzab, more than five hundred miles away. In fact, the escorts were both new P-38Js, which carried extra fuel in their outboard wings, and earlier models of the P-38 that had been similarly modified. At the time, the Fifth Air Force operated more than a hundred of these longer-range variants of the P-38.

A B-24 strike preceded the B-25s and A-20s on April 3 by more than two hours. Notwithstanding that attack or those flown since March 30, there was still plenty of trade for the forty B-25s, ten from each squadron, which the 345th put airborne that day. Specifically, the group was tasked with strafing and bombing Hollandia's three airfields as well as supply dumps located along one of the area's main roads. Geographically, the airfields were obligingly situated such that they could be attacked sequentially—Hollandia, Sentani, and Cyclops—on a generally easterly heading with little need to change course.

Japanese fighters attempted to drive the total force of 233 bombers away but, for the most part, were not aggressive and achieved little success. And many of those that did get airborne were quickly engaged by the escorting P-38s. Only one of the 345th's B-25s, flown by Robert Best of the 498th Bomb Squadron, was attacked. The squadron's mission summary report recorded, "A Zeke attacked this airplane from 12 o'clock at 100 feet." The enemy pilot put three holes in Best's aircraft and blew the Plexiglas out of the top turret, injuring the engineer. As the fighter ripped past the 498th's formation, the crews counted four P-38s in hot pursuit.

As the 345th's men had hoped, the three airfields were thick with enemy aircraft. But many of them had already been hit by previous raids. And traveling just above the ground at more than two hundred miles per hour, the crews had difficulty distinguishing damaged aircraft from others that were undamaged and armed, fueled, and ready for takeoff. The 498th alone claimed to have destroyed twelve enemy aircraft, but later evaluation of their strike photographs was inconclusive. "Photos disclose extensive damage to grounded planes by previous raids. Destruction and damage to planes on this strike not determinable as previous condition of planes is unknown. Few serviceable planes are visible in the photos."

Regardless of the definite fact that some of the aircraft claimed as destroyed had already been rendered unserviceable, dozens more had not been. The mission was a tremendous triumph, with all of the group's crews returning to base, a few with only minor damage. The monthly narrative was almost giddy with the successes that the 345th—together with the rest of the Fifth Air Force—had achieved: "Heavy bombing and minimum altitude, savage strafing, and peerless [fighter] cover upstairs combined to crush, literally, this arsenal of Jap air power. Why he did not use those bombers based at Hollandia we were at a loss to fathom. At any rate, there they were, waiting to be knocked out, and we 'dood' it."

J. R. Jones didn't fly on the April 3 mission to Hollandia. His letter to Elnora that day conveyed a feeling of frustration. "I've been slightly off the ball on this letter writing. I don't know what's wrong with me. I'm still grounded, but my cold has improved to some extent and my sense of smell isn't too sharp yet. It seems to be my sinus acting up, but it never bothered me before."[18]

Among other missions to other targets on New Guinea, the 345th returned to the Hollandia area on April 5 and 12. As with the mission on April 3, emphasis was put on the destruction of enemy aircraft; however, supply dumps and coastal barges were also targeted. Also consistent with the April 3 mission was the general ineffectiveness of the Japanese defenses as the 345th suffered no losses. Antiaircraft fire proved generally inaccurate, and the defending fighters were well handled by escorting P-38s. Hollandia was proving to be no Rabaul.

For no reason explained in the 345th's records, the group flew the April 12 mission at medium altitude. Doing so was less dangerous, but it was also less effective as the bombs could not be dropped as accurately and the crews weren't able to strafe. It is possible that Fifth Air Force headquarters wanted to give the men a respite from the risky low-altitude work or to preserve crews and aircraft for future operations. The group's monthly narrative considered this latter explanation. "We were constantly admonished to stay clear of all antiaircraft [fire]; we were being saved, it seems, for more important tasks ahead." Regardless, the 345th flew only three strafing missions during all of April 1944.

After operating as low-level strafers for so long, the 345th's crews had invariably lost some of their prowess at medium-altitude bombing, especially as many of the original bombardiers had been transferred to B-24 units; the big, four-engine B-24 typically operated at the sorts of high altitudes that required a traditional bombardier. The group's summary of operations, forwarded to the Fifth Air Force, described how the unit adapted: "We found that good results could be obtained by using a B-25D medium bomber, or a D-2—a later version of the strafer but with a position for the bombardier and a bomb sight—to lead the strafers on the bomb run. By this plan, the number one plane of each flight carried a bombardier, and the pilots of the number two and three planes, right and left wing respectively, dropped their bombs 'on him.' In other words, when he dropped, they dropped."

This transition back to medium bombing felt odd to some of the men. The pilots in particular were unable to fire their heavy battery of .50-caliber machine guns; nor were they able to streak low over the target, using terrain for cover. "Strafing is definitely more exciting than medium bombardment," wrote Jones, who had recovered enough from his sinus infection to fly the April 12 mission to Hollandia. "You feel so naked way up there."[19]

———

Hollandia was well softened by the middle of April 1944. Although the Japanese were still very capable and dangerous foes, the Allies were ascendant, and America's military and industrial power had already tipped the balance; Japan was irrevocably on the strategic defensive. Nevertheless, there would be setbacks. One of them would take place on April 16, 1944. On that day the Fifth Air Force would endure its greatest tragedy. But it would be one in which the Japanese would play only an ancillary role.

MacArthur was understandably and obviously anxious for the upcoming invasion of Hollandia to go as smoothly as possible. And he was counting on George Kenney's Fifth Air Force—among other entities, including the Navy—to ensure that the defending Japanese would have little say in the matter. Indications were that previous air raids had been quite successful toward that end. The mission of April 16 was intended to build on those successes.

It was a large strike that included 297 aircraft: 68 B-24s, 51 B-25s, 88 A-20s, and 76 P-38 fighter escorts, as well as 14 photoreconnaissance aircraft. The B-24s were to lead the effort and hit supply dumps and antiaircraft positions. The 345th's target area was on the western shore of Jautepa Bay, where the Japanese had concentrated personnel and stockpiles of material. As on the April 12 raid, the 345th was assigned to bomb from medium altitude. The task of shredding and bouncing the debris at Hollandia's three airfields was left to the A-20 groups.

The 345th contributed twenty-seven aircraft from only three squadrons as the 498th was transitioning to the B-25H, which was equipped with a nose-mounted seventy-five-millimeter cannon. It had rained considerably the night before, and the men awoke to sodden camps and damp clothes. They tromped in wet boots across muddy paths to get chow and then went to their briefings. In the meantime, weather reconnaissance flights radioed back troubling reports of cloud fronts along and adjacent to the route that might make such a large strike difficult. In fact, storms around Nadzab forced the mission to be delayed. The delay made many of the fliers nervous as powerful afternoon storms were a daily feature, as predictable as nightfall. If the takeoff was delayed too long, the men would be caught in the thick of those storms as they returned from the strike.

Even before the takeoff was delayed, the chief meteorologist recommended the operation be scrubbed. He was overridden. MacArthur's invasion of Hollandia was imminent, and reducing the Japanese forces there was imperative. The first 345th squadron, the 500th, led by Dale Speicher, began taking off from Nadzab at 1000, followed by the 501st and 499th in that order. Each B-25 was loaded with ten 250-pound fragmentation bombs.

The weather up to Hollandia proved to be fine, and the 345th's three squadrons had no problem getting formed and then making a rendezvous with B-25s from the 38th Bomb Group. At Buriu, the two bomb groups were joined by their P-38 escorts. All eyes scanned the sky for enemy fighters that never appeared.

The strike was almost a nonevent. The 345th put a good percentage of its bombs into its assigned target area but also dumped some into an adjacent swamp and additionally splashed an embarrassing number into the bay. Japanese resistance was essentially nil, and none of the 345th's B-25s were damaged. In fact, of the nearly three hundred aircraft that participated in the strike, none went down as a result of enemy action.

Smoke from the burning target rose to six thousand feet and higher as the bombers winged southeastward away from Hollandia, across New Guinea and toward home. The escorting P-38 pilots had little to do and entertained themselves and the bomber crews by flitting through their formations, waving and otherwise gesturing as they did so. The bomber crews replied in kind.

And then, more than halfway home, a colossal mass of wicked weather blotted out the horizon. The aerial horseplay stopped as the airmen took in the maelstrom before them. "The front was white and silver and black and fascinating to see," recalled one of the P-38 pilots, "but at the base where it wisped into the heavy foliage of the jungle, it was black and mean-looking."[20] Afternoon storms over that part of New Guinea were a daily feature, but for whatever reason that day's convective weather produced towering black billows of behemoth thunderheads that far surpassed anything the men had experienced to that point. Every pilot in the strung-out formation reflexively checked his aircraft's fuel state. The P-38 pilots instantly regretted their fuel-consuming aerial shenanigans and soon separated from the 345th to find their own way home.

The visibility worsened, and wingmen instinctively tucked in close to their flight leaders; losing sight of the formation heightened the risks of a midair collision. Moreover, the flight leaders were generally more experienced and had on board the most competent navigators; some of the wingmen didn't even have navigators. And, of course, danger was better braved in the company of comrades.

The weather front was located about 40 miles northwest of Dumpu, approximately 120 miles from Nadzab. Initially, when the 345th's pilots plowed into the first thin veils of clouds, they maintained their cruising altitude of about eight thousand feet. But Dale Speicher, leading the group at the head of the 500th, soon climbed to ten thousand feet, where he found a clear area. He circled the formation for a few minutes before the clouds closed the gap. Knowing that the weather was too high to clear, Speicher turned the group northeast toward Astrolabe Bay and started a descent. The weather thickened.

Speicher eventually released the three squadrons to recover back to Nadzab on their own. It was a moot point as the worsening visibility had already forced them apart. Leading the 500th, he directed the pilots to fall into a trail formation and descend to just over the water. From there, they were to fly the course he provided. He followed the last aircraft down and bottomed out at fifty feet under the glowering black clouds.

Rain and hail drummed against and into the B-25s. Wings were wrenched up and down—almost flapping—as pockets of turbulence snatched at the aircraft. Crewmen watched their flight leaders and wingmen disappear and reappear and disappear again behind shrouds of gray mist. Pilots white-knuckled their controls, leaned forward, and squinted into the gloom.

The 345th's men were ill prepared for the sort of serious instrument flying that the weather demanded that afternoon. Because they were difficult to maintain and parts were scarce, many of the aircraft had inoperative artificial horizons, or none at all. In fact, as recalled by Roman Ohnemus, many of the most basic instruments were often missing. "On my first flight [with the 345th] I climbed into the airplane and about half of the gauges in the instrument panel were gone—no airspeed indicator, no altimeter, and a couple of others were gone as well. When I pointed this out to my instructor he looked at me like I was slime and asked me if I had a problem flying without the instruments."[21]

The artificial horizon was the primary instrument used for foul-weather flying, but it simply wasn't needed very often as the group typically stayed clear of clouds. Accordingly, the instrument flying skills the men had learned during their stateside training were stale. And stale skills were a poor match for the backup instrument that was available on most aircraft—the turn and bank indicator, also known as "needle and ball." It was a primitive device that lagged the true nature of an aircraft's disposition by seconds at a time. Using it effectively was almost an art form and was especially difficult in turbulent weather.

Inevitably, just as the 345th's squadrons became separated, some of the three-plane flights within each squadron also lost contact with each other. And the weather skimmed wingmen away from some of the flights until the storm-whipped sky was filled with small clutches of aircraft and errant singles. The crews aboard all of them desperately sought a safe place to land.

The 345th comprised less than 10 percent of the aircraft fighting the weather that afternoon. Radio frequencies were clobbered by distress calls. Especially urgent were those of the P-38 and A-20 pilots. Although the P-38s had longer legs than they'd had before they were modified, those legs weren't overly long. And the A-20 had never been as long-ranged as the B-25. The B-24s could fly the farthest, but even some of those crews were desperately lost.

When Dale Speicher directed the 500th through the clouds while he circled overhead, the rest of the squadron followed Hobart Rankin's aircraft. Rankin brought the other pilots down to just above the wave tops and turned out of Astrolabe Bay before threading his way between a set of islands and back toward the coast. James Waggle's aircraft went missing during this time and was last seen "about 15 miles west of Saidor."

Rankin continued with the rest of the 500th toward the coast until arriving just abeam the airfield at Saidor. There, the flash of a violent explosion split the failing light of dusk. An F-5B—the photoreconnaissance variant of the P-38—collided head-on with a B-25 from the 38th Bomb Group. The pilot of the F-5B and three of the B-25 crewmen were killed. In fact six of the eleven 38th Bomb Group aircraft that recovered into Saidor that afternoon were destroyed or badly damaged, as were many other aircraft of various types.

Notwithstanding the burning carnage on Saidor's runway, Robert Whitsell, low on fuel, dipped a wing and separated from the rest of the formation. Against the odds, he made a successful landing. Rankin directed the remainder of the flight to illuminate their running lights and led them to Lae, where they recovered in darkness.

The 501st, led by Henry Kortemeyer—who had by that time recovered from the injuries he sustained during the Cape Gloucester raid the previous December—stayed relatively intact during the descent through the weather but started crumbling soon after. Low on fuel and alarmed by the weather, two pilots, Daniel Monaghan and Gordon Bedell, swung north toward recently captured Cape Gloucester on the western tip of New Britain. They cleared the clouds and landed without incident excepting a blown tire on one aircraft.

Robert Gentry's left engine coughed and stopped. The tank that fed it was out of fuel. He quickly trimmed his aircraft and evaluated his fuel situation but lost sight of the rest of the squadron. Believing he had no reasonable option but to ditch the aircraft, he dropped tentatively toward the water. But immediately after calling out that he was ditching, Gentry spotted Saidor almost directly ahead of him. He landed safely on one engine and sustained no damage other than a tire that was badly cut by wreckage still on the runway.

Saidor was a crowded mess of wrecks and panicked aircrews. Ground personnel raced to clear debris and pull immobile aircraft clear of the runway. Injured crewmen were wrenched from burning, twisted wrecks. Meanwhile, more aircraft continued to drop out of the clouds and onto the airfield. A P-38 pilot who only barely managed to put down at Saidor just as his left engine failed for lack of fuel recalled, "There were hundreds of GIs lining the strip, watching the Fifth Air Force destroy itself."[22]

Kortemeyer continued toward Nadzab with the rest of the 501st. Along the way, the formation shed Thomas Lewis and Ellis Mays, who, low on fuel, put into the airfield at Finschafen. Finally, with J. R. Jones and two other crews on his wing, Kortemeyer threaded his way out of the weather and landed safely back at Nadzab. Of the three squadrons the 345th put airborne that day, only the 501st recovered all its aircraft safely.

The 499th, led by Dick Baker, was the last squadron to drop through the clouds toward Astrolabe Bay. The formation broke into individual three-plane flights over the water. The first two of these motored just above the rain-beaten sea. Radio traffic indicated that the situation at Saidor was nothing short of pandemonium, so the 499th aircraft continued to Finschafen, where they landed with no issues. The third flight likewise set down at Finschafen except for the crew of James MacWilliam. His right engine had developed an oil leak, which subsequently caused the propeller to run away. The engine finally caught fire, and he turned toward land before putting the aircraft into the water. The crew scrambled clear of the sinking bomber and spent the night paddling clear of Japanese-held Karkar Island.

April 16, 1944—which came to be known as "Black Sunday"—saw the 345th lose two aircraft. The unit had suffered worse losses and would suffer worse losses again, but never to weather. Other groups suffered much more terribly. For instance, nine 475th Fighter Group P-38s crashed or otherwise failed to return. And the three groups operating A-20s lost a total of fourteen machines. In all, the Fifth Air Force wrote off thirty-eight aircraft, a loss rate that approached 15 percent. The casualty list included fifty-four men killed or missing. Although the Fifth Air Force was much larger than it had been during the early days of the war, the losses still stung. Its commander, George Kenney, took the tragedy hard and personally. He later noted, "It was the worst blow I took in the whole war."[23]

"Yesterday was another of those rugged jobs, and I couldn't have written if I had wanted to," J. R. Jones wrote to Elnora on the following day. "The less said about that, the better. Didn't even feel like going to the show tonight. Think I'll hit the sack early and get some slumber."[24]

While Jones was left off the flight schedule on the Monday following Black Sunday, others were sent airborne to look for their fallen comrades. Virtually every unit in the Fifth, including the 345th, contributed aircraft and crews to the effort. The 499th reported that it launched three B-25s to search different sectors. "Each plane carried packages of supplies, rations and emergency equipment, as well as messages. In event of location of grounded planes, packages and messages were to be dropped and positions were to be reported by radio using the Fighter Grid coordinates. In event of locating crews in water, life rafts and emergency supplies were to be dropped and positions on Fighter Grid given to patrolling [PBY] Catalinas."

Julian Baird of the 499th spotted a pair of B-25 wheels floating several hundred yards apart, about twenty miles west of Saidor and close to the beach. He flew low over a trio of barges and directed them to the area. Later he circled Manam Island, where his top turret gunner fired on a group of Japanese troops. "In this attack, one Japanese soldier in a plantation on the east side of Manam Island was observed to be hit." Later, the crew overflew the village of Lilau, where they "spotted a camouflaged serviceable truck with almost new tires parked in a coconut grove." How they ascertained that the truck had "almost new tires" is uncertain.

Baird and his crew stayed busy. At the village of Malas, "an A-20 was observed on the beach. The plane was on the north side of the river and had made an excellent crash landing with a minimum of damage to the plane. Two crew members were observed lying under the life raft and apparently not seriously injured."

Baird made three passes over the men and dropped a bag of supplies almost on top of them. "One man stepped over and picked up the bundle and waved. The other continued to lie on the ground, but waved as well." At that point, three P-38s arrived overhead, and Baird climbed a short distance out to sea to radio the position of the downed airmen. However, his radio had failed. Refusing to be stymied, Baird flew to Saidor, landed, and reported the position of the A-20 and its crew. After taking off from Saidor, he stopped at Finschafen for fuel before returning to Nadzab.

The 500th also sent search crews. They returned to base without sighting anything noteworthy, and the squadron observed that the "crews were a bit disappointed in the results." They waited for news of their comrade James Waggle and his missing crew. It didn't come. He is presumed to have smashed into the water as no trace of the aircraft or the men aboard it was ever found. That being said, the aircraft wheels Julian Baird had spotted floating west of Saidor might have belonged to Waggle's aircraft.

James MacWilliam and his crew had spent the wet and wave-tossed night in their raft. They kept busy by paddling clear of Karkar Island, rightly suspecting that it was held by the Japanese. Not long after dawn the sky buzzed with Allied aircraft searching for survivors of the previous day's mayhem. Although they signaled, MacWilliam's men failed to attract any attention until around noon, when they were spotted by a flight of P-47s.

Not long afterward, they were heartened by the sight of a Navy PBY flying boat. The aircraft made a couple of turns to judge the wind, dropped a smoke marker, and shortly thereafter splashed down and water-taxied to where MacWilliam's crew bobbed in the waves. A few minutes later the men were safely aboard, and the PBY crew machine-gunned the raft into shreds. Left afloat, it might have sidetracked other rescuers, wasting valuable time and resources.

Once airborne, the PBY pilot set a course for the New Guinea coast. Near Malas, about thirty miles down the coast from Madang, the Navy men looked for the downed A-20 and the two-man crew reported by Julian Baird earlier that morning. They spotted them, put the PBY down on the water, and coasted up to the beach where both men waited. The wrecked bomber was the 3rd Attack Group's *Joy Baby*, crewed by pilot William Sanders and his gunner.

When they crash-landed on the beach the previous evening, they mistakenly believed they were safely behind Allied lines. Consequently, after crawling clear of their aircraft, they set up camp and built a big, crackling bonfire. They were additionally ignorant of a road, only a short distance away, over which the Japanese moved men, supplies, and equipment. Indeed, as the PBY pilot readied to put down on the water, his crew spied Japanese troops less than a mile away.

The A-20 men, glad to see their rescuers, invited everyone to disembark from the PBY to enjoy a refreshing swim. They were dumbstruck when apprised of the imminent threat and wasted no time in hustling aboard the flying boat. Happily, both rescued crews were soon reunited with their units.

The PBY was captained by James Merritt of VP-34. Although the rescue was a life-or-death event for MacWilliam and Sanders and their crews—and an existential one for their future progeny—VP-34's war diary description was laconic and matter-of-fact. The event was just part of an honest day's work: "Lieutenant Merritt, plane #73 (08491) searched along coast and offshore islands for missing air crews. Rescued a B-25 crew in open sea southeast of Bagabag Island and crew of A-20 along beach of New Guinea coast near Sarong Harbor. Total of Seven Persons." And that was it.[25]

Although other men were rescued from both the sea and the jungle, such satisfactory endings were not necessarily foregone conclusions. One A-20 crew was observed safely aboard their raft, not far from the coast. They were never seen again. At least six P-38 pilots parachuted or crashed into the jungle and likewise were never rescued, although the dog tags of one were later found on the body of a Japanese soldier.[26] Lost over New Guinea with no trace were four B-24s and their complete crews. Another B-24 crew bailed out over the jungle; remarkably, eight of those ten men walked back to civilization. But the fates of many others remain unknown to this day.

News did not travel accurately or fast in New Guinea, and men of the 345th had little idea how deadly the Black Sunday mission had been. The group's monthly narrative report correctly noted that the strike against Hollandia on April 16, 1944, had yielded "dire results for the Fifth Air Force"; it also acknowledged that "weather was the enemy that day." But curiously, it declared, "One of our planes failed to get through," when in fact two 345th aircraft were lost. The narrative was additionally mistaken when it stated, "All-in-all, [the] Fifth Air Force lost 4 bombers and 9 fighters." In reality, thirty-eight Fifth Air Force aircraft were lost or destroyed. Ultimately, however, whether the men understood how many aircraft were lost didn't matter. They still had a war to fight.

And they continued to fight it, although they didn't mount their next mission until April 21, the day prior to the Hollandia invasion. The group sent twenty-five aircraft to hit the Tadji airfield, just east of Aitape, which was scheduled to be seized simultaneously with Hollandia. The attack was made from medium altitude and was utterly uneventful. The 500th Bomb Squadron's mission summary report was uncharacteristically breezy: "Enemy reaction was nil, not even a rock being thrown at our planes and all returned safely to base. One Jap thumbed his nose at our planes and a force of 150 bombers will be sent up next week to get him, it was authoritatively stated. As was so aptly put by our squadron leader, 'It is this sort of thing that breeds future wars.'"

On the following day, April 22, the day that MacArthur's troops went ashore at Hollandia, a line of clouds at Wewak forced the 345th—perhaps now a bit shy of foul weather—to hit its alternate target at Hansa Bay. The strike was every bit as lackluster as the mission to Tadji had been the previous day. As it developed, the Army did very well at Hollandia without the 345th. The eleven thousand Japanese defenders—mostly made up of antiaircraft and support personnel—put up little resistance to the fifty thousand American invaders. Rather than fighting, most of the enemy troops simply abandoned their positions and melted away to the west.

CHAPTER NINE

"I Hate to See Them Go"

THE 345TH'S 498TH SQUADRON FLEW THE APRIL 5 MISSION TO THE Hollandia area but missed the remainder of the campaign. It did not fly again until April 23. In the interim it busied itself with handing off its complement of older aircraft and learning how to operate the new B-25H.

Among the B-25's many fine attributes was its adaptability. It was a big, sturdy, and powerful machine that readily accommodated a variety of modifications throughout its service career. Some of these changes increased its general usability, while others enhanced its effectiveness in certain roles. For instance, the addition of the solid nose and fixed, forward-firing .50-caliber machine guns made the 345th's crews deadly strafers.

One of the more famous but least loved adaptations was a single 75-millimeter cannon mounted in the left side of the nose. It was believed that the big, tank-caliber gun would be especially useful against a spectrum of targets, but particularly against maritime vessels such as the barges that had become so important to Japanese resupply efforts.

The installation was primitive and awkward. To accommodate the weapon and its twenty-one rounds of ammunition, the barrel was passed under the pilot's seat. The breech, where the gun was reloaded, extended behind the seat and was manually fed by the navigator, who also acted as a cannoneer in the target area.

During the gun's actual use, the pilot approached the target in a slight dive and fired from a range of about two thousand yards. Crouched behind the pilot's seat, the navigator had to reach up and pull one of the fifteen-pound shells from the armor-protected ammunition rack, load it, close the breech, and notify the pilot. And he had to do this under fire while the pilot fine-tuned his aim and fired his .50-caliber machine guns. Normally, a crew could fire only three rounds before the pilot had to pull out of his dive.

The pilot could not maneuver during his firing run without spoiling his aim, so the aircraft was especially vulnerable to antiaircraft guns. The weapon was also loud and sent a concussive shock through the front of the aircraft that rattled the men almost as if they had taken a body blow. And smoke filled the cockpit, making it difficult to see and breathe. Moreover, no matter how much the airframe was strengthened—and it was strengthened considerably—the gun still gave it a considerable beating, often popping rivets. Pilot John Baeta's observations confirmed everything that was wrong with the concept. "Oh, it was horrible. It was so loud, and there was a big blast of flame and smoke in the cockpit when it was fired. And it just tore the airplane apart. And its rate of fire was too slow."

The first B-25 variant to carry this tank-caliber weapon was the B-25G, which the 345th's counterpart, the 38th Bomb Group, used extensively. The 38th introduced it to combat in October 1943, six months before the 345th's 498th Bomb Squadron received their similarly equipped B-25H aircraft. The chief armament difference between the B-25G and the 498th's newer B-25H was replacement of the older M4 75-millimeter cannon in the B-25G with the lighter T13E1 of the same caliber. The B-25H also carried four .50-caliber machine guns in the nose rather than the two of the B-25G. And the B-25H did not have a bottom or ventral turret as did older models of the B-25G. The greatest visible change was the relocation of the top gun turret forward from behind the bomb bay to a point just behind the cockpit. From a recognition standpoint, this was the chief distinction between the older and newer models of the aircraft.

Moreover, unlike the B-25Ds with which the 345th did much of its fighting during its early career, the B-25H had a factory-installed tail turret with two .50-caliber machine guns and a Plexiglas canopy for the gunner's head. Further, the single .30-caliber machine guns mounted at each side of the rear fuselage were replaced by .50-caliber machine guns fired from waist positions farther forward, just behind the bomb bay. These guns were mounted on a trunnion yoke and projected through a canvas boot attached to an opening in a transparent Plexiglas panel that was much larger than the earlier ports through which the .30-caliber guns were fired. Each gun was stabilized with bungee cables to help the gunner control it when the pilot maneuvered aggressively.

The B-25H also differed in not having a copilot. His place was taken by the navigator, or "cannoneer," who sat in that same area on a little jump seat. But without a copilot, the pilot had a considerable workload; fatigue became an issue on longer flights. Additionally, this raised a logical question: If copilots weren't required on the B-25H, why were they necessary on the B-25 at all? Of course, there was no good answer to the question, and most crews preferred to fly with copilots.

In fact, the cannon-equipped B-25 had seen its best days by early 1944 as the heavy barge and lugger traffic against which it was most effective had started to dry up around New Guinea. The 38th Bomb Group began removing the cannons and modifying some of their B-25Gs to strafer configurations beginning in February, a couple of months before the 498th even received their cannon-equipped B-25H aircraft. And most of the rest of the B-25Gs were sent away during the following months.

The 498th used their new B-25H aircraft for the first time on April 23 and then again on April 24. On both days the 345th went to Hansa Bay and bombed from medium altitude. And on both days the 498th's six cannon-equipped aircraft went hunting for targets of opportunity. On April 24 these aircraft fired more than a hundred 75-millimeter rounds, "destroying many huts in native villages by direct hits. A machine-gun position at Bogia was thoroughly strafed and ceased firing. A truck along the side of the road near Bogia Village and the woods near the truck were strafed." These targets seemed trifling; however an antiaircraft position at Uligan Harbor "was completely destroyed by direct hits from seven 75-millimeter shells. This position was completely silenced and contained two guns which appeared to be one heavy and one medium."

Still, by the end of the day, the case for the new aircraft was unconvincing. The squadron noted, "Airplane 130 had a hydraulic failure which was believed caused from firing of cannon. Airplane 164 had compass failure of all its compasses which was believed caused by firing of cannon." Floyd Jensen was at the controls of the aircraft that had lost its compasses. He ended up at Port Moresby. His wingman, Howell Stapleton, ran out of gas and crash-landed on a beach. The squadron opined, "This plane is believed not repairable."

The B-25H earned an indifferent reputation for very good reasons.

—◦—

As he started what he believed were his last few months of combat at the end of May 1944, J. R. Jones continued to be envious of friends who had been given orders for the States, but he still celebrated their good fortune with congratulatory gladness. "Four more of the boys are going home, and I have to go over and have a farewell drink this evening. It won't be a very long one though, as I have to fly tomorrow. I hate to see them go, and yet I'm glad for them. They are a grand bunch of fellows and they deserve it."[1]

The tempo of operations had picked up considerably, as he wrote to Elnora a couple of days later on June 1. "I'm getting my share of flying. In fact, more than I'd like to be doing. If I'm not heard from for a couple of days, I'll be out doing a little work, and facilities for writing won't be too handy. I hate to start roughing it again, but we're off again. I can't even keep track of what's going on any more."[2]

It was little wonder that Jones had difficulty keeping track of what was going on. The 345th had spent much of the second half of May flying missions against Biak Island and the Wewak complex. The pace was unrelenting, and the men were tired. That tiredness took its toll. For instance, during an attack on Biak Island on May 29, 1944, the B-25 flown by Elmer Kirkland of the 498th Bomb Squadron was shot down. Cecil Barnes was part of Kirkland's crew. Barnes's good friend, Owen Bianconi, was flying aboard the B-25 on Kirkland's wing. He was understandably rattled by the sight of the explosion that killed Kirkland's crew, including his friend Cecil.

Once Bianconi was back on the ground at Nadzab, he cataloged and boxed Barnes's belongings as well as those of others in the crew who shared the same tent. When he finished he took them to the quarter-master's tent for dispositioning and shipment to the families.

And then he came undone.

It took time and effort to get him back under control and to seques-ter him from the other men. James Baross visited him shortly afterward. "It was sad to see him, by then somewhat rational again, clinging to the wire of his cage, saddened by the crash of Barnes and both confused and embarrassed by his reaction to it."[3] Bianconi never flew again. However, to his credit, he stayed with the squadron and continued to repair, install, and otherwise service radios.

Baross also recalled another of Cecil Barnes's friends, Marty Berman, who had been a musician with many of the era's big dance bands. "Barnes had played a lot of card games and, at the time he was killed, owed a considerable amount of money to various troops in the squadron. Marty took it upon himself to pay off all of Cecil Barnes's debts and never said a word about it."[4]

J. R. Jones returned to Nadzab on June 10 after spending more than a week flying missions from Hollandia and newly seized Wakde Island. "Hello darling," he wrote Elnora. "Sorry to keep you waiting a few days, but I've been up in the forward areas. It's definitely no picnic there either. I have never been so tired and dirty in my life. Hollandia and Wakde are no places for a vacation. We ate emergency rations all the while we were gone, and I have tasted better food in my lifetime."

It is interesting that Jones named specific locations—something he had never done before. Either the censorship guidelines had eased, or, nearing the end of his combat tour, he just didn't care. "Hollandia is just about the dustiest place it has ever been my pleasure to land at. As soon as you touch the ground, everything disappears. Some fun, but I can think of a better way to make a living."

Evidently the medical authorities agreed that Jones was exhausted. "When I got home again, I was shot [greatly fatigued]. The flight surgeon promptly grounded me, saying I had been flying too much. I guess I am pretty nervous. I have fifty missions now and 235 combat hours. As a result, I'm being sent to Sydney in the next few days."[5]

It is quite possible that the flight surgeon removed Jones from flight operations because he had reached the fifty-mission mark, which until just a short time previously had been the required tally for completing a combat tour. There was no doubt that Jones was tired—anyone who flew fifty combat missions in that environment was bound to be worn out. Exhaustion being a subjective matter, the surgeon could have simply declared that Jones was no longer fit for combat without extensive rest and recommended his return to the States.

In fact, the previous two months had exhausted a great many of the 345th's men. Of the seventy-six crews assigned to the group, only twenty-four were considered combat ready during June. Ennis White-head, commander of Fifth Bomber Command, observed that many of the men appeared "practically punch drunk." More than six hundred airmen from across the organization were sent home during July—a record. Whitehead believed that "a half-strength squadron of willing boys is better than a full-strength squadron of worn out ones."[6]

Aside from sickness and nerves, the heat also wore on the men. J. R. Jones, like many, found that he grew lethargic in the tropical warmth. "Under this blasted sun, even a game of marbles is too strenuous. It seems that no matter what you did before you got in the Air Force, you just get naturally lazy after a time and avoid all forms of exercise."[7] Still, the men evidently did find ways to entertain themselves in the heat. "There is quite a golf game going on outside," he later wrote Elnora. "They have one, left-handed club, and all the boys are right-handed except one. They have fun anyhow as the game consists mainly of arguments."[8]

The tropics not only sucked the energy from the 345th's men but also killed any idea of proper military dress during normal day-to-day operations. "Latest style notes," Jones wrote, "if you could see the way we dress, you would give me up for lost."[9] Indeed, consistent with Jones's observation, photos show the men were often shirtless, even in the mess hall. Short trousers and all manner of footgear were worn, to include loafers and athletic shoes. Hats, when worn at all, were usually baseball caps intended for protection from the sun. Clothing articles often didn't match.

There were many reasons for this. First, the men went about shirtless and in shorts because it was so hot and humid. Shirts quickly became sopping rags, especially when worn by the maintenance men who worked outside in the elements. And clothing articles could only endure a certain amount of wear and tear before simply rotting away. Harsh laundering either by hand or primitive machines exacerbated the problem. Moreover, clothing was often lost or pilfered either by natives or comrades. Replacement items, especially in the right size, were difficult to get. That said, most men had at least one set of serviceable uniform items for parades or other formal occasions.

In fact, the medical profession had long recognized and understood the tropical lassitude exhibited by Jones and his comrades. "It has been recognized that long residence in a tropical environment undoubtedly influences the mental and emotional activity of white people from the Temperate Zone," observed one study. "Physiological changes occur, such as lowered basal metabolism rates, and changes in kidney function which tend to produce an over-all decreased activity often associated with large numbers of psychosomatic symptoms."[10]

The 345th's men were quite at home at Nadzab by June 1944. Indeed, by that time they had completed their club—a place to relax and enjoy a drink or nine. Aldridge Nichols remembered that "during the month of June, each squadron and the group headquarters had a party in the new Group Officers Mess. Each was quite an affair, for New Guinea, and was well attended by officers, nurses and Red Cross girls."[11]

J. R. Jones wrote Elnora, "It seems that no matter where you go, the officers will have a club. I have really seen some beauties since I've been gone. Over here, the Army nurse seems to have undergone a change for the better. I have seen quite a few good-looking numbers about. It makes a pleasant atmosphere anyhow."[12]

However, Jones noted that "pleasant atmosphere" or not, there was no getting around the effects of overimbibing. "We really threw a party in the club last night. One of the boys discovered that he was a father yesterday, and we all helped him celebrate. As a result, I've felt far from good all day.

This climate is definitely not an aid to a hangover. We'll hold a party at the drop of a hat, and we don't have to strive very hard to dig up an occasion. Last night, however, was a super blast and today I am repenting."[13]

Clinton True completed his combat tour during that time and was relieved as commander of the 345th on June 24, 1944. The much-liked leader was feted at the new officers' club. "The group party was really a farewell party for our colonel, Clinton U. True, who had received orders to return to the States," said Nichols. "He had led the group well, to many successful missions, and had been nicknamed 'Fearless,' which he was well aware of, and merely grinned about."[14]

So True, who was remembered as "stern, fair and very efficient," had survived his combat tour. True's replacement was Chester Coltharp, who "was very popular with the men of the group. He has led many missions of the group and already holds the Distinguished Service Cross."[15] Coltharp had won the medal for his actions at Kavieng a few months earlier on February 15. He was a qualified and well-regarded replacement for True.

Aside from relaxing or celebrating in their clubs—when and where they were available—the men enjoyed more ad hoc galas. These were informal gatherings held to commemorate anything that needed commemorating—the news of a baby, the recovery of a downed crew, the completion of a combat tour, a promotion, or even the memory of lost comrades.

They were called, tongue-in-cheek, "prayer meetings." A prayer meeting might start with just a handful of men and a bottle of liquor and, as it picked up steam and created noise, attract more men and more liquor. Ultimately, some of these parties spread until entire sections of billeting were in a celebratory uproar. Indeed, 501st Bomb Squadron pilot Ralph "Peppy" Blount said, only partly tongue in cheek, "I have never associated with a bunch of people who were bigger drunks."[16]

But there was a downside to these celebrations besides the obvious hangovers. Howard Thompson, a pilot with the 500th Bomb Squadron, rightly noted that when the pilots drank hard, they put their crews at risk. "It was hard on the boys that had to fly with a pilot that had partied all night," he said.[17]

The liquor originated from various sources. Individuals brought some of it back from Australia. Some of it was bought on the black market. Some of it was moonshine—distilled in some remote corner of the airfield or in the jungle beyond. Some of it came from the post exchange. And the flight surgeon sometimes contributed medicinal alcohol, often cutting it with juice or soda.

Indeed, the men spent considerable energy and cash to get as much booze as they could. James Mahaffey of the 499th Bomb Squadron recalled an incident that was particularly upsetting to the squadron's officers. "We'd taken up collections to stock an officers club," he said. "So, everybody contributed and I think we had about ten thousand dollars. They flew down to Australia to get it, and when they came back the landing gear wouldn't come down. They pulled the nose up sharply to get the landing gear to drop down into place. They tried that two or three times, making passes over the runway." The crew made another attempt and pulled up especially abruptly. As the nose of the aircraft snapped skyward, $10,000 worth of liquor broke through the wooden slats upon which it sat, then smashed through the bomb bay doors and down to the runway, where it exploded in a glittering spray of glass and atomized spirits.

Ultimately, where the booze came from was of little importance to the 345th's men, and they scavenged it from wherever they could. In fact, scavenging was a way of life for them, and aside from liquor, they picked up many of the items and much of the material they used in their daily lives from all across the Southwest Pacific. The men brought home all manner of items and often determined what was and wasn't useful only after it was safely back in their tents. Those things that had value were put directly to use or bartered for something else.

But the men were occasionally surprised by what they found. Robert Scudder, a pilot with the 500th Bomb Squadron, recalled that his copilot, Floyd Good, "found an unopened wooden case he thought contained Japanese sake. He brought the case home and stored it under my bed. When we finally opened the case, it contained live Japanese antiaircraft shells."[18]

Good, Scudder, and their comrades were lucky there had been no mishap. In fact, many of the men believed in luck and carried good-luck charms or practiced good-luck rituals. J. R. Jones, since the early days of the 345th's combat career, carried the silver dollar that Elnora had given him. McKinley Sizemore, a radio operator with the 500th Bomb Squadron, did not carry a lucky charm or have any rituals, but he recalled a tent mate who did. "One of my buddies, he wouldn't make his bed. His thing was that he was always going to come back, and make that bed when he got back. But one time he didn't come back. That bed didn't get made. He was killed. A good friend of mine. I lost a lot of good buddies over there."[19]

Cal Peckham escaped the very worst luck a number of times. A turret specialist with the 500th Bomb Squadron's armament section, he was one of several men who had missed the ill-fated C-47 flight to Sydney on August 7, 1943. Peckham had been excited by the opportunity to see Sydney, "but at the last minute, Captain [John] O'Brien said I couldn't go because he needed me in Townsville." O'Brien, the head of the squadron's armament section, had inadvertently saved Peckham's life.

Almost two months later, on September 29, Peckham wangled a spot aboard Cecil Jones's aircraft, which was scheduled for practice gunnery at the Moresby Wreck. "I had already made arrangements to go along so that I could check out the turret," Peckham remembered. "However, Captain O'Brien said I couldn't go on the flight because he needed me to work on something. I was replaced on the flight by Private Henry Just." For reasons unknown, Jones's aircraft went down, and the seven personnel aboard were all killed.

Peckham consequently gained a reputation as a jinx. Several months later, as the group staged men and equipment from Nadzab to Hollandia, O'Brien pulled Peckham from a C-47 that was readying to taxi for take-off. "When I got off the plane to go with Captain O'Brien," said Peckham, "all the rest of the guys on the plane got off too. Captain O'Brien said, 'No, no, all I need is Peckham.'"

The men would have none of it and, perhaps with some justification, reminded O'Brien of Peckham's history. They wouldn't get back on the aircraft without him. "So, Captain O'Brien arranged to have another C-47 take the men to Hollandia without me."[20]

They all arrived safely.

Many other 345th men had "near miss" stories wholly attributable to luck. Sil Mawrence came to New Guinea with an engineer unit but was later commissioned and assigned to the 500th Bomb Squadron as a supply officer. "My tent mates were mostly aircrew members whom I admired greatly and who were, are, and always will be my heroes. I lost many tent mates and other friends among them. As a result, I learned to distance myself from them somewhat, on a social basis, because their loss hit me hard and I was afraid to get too close to them."

Mawrence made an exception with Charles Blakemore. "He was a great guy and was so proud that he was finally being checked out as a first pilot. He asked if I would go along with him on his check ride and I agreed." However, upon reaching the flight line, Mawrence chanced upon an old friend who was flying to where his former engineer unit was based. Anxious to see his "long-lost" comrades, he talked with Blakemore and changed his plans.

"I had a great time with my engineer buddies, albeit for only a short time," Mawrence said. "However, on my return to Nadzab, the flight line and base personnel greeted me with astonishment. The check ride I had told everyone I was going on with my tent mate, Lieutenant Blakemore, had crashed." The wreck had been so violent—and the bodies of the crew so badly sundered—that the personnel who reached the scene mistakenly thought that Mawrence was among the pieces.[21]

Jerry Chealander, a pilot with the 501st, had seen considerable action. His aircraft had been hit by enemy fire on nine different missions— his navigator had been killed on one of them. But none of those missions were what brought him closest to death during his time with the 345th. He sat astride his cot on one occasion playing gin rummy with his copilot. "Another copilot, Don Trip," said Chealander, "was sitting on his cot nearby, preparing to clean his .45 pistol. Don apparently had his finger on the trigger as he pulled the slide back to clear the weapon. He released the slide, putting a shell into the firing chamber, and the gun went off. The bullet passed so close to my head that it grazed the hair on my temple."[22]

Benjamin Muller, a radio-gunner in the 500th Bomb Squadron, was part of a mission that landed on recently captured Wakde Island to refuel. "Wakde was so small there was only one airstrip and it extended from beach-to-beach across the island, and there were aircraft hardstands everywhere," Muller recalled. "Apparently, cleanup had not yet been completed since there were still some dead Japs scattered around." A foray by Muller and some of the crew to extract gold teeth from the enemy corpses was unproductive, and the men made ready to spend the night.

"Fortunately, we found some tents that were already in place," Muller recalled. "The tent that I shared with others had a slit trench next to it and was close to a hardstand. Later a P-38 taxied into the hardstand next to us and the pilot proceeded to make ready for the night by hanging a hammock between the tail booms of his plane."

Wakde was harassed by a Japanese raider that night. "I jumped into the slit trench," Muller said, "and landed right on top of another guy, and then another guy landed on top of me. The bombs fell all around us with one of them exploding so close it really shook us. Some of the guys were yelling and crying."

Muller and the other men explored the immediate area after daylight. "There, only a short distance from our slit trench we saw what was left of a direct hit on the P-38. The tail booms, hammock and the pilot were all goners."[23]

When luck ran out, whether in combat or in garrison, men often perished. And the families of the perished deserved to know something of the circumstances that took the lives of their loved ones. The task of informing them fell to the unit's leadership. It was a particularly wearying duty for the officers of the 345th. It took time, and it took heart. And it was required far too often. And because it was required far too often, it was difficult for the letters not to sound formulaic.

The letters from close friends were often more personal, direct, and heartfelt. When Roy E. Smith, a pilot with the 500th Bomb Squadron, was killed on a raid to Negros, Anton Kusebauch wrote to Smith's widow: "He was a swell guy and a wonderful friend. He was like a big brother to me, always taking care of me. The day Roy was shot down, I sat on my cot and cried like a baby."

Even with as many letters as the leadership had to write, many still tried to make their observations heartfelt and real. Indeed, the letter Max

Mortensen wrote to Smith's widow indicated that he knew and appreciated the same attributes that Smith's peers valued: "He will be remembered as a pilot who brought to the 500th Squadron Rough Raiders a brighter spirit and cheerfulness than any ever shown by a new combat crewman. We feel indeed honored to have known him."[24]

About these letters, J. R. Jones wrote to Elnora, "I must get up early tomorrow and go to church. It's not a very pleasant reason, I assure you. I must also write the boy's mother. What does a man say at such times? I don't know—it's very difficult—I do know that."[25]

By the middle of June 1944, Japanese air power in New Guinea was a ghost of what it had once been—George Kenney's men dominated the Japanese in the sky, virtually at will. Certainly, during the period that followed the seizure of Hollandia, although there was still plenty of war to be fought and lots of dying yet to be done, there seemed to be a lull in the intensity of the action. "It's not so bad now as it was in the days when we used to shoot up Rabaul and Wewak," J. R. Jones wrote to Elnora. "It seems odd to fly over Wewak [en route to elsewhere] and not be shot at. With the fall of Hollandia, it rather narrows things down. . . . I'm not too sorry the war has quieted down. Still plenty of work to be done, though."[26]

Much of the remaining Japanese air power in New Guinea was pushed to two airfields at the very northwestern tip of the island on the unusually shaped peninsula known as the Bird's Head, or Vogelkop. One of the airfields, Samate, was situated on the peninsula, while the other, Jefman, was located on an island of the same name, just a couple of miles east of Samate. Destroying the units there would effectively end Japanese air resistance on New Guinea.

The two airfields were out of reach of the units based at Nadzab. Accordingly, the Fifth Air Force ordered both the 345th Bomb Group and its sister group, the 38th, to send aircraft and crews to Hollandia. The aircraft were staged and ready for action against Samate and Jefman on June 15. On the following morning, their bomb bays stuffed with 215-gallon auxiliary fuel tanks and a dozen one-hundred-pound parademolition bombs, twenty-two B-25s of the 38th Bomb Group took off, followed by an equal number of 345th Bomb Group aircraft. The 345th left behind two B-25s that had gotten tangled together in a taxiing accident.

The mission, at a straight-line distance of nearly seven hundred miles, was the longest yet undertaken by B-25s in the Southwest Pacific. The flight to the target was largely uneventful, and the two bomb groups were joined by four squadrons of P-38s at Mios Waar Island, near Biak, at the approximate halfway point. The 38th, leading the 345th, dropped to low level and pressed west until Samate was to the right and behind the formation. Then the line of B-25s made a right turn to the northeast, put Samate on its nose, and readied for the attack.

Approaching the target, the P-38 escort flying above the two bomb groups was engaged by more than two dozen Japanese fighters. The 38th Bomb Group, in two line-abreast formations of eleven aircraft each, dropped their bombs and strafed parked aircraft while knocking down several others that were just lifting from the airstrips. Behind them, the six aircraft of the 501st squadron led the 345th in a line-abreast formation.

A ridge to the south of Samate spoiled the 501st's bombing run but did not stop it from strafing aircraft and other targets. Once clear of that airfield, the squadron's pilots made a quick right-hand turn and roared across the three miles of water that separated Samate from Jefman Island. As the squadron approached Jefman, Japanese fighters dropped aerial bombs in its path. The bombs exploded at about five hundred feet and sent tentacles of fiery phosphorous in all directions.

The aerial bombs were as ineffective as they had always been and did no harm. Likewise, the traditional attacks made by enemy fighters at the same time were unsuccessful. The 501st observed, "The squadron was intercepted by 5–6 Oscars [Nakajima Ki-43 fighters] and Hamps [Mitsubishi A6M fighters]. Several passes were made from 1,000 feet, but attacks were not pressed too closely and, in each case, the enemy planes were driven off by the excellent fighter cover of the P-38s." Indeed, the escorting P-38s claimed twenty-five aerial victories over the Japanese.

But they weren't the only pilots to score in the air. Henry Kortemeyer also did well with his aircraft's guns. "A Hamp came in between 11 o'clock and 12 o'clock on a diving pass from 1,000 feet to within 300 feet of Lieutenant Kortemeyer's plane. At this range, Lieutenant Kortemeyer opened fire with his forward firing .50s in the nose and got in a four-second burst with tracers seen going directly into the Hamp. The enemy plane just flipped over on its back, turned to the right and when last seen by members of the crew was flying upside down, 250 feet above the water." The 498th, following immediately behind the 501st, confirmed that the enemy fighter had crashed into the water.

The 345th's other three squadrons likewise bombed and strafed the two airfields. Aircraft, supply dumps, and barracks were particularly hard-hit. The 500th's Hobart Rankin poured machine-gun fire into a number of enemy aircraft. "Lieutenant Rankin," observed the squadron's report, "gave concentrated fire to four inline engine [Kawasaki Ki-61] fighters on the eastern edge of the strip and 500 yards from the north end, and to a twin-engine bomber and two fighters on the north end. Although heavy fire was seen to enter these planes, they did not burn, but were obviously considerably damaged."

That none of these aircraft was set afire indicated that their fuel tanks were empty, perhaps a sign that there was no fuel to put into them or that such fuel as was available was carefully husbanded. Other 345th pilots reported experiences similar to Rankin's. There could be little doubt that the Fifth Air Force's efforts to strangle the Japanese on New Guinea had been effective.

However, it was apparent that the Japanese at both Samate and Jefman had plenty of ammunition. Antiaircraft fire over parts of the two targets was described as heavy and accurate. The right wingtip was blown from a 500th Bomb Squadron aircraft flown by Roland Thomas, but he kept it under control. William Selby of the 499th was tragically less fortunate. The squadron reported that his aircraft "was hit by ack-ack and was seen to veer off to the north, flip over and explode as it hit the water just north of the center of the island." The report also noted, "In the opinion of crews witnessing the crash, there could have been no possible survivors on this plane."

The attacking B-25s headed southeast, having turned both enemy airfields into pyres of smoke and fire. As they passed Doom Island, a

Japanese destroyer lobbed shells at the fleeing aircraft. They dropped harmlessly short.

A follow-up raid was launched the following day against the two airfields and nearby shipping. It was a bust, as the area was a jumbled disarray of wrecks and ruin that presented few worthwhile targets. Virtually no resistance was met, and no losses were suffered.

That fact gave no solace to the family and friends of William Selby and his crew, several of whom had not only family but romantic attachments in the States. Sadly, many tens of thousands of American wives, girlfriends, and fiancées lost their men to combat during World War II. Aside from memories, these women were left with little more than worn, oft-read letters, old uniforms, and a footlocker filled with odds and ends. The pain of those losses often lingered with the women for the rest of their lives.

Hundreds of those lost men served with the 345th. But J. R. Jones was not among them. He had not seen combat since flying his fiftieth mission, and on June 25, 1944, he wrote Elnora. "I may have a very big surprise for you [in] three or four weeks, darling, bigger than you think. Now don't go straight up in the air, but I think it's going to happen this time. In fact, the orders are in. Think you could stand me around, darling?"[27]

Jones was going home.

━ ◡ ━

The 345th launched two fewer aircraft than planned to Samate and Jefman that day because of an accident on the ground. Unlike with other aircraft, taxiing the B-25—with its tricycle landing gear—required equal parts skill and sorcery. Taxiing was normally an unremarkable part of piloting, but the B-25's size, combined with its free-swiveling nosewheel and extremely sensitive brakes, demanded a very light touch and no small measure of experience. Novices were easily recognized as they lurched back and forth or even trapped themselves in place when the nosewheel became misaligned. The rough taxiways and runways characteristic of the Southwest Pacific further exacerbated the problem. Indeed, extremely bad handling could—and sometimes did—snap the entire nose strut.

CHAPTER TEN

"Torn to Death"

MANY OF THE 345TH'S YOUNG MEN SEEMED TO SENSE AND ACCEPT that they would not survive. Robert Scudder of the 500th Bomb Squadron remembered that his friend and onetime copilot Floyd Good "often spoke of his mother, whom he loved dearly. She was his idol and best friend. While I never met her, I felt I knew his mother well. While in training and overseas, many evenings I would listen to Good write letters to his mother out loud. Somehow or other, I believe Good seemed to feel he would never return home alive. This gave him an underlying sense of bravery none of us had."[1]

On July 2, 1944, the 345th sent twelve aircraft—six each from the 499th and 500th Bomb Squadrons—to fly a barge sweep to western New Guinea near the coastal town of Manokwari. They were staged in advance out of Hollandia. Floyd Good flew on the mission. The two squadrons took off early in the morning, but dust from the airstrip and hazy skies kept them from joining.

It was a desultory effort. The 499th found little that was worthwhile and consequently strafed and bombed various nondescript buildings and native huts. For its part, the 500th did find a pair of barges but only managed to sink one while leaving the other foundering but still afloat. The men complained about the aircraft being loaded with parademolition bombs that malfunctioned too often and were unsuited for maritime targets. They had a point as the bombs—suspended beneath parachutes—couldn't be skipped into the vessels, and it was too difficult to drop them accurately on a moving target, especially considering the wind.

Neither squadron noted opposition either from the air or the ground, and the recovery back to Hollandia was uneventful. Both squadrons landed separately and taxied back to their respective parking areas. Only then did the day turn disastrous. "All planes had landed safely and the pilots were cutting their engines after taxiing to their hardstandings [*sic*]. The bombay [*sic*] doors in Lieutenant Good's airplane were opened and two 100-pound parademo bombs fell out, apparently having failed to release while over the target. The bombs lay there for seconds and then burst with a terrific explosion, blasting the airplane in two and causing it to explode. Crews of nearby airplanes scurried for cover and other men, still in their planes, tumbled out, headed for the ditches."

The scene, backdropped by the inferno that had been Good's plane only seconds earlier, was a gruesome one. Good, together with his copilot and navigator, perished in the explosion. The radio operator's arm was blown away, and he died later that day. The engineer had been under the wing, chocking the wheels with large rocks, when the bombs detonated. He was badly injured but survived. Miraculously, the crew's gunner walked away.

A jeep jammed with seven ground crewmen had pulled close to the aircraft so that they could perform postmission maintenance after the aircrew climbed down. They "were torn to death by the explosion which left them draped in grotesque fashion over the vehicle, and six more were injured, some seriously. An officer from a service unit and an enlisted man from a chemical warfare unit were also injured, the enlisted man seriously."

George Hurt, a bombardier with the 500th, was part of the mission that day. "My plane was sitting about fifty feet away," he wrote in his diary. "Received 23 shell holes on the side of the explosion. Good thing I was slow getting out, or I might have gotten my ass blown off."[2]

There were heroes that day. Men ran to the burning wreck and braved the skin-melting heat and exploding ammunition to pull the dead and injured away. Others manned nearby aircraft and taxied them out of harm's way. Fire crews raced to extinguish the blaze.

Heroics aside, the accident took a gruesome toll. At the end of the day, the count was eleven dead and five injured. The disaster could have been prevented. It was the navigator's duty to check the bomb bay after a mission and to let the pilot know whether it was clear. If it wasn't, the pilot had the option of salvoing the remaining bombs into the ocean or jungle or taking other precautions to ensure they could be safely brought back to base.

"It so happened that the airplane Good flew on that day was a new model B-25D-2," said Robert Scudder. "One of the changes on that airplane was the elimination of the manhole-sized cover on top of the bomb bay where the crew could get a good look inside the bomb bay in flight. In the new model, a small two-inch peephole replaced the manhole."

Francis Cantanzarita was one of the men killed in the explosion. Beforehand he was excited about his job and wrote his father, "Maybe you've read about us fellows in the squadron. We are known as the Rough Raiders and our ships are out a lot. . . . I do some work on the flight line, which isn't too dangerous, but we have to be careful. I'm going to have a lot of interesting things to tell you when I see you again." He closed his letter with "I'll be home soon and hope none of you are worrying."[3]

The mission that day had been a barge sweep. Although they operated large cargo ships and tankers, the Japanese were especially reliant on barges, luggers, and smaller classes of freighters to move men and material to their more isolated outposts. The reasons were several. Chief among them was the fact that Japan lacked the resources and industrial capacity to manufacture large numbers of big ships; certainly it was incapable of matching the output of the United States. But moving the big ships between major ports, where their cargoes could be offloaded and redistributed by the smaller freighters, was also more efficient. Moreover, when a large vessel was destroyed, its large cargo was also destroyed, whereas relatively less material went down with the smaller freighters. Another advantage of the smaller vessels was that U.S. submarine commanders were sometimes reluctant to "waste" torpedoes on them. On the other hand, those same commanders often surfaced and destroyed them with surface guns.

The most ubiquitous of these freighters were steel or wood "sea trucks." Generally about a hundred feet in length and twenty feet at the beam, they were lightly armed, carried a crew of less than a dozen, and had cargo capacities of up to three hundred tons. Designated "Sugar Dogs" by the U.S. Navy, they were very basic and often didn't even carry radio transmitters.

But best of all—for the Japanese—they could be built quickly and cheaply. Mahogany and teak were plentiful in the Philippines, Indochina, and the South Pacific. With almost unlimited construction material, Japanese experts formed teams of skilled craftsmen and unskilled laborers capable of delivering finished vessels in less than two months. This was particularly important as U.S. air and naval units—the 345th among them—were very proficient at destroying them.

The accident that blew Floyd Good and so many other men to bits was spectacularly gruesome. Sadly, although they were generally less remarkable, ground mishaps took lives all through the war. For example, Fred DeCobellis of the 345th's 501st Bomb Squadron was working on the flight line when an Australian aircraft attempted a forced landing. The aircraft missed the airstrip, and DeCobellis was struck by one of its wings and thrown into the turning propeller of another aircraft. He was killed instantly. The squadron noted that DeCobellis "had always been one of the most reliable and dependable mechanics" and that squadron members attended his funeral the next day "with a feeling of respect and sorrow."[4]

DeCobellis's parents were obviously devastated when they learned of Fred's death. They were doubly devastated when they learned that their other son, Ernest, had been killed in Sicily only a few days earlier.

Bad luck killed DeCobellis, but inattention was just as deadly. James Walker of the 500th Bomb Squadron was helping to park an aircraft. His good friend Ben Muller recalled him as a "tall, nice-looking man" and recounted how he was killed: "His plane had come in and he'd put the chocks under the wheels and the prop was just barely turning and he stepped into it and it killed him."[5]

Combat deaths were disturbing, but senseless and preventable loss of life caused a special and empty hurt. The men who lifted Walker's body away certainly carried the grisly experience with them all their days.

⚊ ⚊

Crews fresh from the States continued to arrive at the 345th. Jay Moore was a new pilot assigned to the 501st. He arrived at Nadzab during mid-July and was duly impressed by the vista. "Gee hon, you should be here," he wrote his girlfriend, Billie Riddle. "This valley and the mountains are beautiful." And he was at least as impressed and excited about being assigned to the 345th. "I believe it's a swell outfit and the guys are rough, tough, and all men. They're all swell guys and I'm proud to be part of the outfit. Our group is known as the Tree Top Terrors, so we really get down where they play for keeps."[6]

⚊ ⚊

The 345th pulled up stakes again at the end of July. The campaigns to which the group had contributed were successful and had forced the Japanese further back toward their Home Islands. Consequently, continued operations required that the 345th's men and aircraft be moved closer to where the Japanese could be found and killed.

For that reason, comfortable, organized, well-provisioned Nadzab was left behind. The 345th was sent to the recently captured island of Biak at the mouth of Geelvink Bay on New Guinea's northwest coast. The island was a major Japanese base when the American Army landed on May 27, 1944. But Japanese resistance was surprisingly violent, and Biak wasn't declared secure until mid-August—after the 345th arrived.

Irving Horwitz, a navigator with the 500th Bomb Squadron, recalled that he and pilot Lynn Daker flew a courier mission to Biak while the island was still being contested. "They were getting ready to move airplanes in," he said, "and the engineers were busy cutting back the jungle and grading the runways and such. Shortly after we landed, the Japs attacked with a bunch of airplanes and started strafing everything in sight. Lynn and I ran for our lives and dived into a thick section of brush, right into a slit trench—a latrine. Fortunately, the beach was just a short distance away and we were able to wash ourselves clean once the Japs left."

As when the 345th moved to Dobodura and then to Nadzab, the group's aircraft were used to move material and equipment. And they were stuffed with as much as they could carry. "We had refrigerators in the bomb bay, and lumber sticking out the tail comb," said Jay Moore. "And you didn't worry about weight and balance. If you could chin yourself on the tail skid and the nose wheel stayed on the ground, then you flew it."[7]

When the 345th's men reached Biak, they found that the airfield to which they were assigned, Mokmer, was only barely operational, and living conditions were primitive. "This is really quite a place," wrote Moore to his sweetheart. "We had to hack out a place in the jungle with machetes to put up our tent, and if you think that isn't a job, just try it." And evidence of the recent fighting was everywhere. Moore recalled his first walk to evening chow: "I counted twenty-five dead Japanese between our tent and the mess hall in various states of decay and everything else."[8]

Some of the men lived with the dead on Biak. James Baross of the 501st Bomb Squadron recalled that they were directed to prepare an area for their tents and that he and his tent mates cleared vegetation and debris away from a section of white coral soil. "As luck would have it, the flattest, most desirable spot had a Japanese body almost dead center. We had been told to not touch bodies—that they were often booby-trapped and would explode if moved."

Refusing to be stymied, the men simply built up the area with more soil and covered the body. "From time-to-time the Japanese soldier would wear through and a few helmets full of coral [soil] would be required to put him to rest."[9]

Water at Biak was also a problem. "We had almost no fresh water for a period of weeks," said Ben Miller. "Since it rained so often, we all pulled out the flaps of our tents and caught the water, running it into containers. This was almost enough to keep us clean by using our helmets as wash basins."[10]

Jay Moore's recollection nearly mirrored Ben Miller's. "Getting cleaned up today was simple," he wrote his girlfriend. "All I did was step out in the rain for a nice shower. While I was taking a shower I caught my helmet full of water and shaved. Now, if the ants, bugs, flies and what-have-you would leave me alone, I'd be alright."[11]

"Morale is good, but it has been better," declared the group's head-quarters. "Officers and non-commissioned officers have done the physical work to clear jungle from coral, dig post holes and set up places to work. Approximately half the enlisted personnel are constantly on detail clearing the jungle all the time."

Ben Miller was put to work with an air hammer and a case of dynamite to bore a freshwater well out of the unyielding coral of which Biak was made. After punching to a depth of more than thirty feet and finding no water, the men declared the effort a bust. "We could not abandon this splendid piece of engineering," Miller remembered, "so we had the carpenter put a platform on it with several latrine holes, and a sign that read, 'The Damndest, Deepest ****house in the Pacific.'"[12]

Still, conditions improved, as radio operator Ray Link of the 501st Bomb Squadron wrote in a letter home: "You can't buy anything here. They give you everything: Cigarettes, tooth paste, shaving cream, soap, razor blades, etc. We have real good food. Fresh eggs for the last 3 mornings." His letter also highlighted the fact that the American military leadership was committed to keeping its men healthy. "We have to take vitamin pills to make up for the green vegetables we miss. We take an atabrine tablet every day or two to guard against malaria. It turns your skin a little yellow, but doesn't harm you."[13]

The scattered remnants of Japan's 35th and 36th Infantry Divisions still prowling the island certainly did not enjoy the same support. Despite the fact that the island had been declared secure, they remained a danger. "One day," said James Baross, "they came down and set up a machine gun and sprayed our squadron area, hitting one of our cooks but doing no other damage. We had lots of cooks."[14]

In fact, the starving Japanese grew to be persistent pests; they sneaked onto the airfield to steal food and clothing and other material. They commonly slipped into tents at night to thieve items from under the noses of the 345th's sleeping men. Stories spread of Japanese soldiers standing in the chow line in stolen uniforms.

Consequently, the 345th's men carried side arms and other weapons much more often than they had at Nadzab. "Some of the Japs up in the hills are getting hungry and desperate," wrote Jay Moore, "so they're sneaking down at nite, stealing things. A bunch came down last night and one of them stopped enough lead for ten guys."[15]

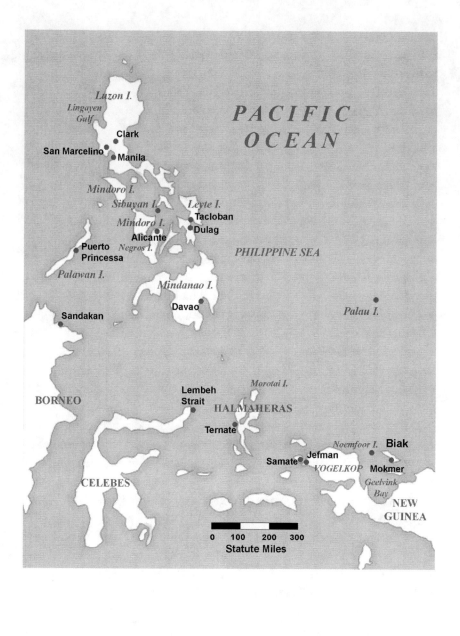

Luzon I.

Lingayen Gulf

Clark

San Marcelino

Manila

PACIFIC OCEAN

Mindoro I.

Sibuyan I.

Leyte I.

Tacloban

Mindoro I.

Dulag

Alicante

Puerto Princessa

Negros I.

PHILIPPINE SEA

Palawan I.

Mindanao I.

Davao

Palau I.

Sandakan

Morotai I.

Lembeh Strait

BORNEO

HALMAHERAS

Ternate

Noemfoor I.

Biak

Samate

Jefman

VOGELKOP

Mokmer

Geelvink Bay

CELEBES

NEW GUINEA

0   100   200   300
Statute Miles

Another incident was described by Bert Rosenbaum, whose friend Johnson Craig had always complained that, as a nonflyer, he would never have an opportunity to "kill a Jap." Rosenbaum recalled, "One day, a very little Jap came into camp pointing his finger at himself saying, 'bang!'"

Joking, Rosenbaum suggested the man ought to be taken to Craig so that he might have a chance to kill an enemy soldier. "This was done," said Rosenbaum. "Johnson was eating a candy bar when he was told he could kill the little Jap. He looked at him and said, 'Kill that little thing?' And to the Jap he said, 'Here, have a candy bar.'"[16]

Even though enemy troops still skulked about the island, the threat wasn't enough to dissuade the 345th's men from exploring. Ben Miller remembered, "Partway up the hill was a large post with an [Japanese] officer tied to it. He wore breeches and boots, but no shirt. We figured perhaps he wanted to give up and was tied to the post and executed as the top of his head was blown off. We called him Willie. Near him were several dozen women in a circle, totally undressed and decomposing in the tropical heat."[17]

There were caves in the hills near where the men were billeted, and James Baross and a couple of comrades grabbed their pistols and flashlights and climbed into one of them. He let his eyes adjust to the dark rather than use his flashlight—batteries were scarce. "Inside there was little light, but by carefully stepping upon the hundreds of coconuts on the floor we could keep our feet out of the muck that covered the cavern floor."

Despite his caution, Baross slipped and fell. "I turned on my flashlight to better see to get up and found, to my complete dismay, that what I had been walking on so carefully were not coconuts at all. They were skulls! Japanese skulls. We left soon after that."[18]

Adding to all the friction associated with the move to Biak was the fact that the 498th's B-25Hs had been reconfigured. "Early in the month," noted the group headquarters, "the 498th [Bomb] Squadron was withdrawn from operation to allow modification of their Hs, the removal of the 75-millimeter cannon. It had been found that this weapon not only had a very limited use, but that its use involved serious maintenance problems. So, meanwhile, the other three squadrons carried on."

Despite the primitive conditions, the 498th's temporary removal from combat operations, and still-at-large Japanese soldiers, the 345th's men buckled down and went to work. "Although our four squadrons were not quite settled," said Aldridge Nichols, "still and all we were ready to carry the ball as Fifth Bomber Command called the signals. And carry it we did, starting off with three strikes on the very first day of the month [August]."

This was during the same period that the criteria for rotating air-crews home was changed. A complete tour was no longer based on the number of combat missions a man had flown. "At about this time, a point system was devised to determine when we had our fill of flying missions and would be sent back to the States," said James Baross. "A simple mission would yield just a few points, while a particularly hazard-ous mission would yield a lot more. We did not know just how or who did the record keeping, or evaluating, but 'ours was not to reason why,' so we simply did what we were told to do. It was all a mystery to us."[19]

Baross recalled that the concept of mission counting had also been imperfect and confounding. Missions to targets that had already been neutralized or softened were sometimes disallowed after the fact. "So when we had flown fifteen missions we would go back to thirteen, and after flying twenty-six, we would go back to twenty-three, and so on. This was disconcerting, and a real problem."[20]

William Welch, like Baross, was a radio-gunner. Baross recalled that Welch "had finally completed his fifty missions and was all set to go back to the States. But a directive came through eliminating two of the mis-sions Bill had flown." Accordingly, Welch was put back on flight status.

Baross was anxious for Welch to complete his missions and go home to his new wife. But he was somewhat upset when Welch was assigned in his place to fly with Eugene Nirdlinger's crew on a barge sweep to the west of the Halmahera island group on August 15, 1944. Baross was Nirdlinger's normal radio operator and Baross liked flying with him as he was widely considered a very competent pilot who always got his crew home. Flying with Nirdlinger—in Baross's place—Welch stood a good chance of finally completing his missions.

Baross was assigned to fly with a new lieutenant whom he did not respect. "He was a poor pilot," Baross said. "We used to call him 'the room clerk,' that being his civilian position prior to going into the service."

Baross approached Nirdlinger to plead his case. "Lieutenant Nirdlinger said he understood, but that tomorrow would be the last mission Bill Welch needed to have enough to go home, and after that I would be back on the crew and all would be well. I had to be satisfied with that."

The mission was not expected to be a particularly tough one. "We had been flying there for some time and had it pretty well softened up," said Baross. Three of the 345th's four squadrons—the 499th, 500th, and 501st—put up six aircraft each loaded with four five-hundred-pound bombs. After the group got airborne out of Biak and rendezvoused, the long overwater flight was uneventful, and the fighter escort picked up over Ajoe Island had no trade. In fact, the group found nothing worthwhile to attack and consequently headed for the secondary target of Ternate, where they were to hit "enemy supplies, installations and personnel."

"As we approached the target, on the shore of a large island," Baross said, "we dropped down to minimum altitude and made our approach from over the water. We made our pass, dropped our bombs, did our strafing, and pulled away—bearing a bit off to the right." Most of the rest of the group made similar attacks against the town's jetty, various buildings, "native quarters," and the sultan of Ternate's palace, which dated from 1796.

Nirdlinger's attack did not go smoothly. For undetermined reasons he either didn't or couldn't release his bombs over Ternate. Rather than make another attack on the same target—which was now fully alert—he gathered the rest of the squadron and flew to the western end of Halmahera Island. Approaching Dodinga Bay, Nirdlinger attacked the jetty with John Nolan on his wing. Nolan's crew submitted a statement: "We were coming in for a run on the jetty, intending to make a strafing pass on some buildings about 300 feet north of the jetty. Lt. Nirdlinger was to bomb the jetty itself. We were flying about 200 feet altitude when suddenly airplane 383 [Nirdlinger's aircraft] climbed sharply and its tail hit our right wing. Our plane went out of control immediately, but we managed to climb the hill directly ahead of us."

The tail of Nirdlinger's aircraft broke away when it hit the right wing of Nolan's bomber. Nirdlinger's bomber and his crew—including William Welch—plunged into the jungled hills and perished in the resultant explosion. Nolan and his copilot, Ed Bina, ordered the crew to prepare for a water landing but soon discovered that the aircraft was flyable despite the fact that the right aileron was damaged and five feet of the outer wing was bent upward. "It took all of our strength to hold the plane under control—both pilot and copilot working the controls continuously," wrote Nolan. "We trimmed the plane with full right aileron and full right rudder, boosted the manifold of our left engine to 10 inches above that of the right engine and 100 RPM greater than the right engine. The plane flew at a 15-degree bank." So configured, Nolan and Bina gradually coaxed the aircraft up to five thousand feet.

Exhausted, their arms and legs numb and shaking with fatigue, Nolan and Bina wrestled with their aircraft for more than three hours before the island of Noemfoor came into view. Finally assured of reaching safety, they readied to land at Kamiri airfield. However, as they made their approach, the right engine failed.

> Our plane started to skid and drop about 1,000 feet per minute. We were unable to straighten it out. We pulled our wheels up quickly, feathered both props, got the plane under control, cut the disconnects, and opened the hatch. Our tail hit first and the plane maintained a level attitude. The water rushed in as soon as the nose hit and we landed in smooth water about 4–5 feet deep over a coral shelf. Our crew got out in an orderly fashion and got away from the plane as quickly as possible, as the nose had begun to smoke. An Army "Duck" [DUKW amphibious wheeled transport] was about one half mile away when we crash landed, and they came over and picked us up.

Nolan—one of the 345th's stalwarts—was physically and mentally exhausted. He was removed from flight status and eventually returned to the States.

James Baross was crushed. Although he had safely completed the mission—and with a pilot for whom he had little regard—he despaired at the loss of Nirdlinger and his friends. "Losing my whole crew was terrible. I felt bad about that. And Bill Welch, on the eve of his going home, getting killed that way. That was my worst day overseas." He spent the rest of it boxing the personal belongings of the deceased.

Although the reason is not captured in the group or mission summary reports for the attack on Ternate on August 15, 1944, the crews' debriefings reveal that they were instructed to avoid hitting Fort Oranje, which was located well within the town. For instance, Robert Erskine reported that he "completed his run 1,000 feet south of Fort Oranje," while Edmund Kasten "resumed strafing, having ceased strafing while flying over Fort Oranje." Roland Thomas "swung sharply to the right in order to avoid Fort Oranje and was unable to release his three bombs. These were later salvoed at sea en route back to Mokmer." The explanation emerges in James Baross's diary entry describing Ternate as a "town of 30,000 and prison camp for the Allies." Fort Oranje held Allied POWs.

Jay Moore flew his first combat mission, a nighttime weather reconnaissance, from Biak. He was assigned as the copilot. The purpose was to confirm that the weather over the next day's target was clear enough to fly the mission.

After accidentally penetrating a thunderstorm, the crew was spit out the other side and into the clear. The rest of the route was uneventful, and the weather over the objective was clear. "Well," remembered Moore, "this pilot thought the target was a Japanese fighter base. He said, 'I'm going to stay up here until about daylight and see if we can't stir up some of those fighters; get them up and get a scrap out of them.'"

The crew's navigator was at the end of his combat tour and was decidedly against the pilot's idea. He made an unequivocal declaration: "You are like hell. We've done what we came here for. Get this airplane headed for home because if you don't, I'm gonna put this .45 [pistol] right over your head."[21]

The pilot needed no time to consider the navigator's instructions and immediately headed back to Biak.

Whereas flying personnel were assured of returning to the States following completion of their combat tours—regardless of whether it was determined by counting missions or tallying points—the ground men, except for few exceptions, were stuck for the duration. Douglas MacArthur, short of everything but disease and Japanese, had declared in mid-1943, "Except for the physically unfit, for air crew personnel returned under a special policy [mission or point count], and for personnel definitely unqualified [e.g., mental issues and criminals] for duty in the command, personnel can be returned only under the most exceptional circumstances."[22]

This policy remained in effect for the remainder of the war and was derided by many of the men. "Join Mac and never come back" was only one of many phrases heard throughout the theater.[23] Some higher-performing outfits, such as the 345th, suffered less from morale problems than others, in part because of good leadership. But the group also didn't start combat operations until the summer of 1943, whereas others had been fighting since the start of the war.

An additional point of friction was the disparity in the furlough policies for airmen and ground personnel. The aircrews—both officers and enlisted men—were sent to Sydney for rest every couple of months or so, which paid dividends in improved morale. And the practice made sense as the flyers faced death on every mission.

The ground-support men—as essential as they were and as hard as they worked—were rarely, if ever, sent away for rest. This, as expected, caused at least some grumbling and resentment. The 501st Bomb Squadron noted the difference in treatment: "Any system that results in enlisted men going a year or more without one day's leave is obviously inadequate. The necessity of rest for men stationed in this area has been recognized by all parties concerned. However, at present there are inadequate facilities for getting them to the Mainland. At the present rate, there will be men in our unit who will not be able to go on furlough for many months to come." The situation did improve over the course of the war, but never to anyone's satisfaction.

Although hardly equal to furloughs to Sydney, one change made during this time had a small impact on morale but ultimately made an enormous contribution to the 345th's legacy. "We tired of calling our-selves the Tree Top Terrors," the group noted, "and set about renaming the 345th." A contest was held, and the winning name was "Air Apaches." The head of an Indian brave in profile, submitted by Charles Pusheton-equa, was chosen as the accompanying emblem.

"The Apaches were an extremely warlike tribe," the group observed, "noted for savagery and violence.... [T]he name seemed to fit our mission in this war. We came upon our enemy with sudden speed and without warning."[24] Indeed, the nickname was a good fit, came out of the mouth more easily than the previous one and conjured vivid imagery. It was immediately embraced both inside and outside the group, and newspaper copy detailing the exploits of the Air Apaches started to appear Stateside.

As they always had, accidents continued to take a toll on the 345th. Jay Moore and others watched as Edmund Kasten of the 501st Bomb Squadron returned to Mokmer Airfield at Biak on August 30, 1944. "He was in trouble," said Moore. "One engine was out and he was trying to make it to the strip. He wasn't a hundred yards off of the strip but he wasn't going to make it." A cliff fronted the approach end of the runway, and Kasten, realizing that he wouldn't clear it, turned to land on the beach at its foot. He didn't make it.

"We were all out in the squadron area watching him and everybody ran down to the wreck," said Moore. "I got to the cliff, looked down, and here come a guy up from the wreckage. He had a guy's leg—from the knee up to the thigh—in his arms, and he was carrying it very tenderly. I can still see him walk up, lay it on the ground, and then run back to see if he could do some more."[25]

The Air Apaches were well settled on Biak by early September 1944. Indeed, the open-air movies to which the group had grown accustomed were enhanced by the special efforts of individuals, as described in the monthly report: "Corporal Michalowsky brought forth one of the finest theatres we've ever had—painted, parachuted [for curtains], and com-plete, even to the point of the classic masks on either side of the proscenium." Aside from cosmetics, the new "Apache Theater" was lauded for the technical excellence of its projection and sound.

The Japanese were evidently unimpressed with the new theater and continued to harry the island with single-aircraft bombing attacks, especially at night. William Witherell was the 345th's photography officer and also served as the historian. He described the attack of September 1: "A full moon brought evidence that the enemy's air offensive was not ineffectual. A one-hour alert, starting at 2125 resulted in three men killed, three hospitalized and three planes damaged. The morning of the 2nd found a great many new and improved foxholes under construction. We had a brutal reminder that the war was still on." The three dead men were from the 501st Bomb Squadron, and their number rose to four when one of the wounded men died a few days later.

James Baross wrote in his diary the effects these harrying raids had: "Was no fun getting up this morning as we have been bombed every night lately. 14 men killed and 25 injured. Started a foxhole today."[26] Ray Link, still new to combat, wrote his mother about his fear of these sorts of raids: "I have undergone a few enemy air raids. It is quite exciting. The first one gave me a funny feeling, if you know what I mean—scared."[27]

The group launched a mission the following day, September 2, 1944. The 499th, 500th, and 501st Bomb Squadrons were tasked with hitting enemy aircraft parked at Langoan Airfield in the northeastern Celebes. However, when the expected fighter escort of P-38s failed to make the rendezvous over Tifou Island, the group's fourteen B-25s flexed to the secondary target: shipping, wharves, and warehousing at Lembeh Town in Lembeh Strait, just off the northeast tip of the Celebes. Each aircraft carried seventy-two twenty-three-pound parafrag bombs in new, recently fielded racks.

The three squadrons dropped low over the Molucca Sea and headed northeast into the bay that funneled into the narrow passage leading to Lembeh Town. By unhappy coincidence they encountered a Japanese minelayer exiting the strait. The 499th reported that the formation was "met by intense, heavy and medium antiaircraft fire from a C/M [coastal minelayer] which at that moment was coming out of the bay."

The unit further observed, "The field of fire was excellent for this vessel throughout the run."

The small ship directed the brunt of its fire at the six aircraft of the 500th Bomb Squadron, which led the group. The two flights of three aircraft each, with Max Mortensen at the head, flogged through the antiaircraft fire only to be met with more from the surrounding hills and the town's main road. The 501st and 499th Bomb Squadrons, with four aircraft each, followed.

Mortensen's bomb rack malfunctioned and failed to release any bombs. Nevertheless he thoroughly strafed the target as well as a small transport ship. Flying on Mortensen's right wing, Lynn Daker's aircraft was hit, but he dumped his bombs into the warehouses and wharves and used his guns to silence a four-gun antiaircraft pit. Thomas Symington, to Mortensen's left, likewise released his load of parafrags and, like Daker, was hit by antiaircraft fire. He could push his control column no further forward than the neutral position and was forced to resort to trim tabs to climb or descend his aircraft.

Behind Mortensen's flight, Robert Truman's bomb racks also failed. His two wingmen, Allan Lay and Lloyd Bardwell, were shot down. Bardwell's aircraft was hit by antiaircraft fire. The 500th's mission summary report noted, "Lieutenant Lay broke formation to give aid to Lieutenant Bardwell who, at the time, was barely keeping his airplane under control. While in his turn he was attacked by two enemy SSF [single-seat fighter] and shot down." Lay's aircraft streamed smoke and went into a gradual descent. A short time later it crashed into Mount Tongkoko and exploded—there could have been no survivors. Bardwell made a water landing northeast of Lembeh Town.

Behind the 500th, the four aircraft of the 499th skirted the minelayer's antiaircraft fire and flew too far off course. Consequently, they put only a very few parafrags on the target. As they sped away to the northeast, Bardwell's aircraft and crew were spotted in the water. The 499th reported,

Lieutenant [Irving] Mosser, bringing up the rear, saw the 500th plane down in the water . . . at the same time perceiving an enemy

fighter heading in the same direction. Without hesitation, Lieutenant Mosser increased his speed and changed his course to intercept the enemy fighter, now definitely described as a Zeke. As the Zeke made a pass at the members of the crew now floating defenseless in the water, Lieutenant Mosser made a pass getting in several bursts with his guns and probably scoring some hits. The Zeke did not attempt to retaliate, but continued on over the stricken ship, breaking [off] the attack.

Meanwhile the four 501st B-25s put all their bombs into the target area and strafed it for good measure. Flying away from Lembeh Town, Hilding Jacobson, at the head of the 501st, spotted Bardwell's aircraft and crew in the water. The squadron stated that Jacobson "led his flight back to the crippled plane where he and his two wingmen, Lieutenant [Harold] Billig and Lieutenant [Robert] Erskine, dropped supplies, life rafts, etc."

"Jacobson," the report continued, "notified his wingmen that he was going to stay over the downed plane and told them that they could stay or return to base, reminding them their gas supply was low. Both pilots elected to stay and remained with Lieutenant Jacobson in the area for approximately forty-five minutes."

"Five survivors were seen to have gotten out of the plane and cling to a partially inflated life raft," the report declared, "but as the last circling airplane left the scene, the life raft had vanished and only three men were seen struggling in the water." The fate of Bardwell and his crew remains unknown.

Despite the antiaircraft fire and malfunctioning bomb racks, the Air Apaches left Lembeh Town burning. They had little interest in returning. The 500th reported that their crews "reiterated the unsuitability of this target for strafers, due to the ideal defensive nature of the terrain." The squadron additionally declared, "The target was very well defended and seasoned veterans participating in the raid stated that the A/A was the most intense they had seen since Rabaul."

The 345th's missions through the rest of September 1944 were similar to, if not so deadly as, the September 2 raid on Lembeh Town. The September 19 mission to Sidate, an airfield in the northeastern Celebes, was noteworthy only for a gimmick that received publicity back in the

States. "Tired of hearing that the Japs had been 'hit with everything *but* the kitchen sink,'" noted the 500th Bomb Squadron's mission summary report, "the squadron decided to include that item of plumbing as the last word in suitable missiles."

In fact, the men crafted and painted a kitchen sink, which was loaded aboard Max Mortensen's aircraft, *Rita's Wagon*. With Tal Epps as his gunner, he led all four of the group's squadrons across the enemy airfield. "Captain Mortensen," the report continued, "with unerring accuracy, toggled out the sink just south of the airstrip, while the cameras clicked." What the Japanese thought of the curious artifact—if they ever found it—remains unrecorded. The actual strike was unremarkable, and the aircrews found little of value upon which to expend their bombs and bullets.

If nothing else, September was noteworthy for the fact that the 345th attacked the Philippines for the first time. However, poor weather curtailed operations to a very great degree at the end of the month, and in fact the last mission was launched on September 23.

―◆―

Jay Moore described in a letter to his girlfriend what the 345th's men wore during their missions at this time. Because they flew at low altitude in the tropics, they had no need of the sheep-lined jackets and heated suits worn by their European counterparts. Rather, their kit was more everyday in appearance: "On our missions we wear a khaki uniform—no zippers of any kind because in case you're forced [down] zippers rust and you either won't be able to get your clothes on or off. Oh, yes," he continued, "we wear a parachute, Mae West [life vest], headset, mike [microphone], carry a .45 [pistol], a knife, ammunition and over the target, a flak suit and flak helmet."[28]

―◆―

Throughout the 345th's combat career, many of its crews flew back to base with holes in their aircraft created by Japanese bullets and shells. But few actually brought the enemy munitions back with them. "Lynn Daker and I came off the target on one mission," Irving Horwitz said, "and saw something rolling around on the floor of the cockpit between us."

The two pilots knew that their ship had been hit but were additionally alarmed when they realized that the out-of-place object was a medium-caliber antiaircraft cannon round. "We didn't know if it had a timed fuze that was set to explode any moment, or it had some sort of contact fuze that would set it off if we tried to touch it. Or, if it was just a dud."

Daker and Horwitz decided not to diddle with the enemy shell and ignored it as best they could as it rattled around for the next several hours. "We landed with no problem," Horwitz said, "and the ordnance men came and took it away."

CHAPTER ELEVEN

"Love to All and Write Real Often"

OPERATIONALLY, OCTOBER 1944 WAS A JEKYLL AND HYDE MONTH AS the 345th flew eleven missions during the first eleven days and only one mission during the remainder. Most of the month's efforts primarily targeted any type of shipping that might support Japanese defensive operations in the Philippines, as the archipelago was the obvious next step for the Allied advance from New Guinea. In fact, the 345th's monthly summary declared, "We were out to hit and sink everything that could carry men and supplies across water. If there had been a water wing factory within range of our aircraft, we would have hit that, too."

And during this time, the young men of the 345th continued to be young men. Ray Link, a radio operator with the 501st, had flown six missions by this time and made many friends. A letter to his aunt reveals that the opposite sex was at the forefront of their minds. "Tell Mary Sue again to please send me the tinted portrait of her. Tell her to send me a lot more pictures of her and her girlfriends. Especially the ones in their bathing suits—the boys like them."[1]

The group did manage to mount a notable effort toward the end of the month. Staging from Biak into Morotai on October 23, seventeen B-25s were sent against Sandakan on the northeast coast of Borneo the following day. There they found the water "fat with shipping." After making three low-level bombing and strafing passes, the Air Apaches left several vessels sinking and multiple shore installations afire. No casualties were sustained.

The slowdown in operations during the latter part of the month was due to many factors, among them the fact that, from September and into October, the group had swapped out many of its older aircraft for new. The operations and maintenance men transferred out forty B-25D and B-25G aircraft and accepted forty-three new B-25Js. This was more than a paperwork exercise as it involved quite a bit of maintenance work and check flights on both the outgoing and the incoming aircraft. By the end of the month the group had sixty-three aircraft on hand as opposed to fifty-six at the beginning. Happily—and unusually—the 345th counted zero men killed, missing, or wounded for all of October.

During the previous month, September 1944, the 345th started receiving its first B-25Js. Drawing on lessons learned from all the combat theaters, North American Aviation made a number of improvements to this final model of the venerable aircraft that had served the group so well since its inception. Improved as it was, the plane proved the deadliest that the 345th operated during its combat career.

The B-25J was produced in two variants. A traditional glazed-nosed model was best suited to the medium-altitude bombing missions flown by the B-25 units in the Mediterranean and southern Europe. Those received by the Air Apaches were modified to carry up to four forward-firing guns in the nose.

But the 345th's crews most favored the solid-nosed strafing variant of the B-25J. Like the glazed-nosed model, it no longer carried the unpopular and ineffective seventy-five-millimeter cannon. In fact, the cannons aboard the Air Apache B-25Hs had been removed much earlier. Instead, the solid-nosed B-25J carried a total of eight .50-caliber machine guns in the nose. Moreover, it retained the .50-caliber blister guns—two below each side of the cockpit. These twelve fixed, forward-firing guns gave the pilot control over a withering degree of firepower that equated to more than 110 rounds per second. The B-25J also retained the two .50-caliber machine guns in the top turret, as well as the two waist guns and the two tail guns. So armed, the aircraft carried more guns than the much larger B-17 and B-24.

Other enhancements included factory-installed armor for the pilots below, behind, in front, and to the sides of the cockpit. The bomb bays were modified to carry up to two sixteen-hundred-pound bombs. Additionally, the radio compartment was modified to accommodate a 150-gallon fuel tank, and the wings could be fitted with racks to carry the five-inch rockets that were just then being fielded. A more powerful variant of the Wright Cyclone R-2600 engine powered the aircraft. This upgraded engine was as loud or louder than its predecessors. Indeed, the B-25 cockpit had always been very noisy compared to those of other aircraft in part due to the location of the engines. But, as one pilot observed, "the B-25 was built for combat, not for comfort."

The new engine was intended to help offset the added weight of the improvements, but it still wasn't powerful enough. A loaded B-25J on a single engine struggled to maintain flying speed. The coming months would see many Air Apaches, flying on just one engine, stagger into the sea.

Curiously, for a short time the 345th had to do without strike camera photography. The 498th Bomb Squadron reported, "No cameras have been installed in the B-25Js, for no provisions were made for cameras. Modifications will be made in the near future."

The receipt of new aircraft aside, the second half of October was operationally slow because the Air Apaches were readying to move to the Philippines. In fact, American Army units came ashore at Leyte Gulf on October 20, 1944. However, the Navy provided the preponderance of the air cover those units received. Most of the Army's air units, the 345th being an example, were still based too far south to travel so far and spend any meaningful time in the area.

Of course, both Douglas MacArthur and George Kenney—by this time commander of the Far East Air Forces, which included both the Fifth and Thirteenth Air Forces—were anxious to move their air groups closer to the fight, to a base where they could not only fly support missions for the ground units but also hit a greater range of targets without first staging forward.

To that end, anticipating the invasion's success, Kenney embarked some of his organizations before the first soldiers ever set foot on Philippine soil. Indeed, the bulk of the 345th's ground echelon and a portion of its aircrews were put aboard two Liberty ships, the *Orland Loomis* and

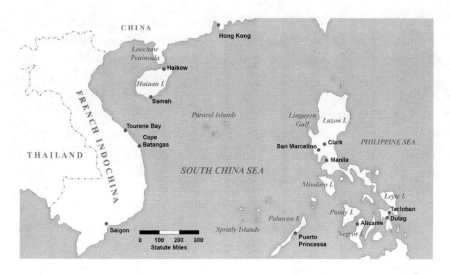

the *Thomas Nelson*, on October 15. The men aboard the Loomis, which had proved quite comfortable, were transferred to the much less accom-modating *Morrison R. Waite* a few days later. The *Nelson* carried men from the 498th and 499th Bomb Squadrons, while the *Waite* carried the men of the 500th and 501st. Much of their equipment was loaded onto another Liberty ship, the *Leonidas Merritt*. By the evening of October 18, after sailing east away from the Philippines, the ships had joined a large convoy in Hollandia's Humboldt Bay.

There the Air Apaches waited for a couple of days as equipment and material was loaded and other ships joined the rapidly growing force. Most of the group's men had little to do. The men aboard the *Nelson* were allowed to swim, and only after jumping from the ship's rigging and spending quite some time in the water did Ben Miller discover that his previously filthy life jacket was actually light blue. He additionally recalled, "Two of the fellows bet they could dive off the ship and swim under the hull from one side to the other." However, once under the ship they found themselves caught by a strong current. "One was dragged against the bottom of the ship's hull which was covered with barnacles and his back was all cut up."[2]

But mostly the men were bored and spent the bulk of their time reading, playing cards, writing letters, or just trying to stay comfortable aboard the grossly overcrowded ships. Ray Link understood that mail service would be spotty during the coming weeks and sought to ease any anxiety his family might experience when he wrote, "I expect to be busy for a while, so don't be expecting any letters for a while. If you don't hear from me, don't worry. I'm going to write when I have the time. Love to all and write real often."[3]

The convoy started for the Philippines on the night of October 23. Kent Sanborn, a seaman aboard the *Nelson*, remembered that the warships attached to the convoy communicated through the dark night with coded lights that flashed from their mastheads. "Sometime after midnight I stood on our flying bridge with the second mate and watched as the Navy pulled out, ghosting past us almost without a sound." He wondered "how it was possible to go through all the commotion of hoisting anchors on several large ships and stow them away in nearly total silence. By dawn they were gone."[4]

The transport ships followed, including the *Nelson*, *Waite*, and *Merritt*. The convoy sailed unmolested, and the trip was marked by "pleasant weather, bright skies, a gentle rolling motion and time spent lolling against the rail, watching the flying fish do their thing." Finally, on October 29, the convoy arrived at San Pedro Harbor near Dulag on the eastern coast of Leyte. There, the *Nelson* collided with a smaller vessel that was already at anchor, but the arrival was otherwise unremarkable.

"We were the first bomb group to arrive in the Philippines," noted William Witherell of the group's headquarters, "and were proud to have been so selected. Although we felt not ungrateful to our past hosts, we were pleased to be so close to what might have been called American soil."

A typhoon brushed the area a few hours after the *Waite* and *Nelson* anchored. "All of us that were camped on deck had to find some other place to go," said Ken Gasteb, a clerk with the 498th. "Several of us took shelter in one of the deck storage areas. At times we thought the ship was going to roll over." But the storm passed quickly, and Gasteb recalled, "After a memorable night, the next day was spent laying out clothes to dry in the tropical sun."[5]

And then the 345th's men sat in their ships. Although the invasion was progressing reasonably well, heavier than normal rainfall turned the countryside into transportation-choking mud, and the beaches were already clogged with units unable to move inland. It seemed insensible to dump everything and everyone ashore when there was nowhere to go. Moreover, units concentrated and stuck on the shoreline would be dangerously vulnerable to air attack. And so the men bobbed offshore and waited. They did their best to entertain themselves and were helped by natives who paddled alongside to sell trinkets, fruit, and other goods.

Ray Link was with many of the 501st Bomb Squadron's men aboard the *Waite*. "The reason for my long silence," he wrote home on November 2, "has been that I have been aboard a boat for some time, and of course was unable to write. Imagine me in the Air Corps, riding a boat. Very boring. Never got sea sick or anything."

In his letter, Link expressed a source of frustration felt by many men who fought in the Pacific. "You civilians back home seem to think that the only war is in Europe. You seem to think that when that war is over, then the whole war is over. I'm glad you are optimistic; I hope you are right; but don't start relaxing and think that the war is over just because it looks so good over there. There is still a war over here. The newspapers only write about the stuff in Europe as if that is the only important place."[6] Of course, Link exaggerated somewhat, as the Pacific theater did indeed receive press coverage. However, the media's reporting probably reflected, to a degree, the priority the Allies had put on defeating Germany first.

The Air Apaches aboard both the *Nelson* and the *Waite* actually spent much of their time scrambling in response to regular air raid alerts. The group remarked that the attacks "kept us running around like civilians with draft notices." Nevertheless, the ships were not often attacked. "We watched the shoreline and could see the Jap planes bombing and strafing areas along the beach," said Ken Gasteb.[7] Still, although most of the Japanese air attacks were directed against units already ashore, the waiting transports were repositioned at least once each day to make it more difficult for the enemy to plan attacks against them.

A small advance party went ashore after about a week to scout the 345th's future airfield, but most of the men remained stuck aboard the transports. The monotony was broken on November 8 when another typhoon hit Leyte. This second typhoon in as many weeks was worse than the first. Ben Miller recalled, "They dragged the anchor and ran the engines, but the ship was at quite an angle. Every time the wind let up, there was a squeaking of bunks being pushed from the lower side, then the wind hit, and all of the bunk legs screeching on the steel floor. All this was done in total darkness. The crew said whenever the ship was listing so bad, we were within two degrees of capsizing."[8]

The 345th's men dried their gear and themselves after the typhoon passed and settled back into what had become a regular routine of trifling diversions that did little more than pass the time. "Several of us often got together at day's end and sang a lot," said Ben Miller. They did so again on the night of November 11. One among the small group, perched atop a life boat and dressed in yellow and white striped pajamas and a winter uniform cap, was Constantinos Macropoulos, the squadron's barber. Miller recalled that Macropoulos, a dark, curly-haired Greek, "must have been well trained in music because he had a great voice and sang a lot of classical and operatic songs."

But the musical confab took a melancholy turn. "After a while he broke down and started crying, with tears running down his cheeks," said Miller. "We asked him what was the reason and he said that it would be his last day alive on this earth."[9] The men offered him reassurances and platitudes before going to bed. Inasmuch as they were in a war zone, Miller and his friends certainly considered that any one of them might be killed at any time, but no one took Macropoulos's breakdown seriously.

William Witherell of the headquarters element recorded the limited operations flown by the Air Apaches during November: "The flight echelon continued its operations from Biak, sometimes staging from Morotai with the 13th Air Force. With one exception, the month's bombing missions went to the Philippines, many in direct support of the Leyte campaign." In truth, "many" was a misleading word as was apparent later in the report. "A disappointing total of only five combat missions were flown," wrote Witherell, "but there were forty-one courier [missions], three supply drops, three search [missions] and one weather recce [mission] winged."

Although the number of combat missions flown during November was small, some of them were dangerous. Late during the rainy afternoon of November 2, 1944, the 345th staged twenty aircraft and crews from Biak to the Pitoe airstrip on Morotai in the Halmahera island group. They brought with them a skeleton cadre of ground personnel. Operations were difficult during this period as most of the ground-support men were still bobbing about in San Pedro Harbor aboard the *Nelson* and *Waite*. Consequently, the 345th relied on an undermanned rear echelon at Biak, as well as the support that the other units still located there were able and willing to provide. In fact, after landing at Morotai the few available ordnance men drafted the enlisted aircrews to help load bombs.

It was already after dark when trucks arrived to take the crews from the airfield to the transient camp. A Japanese bomber rumbled through the inky sky, and the trucks slid to a stop on the muddy track. The enemy bomber was not part of a larger strike but rather a single aircraft on a harassment mission. The Japanese sent these raids over Allied bases during all hours of the night to harry the men—to try their nerves and rob them of sleep. These enemy fliers were collectively dubbed "Piss-call Charlie." They stayed overhead for long periods and usually dropped their bombs one at a time, just often enough to force the men to stay under cover.

John Stone, a copilot with the 501st Bomb Squadron, was aboard one of the trucks. He and his comrades leapt out and ran into the brush. A few seconds later he stumbled into a cleared area and took cover next to a stack of crates. "I didn't know what they were," he said.[10] The enemy aircraft dropped a white phosphorous bomb that cast a weird chemical light across the entire area. Stone blinked through the eerily illuminated night and was discomfited to discover that he was crouched at the edge of the airfield's ammunition dump.

The Japanese intruder did no harm, and that same night the Air Apaches received tasking for the following day, November 3. Specifically, the group was ordered to hit a pair of Japanese airfields, Alicante and Fabrica, on Negros Island in the Philippines. The Japanese had intensified their recently initiated kamikaze attacks against the American naval forces supporting the invasion of the Philippines at Leyte, and MacArthur was keen to stop them. Accordingly, operations against Japanese airfields in the region were stepped up.

The name "kamikaze," translated as "spirit wind" or "divine wind," referred to the propitious storms that scuttled the fleet with which Kublai Khan meant to invade Japan in 1281. Certainly there were instances before 1944 when the Japanese pilots of mortally stricken aircraft or exceptionally fervent men flew themselves into Allied warships. But the first documented attacks by a dedicated kamikaze organization were flown during the Battle of Leyte Gulf. On October 25, 1944, and during the next day, the "Special Attack Force," based at Clark Field in the Philippines, sank the American escort carrier *St. Lo* and hit six more of the small carriers. More than three dozen other ships were also hit, and five of them went under. Throughout the rest of the war, kamikaze attacks caused more damage than conventional attacks.

Aside from the material damage they inflicted, the suicidal Japanese pilots' effects on morale were palpable. Indeed, it was one thing to fight a rational if doggedly determined enemy, but it was quite another, very unnerving thing to combat an enemy who deliberately—and enthusiastically—sacrificed himself in battle.

The air arms of both the Japanese army and navy had once been among the most formidable in the world. But by late 1944, after nearly three years of constant battle with increasingly more numerous and capable American forces, that was no longer the case. The Japanese had proved unable to match the Americans in the production of modern, more capable aircraft. Perhaps worse, they had failed to keep up even remotely with the Americans in the training of skilled replacement pilots. Rather, the quality of Japanese aircrews had diminished noticeably. Consequently, at the commencement of the last year of fighting, Japan had essentially already lost the air war in the Pacific.

And so, Japan's military leadership more closely considered the proposals of different officers who advocated suicide attacks with bomb-laden aircraft. As abominable as the notion was—even to some Japanese sensibilities—there was logic to it. To be sure, the skill required to make an accurate dive-bombing attack against a ship was difficult and expensive to develop. Essentially, a pilot had to aim his aircraft at the target and release the bomb at the single fleeting instant when the correct dive angle, airspeed, and altitude all intersected. And the wind had to be accounted for, as did the targeted ship's speed and direction. If one component changed by even a fraction, the other components likewise had to be adjusted.

It took time and resources to train men to fine levels of dive-bombing expertise, just as it took time and resources to teach them the more mundane aspects of combat flying, such as navigation, taking off and landing, instrument flight, formation flying, and so forth. In fact, the neophyte pilots arriving at the 345th during that period had joined the service nearly two years earlier—or even prior. The U.S. military had the men and resources, as well as the foresight, required for a massive, protracted air war. Its foes, both Japan and Germany, did not.

Consequently, Japan embraced the kamikaze concept. It was much easier to fly an aircraft into a target than to hit it with a bomb. Even the most rudimentarily trained pilots could handle their aircraft well enough to do so. In fact, the probability of a barely skilled kamikaze pilot hitting a ship was greater than the odds of an accomplished pilot making a successful dive-bombing attack. And Japan had many young men willing to immolate themselves in the name of the emperor.

John Stone of the 501st Bomb Squadron was awakened early the morning of November 3, 1944, at Morotai. The date marked his first combat mission, and he was assigned to fly as copilot to William Leggett. After eating breakfast and attending the briefing, the two men rode to the airfield, met the rest of their crew, checked their aircraft, started the engines, completed their checks, and taxied to the runway. Stone remembered that it was still "black . . . dark."

"Just prior to our moving into takeoff position," Stone said, "a jeep came up and it was the flight operations officer of the day and he was waving and pointing at the ground." Such a thing was very unusual. After consulting with Leggett, Stone climbed down from the aircraft and approached the other man.

The combined roar of the engines from so many aircraft forced Stone to lean in close. "He said, 'Stoney, get in this plane over here with George Blair.'" Stone was given no reason for the change. He climbed back into his original aircraft, grabbed his gear, stepped back down, and—buffeted by a propeller-churned wind—hurried over to the other bomber, where he changed places with its copilot. "His name was Jim Waldo," said Stone. "He was from Washington and was married. I graduated from flight school with him."

Both Stone and Waldo settled into their new positions, and the group's takeoff and rendezvous went without incident. Although the men had been briefed that little opposition was expected, an escort of six P-38s joined them midway along their route. Mechanical trouble forced two aircraft from the 498th to return to Morotai, but otherwise the route northwest across the Celebes Sea and the island of Mindanao, then north along the western coast of Negros Island was uneventful.

It didn't remain so as the Air Apaches neared Alicante, almost eight hundred miles from Morotai. Enemy fighters from the nearby base at Bacolod attacked the formation. The 501st, followed in order by the 498th, 499th, and 500th, descended to just above the waves and roared on a northeasterly heading toward the enemy airfield. Behind them, a veil of propeller-flung spray caught the sunlight in an incongruous display of rainbows. Beyond those rainbows, the Japanese fighters retreated without doing the 345th crews any harm.

"Usually, we tried to hide our approach by coming in from behind hills, and through ravines and so forth," recalled Roman Ohnemus, a pilot with the 501st.[11] The 501st's six aircraft, the first to hit the target, arranged themselves in a line-abreast formation to make their attack. "But this time we had to come in from over the water and the Japanese could see us coming. We saw the dust from their fighters as they took off, and people scrambling around as we started our run."

High above the attacking B-25s, the escort of P-38s engaged a mixed bag of defending Japanese fighters. A Nakajima Ki-44, code-named "Tojo," attacked the 499th from behind and was caught by a cone of defensive fire from the formation's .50-caliber machine guns. "As a result of the fire," the squadron recorded, "the Tojo pulled up almost vertically, trailing smoke, and fell off heading straight for the water, still trailing smoke. Since all the interception occurred only 50 feet above the water, this Tojo probably could not have recovered from his dive and is claimed as a probable." In the distance a Nakajima Ki-61, code-named "Tony," hit by the P-38s, fell from the sky, burning.

Medium-caliber antiaircraft fire reached out for the attacking B-25s. William Leggett's aircraft was hit. "You could see that he was fighting for control," said Stone, Leggett's copilot until he swapped places with Jim Waldo that morning. Nevertheless, Leggett and Waldo pressed their attack with the rest of the 501st. The squadron's crews ripped the airfield with deadly streams of .50-caliber gunfire as they dropped their bombs. Roman Ohnemus glanced at Leggett's aircraft, which "was burning and trailing a lot of flames."

The 501st finished its attack and turned away from Alicante, followed by the other three squadrons as they completed their own bombing and strafing runs. Although the airfield was littered with aircraft damaged or destroyed by previous raids, many were still serviceable, and John McKinney of the 498th "destroyed by strafing, one parked serviceable Tony on the west side of the runway." The 499th, in trail of the 501st and 498th, observed, "Three enemy planes were burning on the ground as a result of the attack by the two leading squadrons." For its part, the 499th "strafed and definitely damaged" four enemy aircraft.

The 500th was the last squadron across the target. "Lieutenant [Jack] Landon, on the extreme right of the four-plane element, strafed a Tojo with its prop turning, ready for takeoff. Its pilot was seen to scramble out as our planes approached and hid under the plane which exploded with a satisfying bang from Lieutenant Landon's strafing."

The enemy fighter attacks increased in intensity as the group fled Alicante. The 499th noted, "Fighter cover over the target was excellent considering the fact that the six P-38s seen over the target were outnumbered by approximately 3–1. Consequently," the 499th declared, "the fighter cover was too busily engaged to give the bomber formation adequate protection. As a matter of fact, one P-38 pulled up under our wings when ganged up on by enemy fighters."

"In general," the 499th report observed, "the Jap pilots seemed experienced and somewhat eager to press attacks but were puzzled by the tail turret which they apparently did not expect." The 498th's experience was similar: "As the formation pulled off the target, three Tonys came in to attack from five and six o'clock high. A short burst from the tail gunners and the Jap pilots broke away."

Not all the enemy fighter attacks were ineffectual. Walter Vonflotow, a 499th tail gunner, was hit in his right forearm and thigh by cannon fire. The squadron recorded, "He crawled from his tail gun position—which was rendered useless—to the right waist gun where he kept enemy fighters at bay for fifteen minutes [until] he finally collapsed because of loss of blood and shock."

Meanwhile, William Leggett's B-25 was still afire, as described by the 501st's mission summary report:

He [Leggett] started to make a ditching at sea, but he observed instead, 3 Tojos were preparing to make an attack from three o'clock upon the squadron. At this time his right main gear was seen to fall out of his plane. He immediately got back into formation knowing the disaster which would follow. He stayed in formation until the bright red flames were trailing at least 50 feet behind his right engine nacelle. Pulling out of formation, his right wing was seen to fold and break off. He did a half roll and crashed into the bay, 12 miles northeast of Alicante airdrome at position 12305E-1058N. There were no survivors of this crash.

Still harried by enemy fighters, the group decided to forego the attack on the airfield at Fabrica—there was little possibility of achieving surprise. Accordingly, those aircraft that still had bombs dumped them into the sea, and the formation turned for Morotai, where it landed more than four hours later. Vonflotow, the wounded tail gunner who had collapsed "because of loss of blood and shock," survived the flight and eventually recovered.

Roman Ohnemus reflected on the loss of his friend William Leggett: "I had played cards with Leggett the night before. And that morning, before we took off, I had lent my hack watch to his navigator, James Chance. He had lost his. And then . . . they were all gone."

William Stone, who had taxied for takeoff as Leggett's copilot before inexplicably being directed to swap places with James Waldo, was likewise affected. "That makes you wonder why somebody would come and say 'change seats.' Why would they change planes at the takeoff position? What goes on in this world that would cause that to happen? It makes you think a little bit about religion. It excites you spiritually." Not long afterward, as a direct result of his experience, Stone "was baptized in a water-filled, mud-filled bomb crater on Biak by a Baptist minister."

━ ～ ━

Fragmented as it was during this period, the 345th still served when called. On November 9, two aircraft each from the 498th and 499th Bomb Squadrons landed at recently captured Tacloban Airfield on Leyte. They had no expectation of action when they were surprised by orders from the 308th Bomb Wing—the 345th's parent organization. They were directed to make an attack on a Japanese convoy that was approaching Ormoc on the other side of Leyte Island, only about forty miles to the southwest. The Army's foothold on Leyte was still tenuous, and turning back the enemy reinforcements was paramount.

The four aircraft were loaded with two one-thousand-pound bombs each. Led by Fred Dick, the four-ship flight took off and joined with an escort of sixteen P-38s from the 49th Fighter Group. "The P-38s preceded the attack," noted the 345th's report, "and dive bombed the string of six destroyers surrounding the large enemy troop transport which was busily unloading troops and supplies into barges a mile-and-a-half offshore. Heavy ack-ack forced our planes, led by Lieutenant Dick, up over a ridge and then down on the transport at mast-height level."

Dick's wingman, George Frazier, hosed down the antiaircraft positions on the rear of the large transport with his guns. At the same time, Dick's aircraft was hit by heavy-caliber antiaircraft fire, and his right vertical stabilizer was blown away. The aircraft did a complete snap roll just above the water. Dick recovered the aircraft momentarily before it went out of control once more. Dick's airmanship exceeded the instability of the aircraft, and he righted the ship again, just before releasing his bombs against a Japanese destroyer.

Lightened of his bomb load, Dick turned toward Tacloban and feathered an engine. He continued away from the fight and was soon out of sight. He and his crew were never seen again.

The other three aircraft strafed troop-laden barges as they closed to bombing range. The storm of bullets ripped the men aboard the small craft into chunks of bone and flesh and mists of red blood. Glenn Doolittle dipped a wing and flew directly at the largest transport. He slammed his two bombs into the ship, which caught fire and started to list. Wendell Decker's aircraft, like Dick's, was hit in one of its stabilizers. Doolittle escorted Decker as he cleared the area. Frazier, free of his bombs, searched vainly for Dick before also flying out of Ormoc Bay.

Frazier, Doolittle, and Decker made it safely back to Tacloban. Although the damaged Japanese transport was able to clear the area and escape to safety, the hurt caused by the 345th's attack was such that much of the equipment it carried did not get ashore. Moreover, many men in the barges were killed.

The following day, November 10, the 345th's sister group, the 38th, sent thirty-two B-25s to Ormoc Bay from Morotai. Upon arriving they found and immediately attacked a host of cargo vessels and warships. During the truly epic action, the 38th sank two large transport ships and a coastal defense vessel. Several other ships were heavily damaged, including a destroyer that survived despite a bomb hit that blew its bow off. The attack, though successful, cost the 38th seven aircraft and twenty-five men.

The morning of November 12, 1944, offered no particular promise of excitement to the Air Apaches aboard the *Nelson* and *Waite*. Indeed, the first half of the day was essentially indistinguishable from most of the days since the convoy arrived nearly two weeks earlier. While playing cards with his best friend, Francis Bobay, and another man, Ben Miller was struck by a sudden urge for a cigar. "Bobay said to bring one for him also," said Miller. "I ran, I don't know why, to get to the ladder that led down to my bunk, when there was a huge explosion."[12]

It was 1125, and a Zero fighter had just smashed itself into the *Nelson* aft of the midships housing. The bomb it carried exploded. "I went flying through the air and slammed into the side of the hold," said Miller. "It took quite a while before I could turn my head both ways." Despite his shock, Miller got himself upright, found his gear, and quickly donned his fatigues, helmet, and canteen.

"I went topside," said Miller, "and everything was smoke and fire. Dead and wounded were everywhere; oil and blood everywhere." Miller nearly stumbled over the body of his coworker William Shane, who had been struck by a twenty-millimeter cannon round fired by the Japanese aircraft as it approached the *Nelson*. "It killed him so suddenly that he didn't bleed at all," said Miller. Miller went back below decks and saw that his best friend, Francis Bobay, "lay right by the bunk I had occupied seconds before. He too was gone. I picked up his one hand and forearm and placed them with his body."

Miller climbed topside once more and recognized a big wounded man as one of the group's mechanics. "He asked me for a drink of water, but before I could do it, he quit breathing. His one arm was ripped from his chest, and we could see his heart beating and his lungs moving. Everything in his chest looked as though it was in a clear plastic sack."

Miller also spied his curly-haired singing friend, Constantinos Macropoulos. He was still dressed in his pajamas. And he was dead, just as he had predicted the previous night.

Miller helped with the wounded. "For a while, I held up three bottles of plasma for the Navy medics [corpsmen] who had come aboard. I was covered with black oil and blood." Miller passed the plasma bottles on to someone else. "Everything on the back part of the ship was on fire. Also, flames were coming up from the deck below us. We hunted for a hose on the aft part of the ship that wasn't destroyed and found only one. They had barrels of some kind of very sticky oil on the back, and a lot of these were punctured, with gummy oil everywhere. Many of the dead were covered with this, and much blood." Miller and another man worked the hose against the fire for more than an hour.

Lincoln Grush was a pilot with the 500th. "Another Lieutenant and I headed down a small metal ladder into the quarters to see how we could help," he said. "It was a scene I'll never forget. There was smoke and flames, wounded men, some already dead . . . body parts. I saw a man trying to climb up the metal ladder. His right arm was blown off at the shoulder. I went over to help him and he said, 'Never mind me, Lieutenant, just help the guys that really need you.'"[13]

Ken Haller was a communications man with the 498th Bomb Squadron aboard the *Nelson*. He dived for the deck of the number four hold when the kamikaze hit the ship. The explosion blew dust, debris, and water over the ship, and the wooden stairway that had been installed to accommodate the large numbers of men who were embarked aboard the ship fell away. Haller recovered his wits and scrambled up the ship's steel ladder to the top deck.

> *The scene before me was ghastly. There were bodies scattered all over the deck, some blown apart; legs and arms here and there with blood everywhere. Many fellows were badly wounded but still alive. Some were blown overboard and were swimming in the water. Ducks [DUKW], barges and small boats were picking them up. A big fire was burning at the stern of the ship. Confusion reigned. . . . Some of us went to get the fire hose but it was useless as it was shredded from shrapnel. A Navy DE [destroyer escort] came alongside that brought doctors and nurses from the hospital ship.*[14]

Kamikaze attacks continued through the afternoon while the men aboard the *Nelson* worked to save their ship. Miller was sent to the stern where the bodies were being moved. "Fred Bacelli, sort of a clown, and I got a long-handled coal shovel and a large metal basket. We were wading in blood and pieces of our outfit. When the basket was full we dumped it over the rail and fed all the sharks below."

The men aboard the *Nelson*, badly battered and exhausted, had the fires and carnage under control by 1830, more than six hours after the kamikaze hit their ship. It was then that a Zero smashed into the *Waite*. It struck the port side, forward of amidships, and blew a hole through the hull. The aircraft's engine caught just inside the ship's frame while the fuel tank penetrated further and started fires in a hold where many of the men were bunked. Pieces of the pilot and a photo of his girlfriend were found nearby.[15]

Pete Prunty, a communications specialist with the 501st, helped to clear the carnage and "scour[ed] the stowed cargo below for any still alive. I came upon one of the dead sprawled on his back over some crates in the back of a truck. A hatch cover had landed on him with one of its corners stuck in his throat. He was gazing up at me—pleading, I thought—to remove the hatch cover. I did, and his head fell away from his shoulders."[16]

Day quickly turned to night, and men of all ranks and specialties pitched in to move the wounded from the *Waite* to other vessels. Fred Deady, a communications specialist with the 501st Bomb Squadron, labored alongside one of his coworkers, Harold Morrison. Morrison had been a dynamo since the attack, not only evacuating the wounded but also helping with damage control. Before the war, Morrison had been a mechanical engineer who, because of the Depression, had only been able to find employment as a lathe operator.

Deady noted that Morrison was knowledgeable, able, and reliable but "tended to be on the bitter side" because he had been drafted into the enlisted ranks and "was not much of a mixer."[17] He had no close friends. Still, his actions that night were heroic. "The line [of wounded] seemed endless," said Deady. When the last of the injured men were finally moved to a nearby vessel, Deady turned to Morrison as if to throw his arm around the other man's shoulders. "He flinched violently away and almost screamed, 'Don't touch me!'"

It was then that the moon peeked from behind the clouds and Deady saw that Morrison's shoulders and back were terribly burned. "Reluctantly, very reluctantly, he finally agreed to join the others on the hospital ship," said Deady. "He crossed over just as they were about to move away, and the last thing I heard was him sharply telling people on the other ship not to touch him."

Harold Morrison died of his wounds later that night.

The 345th lost 92 men killed outright and suffered 156 wounded; during the next few weeks, 15 more men died of their injuries. William Witherell's commentary was frank: "The effect upon the outfit's morale, as may well be imagined, was devastating. Not only the loss of close friends, but the shock of working amidst wreckage that was actually wet with blood, the herculean task of unloading the dead and wounded, made an impression on the men that will never be forgotten."

Ray Link, who had written home to ask for photos of girls in bathing suits and admonished his family not to forget the fighting in the Pacific, was killed aboard the *Waite*. Reggie Dunnavant, a friend from his hometown who also served with the 345th, wrote home of Link's death. Censorship constraints prohibited the men from writing about who was killed, when, and where, but Dunnavant got around the regulations by referencing his uncle, Cary Johns, who had been killed months earlier in the fighting around Anzio, Italy. "I haven't heard from Uncle Cary lately but Ray is with him now. We were together for a while, but you know how the Army is. It will certainly separate friends." His letter arrived in the States before the official telegram to the Link family, which was dated December 23, 1944.[18]

If nothing else, the kamikaze attacks on the *Nelson* and *Waite* underscored the fact that death was just around every corner. The 345th's men might be anxious about it, or they might not, but it was there. And it would claim more of them before the fighting was done.

In fact, many of the men did worry about dying, as recalled by Jay Moore, who was assigned to fly as copilot with his friend Henry Muster. "Now, Moose was just a tremendous guy," said Moore, "but he wasn't meant to be a first pilot. He heard bugs in the engine and he got me so nervous that I just almost hated to get in the airplane to fly. Boy, he was a basket case."

As it developed, Muster requested to be either grounded or relieved of first pilot duties—he didn't want to be responsible for a crew. "So," said Moore, "they didn't argue, they just took him off and sent him back [as a copilot] to his old pilot who was down in the 498th."[19] Muster was subsequently killed on January 3, 1945, during an attack on Lahug Airfield on Cebu Island. He was flying as copilot to Edgar Girdler. The 498th recorded their ending: "Airplane 122 was shot down and crashed in the north edge of Cebu Town, with nil survivors. Airplane caught fire and exploded upon crashing."

Moore admitted that he also became "pretty spastic" during this time, despite having written to his sweetheart during the previous month, "We live dangerously, there's no getting around that, but I guess every pilot is kinda proud of that fact. That's what makes flying the wonderful thing it is."

To help settle his nerves, Moore was assigned to fly with the squadron's assistant operation's officer. When Moore observed that one of the aircraft's engines was running a bit rough, the other man said, "Rough? You don't know what rough is. Just shut up and fly the airplane."

Moore did just that, and it produced good results. He recalled that the other man "got me back to where my nerves were settled down a bit. It wasn't long after that until I started checking out to be first pilot and got my own crew."[20]

Combat operations during November and December 1944 were hindered by limited basing and ground support. The raids that the group managed to launch were almost "catch-as-catch-can" efforts mostly supported by other units. The biggest problem was that the bulk of the 345th's support elements were stuck in San Pedro Harbor until after the kamikaze attacks of November 12. And once the ground men were put ashore, there was no good airfield ready for them to occupy immediately.

That fact aside, there was the very real issue that because so many men had been killed or wounded, the squadrons were compelled to reorganize to a certain degree. And finally, even had the kamikaze attacks never happened, and even if there had been an airfield ready for operations, it simply took time to set up an organization as large and complex as the 345th.

Moreover, the Japanese still contested the American invasion with both ground forces and aircraft. Ben Miller helped man a machine-gun position one night and recalled being strafed several times. Although the air attacks did little damage, the men wearied of taking cover in protective holes that were filled with mud and water. "After several passes, one of our cooks said we could do what we pleased, but he was wearing his dry uniform and would not jump into the water-filled trench. When the bullets started to fly, he jumped in. Upon looking at his bunk, we saw that a bullet had slit the top of his bunk from one end to the other. He complained no more."[21]

Not long after coming ashore following the kamikaze attacks on the *Nelson* and *Waite*, the 345th's ground elements moved to the beach at Rizal, south of Dulag, where an airfield was being readied. At the same time, they waited through most of November 1944 to retrieve their equipment. Lack of transportation, poor roads, and enemy action all conspired against them. "At Rizal," noted William Witherell, "we spent the remainder of the month. Constant and usually futile negotiations continued in an effort to get the ships unloaded."

Still, Witherell's observations confirmed that the time and place wasn't wholly unpleasant. "Our beachside area became quite livable. A mess hall replaced the tent we had been serving in. Latrines and showers were evidence of our intention to stay for a while. The absence of mud and the presence of the ocean made the area very agreeable. If we had to sit and wait for our planes, this was the place to do it."

The men also enjoyed mixing with the Filipinos. "The civilians had become used to us and we to them. We enjoyed talking to natives that understood our tongue and we were impressed by their cleanliness and willingness to help. They, in turn, marveled at our array of equipment and our foul language."

And still the enemy continued to resist. On the evening of December 6, 1944, the Japanese launched an operation, Te-Go, that combined an airborne assault with an overland attack. Almost three hundred Japanese paratroopers were dropped near where the 345th's ground element was encamped along with other Fifth Air Force units. The Japanese sought to seize nearby San Pablo and Buri airfields. The confusion on both sides was considerable, and antiaircraft fire knocked down at least two of the enemy troop carriers. Navy ships offshore added their fire to the confusion.

Robert Elliot was part of the nearby 3rd Bomb Group. He was especially awed by the antiaircraft fire that zipped low over the 3rd's encampment. Once the enemy transports flew away and the Japanese paratroopers launched their attacks, he helped coordinate defensive positions. "Ordnance men heard noise to the south between us and 345th group," he wrote in his diary. "I drew a pistol and ventured about 30 yards but saw nothing and was afraid to go further for fear of drawing fire from [the] 345th. They are jittery as hell, possibly from having so many men killed when Nip planes dove into their ship in the harbor."[22]

The Japanese troops did capture some positions but never came together as a coherent force. They had landed in an area held largely by support organizations rather than frontline infantry units. Even so, they were killed or driven away after only a few days.

Although the group's equipment had started to come off the ships at the end of November, the Air Apaches continued to operate out of Biak until the last few days of December. In fact, no combat operations at all were flown during the first eleven days of the month. When strikes did get underway, they were relatively unremarkable and were mostly flown against barges and luggers, secondary, largely abandoned Japanese airfields, and other outposts. While not spectacular, these sorts of sorties kept the enemy beaten down. Indeed, the only six men killed during the entire month were lost in a noncombat aircraft crash.

That crash occurred on December 2, 1944, when the group sent twenty-four aircraft to hit enemy airfields on Mindanao. After getting airborne Purrine Reed of the 500th Bomb Squadron maneuvered to get into formation and was caught in the propeller wash of a preceding aircraft. "It seems that Lieutenant Reed made too steep a bank," noted the 500th, "as his plane slid off on its right wing, flipped over on its back and then plummeted down into the ocean. The plane exploded upon impact, killing the entire crew."

Weeks later, Christmas was a very festive day with two remarkably bounteous and satisfying meals. "Improvised decorations adorned many tents," said William Witherell, "and one canvas home boasted a small tree with colored lights. The rather direct hint of an expected gift practiced by the Filipinos, 'Where's my Merry Christmas?' irked some, but amused more."

The 345th's aircraft were finally—and prematurely—flown up to Luzon following Christmas. "The night of the 26th," remembered Witherell, "the flight and ground echelons, separated since the 15th of October, had a hectic reunion." But no one airfield could take them all. Dulag had been the original destination, but it couldn't handle all four squadrons. Accordingly, the group's B-25s and crews were split between the airfields at Dulag, Tanauan, and Tacloban.

It was a logistical and operational mess. Coordinating between the sites, not to mention moving material and personnel, was exceedingly difficult as the roads were little more than muddy tracks. Getting bombs to the aircraft at the three different airfields was particularly tough, and the ordnance men "spent many a soggy night obtaining bombs from mud-coated dumps." Sleeping and messing provisions were deficient, and the nature of operations was such that men often found themselves at one site while their unit was at another. "Pilots and crews ate and slept when [and where] they could," said Witherell.

James Baross's diary entry of December 30 indicated the confusion—the men had no idea to which airfield the group would move. "Am stationed on Leyte permanently, either on Dulag or Tacloban strip. Am on Dulag now."[23] Nevertheless, the Air Apaches, just as they always had, turned to the task. During the last five days of the month, seven strikes were launched.

CHAPTER TWELVE

"A Perfect Swan Dive"

THE 500TH BOMB SQUADRON SENT A THREE-SHIP TO ATTACK AIR-fields at Los Negros Island on January 3, 1945. That three-ship became a two-ship when one of the aircraft experienced mechanical issues and was forced back to base. "When we arrived over our assigned target," said Joe Mallard, the navigator aboard William Bagwell's aircraft, "we made several passes on the Japanese airstrips."[1]

From his vantage point in the top turret of Bagwell's B-25, William Caputo saw that the other aircraft, piloted by Thomas Symington, had been hit in the right engine—it was afire. Caputo passed the word to Bagwell, who swung the aircraft around and silenced the enemy anti-aircraft position with a torrent of .50-caliber gunfire. That done, he pointed the B-25 out over the water and chased after Symington.

"Enemy ground fire hit our right engine and knocked off part of the cowling," said Symington's gunner, Donald Goehring.[2] "The right engine caught fire and it spread to broken hydraulic lines leading to the right landing gear." At that point, Symington let the crew know that he planned to ditch the aircraft.

"Despite the fact that the right side of the aircraft was on fire, and the right landing gear had extended with the tire burned off," said Goehring, "Lieutenant Symington made a good ditching. After we hit the water, the first thing I remembered was the cold water rushing through the escape hatch."

The crew's engineer, Nelson Peregoy, and the radio operator, Don Williams, helped Goehring get the escape hatch open. With fuel burning atop the water around them, the crewmen helped each other into a life raft. But Williams apparently went into shock and drifted away. Symington, atop the B-25's nose, tossed him a seat cushion, but Williams failed to grab it. Finally, Symington made what Goehring described as "a perfect swan dive," splashed through the burning water, and dragged Williams back to the life raft.

Joe Mallard simply observed, "Lieutenant Symington made a successful ditching just off the coast of Los Negros. We circled the downed crew and spotted canoes heading toward the ditched aircraft. Lieutenant Bagwell buzzed them, ready to blow them out of the water, but saw that they were not Japanese soldiers, but apparently, Philippine guerrillas."

Bagwell's men dropped a raft to the Symington crew and tried to raise a rescue aircraft on the radio, but with no success as Japanese jamming made the frequencies unusable. "We spotted Japanese aircraft," said Mallard, "and flew low over a rocky area near a small island." Not long after, the radio interference cleared, and Symington's location was passed to a PBY.

When the Japanese aircraft cleared the area, Bagwell piloted his B-25 back over Symington and his men. By that time, the Filipino canoes had reached the downed crew. Mallard hurriedly jotted a message and dropped it to Symington and his men. The message read, "Air-Sea Rescue on the way. Do not go with the guerrillas. See you at dinner."

In fact, the Filipinos were not guerillas, were not friendly, and might have been aligned with the Japanese. Upon reaching the downed fliers, they tried to knock them out of their rafts. Symington would have none of it. He threatened them with his .45-caliber pistol until they paddled away.

Bagwell turned his B-25 for home but was anxious to ensure that Symington and his crew were saved. He spotted the rescue aircraft, a PBY with an escort of two fighters, and joined with it. The downed crew was ecstatic when, just as promised, the little rescue force appeared over the horizon. The pickup went without incident, and Symington and his crew—although they didn't make it back in time for dinner—were returned to safety.

Douglas MacArthur's offensive in the Philippines, supported by the Navy, the Marine Corps, and George Kenney's Far East Air Forces—including the Fifth Air Force and the 345th Bomb Group—was progressing well as 1944 gave way to 1945. However, it was far from complete. One of the obstacles was Clark Airfield. Once the main American air base in the Far East, it had been captured by the Japanese in 1942. Since that time Clark had served as an aviation maintenance and logistics point, as well as a primary staging base for aircraft moving between Japan and its bases to the south. It additionally hosted major Japanese army and navy aviation commands.

Although Japanese air units in the Philippines had been badly rocked by that point in the war, they were not fully defeated. And Clark's complex of airstrips was their center of gravity. It continued to launch both conventional and kamikaze missions, and MacArthur's planners wanted it neutralized once and for all.

Clark had endured air attacks for many months, including a B-24 raid on January 6, and the final knockout blow was planned for January 7, 1945. This was one of many actions planned in preparation for the invasion of Luzon at Lingayen Gulf, which was to take place on January 9. The scheme to hit Clark included 136 bombers—48 A-20 aircraft each from the 312th and 417th Bomb Groups and 40 B-25s from the 345th Bomb Group—escorted by 24 P-38s of the 8th Fighter Group. It was to be the largest combined force of medium and light bombers to that point in the Pacific theater.

The Air Apaches—by now all based with their aircraft at Tacloban—were briefed on the evening of January 6. William Caputo, an engineer with the 500th Bomb Squadron, learned that the crew's normal pilot, William Bagwell, was sick and that Lynn Daker would take his place. "When our radio operator heard this," Caputo said, "he let out a loud groan and started to complain in a low voice. He was used to flying with Bagwell and apparently felt that change at this time wasn't good."[3]

Caputo told the other man, John Olsen, to keep his feelings to himself. "Daker is a damned good pilot. On the way back to our tent, Olsen said, 'You better be right about Daker, because it's our ass that will be on the line.' The next morning, while riding out to our plane, I could see that Olsen was glum. We had heard that the medics were making preparations for a busy day after the mission."

The 345th's forty aircraft—ten from each squadron—launched on the morning of January 7 with Chester Coltharp in the lead and flying with the 498th Bomb Squadron. Roman Ohnemus, a pilot with the 501st Bomb Squadron, had a rough start. "After takeoff I had a fire in my right engine. The tower told me to wait while the rest of the planes took off. I told them that they could do what they wanted with those other planes, but I was going to land! Anyway, I landed and jumped in a spare plane and took off again."[4]

Soon after getting airborne, with Ohnemus scrambling to catch up, the Air Apaches were joined by the 312th's A-20s, which were based out of the nearby airfield at Tanauan. The formation set a course northwest and rendezvoused with the 417th's A-20s over southeastern Mindoro Island. The 8th's P-38s picked up the bombers west of Mindoro. From there, the attack force continued northwest over the water and turned north to parallel the Luzon coast.

William Caputo, aboard Lynn Daker's aircraft, enjoyed a tremendous view. "On the way to the target, I could not believe my eyes. Down below were more ships than I had ever seen—warships and troop transports, comprising the invasion force headed for Lingayen Gulf." In fact, the invasion fleet numbered more than 850 ships carrying more than two hundred thousand soldiers.

The big mixed formation of B-25s and A-20s continued northward, just off the coast of Luzon. The plan, formulated by the parent wing of the A-20 groups, the 310th Bomb Wing, called for the 345th's forty B-25s, flanked by twenty A-20s of the 312th, to turn east and cross the western coast of Luzon northwest of Clark. Once through the Zambales Mountains that guarded the central plain upon which Clark was situated, the massive formation was supposed to spread out in a line abreast and make its attack to the southwest. Another sixty A-20s were to penetrate further east from the coast before turning back and attacking in a line abreast from the northeast.

In effect, the attack was to be made by two crisscrossing formations. The Air Apaches were to lead the attack from the northwest, and the attack from the northeast was to follow a short time later. The intent was to plow Clark's entire complex of airstrips, workshops, and other infrastructure with an irresistible fusillade of .50-caliber machine-gun fire while simultaneously blanketing it with nearly eight thousand para-fragmentation bombs.

The plan was laudable for its ambitious nature but execrable for its executability. That a supposedly experienced staff put such an amateurish scheme together is curious. In short, it was not doable in the manner planned. It simply was not possible—especially without practice—for a formation of sixty aircraft to come out of a turn and spread out into a uniform line abreast ready to make an immediate attack. And it certainly was not possible when traversing mountain passes in poor weather.

The 499th's mission summary report bore this out. "Events did not go entirely according to plan, however, because the route chosen as the best approach offering maximum radar evasion led through a mountain pass which upon arrival was found to be cloud-obstructed. These clouds, clustering around the mountain top, precluded a smooth formation through the pass. . . . [T]he planes had more or less to pick their way from one opening to the next to avoid possible peaks."

In fact, the formation came apart, and the aircraft bunched together in small groups, their crews worried about smashing not only into the mountains but into each other. When Clark hove into view, the pilots did their best to get into position and employ their weapons without colliding with, shooting down, or inadvertently bombing each other. The defending Japanese gunners added more friction to the disharmony.

But not all the enemy guns were ready. The 498th's crews saw that "many A/A guns were not manned and some guns still had covers on them during the attack." Still, the complex was defended by more than seventy heavy antiaircraft guns, a couple hundred medium-caliber weapons, and many more light machine guns. It was additionally guarded by several radar stations. The reception given to the 345th and the A-20s was plenty hot.

Joseph Rutter, an A-20 pilot with the 312th Bomb Group, was separated from the rest of his unit while navigating through the mountains and the weather on the approach to Clark. He nevertheless pressed his attack and had almost finished when his gunner warned of B-25s to his left. "At the same time, I heard a rattling sound like a wash pan half-full of gravel hitting our tail. It could mean only one thing: I had flown past the distant 312th and was now crossing at an angle in front of the fast-overtaking 345th Bomb Group B-25s. The ricocheting .50-caliber slugs coming from their nose guns were skipping around and hitting us."[5]

Rutter hauled his A-20 skyward and "made a climbing turn to the right under full power. Without me ever seeing them, the B-25s passed safely underneath our tail as I headed back to where the 312th's formation should have been." Rutter's was only one of many near misses that day.

William Caputo was awed by the mass of the attacking force that approached Clark. "We were in the first wave. The formations were so close it was scary and I could see at once that we would be in trouble. The coordination of flights over the targets was a mess. A-20s were dropping parafrags in front of B-25s. I still don't see how the pilots avoided them. Planes were crossing in front of each other and, to top it off, Jap planes above us were dropping phosphorous bombs." Adding to the confusion were buried bombs that the Japanese triggered remotely as the attackers overflew them. It is believed that these were responsible for knocking down two A-20s.

Lynn Daker—whom radio-gunner John Olsen had considered suspect—flew the aircraft expertly as he avoided antiaircraft fire and the parafrag bombs dropped by other aircraft. At the same time, he fired his guns at Japanese targets and covered the area with his bombs. His machine-gun fire laced two twin-engine bombers, and his bombs "were seen to fall on shacks and a barracks building."

The attack was just short of a free-for-all. Wendell Decker of the 499th, together with his flight, was spit out of the formation and across nearby Fort Stotsenburg. "His attack was limited to strafing," the 499th reported. "No bombs were dropped for fear that his bombs might hit other Allied planes, since, at several points along his run, A-20s were seen crossing his path."

Robert Draper of the 499th had similar issues. He "flew on the far right of the squadron formation but only dropped 24 of his bombs in the assigned area for fear of doing more damage to the friendly planes from the squadron of A-20s flying on the right flank, who were forced to fly on a lower level owing to the crowding-up caused by the trip through the cloud-covered mountain pass."

Roman Ohnemus, after taking off, catching fire, landing, and then taking off again in a spare aircraft, caught up with his squadron in plenty of time to participate in the bedlam.

The B-25s were supposed to come in first from one direction followed by the A-20s from another direction a few minutes later. Well, everyone got there at the same time. We were all dodging each other—flying at fifty feet and below—and strafing and dropping parafrags. We were flying so low that we were blowing camouflaged netting right off of the enemy fighters. I had a buddy from grammar school who also flew on that mission. And he did it with dysentery. He later told me that he knew what it was like to have the "you know what" scared out of him![6]

Howard Thompson led a flight of three 500th B-25s.

We made our run and it was pretty nasty trying to get into formation. . . . I was lined up on a long runway in very tight formation. . . . [A]s we were coming on there was a raised elevation the length of the runway probably fifty or seventy five feet in the air because I was looking up into it. It was above me and there was a line of sheds up there. The whole side of those sheds folded down and there were machineguns in there and I could look right into the guys' eyes watching them strafe us. And they raked us pretty good. We got two hundred holes in our plane that day, lost the hydraulics, lost the engine control in one engine. My radioman got hit, two shots to the thigh. He was in bad shape. And I figured this was it. I was watching for a spot to go in.[7]

Thompson wrestled his damaged aircraft away from the complex and concentrated on keeping it from hitting the ground. His navigator that day was a major on his first mission. "He'd been flying in the Caribbean looking for submarines that weren't there," said Thompson. "He was close to home [the States] and made a lot of rank real quick. Made major. But he was a nervous wreck." Given that he was a participant in a great aerial circus gone wrong—and on his first combat mission—the major's anxiety was understandable.

Lynn Daker, meanwhile, finished his run and also turned clear of the fight. "It was then," remembered his engineer, William Caputo, "that I watched in horror as an A-20 blew up, apparently as it flew over a delayed-action [fuze] bomb. If we had come by ten seconds sooner, that could have been us."

Arthur Browngardt Jr. piloted a 499th B-25, *Sag Harbor Express*. The ship was hit by antiaircraft guns, and the right engine caught fire. A short time later it went out of control and smashed through the roof of Holy Rosary Cathedral in nearby Angeles City. The impact tore it apart, and the flaming pieces smashed into the Holy Angel Academy. The entire crew perished in the crash.

Notwithstanding the fierce attack, a number of Japanese pilots rose to meet the B-25s and A-20s, as described by the 499th. "As planes left the target area, 7 Hamps and Tojos seen taking off, circling for altitude at Florida Blanca. Several P-38s were heading for the airborne enemy." Multiple crews noted that Japanese fighters dropped phosphorous bombs over the field that did no harm.

The crews returned via the western coast of Luzon for the most part and were generally unmolested, although a pair of fighters mildly harried the 501st just a few miles south of Subic Bay. "One Oscar [Ki-43] made a weak pass at our planes from 3 o'clock high, breaking away at 1,200 to 1,500 feet, when fired at by turret gunner." At the time, the 501st aircraft were flying at about seven hundred feet. "About 30 seconds later, another SSF [single-seat fighter] flew 1,000 to 1,500 feet overhead and dropped what seemed to be a phosphorous bomb. The bomb passed 100 yards off the left wing of one of our B-25s and exploded just before hitting the water." The Japanese pilots' aggressiveness was underwhelming—they might just as well have stayed on the ground.

Howard Thompson, whose aircraft had been so badly holed by machine guns hidden in sheds, was joined by a damaged A-20. The two aircraft headed for Hill Field on Mindoro Island. It was busy with recovering aircraft, and Thompson circled overhead while the A-20—also with a wounded crewman—went down first.

The landing gear would not extend, and Thompson set up for a belly landing and removed the escape hatch over the cockpit. As he touched down, he and his copilot cut the fuel to the engines. "But we were full of hydraulic oil everywhere," he said, "so we were pretty nervous about fire." Happily, although the copilot was badly shaken, the aircraft did not catch fire. Thompson, the engineer, and the first-mission navigator pushed the copilot through the escape hatch and followed him out. The crewmen in the back of the aircraft likewise escaped.

In the January 7 raid on Clark Field, John Baeta lost his flight engineer, but not to enemy fire. "His good friend was aboard one of our other aircraft," said Baeta. "He saw it crash into a church and explode, and of course it was obvious that his friend was killed." That his flight engineer was gravely affected wasn't apparent until Baeta landed his aircraft back at Tacloban. "He couldn't speak. Nothing but gibberish came out of his mouth. Of course, he was hospitalized. I wanted to see him, but they had sent him on his way home almost immediately. He did try to come back later, but they wouldn't let him."

Safely back in his tent that night, William Caputo tried to sleep. Olsen and he hadn't talked since the mission. Caputo sensed that Olsen was still angry over their exchange about Daker. "I was really tired," Caputo said, "and as we lay in our sacks I heard Olsen say, 'Bill, are you awake?'"

Caputo didn't feel like talking and responded in a hard voice, "What do you want?" He was surprised and gratified at Olsen's reply: "I just want to say you were right about Daker. He was right on the ball today."

Before dawn, on January 9, 1945—only a couple of days after the mission to Clark Airfield—the Air Apaches put six aircraft airborne from each of its four squadrons. Their primary mission was to support MacArthur's landing at Lingayen. The mission started on a tragic note. The 501st squadron reported that the B-25 piloted by James Underwood "was last seen at 0546 flying about 7,000 feet altitude just on top of the clouds. A few seconds later, a terrific explosion and large flash was seen from the northeast slope of the 6752-foot hill on Sibuyan Island. This plane is believed to have crashed into the mountains." There was nothing for the other crews of the 501st to do but continue with the mission.

Similarly, the 498th reported seeing two large flashes in a mountainous area of Sibuyan Island at 0542 in poor weather. Later, at 0630, the squadron noted another bright flash near a large mountain on Mindoro Island. One of those flashes likely marked the crash and explosion of Wallace Challifoux's aircraft as he was never seen following his takeoff that morning.

After arriving in the vicinity of Lingayen Gulf—with two crews already lost—the group was unable to make contact with the air control officer on the ground, and each squadron pressed ahead with its secondary mission: the interdiction of railroad lines on Luzon. The 500th Bomb Squadron started its attacks on a southbound course beginning at the town of Paniqui. Continuing south and approaching Tarlac, the aircraft flown by James Buffington inexplicably reversed course and disappeared.

When the group's aircrews landed later that day, no one had any idea what had happened to Buffington or his crew. Walter Nelson, Buffington's radio operator, later reported that cannon fire hit the B-25's cockpit and set it afire. Sitting in the middle of that fire, Buffington crashed the aircraft near Angeles, not far from Clark Airfield. He, the navigator, and the gunner burned to death. Nelson, relatively uninjured, pulled the wounded copilot and engineer clear of the aircraft and ran for help.

Nelson reached a village and joined with a group of Filipino guerillas. When they returned to the wrecked aircraft, they found that the Japanese had slit the throats of both the copilot and the engineer and had additionally stripped their bodies.[8] The slain engineer was Reggie Dunnavant, who less than two months earlier had surreptitiously written to his family to tell them of Ray Link's death.

Although the road and rail network in the Philippines was hardly extensive, the Japanese nevertheless relied on it to move men, material, and equipment. The 345th was consequently used to disrupt that movement. On one of those missions, flown on January 13 in central Luzon, the group destroyed a number of locomotives, boxcars, and vehicles.

James Baross of the 501st was the radio operator aboard John Hamner's aircraft. "Had some good hits," he wrote in his diary. "Went over a multiple 20-millimeter [antiaircraft] position and it felt like we got hit. Did get one round over upper right package gun that hit Flight Officer [Gordon] Arnold in upper back. Exploded and killed him instantly."[9]

Arnold, Hamner's navigator, wasn't the only 345th casualty on that day. The 498th aircraft flown by Bertram Weich was seen to ease out of formation during a turn. A statement by a crewman in another aircraft declared, "At the time Lieutenant Weich was last seen, his ship appeared to be in perfect shape, and no signals of distress of any kinds were seen." A search mission launched the following day failed to find any evidence of Weich's aircraft or crew.[10]

***

During this time a revised insignia was applied to the group's aircraft. Although Apache head artwork starting appearing with the adoption of the new nickname the previous August, that artwork was not standardized across the group and was quite complex to paint. That changed with the arrival of Charles Metzel.

Metzel had been a commercial artist in Cincinnati prior to going into the service and was asked to help design a simpler yet more compelling emblem for the 345th. "Although the head is a product of many members of the group," said William Witherell, "Metzel cleaned up the design and added the professional polish that is evident today. Limiting the color scheme to red, white and black, he introduced a stencible simplicity that has made practicable the widespread use of the Indian on everything from stationery to stabilizers." It was only a short time before the newly standardized insignia dressed the vertical stabilizers of all the group's aircraft. Debriefs with Japanese POWs confirmed that the B-25s with the Apache head were readily recognized and feared.

CHAPTER THIRTEEN

"It's All for the Best, Dad"

As THE AIR APACHES WERE FORMED, TRAINED, AND SENT INTO COM-
bat, many hundreds of thousands of young men from all over the country were still being inducted into the Army Air Forces. Once they were
trained, some of them were sent overseas to the 345th. In fact, of all the
men who served with the unit during the war, two-thirds joined after it
had been sent to the Pacific. Melvin Pollock's experience was representative, and a review of his story through his letters home provides unvarnished and valuable context.

Pollock was almost twenty-two when he left his hometown of
Adams, Wisconsin, in early January 1943. A handsome young man—and
an equally handsome dresser—he was artistic and loved to dance. His
father, Manley, was a barber, and his mother, Edna, had passed away in
1941. Both husband and son still grieved for her. When Melvin had been
hit by a car as a young boy, he had spent months in the hospital, but it
was Edna's home care that returned him to full health.

Melvin wanted to be a pilot. Although he had no college experience,
he successfully passed the battery of tests necessary to be considered for
training as an aviation cadet. This was not an inconsiderable accomplish-
ment as the tests covered a broad spectrum of topics that included liberal
arts, science, and math. Moreover, the physical examination to which
candidates were subjected was very thorough.

When Pollock wrote his first letter home to his father on January 19,
1943, he did so from the Aviation Cadet Classification Center in Nash-
ville, Tennessee. Beyond the initial screening and testing done by the

recruiters, the center offered another opportunity to determine the fitness of candidates for service as officers and flyers. It was also decided there whether they were best suited to fly as pilots, bombardiers, or navigators. Most of the men, as was the case with Pollock, wanted to be pilots.

In his letter, Pollock exhibited an almost naive altruism and sense of purpose: "S'pose you're plenty lonely now—but it's all for the best, Dad. I can see right now we're here to go to it, and I'm standing on the threshold of something."[1] Such noble declarations disappeared from his letters almost immediately after he entered the sometimes spirit-sapping machine that was Army Air Forces training.

"I chose pilot for first choice, navigator and then bombardier," Pollock wrote. "I look good in my uniform. Officer hat and large wings on it. And blue band around it. There are planes flying all over, all day. I guess I'm in the Air Force alright."

"I've finally passed," Pollock wrote to his father a couple of weeks later, on February 1, 1943. Earlier he had been told that he was not qualified for service as a pilot due to slight astigmatism in one eye. He was disappointed but made the best of it. "I was recommended for a navigator. We get 27 weeks of training, and then graduate as a 2nd Lt. That's a superior rank to flight officer. Some fun. We can pick up flying time on cross country runs when we get advanced enough. We also go to gunnery school, and a few other details."

Pollock was sent to Selman Army Airfield, near Monroe, Louisiana, a short time later. There he and his classmates started the preflight phase of their training. Aside from classroom studies in various aviation-related subjects, the training emphasized military discipline, physical fitness, and leadership. It was a sort of indoctrination, or "boot camp," for the aviation cadets. "They gave us the Burma road today," he wrote of a conditioning hike. "The damn thing is appropriately named too. Five miles long, and all hills and rough terrain up and down, in and out." Still, he seemed in better shape than most of his classmates. "Had the stiffest cross-country run of all today. Right after breakfast. We all got sick. Thirteen of us finished out of 37. Two more blocks, and I wouldn't have lasted."

Pilots and navigators also trained at Selman. There Pollock likely first felt close—although only by association—to the dangers that were part of aviation during the war. A planeload of cadets from Selman, along with their instructors, went down. "They crashed near Hondo, Texas, and all were killed instantly. Too bad, but it happens to the best of them. Nothing will happen to me though, as I'm too darn ornery."

Pollock's performance during the preflight phase at Selman was good. "Don't worry about me, dad," he wrote. "I'm swell and I've just graduated from preflight. I'm now in the advanced school." Indeed, although there continued to be some focus on physical conditioning and other military subjects, the main thrust of Pollock's training was navigation.

"We got wristwatches," he wrote. "Navigation 'hack' watches worth $75.00. A stop-second hand for resetting to correct time. The most they ever lose is 5 seconds a day. We keep a chart on their accuracy. In the air, you deal in seconds."

"A lot of the guys are wondering if they'll get airsick. They've never been up, a lot of them. I wouldn't have joined without going up first." As always, he let his father know how much he cared for him: "Love to you, Dad."

Pollock's navigation training was well underway by early May 1943 as the 345th started overseas. It came with its bruises and bumps, literally. He wrote his father on May 12, "Flew our third [training] mission yesterday. Ok. Got a front tooth knocked out on the landing. Just cracked off ⅔ of the way up. It'll be easy to fix. They'll put a ¾ enamel crown on. It looks like hell personified. I was in the copilot's seat and was finishing my log. We hit hard, and my jaws snapped together."

All the nation's services were made up almost entirely of young men like Melvin Pollock. They possessed the physical and mental stamina so necessary to military operations. They were strong and healthy. And although they weren't unwise or even completely raw, they had a certain innocence and sense of invulnerability that made them easier to send into combat. But they could also be conflicted. Many got bored easily. Some second-guessed what they didn't completely understand—which was often a great deal. And they could be impulsive and were often easily distracted.

Melvin Pollock seemed all of those things when he wrote home to Adams, Wisconsin, on May 31, 1943. "I've decided to quit navigation," he wrote his father. "I've done alright by it, but I can't get interested in it anymore. I can't see myself sitting up there at a desk, when I could have guns or anything else to occupy my time. I just wasn't cut out for this damn work. I don't really like to be a quitter, Dad," he continued, "but after all, if I had a job in civilian life I didn't like, I'd get another. This is the very same thing to me."

He wanted to be an aerial gunner. "But it goes down on my record that I asked out of navigation. I'll be automatically out of air crew. So, I asked my instructor if he could fix that. He said he could make it into a washout [failure]. I said that'd be OK with me."

"I'm sure not sorry to be out of it," Pollock explained to his father. "I'm glad. I considered it from all angles before I decided. I've got it in my grasp, but what do I do? I sweep it away with one motion. Funny thing, I don't give a damn for those bars [lieutenant's rank] any more. All I want is for this war to end so I can go into art."

Pollock's self-conflict was more evident later in the letter. "I don't know what in hell I want, and that's the truth. Maybe this army is changing me. Sometimes I wonder what in hell is the matter with me. I can't dig into things like I should."

His father, Manley, was disappointed. Proud of his son, he had enjoyed telling patrons in the barbershop about Melvin's latest accomplishments. And now, Melvin had quit his training as a navigator for no reason that Manley was able to reasonably articulate.

Pollock's dissatisfaction did not go away. "I don't know if you're blue, but I know I am," he wrote his father from Keesler Army Airfield on the Gulf Coast of Mississippi. It was June 24, 1943, about a month after he had quit navigator training. "Maybe we can cheer each other up in our solitude, Dad. How about it?"

It was apparent that Pollock regretted his decision. When he quit, he lost his status as an aviation cadet and was made a private. His pay was also substantially cut. Already eager to escape his new enlisted status, he had taken the test to be admitted into Officers Candidate School. "It's only a forty-minute test for 150 questions. I scored 135. I got the highest mark of the 13 who took it." Melvin Pollock's intelligence could not be questioned.

But intelligent or not, Pollock was still just one of many thousands of dog-faced privates at Keesler, a basic training center and mechanics school. He hated it. "If anyone ever catches me south of the Mason-Dixon line when this fracas is all over, they can just put me in the bug house for sure, without even giving me the entrance exam."

Pollock didn't have to endure Keesler for long. He was sent to Amarillo Army Air Field in July 1943 and promoted to private first class. "That's $4.00 a month more. It all helps," he wrote to his father on July 13, 1943. He had been assigned a new specialty: "We'll be in mechanics school. We'll be crew chiefs. Flying sergeants. We'll all be aerial gunners too."

He didn't write his father again for six weeks. "Haven't really much to say," he wrote on August 29. "Still haven't heard from the cadet board. Won't for over a week." Pollock's desire to get back into the aviation cadet program was quite strong, and he commented on rumors that the qualifications for entry had been substantially lowered. "Should make it back in the cadets. Sure hope I do."

In his letter of September 4—while the 345th was just starting strafing operations half a world away—Pollock observed that his chances of being readmitted as an aviation cadet looked even better. "They've got a big drive on to get more. Guess they really want them. They must be building a lot of planes to be so short on men. All that is really very encouraging. Think I'll make it."

But it was not to be. His disappointment was obvious when he wrote his father on September 13. "Well, I got my letter back from the cadets, and it's out. They're refusing all ex-cadets. Or at least 94% of them. Makes me kind of disgusted. Guess I'll have to go thru this damn school to get out. Either that or die. Only two ways."

Salt in the wound came almost a month later when he was visited by one of his aviation cadet classmates from his time at Selman Army Airfield. "He sure made me wish I'd kept at it. Wings, bars and $291.00 a month. Especially the dough." His friend also told him the sad news that one of their classmates, "old Howie Raaven," had been killed in a training accident. "Plane dragged a wing, and exploded and burned." This was likely the first close friend Pollock had lost in the service and his pain was palpable: "Can't get over Raaven. Hard."

On September 30, on the anniversary of his mother's passing, he wrote home again. "Well, I 'spose you're thinking the same thing I am today." That both of them missed her deeply was obvious. "I can't help but think of how great a woman she was. How she always did her best for you and I in spite of all the odds that were against her." He also exhibited a keen sensitivity and understanding when he wrote, "As she looks down on us now, I can't help but think she can't help but be proud of you for the way you've borne up these past two years and kept your nose on the grindstone . . . for yours was the greatest loss—not mine."

Still, his training at Amarillo was apparently going well. "We've been testing engines for 9 days now. All day I test engines, and all nite my ears ring like church bells. Good thing I'm the only one who can hear them, or they'd keep the whole barracks awake."

His letter to his father on November 27, 1943, included a reminder that the wartime generation, just as every generation that preceded and succeeded it, included broken persons capable of the worst depravities. "Just heard on the radio about a gal in Claremont, Minnesota, that ran around the table, and every time she went around she slashed at her 3-year-old kid with a butcher knife, killing the kid finally. What a gal! You can talk about your freaks in the world, but the human mind is the queerest of them all, if you should happen to ask me."

Pollock had graduated from the aircraft mechanics school at Amarillo and was waiting in Las Vegas to start aircraft gunnery school when he wrote his father on December 5, 1943. He had been awarded the Good Conduct Medal, about which he made light: "It means that I've eaten my Wheaties 1 year in a row every morning. All you have to do is stay sober and keep away from an M.P. [military policeman]."

While he and his comrades waited for their gunnery class to start, they did what young men do. "We go over every nite and load up on beer at the P.X. [post exchange]. Then we proceed home gaily and pour ourselves into bed."

The letter also included deeper and more sensitive thoughts. "Illusions are a lie, but I want them near me; hope is another, but I want it to walk before me always." If his letters were sometimes sarcastic, or complaining, or even arrogant, they also showed that he was intelligent, observant, and perceptive. His writing indicated—without him saying it directly—that he felt trapped and badly used. As one of an eventual 16 million young American men who served in uniform during the war, he was far from alone; many men occasionally felt downhearted.

By early January, Pollock's aerial gunnery training was well underway, and his spirits seemed improved. "I've been busier than hell," he wrote to his father on January 8, 1944. "10–11 hours of school and shooting a day. It's fun though. My accuracy is improving. You'd be surprised how they can make a good shot out of you. They spend a lot of money on you here."

His observations on war and combat seemed especially mature. "I see several guys that have DFCs [Distinguished Flying Crosses]. And others have Air Medals and Silver Stars. I don't give a damn for the medals if I can come back in one piece, with the war over, and civilian life waiting for me. I mean it."

At the end of January 1944, Pollock wrote his father of the almost impulsive decision that ultimately led to his service in the 345th: "I was scheduled to go to B-26s at Shreveport, Louisiana, but Matlock and McTavey [his friends] are going to Columbia, South Carolina, and I got the lieutenant to change mine [his orders] to there. I heard they had B-25s there. But don't know for sure. Besides, I've been in Shreveport before, and flew over it, but never have been in South Carolina."

Following his completion of aerial gunnery school in early February 1944, at the same time that the 345th was settling itself at Nadzab, Melvin Pollock received his first furlough home after more than a year in the service. He took it while en route to his new assignment at Columbia Army Air Base. Indications are that he and his father enjoyed each other's company. "We must've been at the top of our lungs in the Beanery," he wrote on February 20. "I was sure in sad shape when I got into Chicago. Hangover. Didn't even eat breakfast at all."

Despite the visit, or perhaps because of it, he was obviously still unsettled in military service. "Don't believe I'll ever be stoic and calm until the war is over and I can throw these clothes away. I just can't wait." About what his flying future held for him, he seemed ambivalent. "They've got A-20 and B-25 planes here. Guess I'll get a B-25. Don't care one way or the other."

As it developed, Pollock, now a flight engineer and gunner, was assigned to a B-25 crew at Columbia Army Air Base during early March. "I have a pilot from New York City, a Chinese navigator-cannoneer from Los Angeles, California, and don't know where the radio-gunner and armorer gunner are from." He observed that "the Chink" had less schooling as a navigator than he had.

His letter of March 18, 1944, included a melancholy remembrance of his mother, to whom both men had been so close. "Well, Mom was 43 [on] the 17th. St. Patrick's. She should still have 20–30 years left instead of 2½ years gone. The mockery of life. You and I have been closer than we ever were before I got in uniform, you know. Guess it's just since Mom died."

A couple of weeks later, Pollock wrote that he was glad he had dropped out of navigation school. He had written two letters to classmates who had finished the school and were subsequently sent to England. "Both letters came back stamped 'Missing in Action,'" he wrote. However, Pollock's suggestion that his decision not to finish navigation training had somehow saved his life is curious. If a navigator was shot down, so was the entire crew—including flight engineers like him.

Through April and into May, Pollock's training intensified and included nearly a month of advanced gunnery training while flying out of Myrtle Beach Army Airfield in South Carolina. "We're in the air day and nite," he wrote on May 8, 1944. "We haven't got long left in the USA. 3–4 weeks, I'd say."

He was mistaken. "Well, I have news for you, old bean," Pollock wrote to his father on May 11, 1944, from Warrensburg, Missouri. Aside from the fact that he had been promoted to sergeant, he announced that he had requested and been granted a transfer to Ferry Command, which was responsible for moving aircraft around the country and overseas. It was an enormous organization capable of coordinating and executing all the many details required for such a large and complex task.

Pollock likely made his request because he would spend most of his time traveling. He would see new places and make new friends. It also offered the prospect of more money. "Every day we're away from home base we get $7.00 a day maintenance [per diem] for hotel bills and food.

Best deal in the Air Corps." He outlined the job and tallied his potential earnings: "We'll ferry ships [large aircraft] all over the country. Also, maybe paratroopers in the South Pacific. What a deal! Travel all the time. $210 a month for maintenance. Plus flight pay. Boy!!"

It all came apart, as he explained a week later. "I held off writing a little bit, hoping I could tell you what I'm doing here, but I can't. They sent a letter back about us to try and find out. Nobody seems to know on the whole field. We're the only 12 gunners here. And the planes, C-47s, don't carry guns. They told us the whole thing was a mistake, and we wouldn't be here too long. Hope not."

Pollock's disappointment was tangible. "I'd take a discharge if I could get one now. Hell's bells! They don't even want me to fight!! That's been proven to me on this last little deal. I would have been already left for overseas by the first of the month."

It took the Army until July to send Pollock to Tampa, Florida, the epicenter of B-26 training. On July 31, he wrote his father, "Well, I heard tonite we were going to Shreveport, Louisiana, for the B-26." Of course, it made very little sense at all as he had nearly completed his training on the B-25 before mistakenly being transferred to Ferry Command. Although the service was churning out prodigious numbers of trained personnel, it wasn't always efficient.

However, in Pollock's instance, someone realized the folly, and he was duly sent back to Columbia Army Air Base during August. Understandably frustrated by it all, Pollock wrote, "They really spent the taxpayer's money foolishly this time, eh?" But the training apparatus clearly wasn't sure what to do with him as a crewman who had already completed nearly the entire course. "We're going over to the Bomb Crew section tomorrow to start RTU [Replacement Training Unit] all over again. Right back where I was 4 months ago."

As it developed, he skipped entire sections of training and was able to go home to see his father. Later, writing to his "best dad" of some photographs taken during that time, he observed that they "weren't bad." And that Manley "looked pretty good in those [photos taken] at the fair. A little tanked, but what the hell."

Pollock was flying again in Columbia by the middle of September 1944. At that time the 345th was flying out of Mokmer Airfield on Biak. However, even though Pollock had yet to serve overseas, he was obviously fed up with the war. His thoughts were reasonable and practical; he wanted to live his own life his own way and didn't want to be compelled to do otherwise simply because faraway tyrants were making war. "I wish those lousy bastards who call themselves human beings would quit, as I'm sick of pissing my young life away in this goddamn neck of the woods."

The tempo of his training picked up during October 1944. The excitement of flying had long ago worn off, and accidents were common. Some men looked for excuses not to fly and hoped that their sorties might be cancelled for mechanical breakdowns, scheduling snafus, or poor weather. Pollock wrote his father on October 2, "All these new guys who were so enthusiastic about flying the first few times are starting to pray to Allah to rain like a bastard when their turns come up, just like us old veterans are." Later he declared, "I'm so damned sick of flying right now, I can't even carry on an intelligent conversation about a B-25."

By that time, combat veterans were returning to teach what they had learned, and this made an impact on the training, as Pollock noted with a measure of approval. "They've got a major back from overseas here now. Now we've got takeoff at a certain time, and arrive over the target at a certain time, etc. All of it's timing, same as overseas. Then we have bombing and cannon runs and fighters jumping at us. We use a camera gun and the pilot does evasive action. Zig-zags to throw the fighter's aim off. Good stuff, I guess."

On November 3, Pollock wrote his father, "Your boy is going to finally fight the war. After nearly two years, it's here." Although Pollock's military career to that point seemed disjointed, it was hardly unique. Men were regularly bounced around to different schools and commands for no apparent good reason. Indeed, of the 2.4 million men in the United States Army Air Forces at its peak strength during 1944, only just more than half ever served overseas.

Pollock finally departed the States in December 1944 and spent most of January 1945 undergoing theater-specific indoctrination at

Nadzab—now a major training base and transportation depot. It had been two years and many detours since he had reported for service. He was moved up to Tacloban and assigned to the 345th's 500th Bomb Squadron. His attitude was upbeat, even if he got the 345th's nickname slightly wrong. "Squadron 500 is called the 'Rough Raiders,'" he wrote to his father on January 27, "and the group is called the 'Apache Raiders.' Tokyo Rose, I hear, calls us the 'White Bellied Bastards' because of how our planes are marked, so I guess the Japs know we're in the war alright."

Complex and sensitive Melvin Pollock, whose experience to that point had made him sometimes jaded, was impressed by the 345th. "Morale is excellent here. No one bitches too much. We have six men to a tent and we use cots and have our own blankets, etc."

Manley Pollock must have experienced a mixture of pride and anxiety when he received the letter his son Melvin had penned to him on February 2, 1945. "I've put a couple of missions in already. One to Cabacaben on Bataan Peninsula to bomb and strafe. It's close to Corregidor. We avoided the island on the way back. Then one to Puerto Princesa on Palawan. We bombed and strafed there also."

Melvin Pollock, after two years, was finally in combat. And he seemed especially proud of the Air Apaches. "We're reputed to be the most hated flight group in the South Pacific. Tokyo Rose mentions us quite often in her little broadcasts. She has pet names for us that aren't complimentary. She plays records, trying to make the guys homesick, and asks us little things like, 'Did you enjoy eating your bully beef and hardtack this morning?' And then proceeds to describe a ten-course dinner to us."

As a morale-boosting stunt, men of the 345th's 500th Bomb Squadron fabricated and signed a kitchen sink. Max Mortensen and his crew dropped it—and a load of bombs—on the Japanese at the Sidate airfield in the Celebes on September 15, 1944. The 500th could then claim to have dropped everything, *including* the kitchen sink, on the Japanese. Pictured left to right are Max Mortensen, Gerald Paquette, William Baily, Talmadge Epps, and Neal Ryan. USAAF

These wrecked Japanese Zeroes at Lae were emblematic of the state of the Japanese air forces on New Guinea by the summer of 1944. The aircraft in the background is a Royal Australian Air Force Wirraway training and general-purpose aircraft. USAAF

A 345th B-25 hitting a Japanese destroyer escort at New Hanover on February 16, 1944. This ship would be destroyed and its survivors strafed. An enemy freighter burns in the background.
USAAF

PBY flying boats saved the lives of many 345th aircrews. USAAF

C-47 transports such as these were invaluable in moving the 345th to different bases. Note the escort of P-40s, nearly hidden by the center aircraft. USAAF

James Baross was a radio operator with the 501st Bomb Squadron. His memoir offers very frank insight into day-to-day 345th operations. JAMES BAROSS

Chester Coltharp was awarded the Distinguished Service Cross for his role in rescuing multiple downed crews at Kavieng on February 15, 1944. He later took command of the 345th from Clinton True. USAAF VIA BYNUM COLLECTION

A PBY rescues a downed 345th crew. Note the life raft pulled close. USAAF

Everywhere they were based, the 345th's men exercised ingenuity to make their lives as comfortable as possible. Here is a field-expedient laundry setup. USAAF VIA BYNUM COLLECTION

Movies, important to morale, were shown virtually every night. Sometimes the same movie screened for a week or more at a time, depending on what was available. USAAF VIA 345TH BOMB GROUP ASSOCIATION

General Crabb presents the Air Medal to Ed Bina, who, as copilot to John Nolan, helped wrestle their mortally stricken bomber to a crash landing in the water off Noemfoor after striking Ternate on August 15, 1944. BINA COLLECTION

Ben Miller, a communications expert with the 499th Bomb Squadron, was the epitome of the hardworking, ingenious American-farm-boy-gone-to-war. MILLER FAMILY

For a short period during 1944, the 345th was known as the "Tree-Top Terrors." The name never really caught on. Soon after, the unit adopted the "Air Apaches" moniker. USAAF

345th B-25s parked at Nadzab in the Markham Valley, New Guinea, March 17, 1944.
USAAF VIA JOHN RAUZON COLLECTION

The Japanese freighter the 345th hit at New Hanover on February 16, 1944, burns. Remarkably, none of the crews reported the Japanese submarine seen next to the burning hulk. PERRY HURT COLLECTION

Turning a propeller prior to start.
PERRY HURT COLLECTION

When a pair of one-hundred-pound bombs accidentally detonated at Hollandia on July 2, 1944, eleven men were killed.
PERRY HURT COLLECTION

The 345th's men encountered Japanese aircraft of all types as they staged through Hollandia. Pictured is a captured Ki-43 "Oscar."
PERRY HURT COLLECTION

C-47 transport aircraft such as this helped the 345th during its many moves across New Guinea, through the Philippines, and to Ie Shima. USAAF

Females were generally scarce where the 345th was based, but there were a few. Pictured is a nurse. USAAF VIA 345TH BOMB GROUP ASSOCIATION

P-40s such as this sometimes escorted the 345th B-25s. USAAF

The P-38 Lightning frequently escorted the 345th's B-25s. USAAF

The P-47 Thunderbolt sometimes escorted the 345th. USAAF

A 345th B-25 from the 500th Bomb Squadron is loaded with bombs at Clark Field sometime in the spring of 1945. USAAF

Japanese seamen struggle to escape one of the destroyer escorts sunk by the 345th on April 6, 1945. USAAF

A B-25 from the 345th's 499th Bomb Squadron taxis at Clark Field during the spring of 1945. Another follows to the far left. USAAF

A glazed-nosed 345th B-25J.
SAN DIEGO AIR & SPACE MUSEUM

The definitive and final version of the Air Apache insignia. It was rendered in white, red, and black. USAAF

A late-war solid-nosed B-25J of the 345th's 499th Bomb Squadron. Note that it was left with a natural aluminum finish. SAN DIEGO AIR & SPACE MUSEUM

The Betty bombers that brought the Japanese surrender delegation to Ie Shima drew huge crowds of curious American servicemen. U.S. NAVY

Japanese antiaircraft defenses on Formosa could be especially effective. Here, a B-25 from the 345th's 498th Bomb Squadron has been hit. It crashes and explodes seconds later. USAAF

This was the April 4, 1945, attack on Mako Town during which Stan Muniz's friend Bartolino Maggi was shot down and killed with the rest of his crew. USAAF

A Japanese destroyer escort founders in the South China Sea after being hit by the 345th on March 29, 1945. USAAF

Parafragmentation bombs fall among at least eight heavily camouflaged Japanese aircraft during the attack on Clark Field on January 7, 1945. USAAF

The eight .50-caliber machine guns placed into the solid-nosed B-25J packed a powerful punch, but they also required powerful and careful maintenance. USAAF

The attack on Clark Field by the 345th and the A-20-equipped 312th and 417th Bomb Groups on January 7, 1945, culminated a series of air raids that effectively ended major Japanese air operations from the Philippines. USAAF

In the background, a Japanese phosphorous bomb explodes during the January 7, 1945, attack on Clark Field. USAAF

A bomb from an Air Apache B-25 lands at the bow of this Japanese freighter in a South China Sea port. Spray from the bomb is just visible. USAAF

The bomb from the previous photo has exploded and blown the bow to pieces. The enemy ship is already sinking as another Air Apache B-25 flashes by overhead. USAAF

Curious men, 345th Air Apaches among them, throng the Japanese Betty bombers that brought the Japanese surrender delegation from Japan to Ie Shima on August 19, 1945. USAAF

The Japanese surrender delegation brought a gift of flowers to Ie Shima on August 19, 1945. They were ignored. USAAF

Below: A 345th aircraft makes a mast-height attack on a Japanese destroyer escort in the South China Sea on March 29, 1945. USAAF

Bottom: The 345th aircraft completes its attack. Note the double-string of bullet splashes in the water from the tail gunner of the B-25 from which the photograph was taken. USAAF

A B-25 from the 345th's 499th Bomb Squadron attacks a Japanese destroyer escort in the South China Sea. USAAF

Japanese destroyer escorts under attack by the Air Apaches in the South China Sea on April 6, 1945. USAAF

Air Apache crews attack a Japanese destroyer escort in the South China Sea on March 29, 1945. USAAF

After being damaged by an American submarine, the Japanese destroyer *Amatsukaze* was fitted with a snub nose and sent back out on operations. The 345th encountered and damaged it on at least two occasions, effectively putting it out of action on April 6, 1945. Note the B-25 in the distance making a bombing run. USAAF

The Betty bombers carrying the Japanese surrender envoys to Ie Shima on August 19, 1945, were escorted by the 345th's B-25s. An SB-17G rescue aircraft flies in the background. STEPHEN QUESINBERRY COLLECTION

Small transport ships moved freight to and around the Japanese Home Islands. This example was destroyed by Donald "Buzz" Wagner. RANDY WAGNER COLLECTION

CHAPTER FOURTEEN

"We Seemed to Be Awfully High"

WILLIAM WITHERELL RECALLED THAT IT WAS EARLY FEBRUARY 1945 when the 345th "got 'rush-rush' orders to scrape the mud from our shoes and become operational by February 13 at San Marcelino. We found the place on the Luzon map, slightly above Subic Bay, but the only photos S-2 had showed a very barren location."

The Air Apaches, which even at that time still had personnel and equipment in Biak, went immediately to work to move itself from Tacloban, on Leyte Island, to San Marcelino, on Luzon Island. During a multiday, around-the-clock tumult of barely organized chaos, tents were knocked down atop men who still slept, and the group's aircraft were stuffed with material and equipment. C-46s were sent to help with the move and were likewise crammed with whatever wouldn't fit inside the B-25s. The equipment and material that the C-46s couldn't accommodate was trucked to the beach, where it was loaded aboard ships. In the end, the group roared into San Marcelino during February 12 and 13 in a state of disarray that the Fifth Bomber Command perversely described as "one of the smoothest air transport operations we have ever had."

San Marcelino was indeed "a very barren location," but it was less crowded than Tacloban and closer to the group's targets. Still, it had its own shortcomings. It was extraordinarily dusty, which made maintenance difficult. The dust found its way not only into the various aircraft mechanicals but through engine filters and seals, causing insidious but deadly damage. Dust-corrupted oil was less efficient at reducing friction and carrying away heat. Consequently, engine failures occurred more

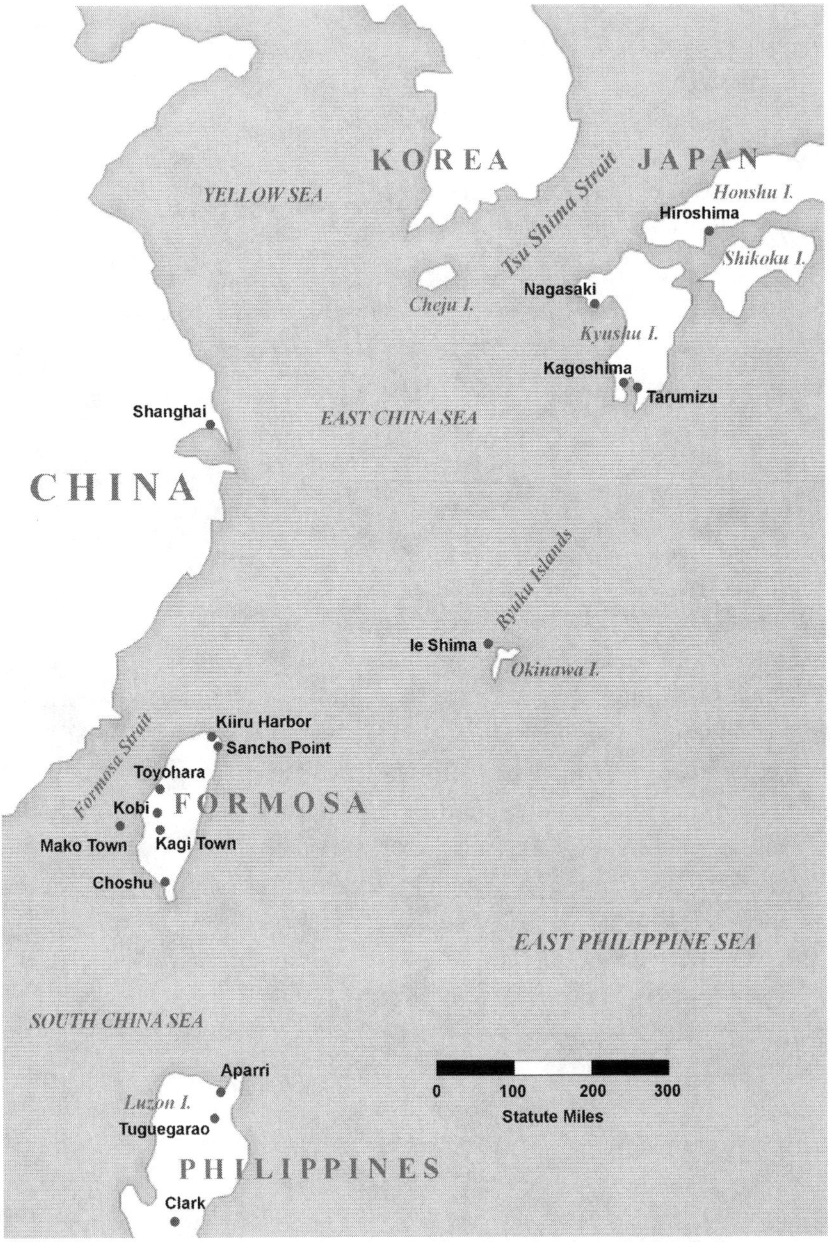

KOREA

JAPAN

YELLOW SEA

Tsu Shima Strait

Honshu I.

Hiroshima

Shikoku I.

Cheju I.

Nagasaki

Kyushu I.

Kagoshima

Shanghai

EAST CHINA SEA

Tarumizu

CHINA

Ryuku Islands

Ie Shima

Okinawa I.

Formosa Strait

Kiiru Harbor

Sancho Point

Toyohara

Kobi

FORMOSA

Mako Town

Kagi Town

Choshu

EAST PHILIPPINE SEA

SOUTH CHINA SEA

Aparri

Luzon I.

Tuguegarao

PHILIPPINES

Clark

| 0 | 100 | 200 | 300 |

Statute Miles

frequently. And during very long-range flights over vast expanses of water, an engine failure could be a death sentence. Chester Coltharp, the group commander, additionally remarked, "The strip was also very rough and tires had to be replaced frequently."

The men did not put as much effort as they might have into improving their lot at San Marcelino. "The stayover was billed as little more than a staging operation," said William Witherell. "It was understood that we would use the unsurfaced strip there until the rainy season started. Consequently, only temporary accommodations were erected for offices and living quarters."

"The landing strip was fashioned out of a north-south road," said Donald "Buzz" Wagner, "and when taking off [to the] north, you made a turn west out through an opening between two low mountain peaks. I always worried about losing power on takeoff, and the possibility of having to jettison the bomb load on the village off the north end of the runway."[1]

The move also meant that the Air Apaches were better able to visit the Navy's base at Subic Bay, although it was a multihour drive along miserable roads. Still, the attraction of twenty-five-cent highballs at the Navy's clubs was hard to resist. The men reciprocated by flying their Navy brothers to Manila for rest-and-relaxation visits. "We used to scare the hell out of them," said Wagner, "when we hit the deck and jumped over sunken ships in Manila Harbor on our way to the airfield at Nichols. I remember one white-as-a-sheet lieutenant, as he got out of the airplane, asked why we didn't put up a periscope coming across the harbor."

During this time the group also negotiated leases on two substantial houses in Manila—one for the officers and one for the enlisted personnel. Furloughs to Sydney were growing difficult as the 345th was operating farther from Australia than it ever had. Consequently, three-day passes to Manila helped to relieve some of the stress of combat operations.

"Much of Manila was pretty well demolished," remembered Al Stone, an ordnance man with the 500th Bomb Squadron.[2] "You could get a drink, and buy some souvenirs. Of course there was prostitution for those that were interested. It seemed that they kept a pretty good handle on that—the doctors did medical inspections in the houses and such."

"Early on," Stone recalled, "there were still Japanese soldiers in some parts of the city." He recalled that not all the fighting was between the Americans and the Japanese. "There was one night that things got out of hand. Black stevedores got into it with an Army unit that had just been pulled in from the battlefield. I'm not sure who said what, but it was a combat zone and everyone had a gun. A fight broke out and sooner or later there was shooting. Most of us headed inside to stay out of the way, but the firing continued all night."

Simply getting to where the 345th was fighting was difficult, if not dangerous. As had those who had joined the group since 1943, most men started out from the San Francisco area and from there proceeded to Hawaii before hopscotching down to New Guinea. From New Guinea—usually following some sort of theater-specific training—they bounced across and up a series of airfields and islands until arriving in the Philippines.

Administrative delays, lack of transportation, accidents, and illness, not to mention enemy air and sea attacks, all took a toll. The experience of George Givens was representative. He completed his indoctrination training at Nadzab during mid-February 1945 and subsequently received orders to report to the 345th at San Marcelino in the Philippines. Trained as a radio operator, he boarded a C-47 with the rest of his crew and two other B-25 crews. The C-47 headed northwest from Nadzab through various airfields.

Still en route on February 22, 1945, Givens and the others climbed aboard a different C-47 at an airfield in the Halmahera Islands. On each side of its nose, the aircraft bore the name *So What?* in big, white letters. *So What?* passed peaceably over Leyte Gulf in the early afternoon, on course for the airfield at Tacloban. Givens and his comrades were mightily impressed by the naval power arrayed below them. Hundreds of cargo vessels, protected by warships, waited to unload equipment and material for the men who fought so desperately in the distant green hills.

The pilot of *So What?* descended and set up to land at Tacloban. However, he didn't lose altitude quickly enough. "As we passed over the end of the runway, we seemed to be awfully high," said Givens.[3] The aircraft still had not touched down as it passed the runway's midpoint. "I noted the alarmed looks on the faces of the men about me." All of the passengers were B-25 crewmen, and they could see that something was not right.

The pilot finally slammed the C-47 to earth too far down the runway. He immediately applied maximum braking, but it was too late. "With the brakes fully locked on the right landing gear," said Givens, "the pilot desperately attempted to steer *So What?* onto the taxiway at the end of the landing strip. Our speed was too great. The aircraft spun to the right, but our momentum carried us straight ahead. The landing gear collapsed under us with a rending, grinding crunch. We careened off the end of the runway and crashed into a drainage ditch."

Givens groped for a handhold. "The last thing I saw before being knocked unconscious was bodies flying through the compartment—and I was one of them." The aircraft did not explode or burn but rather came to rest after passing between two trucks. The men in the trucks paused to be sure there would be no explosion before rushing to aid the badly battered occupants. Givens regained consciousness outside the aircraft. "How I got there I do not know." He had no external injuries, although his neck and shoulders, which had probably been dislocated and relocated, pained him badly.

In fact, no one was seriously injured, although a few of the men sustained gashes and bruises. Medical personnel tended to them, and most were soon on their way. Givens recalled that the worst harm was done by their rescuers, who "robbed us blind. Not of our wallets, but of our .45-caliber pistols, our watches and our very expensive, GI issue, Ray Ban sunglasses."

A day or so later, aboard another C-47, Givens and the others left Tacloban for the 345th's base at San Marcelino. "As we banked over a line of low lying hills I caught a glimpse of the airstrip in the valley below. One dusty road ran the length of the valley. The group headquarters was to the east of the road and the tent area to the western side. Each squadron had its own distinct area layout and it gave the appearance of military neatness. The hard-packed crushed coral runway laid about a fourth of a mile to the west of the bivouac area."

The C-47 set down—without crashing—and Givens and the other men peered through the small windows.

We taxied past rows of B-25s parked on their hardstands. But these were B-25s like we had never seen before. Every one of them had large red, white and black Indian heads painted on the vertical stabilizers. However, the most striking element of their appearance was the nose art. Fierce-looking birds, bats and horse heads covered the entire nose sections of the aircraft. Some of the planes were being serviced by ground crews. Deuce-and-a-half [two-and-a-half-ton] trucks picked us up and delivered us to the headquarters area. In front of the headquarters tent was a large sign identifying the outfit stationed here. It had a large Indian head painted on it like the one on the bombers at the airstrip.

Givens had finally arrived at the 345th Bomb Group.

He was assigned to the 498th Bomb Squadron. After some preliminary instructions, the enlisted men followed a corporal to the squadron's living area. "He then led us to into a tent and assigned us to empty cots. He instructed us not to switch cots with one another as he was the man who came around in the dark of night to wake up men who were scheduled to go out on the mission for that day. He knew the exact location in all the tents in the squadron of where every gunner was assigned. 'Stay put. Stay in your assigned cot, and don't screw me up.' Then he left."[4]

Al Stone, like Givens and many of the men sent to the Air Apaches during this time, wound his way up to the Philippines only after enduring a bewildering series of training stops, detours, delays, and rough rides. "I was put into the 500th Bomb Squadron," Stone said. "They already had enough armorers, so I was put into the ordnance group—bombs. It was typical of the Army. I had been trained as a radio operator, and as a gunner, but had never before been around bombs."

For all he knew about bombs, Al Stone might just as well have been pulled straight out of his high school history class. "I didn't mind it though," he said. "Everyone there had a really good attitude and worked really well as a team. Each man was assigned just one or two jobs that he got really good at. It was an efficient system."

"I'd usually go to the bomb dump in the morning and we'd load bombs on a trailer that we pulled with a pickup truck. The trailer had indentations in it so that the bombs wouldn't roll around. Then, we'd take them to the flight line and kick them off onto the ground next to the airplanes."

"We put the fins on the bombs before we put them in the bomb bay," Stone said. "My other job was to mount the shackles into the bomb bay so that we could hang the bombs. After the mission, I'd take them out. There were different shackles for different sized bombs." He recalled one payload that didn't require shackles: "On one mission—as sort of joke on the Japanese—we loaded a bunch of empty bottles into the bomb bay on top of a normal load of bombs. The bottles whistled as they fell, and we figured it would give them a good scare."

"The fuzes weren't put into the bombs until after they were loaded. I didn't do that because it was a little bit more complicated. One of our old, crusty sergeants who knew everything about everything did the fuzes."

"The parafrag bombs had a plunger fuze and came to us already built with the parachute attached," said Stone. "They hung vertically in the bomb bay. They had a devastating effect on the Japanese troops when our aircrews flew missions in front of the army. We could actually hear the fighting at San Marcelino."

"I went up to Zig-Zag Pass with a couple of mechanics to salvage a Japanese truck," Stone recalled. The area to which he referred had seen two weeks of savage fighting during February 1945 as the U.S. Army pushed east up Highway 7 from the town of Olangapo on Subic Bay. "Our group had done a lot of strafing and bombing with parafrags in that area. There were Japanese bodies everywhere. And I mean everywhere. The stink was terrible—the smell of those Jap bodies. And I saw several parafrag bombs that hadn't exploded. They had gotten hung up on one thing or another and hadn't hit the ground. Anyway, they just ended up bulldozing those Japanese into the ground."

"I was pretty proud—even at the time—of what we were doing and how well we did it," Stone said. "And I think that was the general feeling.

We were part of a team that was doing an important job. We were making a difference in the war."

"There was a lot of respect between everyone—officers and enlisted men, flyers and ground crews" he said. "There wasn't a lot of saluting, but that didn't mean that we were lazy or sloppy. We knew our jobs and we did them well. One of the ways we showed our respect to the aircraft crews was by gathering at the end of the runway as they took off for their missions. We'd stand there and wave or salute as they went by."

"Still, although we respected them, we didn't often try to make close friends with the aircrews," Stone said. "The nature of combat was that they could be there one day, go out on a mission, and not come back. And that could really shake a person up."

Al Stone mentioned the parafrag bombs—quite possibly dropped by the 345th—that he spotted while passing through Zig-Zag Pass. In fact, aside from making shipping sweeps and hitting isolated Japanese outposts, the group flew a great many ground-support sorties during this period. Working under the guidance of a ground controller embedded with infantry units, the 345th's crews bombed and strafed stretches of jungle without ever seeing whatever they were supposed to be killing. Many of the aircrews felt that these missions were unrewarding or even ineffective.

"The jungle was so thick," said one pilot, "that we really couldn't see anything at all down on the ground. If the Jap positions weren't marked, we would have had no idea that anything was down there. A lot of the time we worked with Marine Corps aircraft—Corsairs—and they marked the targets with rockets."[5]

Typical was the mission flown by the 500th Bomb Squadron on February 18, 1945. The squadron sent nine aircraft to the Bataan Peninsula, where they bombed under the control of a ground controller with the callsign "Zombie." The squadron recorded that "a total of eighteen 1,000-pound demolition bombs were dropped in the wooded areas along the Bagac-Pilar Road as directed, but results of both bombing and strafing were unobserved."

Unobserved or not, the missions often caused real damage, as pointed out by John Clifford Hanna, the group's intelligence officer. In his position he occasionally received reports from very grateful infantry units describing the results of the ground-support missions. "In contrast with our 'results unobserved due to terrain,' what they find as they advance into the bombed area provides strike evaluation and intelligence of the highest order."

He relayed the report of a unit supported by the Air Apaches: "An Alamo Scout [6th Army Special Reconnaissance] had reached the area and he reported this damage: 3 trucks destroyed, blood noted all over area, ammo dump destroyed, oil and gas dump destroyed. Five landslides closing road in five places, one bridge knocked out and several houses destroyed." Hanna noted, "This was damage indeed, and a source of immense satisfaction to the crews that had flown the mission, albeit quite a surprise."

Hanna further underscored the validity of the report. "Here was the immediate eyewitness account of the man on the ground—no guesswork, no interpretation of photographs, no probably this or that. Just plain, cold facts." He also observed that, in reaction to this report, the men flew these heretofore unremarkable missions "with much more enthusiasm."

Japan was a maritime nation, and by 1945 its dependence on raw materials convoyed from the territories it had conquered was critical. To the south, oil and other material from Borneo and the Netherlands East Indies was consolidated at Singapore before being moved north to Japan. At that point, American submarines were ubiquitous across virtually the entire Pacific, and Japanese convoys were forced to hug the protective shorelines of Indochina and China. They moved primarily during the night when they were more difficult to detect and track. During the day they laid up in harbors protected by minefields, antisubmarine vessels, aircraft, and antiaircraft guns.

Still, the pressure from the Allies remained relentless. The Philippines had been seized, in part, to serve as a base for interdicting the Japanese convoys. General George Kenney said, "It was quite evident that the Japs realized the decisive nature of the struggle for the Philippines. The islands sat astride the routes from Japan to the Netherlands East Indies and if our aircraft once started flying over the China Sea and cutting off the supplies of oil, rubber, tin and other essential raw materials to the factories in the homeland, the Rising Sun would soon start setting."[6]

Aside from the Philippines, the island of Formosa was critical to Japan's survival. Historically a relatively undeveloped province of China, Formosa was handed to the Japanese in 1895 following the First Sino-Japanese War. Strategically situated between Japan and the Philippines and roughly a hundred miles from the Chinese coast, it presented a heavily fortified threat to Allied operations. And it offered safe refuge to the shipping that moved between Japan's conquests in the south and the Home Islands.

Accordingly, it was, together with the Philippines, considered for invasion. For a number of reasons—moral, political, and military—the decision was made to retake the Philippines, which were still American territory, and bypass Formosa. However, bypassed or not, Formosa had to be neutralized. Regular air raids were key to that neutralization, and the 345th played a significant role beginning on February 20, when the group sent a mission against the railroad marshalling yards at Choshu, on the southern tip of the island. That raid caused indeterminate damage at the cost of one aircraft.

The Air Apaches next went back to Formosa on March 2, 1945. On that day, the group's four squadrons launched a total of thirty-four aircraft out of San Marcelino. They were only one of many Fifth Air Force units scheduled to hit a spectrum of targets across the island. On a heading of almost due north, the 345th's B-25s left the Philippines, crossed the South China Sea, and flew up the west coast of Formosa. Finally, after flying more than six hundred miles, the 500th Bomb Squadron led the group in an easterly turn across the northwest coast and then headed south.

All across Formosa, Japanese defenders were alerted. Certainly, that was the case at Toyohara Airfield, the 345th's target. Finally, with the airfield off the formation's right side, the 500th turned west, directly toward it. Overhead, two squadrons of P-51 fighters provided high cover. Out of the turn, the 500th and the trailing squadrons arranged themselves in line-abreast formations.

Even with as much warning as they had had, the Japanese fighter pilots at Toyohara still failed to get airborne. Nevertheless, the antiaircraft gunners were ready and offered stiff resistance. Machine-gun and twenty-millimeter-cannon fire was particularly fierce and, as described by the 500th, "caught our airplanes in a deadly crossfire over the drome, throwing up a barrage-type fire." The 345th's squadrons nevertheless pressed their attacks and strafed aircraft, buildings, antiaircraft guns, and supply dumps. In their wake, more than a thousand twenty-three-pound parafrags drifted to the ground and exploded in orange-black bursts that sent shrapnel hurtling across the airfield.

Virtually all the enemy aircraft were heavily camouflaged, and many failed to burn when hit by the Air Apaches. This possibly indicated that there wasn't enough fuel to get them airborne or that they were being held in reserve. Nevertheless, many of the various buildings that were strafed and bombed blew apart or erupted into flames.

The B-25 crews stayed at treetop level as they raced away from the airfield. They continued to strafe and bomb military targets as well as towns and villages. One of the 501st's crews dropped a salvo of twelve parafrags on a machine-gun nest southwest of the airfield and reported "destroying two shacks and demolishing the gun positions. Debris, torn clothing, and parts of bodies were seen flying in the area after these bomb bursts."

The Japanese defenders put holes in twenty of the group's aircraft. The B-25 flown by the 500th's Arthur McKinney was hit, turned directly for the coast, and went down shortly after crossing the shoreline. The squadron reported, "The plane exploded and burned on impact and the entire crew was believed to have been killed. However, a P-51 in the area reported the presence of one motionless body atop one of the airplane's tires floating in the water." A rescue aircraft was called to the scene, but to no avail.

The 499th aircraft piloted by Clifford Sisson climbed out of formation with engine problems. The formation leader directed Francis Thompson to escort Sisson, unaware that Thompson's aircraft was also critically hit. Thompson's radio transmitter was out, and his protests went unheard. Nevertheless, he dropped back to protect Sisson, who climbed to six thousand feet after feathering his right engine.

A short time later, for no apparent reason, Sisson's aircraft began dropping to the sea. Streaming fuel, the bomber leveled off just a few hundred feet above the waves. At that point, low on fuel, Thompson had to turn for home. Sisson was last seen under control on a southwesterly heading. Neither he nor his crew was ever heard from again.

Thompson, also losing fuel, barely made it back to the airfield at Lingayen. "Lieutenant Thompson made a crash landing at Lingayen when his nose wheel would not lower," noted the squadron's mission summary report, "and did an excellent job in saving the crew. The airplane was damaged beyond repair but salvage is practical. Three men sustained minor wounds."

Formosa proved itself a tough target. It would demonstrate that toughness many more times to the 345th during the coming months.

⌐⌐

Early in 1945 Kenney had directed Ennis Whitehead, commander of the Fifth Air Force, to "maintain an air blockade of the China Sea, all the way to the China coast, to stop all ship movements from the Netherlands East Indies towards Japan."[7] Whitehead focused a considerable portion of his resources on meeting his boss's directions. The Air Apaches were among those resources.

One of the 345th's men who saw action during these operations was Roger Lovett, a Kansas native. Several years earlier he had been one of those enthusiastic young men who worried that the war might end before he had an opportunity to fight. "I went so far as to write the Royal Air Force and the Royal Canadian Air Force to see if I could leave the States and enroll in their cadet flying programs. They actually replied, but declined my request." His ardor to serve never diminished, and when he turned seventeen he secured his parents' written permission to join the Navy.

One of Lovett's friends was scheduled to leave for an Army aviation screening center in early 1943. "He asked me to ride the train with him from Lawrence to Kansas City," Lovett said. "He wanted a little company on the way. When we got to Kansas City there were a great many young men milling around."

After a time, the crowd of would-be fliers was herded aboard the buses staged nearby. "I said goodbye to my friend and stood around while the place emptied out. Then, there came along a sergeant and he told me—very directly—to get aboard a bus."

Lovett explained that he wasn't part of the group. "The sergeant seemed a little indignant and asked me why, and I explained that I wasn't old enough. He asked me how old I was, and when I declared that I was only seventeen he said that all I needed was permission from my parents. I told him that I had a permission slip from the Navy that my parents had signed—in fact, I had it with me." The sergeant took a brief look at the paper, grabbed Lovett by the elbow, and hurried him into a waiting bus.

"That was how I ended up in the Army."

Following a brief stint as a flight instructor, Lovett was trained as a B-25 pilot, then sent to Nadzab in early 1945 for theater-specific training and a follow-on assignment to a combat unit. "We got called into headquarters a week or so later," said Lovett, "and were handed all our records in manila envelopes. We had orders to join the 345th Bomb Group. We asked where they were and they told us they didn't know. When we asked how we were supposed to get there, we were told to hitch a ride!"

Lovett and the rest of the crew divined that the 345th was somewhere in the Philippines. "We were able to catch a ride to Biak, and then Halmahera. We finally got to Tacloban but the 345th had already left. So, the crew spread out like magazine salesmen to see what we could find out—we'd gotten pretty good at that sort of thing."

It took them three days. "We spotted a 345th truck that was hauling lumber. We found out that the driver was part of a small rear party that was rounding up the unit's wooden flooring and sending it up to San Marcelino via C-47. Wood was a commodity."

The C-47 took Lovett and his companions—and a full load of used lumber—to San Marcelino where they finally caught up with the Air Apaches. "The first thing they wanted to know when we got off the plane," he said, "was whether or not we had any booze. As much as wood was a commodity, booze was even more so. And really, anywhere you landed, whoever was there always wanted to know if you had anything to drink."

Soon after the business of who had liquor and who did not was settled, Lovett was assigned to the 500th Bomb Squadron. He and the rest of the newly joined men were gathered together for what he described as "a brief welcome. It went something like this: 'Welcome to the 500th Bomb Squadron. We're called the Rough Raiders but we're known more familiarly as the Bloody 500th. We deal more misery to the enemy than the other squadrons do, and we pay a higher toll. Take a look at the man on either side of you. One of the three of you will not be going home; those are the odds in this squadron. Enjoy your stay.'"

This declaration was not wrong. Of the four Air Apaches squadrons, the 500th sustained the greatest losses. Other squadrons might have argued with the 500th's belief that it dealt the Japanese the greatest hurt, but no one would ever say that it was not an effective unit.

Lovett's second mission on March 6, 1945, put him square in the middle of the action he had craved for so long. The target was the airfield at Samah, on Hainan Island, from which the Japanese launched aircraft to cover the convoys moving back and forth between the South Pacific and the Home Islands. He flew as a copilot aboard one of the nine aircraft the 500th put airborne that day.

"After getting to the island we swung inland for a while," said Lovett, "before we turned back toward the airfield in a line abreast. Our aircraft was on the far left side, closest to the bay." The Japanese had been alerted, and Lovett saw fighters readying for takeoff. "We achieved some degree of surprise because we jumped a bunch of Zeroes as they were taking off. They were painted a very light color—gray, or white. Or maybe silver."

As low to the ground as they dared fly, the 500th's crews fired their guns as the airfield came into range. "And they kept jamming," said Lovett of the guns in his aircraft's nose. "One of my jobs was to clear the jams and charge the guns by pulling on the T-handles that were connected by cables to each receiver. My pilot, Bill Lentz, kept firing and shouting, 'Charge those damn guns! Charge those damn guns!'"

To their right, eight other B-25s also ripped the airfield with gunfire. Bombs fell from their bellies and skimmed the ground before slamming into their targets. "Our path took us across a revetment and toward a headquarters area," said Lovett. "As we approached one building, a bunch of people dressed all in white rushed out and jumped into a brushy area." The vegetation offered no protection against the streams of bullets that Lentz sent into it.

"We shot up one aircraft in a revetment," Lovett recalled. Getting the bomb bay doors open and dropping the bombs was one of his duties. "There was a toggle switch that released the bombs and our technique was to let them go just before the pilot pulled up to clear whatever it was we were bombing. It was pretty much done by intuition," he said. "I was pretty busy during all of this, but we still put two of our bombs into a very long, low building."

On the other side of the airfield a Zero dove on Vernon Sawyer's aircraft and saddled up from behind. Sawyer's turret gunner, Robert Manley, returned fire and struck it in the engine. The Zero pilot pulled up and away, and Manley stitched its belly with more .50-caliber rounds. The enemy aircraft fell away smoking, no longer a threat. According to Lovett,

As we cleared the target I turned back to the navigator. It was his responsibility to check the bomb bay and make certain that we didn't have any bombs stuck in there before I closed the doors. I shouted at him to do his checks and he nodded at me but just kept staring straight ahead. I shouted at him three more times and he still did nothing—this was also his first time in real combat. Finally, I blessed him very coarsely and just took a chance and closed the doors.

We sped out of there as fast as we could go at about twenty-five feet. The Jap fighters that had been able to get airborne didn't bother us. They followed at a safe distance for only a little while before turning back.

Once we got far enough away from the target we arranged ourselves into three-ship formations and started climbing. One of our aircraft, flown by Jack Barnes, had been hit in the left engine; it had a runaway propeller. We slowed down and climbed with him but the engine finally failed and the propeller wouldn't feather. There was no way that he could stay airborne on one engine with all that drag.

Barnes's crew rode the crippled bomber down until he could keep it from the water no more. "He made a very nice water landing," said Lovett. "And it floated pretty well. We circled them for a while and dropped a large life raft. We counted six crewmen out of the plane—five in one raft and one in another." Ultimately, low on fuel, Lentz and Lovett and the rest of the crew were forced to head back to San Marcelino.

Air Sea Rescue was contacted. A Catalina was on the scene within an hour but did not find Barnes and his men. The 345th sent search missions for three subsequent days without success. Whether Barnes and his crew simply perished at sea or were captured and killed by the Japanese was never determined. "It was a very sad thing," said Lovett.

An incident that occurred soon after he arrived at San Marcelino compelled Lovett to consider the differences between himself and his comrades as compared to the Japanese. "Some of our men caught a Japanese soldier who had been hiding out in the jungle. He was near-starved and had sneaked into our area looking for food. Instead of beating him up or shooting him or beheading him as the Japanese would have done to any one of us, our guys gave him food." Of course, not all American units were so kindly. The savagery of the fighting in the Pacific was such that Americans sometimes killed Japanese rather than make them prisoners.

On March 10, 1945, the Air Apaches sent six aircraft each from the 498th and 500th Bomb Squadrons to comb the coast of Indochina for enemy shipping. The 500th hit pay dirt at Tourane Bay, where it found a large tanker and several smaller vessels. The squadron made two low-level attacks and left the tanker sinking and several other vessels struggling to stay afloat. Having sustained no significant damage, the eight crews sped away but were attacked by four Nakajima Ki-44 "Tojo" fighters as they reached the mouth of the bay.

The first two fighters attacked from high and behind, "closing to 800 yards before breaking away when [the squadron's] gunners opened fire." Another attacked up the formation's left side but turned away as it was struck by fire from the B-25s. The Tojos continued their attacks as described by the crews. "One pass was made at our airplanes from ten o'clock level, skimming level over the top of the formation and breaking away at six o'clock. This Tojo did not fire. All enemy planes were black with no insignias or other markings. Our tactics consisted of turning slightly into Jap attack and tightening of formation." Ultimately, the Japanese fighters did no harm to the 500th's B-25s.

More than a hundred miles down the coast, the 498th's formation also scored when a tanker was spotted moored close to shore. The crews made two bombing runs each, in two-ship formations. Franklin Chambers dropped a pair of bombs against the tanker, and one of the delayed fuzes malfunctioned. Rather than detonating several seconds after impact, it blew up instantaneously. Although rocked hard by the bomb's shock wave, the aircraft seemed to have sustained no great hurt. Chambers's radio operator, Bauduy Grier, recalled that it felt as if his feet had been smashed by a baseball bat.

When the 498th's aircraft turned for home, the tanker was sinking. Behind it, a large petroleum tank—into which an errant bomb had skipped—was split open and burning. Sheets of flame reached a thousand feet or more skyward. A black smoke plume climbed many times higher.

The formation was well out across the South China Sea when the left engine on Chambers's B-25 puked smoke. It failed rapidly, and the propeller refused to feather. The good engine did not have enough power to keep the aircraft aloft, and it fell inexorably toward the water.

Grier and the crew's gunner, Jimmy Lane, threw equipment overboard in an attempt to lighten the aircraft. It did no good. The two men finally sat and braced themselves for the water landing.

The sea was rough, and the bomber hit the water hard, knocking both Grier and Lane unconscious. The aircraft's tail lifted clear of the waves at a forty-five-degree angle. When Grier came to, he threw a one-man raft through a window. "I glanced up to the cockpit, already underwater," Grier said, "and bellowed and hollered hoping for some response at the same time yanking on the lever to release the main life raft."[8] There was no response from the front of the aircraft, and the main life raft refused to deploy.

Grier and Lane, close friends, escaped into the water together. There was no sign of the rest of the crew. Lane could not swim, and Grier kept him calm and afloat until Lane latched onto an oxygen bottle that had broken away during the crash. Paralyzed with fear, he begged Grier, a champion collegiate diver, to help him. At the same time the main life raft rocketed to the surface, having broken clear of the sinking bomber. Grier tried to drag Lane after the wind-blown raft, but he wouldn't let go of the oxygen bottle. Finally, with no other choice, Grier let go of his friend and swam for the raft, which was quickly blowing away.

Grier caught the raft after a great, wave-tossed race. He struggled mightily to get aboard and, exhausted, paddled and thrashed in a vain search for Lane. Swells lifted him up and dropped him down until he lost all sense of direction. There was no sign of his friend. Physically beaten and tormented by the loss of his comrade, he fell to the bottom of the raft, where he sobbed between bouts of vomiting.

George Givens was aboard Elmo Cranford's aircraft that day. Cranford, the 498th's formation leader, circled as Chambers's stricken B-25 slammed into the waves, shrouded by a massive spray of seawater. "We saw only two men come out of the back of the plane," said Givens. "No one got out of the front—the hatch must have jammed."[9]

The sight of the two survivors struggling against the wind-whipped waves was heartbreaking. "One of the guys managed to get a life raft deployed, and get into it," said Givens. "The other guy was on the far side of the fuselage with his Mae West inflated. He tried to swim around the tail to get to the raft, but the wind and the waves pushed him away. Then the airplane started to sink."

Givens and his crewmates hated the helplessness they felt, knowing that four men were drowning in the sinking bomber at that very instant. "And the guy in the raft had an oar and was trying to paddle to the other crewman, but it was obvious that the wind was blowing them apart. The crewman in the water was almost sure to die. We didn't have much fuel and had to leave them. I tossed and turned that night, thinking about the man who didn't get into the raft."

"The next day," Givens said, "we sent out search aircraft, but they found nothing."

The group also mounted operational missions that next day. On March 11, 1945, the 345th's 499th Bomb Squadron sent six ships from San Marcelino to Indochina to harry the enemy's coastal traffic. In addition to shipping, the trains on the rail lines that ran just a short distance inland were also valid targets. When the formation made landfall near Cape Batangas, John Baeta led two other aircraft north, while the other three B-25s headed south.

Motoring along at only a couple hundred feet, Baeta's little formation darted back and forth across the coastline. They discovered nothing particularly noteworthy but fired their guns at targets of opportunity as they presented themselves. After some time, Baeta noted the oil pressure on the right engine was below normal limits and falling. Leaning forward, he saw a thin plume of bluish-white smoke streaming back from the failing engine.

The smoke was followed by a fire, which Baeta quickly suffocated with CO_2 from the engine's fire extinguisher. He immediately aborted the mission, started a climbing turn away from the coast, dumped the ship's bombs, and pressed his navigator, Edward Karnis, for a heading to Triton Reef.

"We had been warned against heroics in the event that we lost an engine," Baeta said. "They didn't want us to try to make it back across all that water on just one engine." Consequently, the men were often briefed to ditch at specific locations where flying boats or submarines might more easily pick them up. On that day, in case of an emergency, they had been told to put down at Triton Reef in the Paracel Islands. Though little more than a coral spit—often submerged at high tide—it was nevertheless a readily identifiable point in an otherwise broad expanse of open sea.

Trailed by his two wingmen, Baeta shut down the failing engine and nursed his aircraft northeast until, nearly an hour later, he spotted Triton Reef. "I circled around until I figured out on which side of the reef the water was calmest." Baeta eased the aircraft down as he turned into the wind. Just prior to making contact with the water, he secured the good engine and held the nose of the B-25 up until it stalled onto the surface.

Notwithstanding his deft touch, the impact was still jarring. "The crews circling above me said it looked like a PBY touching down with sprays of water shooting out from both sides of the nose."

The aircraft's nose ducked momentarily under the surface. "Water came pouring in through the top hatch," said Baeta. "I thought we were all going to drown." There followed a rending screech as a section of the reef tore into the bottom of the fuselage and jerked the B-25 to a stop. "My copilot, Tom Frazier, crushed a vertebra in his neck," said Baeta. "His hand, which was on the control column, was also injured. One of the gunners hurt his head when he tried to dive through the Plexiglas side hatch. The rest of us had a few cuts and bumps and bruises, but we all managed to get out without drowning."

Baeta and his men climbed out of the aircraft and rallied atop the half-submerged B-25. "We walked across the wing and onto the reef. We dragged our life raft with us and waved to our squadron mates who were circling overhead." The other two aircraft dipped low and dropped another raft, emergency rations, and water. "My biggest concern," Baeta said, "was drinking water. I didn't know how long we would be out there." His anxiety grew when the other two crews, low on fuel, wagged their wings and turned for home.

They were alone.

Huddled on the reef, Baeta and his men tended to their injuries as best they could and took stock of their equipment and their situation. It was reasonable to assume that their comrades had radioed for help. Nevertheless, the horizon was empty. "We were worried that maybe the Japanese might find us before our own people did."

At that very moment, Millard Bornstein and the crew of his PBM—a more modern amphibious flying boat than the trusty PBY—were having no luck as they searched for Franklin Chambers and his crew, including Bauduy Grier. They had gone down only the day prior. A message was received that another B-25 had gone down at Triton Reef. Knowing that the odds of recovering this second crew, Baeta's, would be better if he acted immediately, Bornstein broke off his search and headed for Triton Reef. He was anxious to get there before nightfall, when it would be more difficult to spot the stranded men and more dangerous to set his big aircraft down.

It was late in the day—almost dusk—when one of John Baeta's crewmen spotted the aircraft. There was no immediate celebration as the men squinted at the vague form. It might have been Japanese. "And then I saw that it had gull wings," said Baeta, "and knew right away that it was a [Martin] PBM Mariner. So, we fired our Very pistols, and waved and jumped up and down."

"Of course the men in the seaplane were careful, because they didn't know who we were, either," said Baeta. "But after circling for a bit, the PBM landed and we paddled our rafts out to it. They loaded us aboard and took us to Lingayen [about fifty miles north of San Marcelino] where their seaplane tender was moored. They had a dispensary and a doctor there, and he looked us over pretty good and patched us up as best he could. And they gave us new clothes—Navy clothes."

"We carried Colt .45-caliber pistols," Baeta said. "And the Navy folks at Lingayen were really envious as their sidearms were smaller .38-caliber revolvers. They kept after us to horse trade away our .45s."

The 499th sent several aircraft out to Triton Reef the following day to find Baeta and his crew, evidence that communications between the Navy and the Army were difficult. "They didn't find anything," Baeta said. "The aircraft was washed out to sea at high tide, and of course we were gone. It wasn't long until they started packing our personal belongings up to send home. They finally got word we were at Lingayen about three or four days later and sent an airplane to come get us."

❧

George Givens flew several missions across the South China Sea. "If it had a motor, either on shore or out at sea, we shot it up," he recalled. "And because it was so far from where we were based in the Philippines, we didn't take a gunner, or the two .50-caliber machine guns in the waist. Or the ammunition boxes and ammunition that went with them. This saved weight so that we were able to stay airborne longer."

Prior to an attack, the 345th's radiomen typically stepped away from their little position in the radio compartment to man the tail guns. This could be terrifyingly disorienting not only due to the obvious fact that the men were in combat but because many pilots slewed the fire of their nose guns back and forth across the target by alternately stepping on the rudder pedals. Of course, this also "wagged the tail" of the bomber. So then the tail gunner faced backward, racing only dozens of feet over the ground or sea at more than two hundred miles per hour, while being tossed back and forth. And while being shot at. And while shooting back with two powerful .50-caliber machine guns. "It was an exciting ride," said Givens.

The tail gun position obviously pointed to the rear, and Givens had to exercise some resourcefulness to get his guns onto a worthwhile target before it was too late.

The position had a sort of bicycle seat about a foot off the floor that helped to take some pressure from your knees. I would take my helmet off, then twist around and push my head into the small Plexiglas blister above me. Looking forward over the top of the aircraft, I could see what was coming up and get ready in time. It also helped when the copilot called out targets for me. Normally, I'd just fire a short burst to get my aim, and then fire longer bursts afterward. But I had to be pretty quick because we'd fly out of range in just a matter of seconds.

"I was scared my first few times," he said. "And I almost always got nervous as we approached the coast. I was all alone back there—I couldn't see anyone else. But after the first few missions, once the shooting started, I turned into a killer. The smell of cordite was almost like a drug, and I wanted to kill everything."

The frenetic nature of air combat was such that the mind couldn't record every bit of action. And over time, many of the images that were registered faded until they were forgotten. However, some memories, for whatever reason, remained vivid. "I was in the tail gun position," said Marvin "Murph" Leventon, a radio operator with the 500th Bomb Squadron, "and I don't remember where we were on this particular mission, but we were making a low-level attack. I spotted a truck that was moving pretty fast and I covered him with a burst of machine-gun fire. That truck just sort of slowed down and started weaving and then tumbled off the side of the road. It was almost funny. I don't know why that memory sticks in my mind. It just does."[10]

Chapter Fifteen

"He Was Even More Handsome in His Uniform"

"I used to dream of meeting and falling in love with a tall, dark and handsome Prince Charming," remembered Ruth.[1] "But I didn't really meet my Prince Charming. Instead, I sort of grew up with him at church." One evening, at a youth group meeting in their hometown of Glenbrook, Connecticut, sixteen-year-old Ruth disagreed with Robert Jensen and stuck her tongue out. "That was the beginning!"

They started dating. "Bob was tall at six-foot-four, and blonde—not dark—but very handsome." Their relationship continued until they went to study at different colleges in different states. "We decided to cool it off for the time being," Ruth recalled, "and agreed it was okay to see others. Then, December 7, 1941, happened and Bob enlisted sometime after."

Several years passed before Ruth and Jensen had any meaningful contact. During that time he completed pilot training. "On Easter Day, 1944, I was washing dishes, when I looked out the window and saw Bob and a friend walking towards his aunt's house which was next to ours. He was even more handsome in his uniform—my heart missed a beat or two, or more."

"That night, I called his buddy, Lloyd, and told him that I would love to see Bob. Lloyd knew that Bob had gone to the movie. He picked me up and we waited in the car across from the theater. Upon seeing Bob, Lloyd called out, 'Jensen! Come on over here! Someone wants to see you!'" Bob took Ruth home that evening.

The two began dating again with urgency, although Jensen was hard at B-25 training in Greenville, South Carolina. Nevertheless, they married on July 29, 1944, and soon moved to Columbia, South Carolina, where Jensen received orders overseas in October. "So I returned home to Connecticut," said Ruth. "Naturally, it was heartbreaking, but I was happy with the knowledge that his baby would be born in May. Back at home, I wrote a letter to Bob every night, and then left it outside my parents' bedroom door for my dad to mail when he went to work each day in New York City."

Talmadge Epps stopped flying combat during this time. He had been with the group since before it had left the States. Unlike many of his comrades, he'd had extraordinary luck. When his pilot smashed into a New Guinea mountainside on June 27, 1943, he had been at sea, safeguarding equipment. And when he was scheduled to be aboard the ill-fated C-47 flight to Sydney that killed twenty-seven on August 7, 1943, he was not. And when he decided to continue flying combat well beyond his mandated tour—so that he could continue to take furloughs to see the Australian girl who had captured his heart—he survived. Indeed, after most of his squadron mates had returned to the States, he remarked, he continued to fly "for love."

"Anyway, after a lot of praying," he said, "instead of filing papers to go home, I filed an application to marry Miss Ruth Pearson of Australia. In addition to obtaining the young lady's approval, and that of her parents', your commanding general had to ask the International Red Cross to run a check on each applicant. This was due to abuse by personnel marrying more than one person. When I applied, I had about fifty missions. When I received approval, I had survived 109 missions. The odds against this were astronomical." Epps and Ruth Pearson were wed in Australia on March 15, 1945. His combat days were finally over.

The 345th's antishipping operations continued, and the group sent twelve aircraft to sweep the Chinese coast on March 15, 1945, the same day that

Epps was married. Approaching landfall near Henghai Bay, the formation broke up as planned, with six B-25s from the 498th swinging north while the other six aircraft—from the 500th—turned south.

The 498th's formation motored all the way to Swatow and recorded "nil sightings." They regrouped, climbed, and headed southeast back to the 345th's base at San Marcelino. The six aircraft of the 500th, on the other hand, had better hunting. Moving south from Chelang Point, they noted nothing worth their attention until reaching a point approximately fifteen miles south of Hong Kong at the mouth of the Canton River. There, near Tungku Island, a heavily camouflaged freighter of two thousand tons was spotted. "Great pains had been taken by the Japs to make this boat appear as a small wooded island," the 500th reported.

Great pains or not, the camouflage did not fool Herman Reheis, who led the 500th that day. Attacking from the west, Reheis dropped low over the water and raced toward the moored freighter. Once in range, he sprayed it with his machine guns. Behind him, Bob Jensen, flying *Bold Venture*, followed. Only seconds before colliding with the enemy freighter, Reheis released a single five-hundred-pound bomb and pulled up just in time to clear the bridge.

During the time between when the bomb buried itself inside the Japanese ship and the instant it exploded, Jensen closed the distance and released his own bomb. His B-25 was directly overhead the freighter when Reheis's bomb detonated.

The violence of the explosion was spectacular and indicated that the vessel was carrying explosive material of some sort. "The hit," the 500th reported, "caused an explosion amidships almost severing the bow and stern sections." Remarkably, Jensen and his crew were not blown to smithereens.

But they were in big trouble. A friend wrote home about what he was able to learn:

The plane came out wobbly and unsteady—evidently hard hit by the explosion of the Jap vessel. The attack on this vessel occurred very close to the shore and there were some high hills down to the shore line. The plane started a turn to the right to avoid these hills and in the middle of the turn it was seen that the crew feathered its right engine. The plane just barely held its altitude but in its crippled condition was unable to turn inside the hill. The plane mushed into the hill and exploded. The other planes of the squadron circled the wreck for a long time, but there were no signs of any survivors.[2]

Reheis and the others could do nothing for Jensen and his crew. They turned toward home, but before departing the area, they strafed two junks into pieces. It was an almost spiteful act of anger over the loss of their comrades.

On the ground, Chinese villagers raced to the site of the crash. At great risk of Japanese retribution, the villagers secreted the bodies of Jensen and his crew to their cemetery. As they were prepared for burial, an American silver dollar—dated 1920—was discovered on one. It was Bob Jensen's good-luck piece. He had been born in 1920. The Chinese returned the coin to his body and, with great solemnity, buried him and the rest of his crew.

Ruth Jensen was at home on Sunday night, March 25, 1945. The war in Europe was less than two months from its end. Allied advances in the Pacific were encouraging. It seemed clear that the war would be over soon. She remembered,

A policeman came to our door. When my mother and I asked why the officer was there, my dad made up some excuse as to the reason.

I went to bed and wrote my nightly letter. In the morning, my father picked it up as usual, but cried and handed it to my mother and said, "Bob will never receive this." He showed her the telegram the policeman had given him.

They came up to me as I was still in bed. My twenty-year-old life came to a sudden crash. But I thanked God that a part of Bob was alive in me. Little Bobby Jensen, Jr., was born on May 17, 1945.

The air blockade missions continued to consume a significant portion of the 345th's operations through the remainder of March. Only a few days after Ruth Jensen learned of her husband's death, the Air Apaches launched in pursuit of a Japanese convoy spotted sailing northward near Hainan Island. Strategically located in the South China Sea, just south of China's southernmost coast, Hainan had good harbors and airfields; it was well garrisoned and ideally situated to support Japanese ships moving south to the Netherlands East Indies or north to Japan.

On March 28, 1945, a Japanese convoy made up of three tankers and shepherded by the destroyer *Amatsukaze* and at least eight other escorts departed Nha Trang Bay in French Indochina for Japan. Originating from Singapore, the convoy, designated HI-88J, was one of a long series of numbered convoys that moved petroleum and other desperately needed material from the Netherlands East Indies, British Malaya, and French Indochina to Japan. The *Amatsukaze*'s bow had been blown off the previous year by the submarine USS *Redfin*, and a temporary bow had been scabbed to its nose. Likewise, most of the other combatants, a mix of coastal defense ships, submarine chasers, and purpose-made escort vessels, were veterans of earlier actions.

The convoy came under air attack almost immediately. U.S. Army Air Forces B-24s sank one of the tankers and forced another vessel to detach. Less than two hours later, the submarine USS *Bluegill* torpedoed the second of the three tankers. The rest of the convoy pressed northward. As it did, American intelligence officers plotted its projected course.

The Air Apaches were ordered to find and attack the convoy that same afternoon, but it did not, as noted by the 499th Bomb Squadron: "During this time the fighter escort called to report the convoy's position, but the message was not clear. The group leader was notified of the situation but ordered an attack on land targets of opportunity." Consequently, the group's four squadrons bombed and strafed coastal railroad infrastructure and towns. For its trouble, the 345th lost an aircraft from the 501st Bomb Squadron.

That aircraft, with an engine shot out, was piloted by George Blair. He headed for the open sea while the crew broadcast a distress message in hopes of reaching a submarine that might be surfaced. "Message from B-25 squadron leader to any sub," recorded the log of the USS *Guavina*. "We answered and got dope that one plane was in trouble and would probably have to ditch." The *Guavina* responded with its position.

"Sighted B-25 about 300 feet off water, one prop feathered," noted the submarine's log nearly an hour after receiving the first distress call. "Got contact by VHF and talked over plans for rescue. Pilot decided to ditch." It was another fifteen minutes before the *Guavina's* log recorded, "We are crossing our fingers—sea running about condition 4-to-5 [very rough]. What a splash!"

Despite the rough conditions, Blair put the bomber into the water without breaking it apart, though he gashed his head quite badly. He sat slumped in his seat, unconscious, as the aircraft filled with water. In the meantime the rest of the crew crawled clear of the sinking B-25, as observed by the *Guavina's* crewmen, who recorded, "Crew jumping out like 'Mexican jumping beans.'" As the submarine maneuvered to get into position to recover the airmen, Blair's gunner, James Richardson, declared that he could not swim and subsequently disappeared.

Blair regained consciousness a couple of minutes later. Exhausted and bleeding badly, he pulled himself clear of the B-25 and fought against the waves. His Mae West inflated only partially, and he lacked the strength to keep his head above the water. He was about to give up "when I looked up in the sky and saw my girlfriend—in color—just her shoulder and her head. I thought if I am ever going to see her again, I better start fighting for my life."[3] Moments later, sailors from the *Guavina* pulled him and the rest of his crew, minus Richardson, to safety.

The Air Apaches were ordered to launch a force the following morning, March 29, with the objective of intercepting and destroying HI-88J. The 499th declared with erudite vibrancy, "This mission was, in effect, another deep slash in the only shipping artery remaining between the heart and the extremities of the Japanese empire."

The group's 501st Bomb Squadron took off with the 498th at 0700. The 499th led the 500th airborne a half hour later. The weather over the convoy's estimated position was poor, with low cloud ceilings, rain squalls, and visibility hampered by fog and haze. Nevertheless, Jack Jones, the 501st's squadron commander, spotted a pair of the Japanese escorts that were identified as frigates. With the 345th's commander, Chester Coltharp, coordinating the group's attack from his copilot's seat, Jones bore down on the trailing Japanese escort, which heeled hard to starboard and began firing at the American bombers.

Flying just above the wave tops, Jones replied with his own .50-caliber nose guns before releasing a bomb that slammed into the stern, "scoring a damaging hit." Jones's wingman dropped two bombs, both of which went long. "Pilots reported the frigate appeared to be throwing over depth charges," observed the 501st, "possibly intending to protect their ship by setting up water spouts around it."

Although curious, this tactic might have worked. Donald Hardeman, following Jones, "was forced to pull up high over the ship because of water spouts or bomb blasts, and did not drop any bombs." His wingman, Rico Pallotta, "was able to slip in under him, and dropped two bombs, one short for a near miss, and the other skipping squarely up the starboard bow where it exploded for a direct hit." In all, the 501st strafed the enemy ship heavily and dropped six five-hundred-pound bombs, two of which struck home. Following the attacks, the vessel was "observed to be billowing black smoke, blazing fiercely amidships, and starting to settle in the bow." Later-arriving Air Apache crews reported, "The crew was seen to abandon ship."

The 501st's last two aircraft went directly after the leading escort ship, which had yet to be attacked. The ship turned hard to port, and both pilots dropped two bombs apiece, which missed. They were followed by Jones and the other six pilots of the 501st. "Captain Jones," reported the squadron, "made a run on this leading frigate, dropping two bombs, one of which scored a direct hit at the port bow." Pallotta also scored another hit, as did one other pilot, Milton Esty. Like the first vessel, this one was mortally damaged and described as "dead still in the water, burning fiercely and listing very badly to the port bow."

—————

The 345th's crews typically attacked ships while in a shallow dive. As they closed the distance, they leveled out just above the water and released their bombs so that they either skipped across the water before slamming into the ship or hit it directly. As they dived, the pilots also fired their guns. Not only did so many hard-hitting machine guns shred men and material, but the bullets that ricocheted from armor had multiple chances to cause more damage. Importantly, the gunfire also modified the behavior of defending antiaircraft gunners, as noted by a contemporary journalist: "A gunboat, of course, is a fierce target. Its fire is heavy and concentrated. But the [B-25] Mitchell crews have made one comforting discovery—the average Japanese gunner will not stick to his gun for more than a third of a Mitchell's run. 'When we get within a thousand yards, they usually duck for cover.'"[4]

The 345th's waist and tail gunners also fired at the enemy when the opportunity presented itself. But the environment was very dynamic—particularly for the waist gunner—as the pilots maneuvered not only to get into position but also to avoid enemy fire. A waist gunner could not simply stand or crouch in his position while he fired his weapon. McKinley Sizemore explained his first experience. "My head was hitting the ceiling and my feet were hitting the floor. I had no way of holding on except the guns."

Of course, the guns were suspended by flexible cords, and using them as a means of staying put when the aircraft was being flown aggressively was difficult—and dangerous. A more experienced crewman instructed Sizemore to "put your toes up under the ledge of the airplane when you're strafing and put your head into the wall. That way you can shoot that gun with one hand and hang on with the other."

He developed a technique as he gained experience. "I had my .50-caliber machine gun, firing out the left side. I'd empty that machine gun, hang it up, and grab the other one on the other side, and try to empty it."

The 498th presumably attacked the same two escort vessels first hit by Jack Jones and the rest of the 501st. However, the 498th's mission summary report gave no indication that the vessels were even damaged before its aircraft arrived. The 498th's lead two-ship attacked the trailing vessel and scored near misses. The second two-ship attacked next, as described by the squadron's report. "Major Jack McClure and Lieutenant Charles Plumb, following the first airplanes, came in from the west, attacking [the ship] from bow to stern from the starboard quarter." McClure skipped a bomb into the escort vessel with results captured by the strike cameras. "Vessel was left sinking and was confirmed later as sunk."

The 498th, just as the 501st had, next attacked the leading ship. McClure was the first to drop his bombs and missed, and the squadron reported that strike photography from this run "shows the vessel underway and not damaged." Kenneth Jordan dropped three bombs. One missed, one landed topside and rolled into the water without detonating, and the third exploded into the side of the ship.

"Bombs hitting the vessel caused a large explosion verified by four crews," observed the squadron's report. "Later attacks by Lieutenant [Richard] Ranger show the vessel on fire and listing to starboard. The vessel was observed to have a huge hole in the side and sinking rapidly. This vessel was confirmed as sunk by Lieutenant Jordan."

It is difficult to reconcile the reports of the two squadrons. A review of the 501st's mission summary report makes clear that the two escort ships were badly damaged and in the process of sinking. On the other hand the 498th's mission summary report indicates that both enemy vessels, which they presumably attacked shortly after the 501st left the area, were underway, undamaged, and in no material distress.

The possibility exists that the two squadrons attacked different vessels, but existing records—such as they are—don't appear to support the loss of four combatant vessels at that time and place. More likely the stress of attacking through stiff antiaircraft fire, exacerbated by bad weather, rough seas, and the explosions resulting from direct hits and near misses, caused the crews to make inconsistent assessments. Still, considering that the squadrons' mission summary reports were compiled only after careful consolidation of observations from all the relevant participants, and evaluation of strike photos, the discrepancies are perplexing.

Another explanation is that both squadrons attacked the Japanese escorts at the same time. Although neither squadron mentioned making contact with the other, the weather was poor. That being the case, it is possible that the different aircrews did not realize they were intermixed.

At any rate, as the 501st noted, "When the two frigates were seen to have been destroyed, Captain Jones ordered the remaining six planes in his squadron to return to base, while he and wingman, Lieutenant [Heath] Steele, proceeded into the weather front to the north of the sinking frigates to search for the rest of the reported convoy." Jones punched through the fog-shrouded weather and into the clear. There, directly in front of him, was the main body of the convoy—approximately ten Japanese ships.

Chester Coltharp, sitting next to Jones, passed the convoy's position to the two remaining 345th squadrons, the 499th and the 500th. Jones told wingman Steele to remain at a distance while he attacked a tanker; Steele had already dropped all his bombs, and there was little sense in exposing him to the ship's antiaircraft fire.

Jones made his run and blanketed the tanker with heavy gunfire. However, his bomb failed to connect, and immediately after passing overhead, he was forced by the weather to fly on instruments. "Lieutenant Steele," the squadron reported, "had disregarded Captain Jones's instructions . . . and decided to add the extra firepower of his guns by strafing and to help cover Captain Jones's attack."

In fact, Jones came away unscathed. Steele was not so lucky. "A direct hit tore off most of his right elevator, while another burst tore a large hole in the fuselage directly to the rear of the navigator's compartment. Several smaller holes were received, but there were no casualties among his crew."

Meanwhile, the 499th "arrived at the target area and spotted two burning vessels. The squadron immediately peeled off to the north, avoiding the two already damaged escort vessels . . . in an attempt to locate other targets."

Robert Todd flew at the head of the 499th and took the squadron's eight aircraft into a cloud-cloaked area of low visibility. At that point he spotted a merchant vessel and made an abrupt turn to engage it, losing the rest of the squadron in the process. The effort was for naught as he failed to score any hits. He was forced by the clouds to fly on instruments for a short time but then broke back into clear weather, where he spotted an escort ship. He dove to attack and again failed to do any significant damage.

The rest of the 499th's aircraft flailed about in the clouds until they happened upon the ships originally struck by the 501st and 498th. They piled on, leaving one of the vessels more of a wreck than it already was. The other slipped under the waves as it was being strafed.

The eight aircraft of the 500th Bomb Squadron were last to attack. "Fog and rain squalls partially hid the convoy," the squadron observed, "and our pilots had to fly on instruments frequently during the attack." Despite the weather, the 500th had better success at finding and attacking the convoy than did the 499th. The squadron declared, "It has been well established that Lieutenant Cyriaque Loisel scored a direct hit on a Sugar Charlie Love tanker, causing it to explode and sink. This pilot also scored a direct hit on a destroyer escort vessel, leaving it listing badly and burning." Kenneth Waring scored a hit on another escort, and "reports indicate an explosion resulted from his attack." Waring had pressed his attack so closely that he brought home a piece of the ship's mast embedded in his right wing.

The accounts of the 345th's attack on Convoy HI-88J are conflicting and unclear, but there is little doubt that the Japanese suffered great harm. A number of escorting combatant ships were sunk or badly damaged, and all, or nearly all, the tankers were destroyed. And the tankers gave the convoy its reason for existing; they carried fuel for the Japanese war effort, whereas the escorting combatants consumed it.

———

The 500th described the ship that Cyriaque Loisel was credited with sinking as a "Sugar Charlie Love" tanker. This designation came from an identification system developed by the U.S. Navy to better classify Japanese merchant ship types. The system was not particularly intuitive but focused generally on the size of a ship and on particular characteristics, such as the type of construction and the location of the engine, among others.

For instance, the Navy's *ONI 208-J (Revised) Supplement 3* describes the Sugar Charlie Love as having a beam of 50 feet and a length of 315 feet. It further notes, "This ship retains the engines-aft design but adopts the 'economy' hull typical of new Japanese construction. Note the long superstructure with bridge aft, with closely-spaced stack, kingpost at forward edge of bridge, and stick mast far forward in the well but not on forecastle. This type has been observed under construction at Fusan, Korea."

The document, published in January 1945, describes other merchant types, such as Fox Tare Charlie, Sugar Baker Sugar, Sugar Able Love, and others. Frankly, the descriptions and drawings were likely more useful to a photographic analyst than to an aircrew hurtling at wave-top level through antiaircraft fire at more than two hundred miles per hour. That men returned from combat and misidentified the types of ships they engaged is a certainty.

Inasmuch as ship attacks often degenerated into wild, freewheeling melees, the Air Apaches did practice a set of preferred tactics. The group described them to higher headquarters after a particularly successful mission: "Whenever possible, that is, when the enemy ship does not outguess us, our attacks are made fore and aft, or quartering rather than abeam. This not only gives a greater area for bombing, it restricts the enemy's antiaircraft fire. The automatic weapons positions usually placed on the sides of the vessel can be effectively strafed on the approach. The best attack is stern-to-bow. This approach allows us to track the ship and counter his evasive turns, and a hit at the stern will usually disable the ship."

When initiating an attack against a convoy, the group preferred "to make [its] first pass in line abreast formation, hitting simultaneously as many ships as possible." Spreading out the group's B-25s typically caused the enemy ships to scatter. This consequently made it difficult for them to concentrate their antiaircraft fire, and they became easier to pick off. "Circumstances occasionally cause the formation leader to vary his attack from the above," the report declared, "but in the main we have found this plan pays dividends in Jap [shipping] tonnage."

CHAPTER SIXTEEN

"Jap Fighters Making Long Range Passes"

CHOKING JAPAN OF THE RESOURCES IT SO DESPERATELY NEEDED required the United States and its Allies to commit land, sea, and air forces. This was evident in the effort taken to destroy Convoy HI-88J. Aside from air elements—the 345th among them—Navy submarines also tracked the enemy ships.

The USS *Chub* had left Saipan on its first war patrol just more than a month earlier on February 25. Since that time, the submarine passed through the Luzon Strait and hunted in the Java Sea, the Tonkin Gulf, and the South China Sea. Enemy ships were scarce, however, and aside from dodging torpedoes from a Japanese submarine, *Chub* saw little action.

HI-88J represented an opportunity, but it was a frustrating one. Cooperating with two other submarines, *Sea Robin* and *Flounder*, *Chub* worked for two days, beginning on March 29, to get into position for a torpedo attack. Almost three hours after the 345th had made its attacks on the enemy vessels, the *Chub*'s log recorded the receipt of the message that started the chase: "Received delayed contact report from plane. Seven ship convoy, Latitude 15-02N, Longitude 109-29E, course 060°, speed 10 knots."[1] At that point, the convoy was well south of *Chub* and could have veered well clear of the submarine's reach. Nevertheless, anxious for action, its captain set a course to intercept the enemy ships.

Just more than a half hour later, *Chub* submerged upon sighting a Japanese aircraft. The enemy pilot dropped a bomb just as the submarine descended through eighty feet. Although under attack, the ship's crew seemed a glass-half-full sort: "This indicates that the convoy is not swinging wide. . . . Believe we are fairly close to projected track." Finally, it seemed, *Chub* was in the right place at the right time.

Chub surfaced shortly afterward but was forced underwater again after spotting another enemy aircraft. After surfacing once more, the crew set an intercept course for the convoy. On the way a message came in from higher headquarters: "Received message from CTF 71 that zoomies [U.S. Army Air Forces B-24 crews] would bomb the convoy during the hours 2130 to 0100 while they are well offshore in deep water, and for us to remain clear during that time."

Chub increased its speed in hopes of catching the enemy ships before the bombing began. "If not in contact by 2100, plan to reverse course, pull clear, and gain position ahead while awaiting completion of aircraft attacks." As it developed, the submarine crew had to do just that. *Chub* sailed out of the area and, although it was dark, was forced down by another enemy aircraft. After it resurfaced, lookouts spotted the action. "Observed tracer fire, gun fire, and bomb explosions, showing that planes were at work. One ship apparently on fire."

Enemy aircraft forced the submarine to submerge two more times while racing to get ahead of the enemy ships. The crew's frustration and anxiety showed in the log entry made at 0211 the next morning, March 30, 1945. "Observed flashes from gunfire or aircraft bombing. The zoomies are not conforming to the schedule, which called for bombing between hours of 2130 and 0100 only, while the ships were out in deep water. Now that the ships are approaching shallow and uncharted water, the submarines are supposed to have their turn."

Just more than an hour later, it seemed the *Chub* was going to have its "turn" as the enemy ships approached. Although it became apparent that the submarine had been spotted, the crew readied to engage one of the escorts, "which is showing sharp angle on the bow. Sharpened our track as range closed rapidly to 5,500 yards." And then, all the *Chub* crew's work came undone. "At 5,500 yards, the DE [destroyer escort] zigged away and the picture became most confusing. Radar began to pick up decoy targets between us and the ships, making tracking most difficult."

Ultimately, the convoy passed out of range, leaving *Chub* "out on the limb." Later that morning *Chub* met with *Sea Robin* and exchanged information. Neither *Sea Robin* nor *Flounder* had had any better success than *Chub*. "In retrospect," noted the submarine's log, "it appears that pickings are really getting lean when 3 submarines have to chase a group of 6 DDs [destroyers] and DEs [destroyer escorts] all over Tonkin Gulf in an effort to get a shot."

❧

Although they didn't know its designation, the Air Apaches were excited at their March 29 successes against Convoy HI-88J and were anxious to mop up the surviving ships on the following day, March 30, 1945. Accordingly, the group's four squadrons put up a total of twenty-three aircraft at 0640. The squadrons, loosely coordinated, headed northwest and poked around the Paracel Islands with no success. The 500th and the 501st went hunting on their own, whereas the 498th and the 499th pointed north and, as noted by the 499th, "spread out widely in 'abreast' formation and flew to a point just off Cape Gaalong," at the southeast point of Hainan Island.

The 499th then dropped behind the 498th and followed it across the mouth of Yulin Harbor, where several enemy warships were moored. The enemy vessels' guns aside, the harbor was well protected, and the flight's leaders decided against an attack. In fact, as the two squadrons continued across the opening of Samah Bay, the 499th "was crowded into the shore defenses and turned back to Cape Gaalong."

The 498th motored away and attacked the village of Mencheong, where it started a couple of fires and caused an explosion that sent smoke to a thousand feet. At the same time, the 499th's crews spotted "an armed trawler equipped for anti-submarine patrol" and immediately attacked. This ship was likely the auxiliary sub chaser *Shinan Maru*. John Boyd led the attack at wave-top level and dropped two of his four five-hundred-pound bombs. Both missed.

Boyd and the other five B-25s outgunned the hapless enemy ship by a considerable margin. In fact, the machine-gun fire that the enemy sailors sent after the 499th's aircraft was described as "light, meager and inaccurate." Notwithstanding this fact, the performance of the American crews on this day was less than impressive despite multiple bombing and strafing runs.

After missing with two bombs on his first pass, Boyd dropped two more. One of them missed and the other caused "superficial damage to the superstructure" of the enemy ship. "Lieutenant [Thomas] Mangum," the squadron reported, "dropped four bombs, all of which missed." And "Lieutenant [James] Walker dropped two bombs on his first run but both were wide and long." It was Theodore Bronson who finally inflicted real damage. "He scored a near miss on the first run. On his second run he placed a bomb within 10 feet of the vessel which was lifted almost clear and heeled completely over on the port side by the burst."

Still, as impressive as Bronson's near miss was, a crew on loan from the 498th made the killing blow against the *Shinan Maru*. Newly joined pilot Charles "Chuck" Myers scored two near misses, which set the vessel afire and started it sinking by the stern. The 499th declared, "Actual credit should go to the 498th squadron pilot [Myers]." For his trouble, Myers was attacked by an enemy fighter: "The [Mitsubishi J2M] Jack II came in high at nine o'clock holing the airplane from wingtip to wingtip, holing the radio compartment and puncturing the right tire." Apparently undeterred by the sieving the Japanese had given his aircraft, Myers headed for Mencheong with his two remaining bombs. There, he dumped them into the smoking turmoil that the 498th had created.

It had taken sixteen five-hundred-pound bombs and tens of thousands of .50-caliber machine-gun rounds to sink the enemy vessel at the cost of one B-25. Although the lightly armed enemy ship failed to knock down any of the 499th's aircraft, the 499th did the deed to itself. On his second bombing attack, James Walker either followed one of his comrades too closely and flew through an explosion or was struck by shrapnel from his own bombs. The squadron expressed this latter theory in a missing air crew report, which said that Walker's aircraft was "hit by rebound of bomb fragments from its own bombs."[2] Regardless, the B-25's left engine was afire, and Walker turned southeast to get as far away from Hainan as possible before the aircraft came apart.

At the same time—and not too far away—the 498th's B-25s closed formation as Japanese fighters dived after them. "Six [Nakajima Ki-43] Oscars attacked the squadron 2 miles offshore at Samah airdrome," the squadron observed, "making two and three passes from high at eleven and nine o'clock. Only two passes were pressed to 500 feet."

The Japanese also tried to bomb the 498th's formation. This effort failed, as had similar efforts in virtually every instance throughout the war. "Two phosphorous bombs that were dropped 500 feet above airplanes did no damage," the squadron reported, "one exploding to the rear, and one just ahead and above the formation." Unharmed by the enemy fighters, the 499th made an uneventful recovery at San Marcelino.

James Walker and his crew did not. Approximately twenty miles southeast of Hainan, escorted by other aircraft from the 499th, the aircraft went into the water. Walker and his copilot, Richard Lee, managed to escape the quickly sinking hulk, as did the navigator, Morris Perkins. Anthony Marsili, the engineer, and John O'Hop, the radioman, were still in the aircraft when it slipped beneath the waves just more than a minute after coming down.

The aircraft's life raft did not inflate, and the crew was fortunate that the two life rafts dropped by their circling comrades splashed down nearby. Walker crawled aboard one, while Lee and Perkins pulled themselves into another. They drifted apart, however, and Walker cried out in desperation as he struggled vainly to reach the other two men. His efforts were of no avail, and the men soon lost sight of each other behind the swells.

Perkins, the navigator, was badly concussed and had a massive lump on his head. Lee was also in shock and struggled to gain his wits. They treated their wounds and inventoried the gear aboard the raft. Overhead, their squadron mates circled, "attempting to contact rescue subs and 'Cats' [PBY Catalina rescue aircraft] on 4475 KCs (Voice and CW) and all channels of VHF. No answers to these calls were received." Finally, after an hour—and low on fuel—the remainder of the 499th turned southeast for San Marcelino. "As our planes left the scene of the ditching," the squadron observed, "two men were in a life raft waving and apparently in good condition."

It was eerily quiet except for the lap of the sea against their raft. Morris Perkins and Richard Lee squinted against the horizon, wary of

Japanese vessels that might be searching for them. Likewise, they watched the sky for rescue aircraft. There were none. After some time they were startled by a shout and heartened to see James Walker splashing the oars of his raft against the waves. As he approached they reached out and pulled him close. With their two rafts secured together—and no sign of rescue—the three men settled in for a restless night.

The 499th chided its fliers for their lackluster bombing accuracy, especially during shipping attacks. "On numerous missions, including this mission," the report began, "photographs have shown that a minimum of 50% of bombs dropped on shipping targets have been released too late and consequently dropped long. Such consistent inaccuracy should be remedied—possibly by use of the sight, or by purposely dropping short and trying for a skip."

No subsequent documentation indicates whether this issue was ever raised again or resolved.

At the same time that the 498th and 499th were engaged, the 501st made a run on shipping in Hainan's Yulin Bay, situated on the southeast coast of the island. The squadron's six aircraft were jumped by an equal number of enemy fighters, but their attacks were nevertheless effective. "Captain [Robert] Erskine," noted the mission summary report, "dropped a bomb which struck the aft end of an unidentified merchant vessel which was tied to a dock. Crews stated this ship was brownish in color and was probably a transport of 4–5,000 tons. The bomb was seen to blow off the entire aft end of the vessel and crews believe this ship was left in such condition that it would sink." The squadron also hit, but did not claim as destroyed, a patrol craft.

Roger Lovett, a copilot with the 500th, recalled that his squadron also hit shipping at Yulin Bay. Herman Reheis, at the head of the six-aircraft formation, spotted a Japanese warship at the mouth of the bay. Reheis made a heading correction toward the island so that the surrounding terrain would mask the 500th's attack from the enemy ship.

"He directed the squadron to form itself into three two-ship flights," remembered Lovett. "My pilot, Vernon Sawyer, and I were on the left wing of the first three-ship, so we dropped all the way back and formed up with James McGuire as part of the last two-ship." The 500th's three two-ship formations were each separated by a mile as they made landfall at Hainan.

"We wound our way through the hills as we continued toward Yulin Bay," said Lovett. "Finally, we crested the last bit of terrain and started down the other side toward a small ship we spotted directly in front of us." Despite his efforts to make the 500th's attack a surprise, heavy anti-aircraft fire greeted Reheis's formation. Indeed, in addition to antiaircraft guns ashore, a sizeable contingent of smaller combatant ships in the bay added to the fusillade that ripped through the aircraft. The mission narrative cataloged the vessels as "4-to-6 destroyer escorts, 6-to-10 small craft up to 100 feet long, and a large vessel identified as a harbor gunboat."

"As we started down toward the water," said Lovett, "I looked left, behind Sawyer's seat, and spotted my good friend Bill Boyce. He was McGuire's copilot. He looked over at me and smiled and waved. I really liked him. He was from Arkansas and was a really genuine and friendly sort. When I arrived at the squadron he was the first one to actually come over and make friends with me."

Sawyer and Lovett dived toward a coastal patrol vessel that was putting up an effective stream of antiaircraft fire. "The damaged destroyer—which was just off to our right—was also firing heavily and continuously," Lovett said. The destroyer was the 345th's old friend *Amatsukaze*, which it had attacked on March 29. "I looked over to my left again and saw that McGuire had been hit and was burning. And the top turret and cockpit were filled with flames. I saw Bill Boyce in there—it looked like he was on fire."

Lovett's pilot, Vernon Sawyer, appeared hypnotized by the sight of McGuire's flaming aircraft. "He almost seemed to forget what we were doing," said Lovett, who hauled back on the aircraft's controls. "We almost hit the ship we were attacking. We dropped two bombs and flew down its deck, lengthwise. The bombs exploded but we couldn't tell if they were near misses or hits—and our radioman back in the tail gun position forgot to turn on the camera." In fact, the 500th's narrative summary was unflattering in its assessment of the squadron's attack when it reported, "Nine 500-pound bombs were dropped from minimum altitude with poor to generally unobserved results."

McGuire's aircraft went down at the same time that Sawyer and Lovett made their attack. Shaken by their near collision with the ship, they wheeled around to where they guessed McGuire's B-25 had hit the water. "The antiaircraft fire was too heavy and we couldn't really do a good search," Lovett said. "Anyway, we didn't find anything. There was no wreckage and no bodies and no life rafts. Nothing. Our navigator said that the plane had simply hit the water and gone under."

Sawyer and Lovett were at great risk. "Defensive fire," noted the narrative summary, "was so strong that a second pass was inadvisable and not made." Unable to do anything for McGuire's crew—and under continuous fire from ship and shore guns alike—Sawyer and Lovett winged their way out of Yulin Bay and joined the rest of the 500th for the long flight home. It was the second time in three weeks that Lovett was forced to leave squadron mates—friends—in the water. In fact, the narrative summary declared that there were "nil survivors."

It had been nearly two hours since Sawyer and Lovett and the rest of the 500th's aircraft had flown out of sight. James McGuire and his badly wounded navigator, Eugene Harviell, clung to debris from the wreck that had once been their aircraft. A wave lifted them to its crest, and McGuire spotted a Japanese boat motoring straight at them.

On March 30, 1945, the USS *Chub*, like the Air Apaches, had been anxious to find and destroy what remained of the Japanese convoy that the 345th had savaged so viciously the previous day. And like the B-25 crews, the submarine's crew had been not nearly so effective. Much of the day had been spent hiding from enemy aircraft and ships and alternately stalking diaphanous radar and radio signals—all to no satisfactory end. "Surfaced," read the submarine's log entry for 1715. "Received plane report of survivors in raft, southeast of Gaalong. Set course to round Yulinkan and search."

Walker, Lee, and Perkins—who had gone down earlier that day—knew none of this. Nevertheless, they were certain that some sort of search would be initiated. And if it were not already underway, it would certainly start no later than the next morning. No matter what the tempo of operations was, the Air Apaches had always spared aircraft and crews to find its lost comrades.

"Commenced search," read the *Chub's* log entry for 2205, almost five hours after charting a course for the downed flyers. Another entry followed at midnight: "Conducting expanding type search for survivors southeast of Gaalong Point. Have three different positions so far and are trying to cover them all. Moon just past full, visibility excellent." As they had little more than eyeballs with which to search for the tiny rafts, the light of the moon was welcome. Daytime searches were difficult enough. Without moonlight, the odds of finding anything at night were near nil.

The chances of rescue increased when both parties were active participants. To that end, the *Chub* tried to trigger a response from the downed crewmen. "Shining red blinker gun around horizon at periodic intervals, and listening on 500 Kc for the Gibson Girl." The Gibson Girl, officially known as the BC-778, was an emergency transmitter rescue kit that included a hand-cranked transmitter, the SCR-578. The kit also contained both a kite and a balloon intended to lift the 260-foot wire antenna, as well as a weighted grounding wire and a signal light.

Almost a foot in height and depth and nearly as wide, the transmitter was curved inward in the middle on each side, which gave it a pinch-waisted appearance, much like the Gibson Girls so popular during the early part of the century. This waist allowed the operator to more readily wrap his legs around the transmitter while he spun the detachable crank mounted to the top. Properly assembled and operated, the SCR-578 sent a continuous homing signal that could be received at two hundred miles by an aircraft flying as low as two thousand feet. It could also be operated in a Morse code mode. It did not include a receiver.

The *Chub's* log made no entry indicating receipt of an emergency signal. At 0421 the submarine "arrived at new point," the log entry declared, "and started an expanding rectangle type search plan. Night is quiet and sea flat. Started sounding blast on ship's whistle once every mile."

In the rafts, one of the men cocked his head and concentrated in the dark. There it was again. Was it a horn? It had been faint, to be sure. So weak was the noise that he wasn't even sure that it was real. Exhaustion and the shock of the day dulled his senses, and he found it difficult to separate the tangle of imagination, hope, and reality. But the might-be-a-real-noise didn't sound again, and he finally laid back to rest.

Although the *Chub*'s crew increased its chances of finding the downed crewmen by flashing the blinker gun and sounding the whistle, those actions also heightened the odds of discovery by the Japanese. Accordingly the log noted that the submarine was "running trimmed down for fast diving and small silhouette." Of course, the other edge of that sword was that a smaller silhouette was more difficult for the men in the rafts to spot.

March 31, 1945, dawned, and the three 499th men were still adrift. They blinked themselves awake during the next couple of hours and checked the surrounding skies and ocean for any sign of activity. There was none. But unbeknownst to them, Robert Draper and his 499th crew were already en route from San Marcelino with three other B-25s.

And they weren't the only aircraft looking for the three men. "Sighted aircraft headed towards us," recorded the *Chub*'s log at 0855. "Fired recognition signal from mortar. Plane turned and [was] recognized as a [B-24] Liberator. He was followed by a second Liberator. Very glad to see them as we are about 5 miles off Gaalong Point, expecting to be forced down any minute."

The aircraft were actually PB4Y-2 Privateers, a Navy version of the USAAF's B-24 Liberator that was commonly used for long-range bombing, patrol, and air-sea rescue missions. Regardless, their crews quickly got to business as noted by the *Chub*'s log: "First plane searched southwestward while second plane searched our vicinity. About 15 minutes later, first plane reported locating two life rafts 5 miles south of Yulinkan, about 15 miles from where we are searching."

So close to enemy-held Hainan, the *Chub* wasted little time. "Went to flank speed on 4 engines," the log declared, "blew all tanks dry, and came to course given by plane. Signaled planes we would swing wide and approach from south. Asked planes to tell survivors to paddle south. Plane dropped notes to life rafts."

At 1000, the *Chub* recorded that the Yulin Harbor defenses were tracking it and that "planes report that one DD [destroyer] and one DE [destroyer escort] in the harbor are getting up steam." At 1004 the log noted, "Sighted mirror flashes beneath orbiting plane." And then, two minutes later, at 1006, "Sighted two yellow life rafts south of Yulinkan. Mirror flashes soon became more rapid when it looked as if we might pass them by."

Activity increased in all quarters as the *Chub* headed for Walker, Perkins, and Lee on a northwesterly heading. At 1012, "Planes reported Jap DD underway in harbor and 16,000 yards from us. Cannot see him against the harbor background." This was likely the *Amatsukaze*, which had escaped the 345th's attacks two days earlier.

It was also then that Robert Draper and his flight of four B-25s arrived overhead. "We sighted and reported 4 aircraft," reported the *Chub*, "later identified as Mitchells, coming in on quarter. We sighted and reported two enemy fighters circling for altitude ahead. Beginning to look as if Japs may make an issue of this recovery."

At 1015 the submarine's log recorded that the Air Apaches "joined the Liberators in flying a tight low circle around us." The defensive screen worked even as the log noted, "Jap fighters making long range passes and attacks on bombers, trying to get them to break formation. Bombers holding formation and turning the Zeroes back each time."

So close to the island, the submarine's captain worried about uncharted shoals and consequently reduced his ship's speed. The *Chub*'s 1020 log entry described how the submarine "stopped and started swinging towards survivors who are paddling towards us from several hundred yards off. We are now 11,900 yards from shore by radar." And then, at 1021, "Jap Zeroes made quick dive and strafed the life rafts from high altitude without damage. We trimmed down again as a precautionary measure. Careful observation shows the Zeroes are not carrying bombs." The *Chub*'s remarks coincided with those of the 499th crews, who noted, "As the sub approached the raft, three probable Oscars attempted to break through and attack the exposed crew in the raft."

At 1023 the enemy pilots turned their attention from the men in the rafts to the submarine. "Observed Zeroes starting a dive on us. Cleared bridge of all hands except C.O. [commanding officer, Commander Cassius Rhymes] who ducked behind bridge armor plating. First plane made lots of splashes around us but no hits. Second plane was better and rattled quite a few off our plating." The guns of the Japanese fighters were not big enough to do the *Chub* any real harm, and it continued toward the downed airmen. As the submarine brushed against the rafts, a pair of officers scrambled down to the deck and helped Walker, Lee, and Perkins aboard.

The enemy aircraft continued to harry the PB4Ys and B-25s. Draper's aircraft was targeted by two Oscars, which "came in from 10 o'clock high in trail and with all guns blazing." Draper's gunners forced the lead fighter to terminate his attack early. "The second Oscar came in immediately behind and was able to get quite close while the gunners were firing at the first Oscar." However, the Japanese pilot's aim was poor, and he did no damage. Other enemy aircraft dropped phosphorous bombs on the PB4Ys but, as usual, caused no harm.

The *Chub* had everyone aboard at 1029 and raced to leave the area. "Swung left and started opening out to south at flank speed. Our planes damaged one Zero, sending him home, but he was replaced by another." As the submarine sped away, Draper asked if it needed any further protection. The *Chub* replied in the negative and asked if Draper wanted it to remain on station in the event one of the aircraft went down. Draper declined the offer.

Finally, at 1042, the *Chub* recorded, "Zeroes starting in for second run on us. Submerged, notifying planes on the way down. Planes replied they were heading for home. Heard machine gun fire rattle around our sheers as we made our quickest dive on record—passed 100 feet in 50 seconds. Returned to periscope depth to watch our planes out of sight."

News of this rescue quickly spread, reaching James Fife, commander of the Seventh Fleet's Submarine Forces, who "fully concurred" with the following description written by famed Submarine Squadron 30 commander and Navy Cross recipient Karl Hensel:

The highlight of the patrol was the stirring rescue of three Army aviators south of Hainan on 31 March. This rescue was accomplished close to shore in face of strafing by two Zeroes and a report from the air cover that a Jap DD in the harbor only six miles away was getting underway. Two Liberators and four Mitchells provided a very effective low altitude tight defensive screen during this operation. This rescue is outstanding, not only in the courage and determination of the Commanding Officer, but also in the fine flight discipline and courage of the air cover in continuing their tight defensive circle over the submarine for about 25 minutes, up until the submarine dived after rescue. This is an example of air cooperation of the highest order.

It had been two days since the *Chub* pulled Walker, Lee, and Perkins out of the water. And it had been twenty-three days since Franklin Chambers's B-25 slipped beneath the white-capped waves on March 10, 1945. George Givens had watched from high above on that day as one of his squadron mates crawled from Chambers's aircraft into a life raft and desperately— but futilely—tried to save another man in the wind-tossed sea. Now, in the late afternoon of April 2, the man in that raft, Bauduy Grier, dozed fitfully beneath a tarpaulin that protected him from the sun's penetrating rays.

Strange vibrations pulsed through the water and shook Grier awake. He bolted upright and screwed himself around the bottom of the raft. "A ship was coming directly at me!" Grier struggled to keep from falling into the water and waved his arms wildly. At the same time, he scooted to the front of the raft, where he snatched the rescue whistle out of a pocket. He shoved it between his parched lips and blew for all he was worth.

The submarine closed the distance, and Grier pleaded with the armed sailors not to leave him. "Don't worry," they replied. "We're not going to leave you. We're coming around easy. We don't want to knock you over and lose you."[3]

The crew of the USS *Sealion* threw Grier a line and hauled him aboard. When his rescuers reached to help him to his feet, he shoved them aside and tried to walk on his own. Desperately weak, he collapsed immediately. Physically and emotionally exhausted, and literally dying of thirst, Grier begrudgingly allowed the bemused seamen to lower him into the ship. It was no great challenge as he had lost forty pounds. Blinking through the dim light of the submarine, Grier spotted a water fountain and lunged for it. Weak as he was, it took four sailors to peel him away before he could make himself sick. Ultimately, although he was horribly sunburned, dehydrated, and nearly starved—and suffering from a magnificently terrible case of hemorrhoids—Grier made a full recovery.

He had drifted more than five hundred miles south of where Givens had last seen him. Givens recalled his story.

> *He said that the only reason he was able to stay alive was that he was drenched by rain squalls nearly every day and was able to collect just barely enough fresh water. But the rain stopped coming toward the end and he started drinking salt water. It almost killed him.*
>
> *And he hated the damn sharks. He said that they "haunted" him almost continuously. They never tried to pull him from the raft, but they often scared him by brushing up against it. They gave him nightmares.*

Ironically, on the same day he was rescued by the *Sealion*, Grier was joined by George Blair of the 499th Bomb Squadron and the other survivors of his crew. Blair had nearly drowned before being inspired by a vision of his girlfriend "in color." After going down four days earlier, they had been plucked from the sea by the submarine USS *Guavina*. That vessel, en route elsewhere, transferred them to the *Sealion*.

—◦—

Quentin Stambaugh, a radio operator en route from the States to a combat assignment, spent Christmas of 1944 in Hawaii with strep throat. "I was in the hospital and they wouldn't release me. The rest of my crew had to continue with our airplane to the South Pacific, so I was on my own."[4]

When Stambaugh got out of the hospital, he was essentially on his own and started wheedling rides on aircraft headed south toward New

Guinea. "I had orders to the 309th Bomb Wing, but no one seemed to know or care where they were. It was actually hard work because I was dragging all my uniforms and cold-weather flying gear and other stuff with me. It weighed about a hundred pounds."

"There was a colonel, his name was Swanick, who took me under his wing for part of the way," said Stambaugh. "Colonels got better treatment than radio operators." Stambaugh eventually reached Nadzab, where he learned nothing certain about the 309th. However, he knew that most of the fighting was happening in the Philippines and headed in that direction. "I ended up in a transient camp on Biak for a little while and then caught a flight up to the Philippines."

After passing through Baguio and Subic Bay, Stambaugh finally landed at San Marcelino.

At San Marcelino, I spotted a tent that had a sign marking it as the 309th Bomb Wing. So, I walked in and there was Colonel Swanick! He looked at my orders and told me that he was happy to see me and that we had a lot of work to do. Right away, he started me to work putting together orders and strike reports and such—I was a pretty good typist. I told him that I was trained for combat and that I needed to get to a combat unit, but he wasn't really anxious to let me go.

Stambaugh spent a few weeks working for Swanick. "I did the sorts of things for him that a clerk or an aide would do. Aside from office work, I poured his whiskey for him, and that sort of thing. When I reminded him again that I wanted to get to a combat unit and find my original crew, he made the point that no one was shooting at us and that we had a pretty nice arrangement. He also pointed out that we'd be making trips to Hawaii every couple of months."

But Stambaugh was insistent, and Swanick finally relented. "He told me that if I really wanted combat, he'd get me into combat. So, he sent me to the 345th Bomb Group, and they assigned me to the 498th Bomb Squadron. When I dragged my baggage to my tent I saw that there were two empty cots and I picked one. The other men in the tent told me that I couldn't have it—it belonged to someone else."

That "someone else" showed up the next day. It was Bauduy Grier, who had recently been rescued. "Oh, he was almost a skeleton," said Stambaugh. "He was so skinny, and he was covered with scabs and sores. He had almost died."

Stambaugh started flying combat missions a short time later.

Chapter Seventeen

"I Inflated My Mae West"

As the crew of the *Chub* had noted in late March, "It appears that pickings are really getting lean." Such seemed to be the case when the Air Apaches sent six aircraft each from the 499th and the 500th to search for enemy shipping in the area between the Loochow Peninsula and Hainan Island on April 3, 1945. "Six of our airplanes," reported the 500th, "after completing a fruitless shipping search south along the east coast of the Loochow Peninsula, hit the secondary target at Hoi How town on the north Hainan coast."

Visibility was poor, and the 499th, leading the 500th, spotted Hoi How too late and passed the town without making any attacks. Such wasn't the case with the 500th. One pilot dumped his bombs into the town, while the rest of the pilots held theirs in anticipation of the 499th turning the formation around for another attempt. Antiaircraft fire, described as intense and of "all calibers," laced through the bombers. Benjamin Muller, the radioman aboard William Simpson's B-25, recalled, "As we left the coast and headed out to sea, still very low, I started to get very hot as I was in the tail gunner's position. I looked over my shoulder toward the front of the plane and I saw great flames coming from the front and over the bomb bay."[1] Other crews confirmed that "fire broke out in the stricken plane's open bomb bay and around the top turret."

Muller was anxious to not be burned alive. "I opened the escape hatch over my head and when I did, the draft caused the flames to get really big. I stood up to jump out without a parachute, and just when I did, the pilot made a perfect ditch in the ocean." The rest of the squadron, flying close by, confirmed that the crew "made an excellent ditching."

"I inflated my Mae West," said Muller, "stepped onto the horizontal tail surface and then into the water. My legs and arms were burned. Our life raft had ejected and inflated when we hit the water and our squadron circled us and dropped more rafts." In fact, the five remaining aircraft dropped four additional rafts and counted four survivors before they departed for San Marcelino.

"For some unknown reason, our pilot [William Simpson] never got out and went down with the plane after he had made a perfect ditch, saving our lives," said Muller. The four remaining crewmen—Muller, Merritt "Gene" Lawliss, Charles Suey, and Arthur Blum—fought against the waves. Blum, the copilot, was swept away. "We never saw him again," said Muller. "We did hear him firing his .45 [pistol]."

Muller climbed aboard a raft with Lawliss, the crew's navigator. Muller recalled that Lawliss "had hurt his back somehow. He couldn't move his legs for a while."[2] They were joined by Suey, the engineer. In the meantime, the 499th worked to coordinate a rescue. They were successful in contacting a submarine, and "full particulars were passed to the sub commander."

As the downed airmen were only a few miles off the coast, there was little chance that the submarine would reach them before the Japanese. "I heard machine-gun fire after maybe an hour," said Muller, "and a Jap patrol boat came up alongside and picked us up. They took us to shore where we were slapped and beat up a bit. Then the three of us were tied together and paraded through the town we had just bombed. They were mad, mad, mad. They spit on us, hit us, threw things at us, and yelled and hollered."[3]

The three men were taken to the Japanese naval base at Haikou and put into concrete cells. While there, they were kept handcuffed virtually the entire time. "Little cells," said Muller. "Three feet, by five feet, all around the perimeter and an open space in the middle. They had Gene and me in there in the middle, interrogating us and beating on us with boards and different things." Muller recalled one incident when it appeared the Japanese were set to murder Lawliss. "They put me back in my cell and left Gene out there—he was a captain—and had their swords drawn and had him kneeling down. I just knew they were going to cut his head off right there, but they didn't do it."[4]

"The more I think about it," Lawliss later recalled, "the more I believe that if I had shown the fear I felt, he'd have done it. But I don't think I moved a muscle. I was beyond fear. There were about 50 Japanese and Chinese watching, and it was deathly quiet. It seemed like a minute, but it was probably more like 30 seconds, he held the sword over his head, and then he sheathed it."[5]

None of the three survivors from Simpson's crew—not Muller, Lawliss, or Suey—knew there were also more than four hundred Australian and Dutch POWs on the island. They had been moved there in late 1942 and used as slave laborers during the more than two years since. One prisoner recalled, "The first big job was building a ramp about ¾ mile long from nothing up to about 60 feet high to carry about 6 sets of railway lines. This was so that the iron ore they were bringing in by rail from the island could be loaded direct onto the ships. The guards were very cruel and beat the chaps with iron bars, pieces of thick timber, rifles and many had to be carried back to camp by their mates."[6]

Worked hard and cruelly, kept on a starvation diet with virtually no medical care, and maliciously beaten and abused on a regular basis, more than a hundred of these POWs had already died by the spring of 1945, and more were perishing by the day. Likewise, Muller, Lawliss, and Suey, infested with lice and other parasites, besieged by disease-carrying mosquitos, and fed nothing more than rice, soon became sickly.

"We mostly thought and dreamed of food," Muller recalled.[7] "We talked and hoped and prayed. We also learned a bit of the Japanese language. Our diet was rice. A Japanese officer, when questioning us, said, 'From now on, rice is your life.' We got a small rice ball, maybe three times a day. We also sometimes got a few pieces of imo—like a sweet potato."

Japanese refusal to tend the prisoners' injuries exacerbated their poor condition. "They didn't treat our wounds," said Muller. "I was burned on my legs and had maggots in my legs. They didn't treat anything like that."

After a time, the three men were moved. "We were loaded into trucks with some Chinese people—women and goods and all kinds of things,"

Muller said. "We had to stand up and they put a woven basket over our head so we couldn't see." They eventually reached a base somewhere in the interior of Hainan, where they were put together into a makeshift cell.

While there, the men were nearly murdered by a group of intoxicated, sword-waving Japanese officers. Shouting and cursing, they entered the building where the American flyers were kept and accosted the enlisted men guarding their cell. They yelled at, cajoled, and bullied the lower-ranking soldiers, insisting that they release the Americans to them. "But the guards wouldn't let them get us out," said Muller. "They were probably going to do us in, right there, but the guards wouldn't let us out."[8] The enemy officers finally stormed away, their drunken bloodlust unsatisfied.

In that unremarkable location, Charles Suey, the engineer, died of starvation and neglect. Muller recalled that Suey "was burned somewhat more than I was, and he didn't like rice and he wouldn't eat rice. We didn't have anything else to eat but rice. I'd hold his head . . . and try to feed him rice, but it would just kind of dribble out of his mouth. He died right there not long after that."

The men were moved again, this time to the naval base at Samah at the southern tip of Hainan. "We were kept in a bamboo cage that was built on the side of a Jap enlisted sailor's barber shop," Muller said. "There were two cells. Gene and I were in one cell and lo-and-behold, in the other cell was [James] McGuire and [Eugene] Harviell. They were also in our squadron and they had been shot down two days before us."

In effect, the wretched, starving Americans were little more than a zoo display. "We were oddities. Like monkeys in a cage,"[9] Muller said. The men no longer had uniforms and wore only the loincloth-like *fundoshi* and no shoes. Japanese sailors looked at them, threatened them, poked at them, or tried to engage them in conversation as they came and went to and from the barber shop. The four men had little to do with their time. One of their guards—the only kindly Japanese they encountered—gave them matchboxes from which they fabricated a set of playing cards. "We used to play cards together," said Muller. "We'd play gin rummy. In fact, I still owe millions of dollars."[10]

But this small diversion aside, the condition and morale of the men continued to deteriorate. Muller contracted malaria, which indirectly caused him to become infected with dysentery. "I was so thirsty, I just couldn't get enough water." He was driven nearly mad with a malarial, fever-driven thirst. "There was a spigot out in the middle of the ground out in front of us and when they let us out to go to the bathroom, we weren't supposed to touch that because it was not good water. Well, I just went and drank some of that water. . . . I got dysentery from it and so I was wasting away." Muller's feet also swelled from beriberi, a malady caused by a vitamin B, or thiamine, deficiency.

So cruelly neglected and with no prospect of relief, the four Air Apaches slowly slid toward death.

———

The 345th was one of the most effective units fielded by the United States Army Air Forces during the whole of World War II. Its men—the Air Apaches—had caused the Japanese real and meaningful hurt that affected their ability to fight the war. Nevertheless, it was a large organization of approximately fifteen hundred young men. Any notion that they could live and work and fight and die together in primitive conditions against a cruel and capable enemy—and do it harmoniously at all times—would be an unrealistic one. The men were often exhausted and hungry. Sometimes they were sick. They all had different personalities, and some would have clashed with each other in the best of circumstances. So in the hot and stink and general misery of that theater, it was only natural that they occasionally argued or even fought.

McKinley Sizemore, a radio operator with the 500th, offered an instance during which he and a friend, Wood T. Harrell, nearly came to blows. "He was listing all the pilots, naming them, that he wouldn't want to fly with," said Sizemore. "And I said, well somebody has got to fly with them. That's all I said. And he said, 'Say that again and I'll knock you right through that tent.'" Sizemore invited his friend over to argue the point, but ultimately the situation did not devolve into a physical confrontation.

Some friction was more deeply rooted than the sort of momentary hotheadedness described by Sizemore. James Baross of the 501st Bomb Squadron recalled,

Nathan Albert, one of the radio-gunners in the squadron, was not held in high regard by the rest of us. He was old. Too old to be flying. Thirty-seven [actually thirty-three] years old. We considered that pretty ancient.

And he talked constantly about the advantages of communism. He thought it was a far superior type of government. We did not like that one bit!

And every time he flew, he threw up. Every time. And it was an unwritten rule that regardless of who you were, or your rank, if you messed up, you cleaned up! So, after every mission, Nathan Albert had to clean his area of the plane. We did not like to have to fly and use equipment Nathan had used. So, we did not like him.[11]

Despite not being well liked, Albert flew a complete combat tour. Ed Bina, a pilot with the 501st Bomb Squadron, remembered that the radio-gunner, "who flew with me occasionally, came to my tent and asked me, a twenty-year-old, if he should continue flying or return to the States. I recommended that he return to the States. However, he chose to fly again. He went down on his next mission. I had given him up as lost, when he came to my tent later and said, 'I should have taken your advice.' I never saw him again."[12]

Notwithstanding minor personality clashes, the Air Apaches continued to fly and fight, and the interdiction of enemy shipping—and the infrastructure that supported it—remained a primary focus. At that point, the Japanese navy maintained an important base at Mako Town in the Pescadores Islands, situated in the eastern part of the strait between Formosa and the Chinese mainland. It served as a staging point for elements of the invasion force that moved against the Philippines during the early part of the war and subsequently serviced military and commercial shipping moving between Japan, China, and

Singapore. It was also a base for smaller naval combatants, including recently arrived suicide boat units.

Accordingly it was hit several times during the latter part of the war by both Navy and USAAF aircraft. As part of the continuing campaign to isolate Japan from its conquests to the south, the 345th was tasked with hitting shore installations and shipping at Mako Town on April 4, 1945. Stan Muniz, a radio-gunner with the 500th Bomb Squadron, was assigned to fly the mission. Also in the flight was Sergeant Bartolino "Bart" Maggi, who had served in the infantry during the invasion of North Africa and was later retrained as a radio-gunner.

"Bart and I had had a falling out back in gunnery school over something about which I can't remember," said Muniz.[13] "Only that morning we patched things up and were now good friends. We talked for about an hour or so before we had to go to the briefing for the Mako Town mission."

The group put up twelve B-25s just before noon—six from the 498th Bomb Squadron leading six aircraft from the 500th. Muniz recalled that he and Maggi settled into the tail gun positions of their respective aircraft once they got airborne and that they "smiled and waved" across the formation to one another. The 498th led the 500th up the strait until reaching the Pescadores, at which time the formation turned west through intermittent rain showers and then southeast across Boko Island to Mako Town. On the run to the target, the pilots arranged themselves into a string of two-aircraft elements.

The town and harbor were rich with targets. The 498th put five-hundred-pound bombs into various buildings and warehouses as well as vessels in the harbor. The 500th followed suit and recorded the results.

Nine bombs dropped through the central part of Mako scored hits on buildings but resulting damages were difficult to assess. Lieutenant [Joseph] Herick scored a hit on a large warehouse in the west-central section of town causing the structure to blow up in a violent explosion followed by heavy black smoke. Lieutenant Lewis, squadron leader, scored a direct hit on a 2,000-ton tanker tied to a jetty just west of the small boat basin and breakwater. The tanker exploded, throwing flames high into the air with black smoke to 1,500 feet. Flames spread along the water and over the jetty, completely enveloping a 2,500-ton vessel tied to the opposite side.

Stan Muniz fired his guns as his aircraft swept across the target. He additionally kept an eye on Bart Maggi's aircraft, which was flown by Francis Hart. "When we made the run over Mako Town," Muniz said, "I noticed that his plane was drifting to the left and was soon almost in direct line astern and back about a hundred yards or so from our plane." It was apparent to Muniz that Hart was setting up to attack the same two ships that Muniz's pilot was targeting. Antiaircraft fire lashed out at the B-25s.

"Suddenly there was a large burst of flak just behind the tail of our plane which put some holes in our rudders," said Muniz. "The second burst blew off the right wing of Bart's plane just outboard of the right engine. Bart's plane immediately did a snap roll and hit the water a few hundred feet past the end of the jetty and blew up. I sat there stunned, watching the circle in the water and the wing still in the air fluttering down like a falling leaf until it hit the water, hardly making a splash."

On the return flight Muniz considered that the Japanese gunners had actually been targeting his aircraft but had not led it enough and consequently hit Maggi's aircraft. "If Bart's plane had not been in a direct line behind ours," he said, "his plane might not have been hit." Muniz was hurt by the loss of a comrade with whom he had just reconciled but happy "he and I were able to patch things up and become friends as we did. I would have liked to have known him better—he was an okay guy."

Roger Lovett, a copilot with the 500th Bomb Squadron, was airborne on April 15, 1945, for a mission to hit the airfield at Lampsepo in northern Formosa. The 500th was at the head of the group's four squadrons, which put up a total of twenty-five aircraft. "We got airborne and received word sometime later that there were patches of tough weather on the route and that we were going to hit an alternate target," Lovett said. "My pilot was Sam Bennett—he had been one of the most experienced copilots and this was his first flight as a pilot. He grinned and commented that if a target was especially tough—like Formosa usually was—then the flight leader could usually find bad enough weather to justify changing the target."

The secondary target was the airstrip at Tuguegarao in central Luzon. The 500th declared that the purpose of the strike was "to remove any possible threat of enemy use of Tuguegarao strip for strikes against our Philippine forces." In fact, Tuguegarao was an ill-defended backwater and, as it hosted no serviceable aircraft, was no threat to anyone.

"The Japanese in the Philippines were very poorly supplied at this point in the war," said Lovett, "and they didn't even have ammunition for their antiaircraft guns. We attacked right down the runway at minimum altitude firing our guns and dropping parafrags. As we did, I noticed small black objects going past us."

The squadron conjectured that because there were no muzzle flashes and because the projectiles could be seen as they fell to earth, the enemy was reduced to using mortars. The mortars, typically used against infantry, were fired from "a clump of bushes approximately 1½ miles due east of the airdrome." Lovett ducked instinctively as his aircraft's slipstream lifted one of the objects over the windscreen in front of him and into the top turret where it punched a ragged hole through the glass.

"As we pulled away from the airfield," Lovett said, "the engineer stepped down from the top turret and asked us what the objects were. He had a big welt on his face which he said stung a bit, but he wasn't hurt beyond that." In fact, their aircraft was the only one hit by the mortar fire.

On that day, the 500th's men—or at least one of them—were more of a danger than the Japanese. "As we climbed away," Lovett said, "one of the pilots accidentally toggled off a group of parafrags right into the aircraft behind him. It caused a bit of a panic. This same guy had a reputation. Normally, as we came across the target the pilot would cross-control and skid and jink the airplane to make it difficult to hit. Well, this pilot was particularly violent with the controls. On one mission he was so rough that the radio rack was ripped from its mounts! The command eventually handed him all his records and told him, 'Go find someone that wants you.'"

The 345th focused on combat operations but still expended significant effort on training, not only to season newly joined crews but to upgrade copilots to pilots and to familiarize the men with new tactics and new weapons. Although typically not subjected to enemy action during these training missions, the crews still had to be ready for any contingency. Combat aside, flying was still risky.

Pilot John Baeta with the 499th took a new pilot airborne out of San Marcelino on April 4, 1945, with no thought whatsoever of having a mishap. The sortie was a simple training mission to practice skip bombing on a wrecked ship not far off the coast. "We dropped a bunch of one-hundred-pound bombs on this old hulk. It was really pretty uneventful." However, upon returning to base, the aircraft's landing gear failed to fully extend. "Evidently," said Baeta, "one of our bombs hit the wreck and ricocheted back up at us as it exploded and put some shrapnel into our hydraulic lines."

Baeta circled the airfield for more than an hour as he tried multiple maneuvers and procedures to get the recalcitrant landing gear to lock into place. "They even brought a North American technical representative up into the tower to talk to us." Baeta made several low, slow flybys past the control tower. The technical representative and the 345th's commander, Chester Coltharp, called over the radio with several suggestions. "But nothing worked," said Baeta. "Finally, they told us we could either bail out over the airfield or make a crash landing on the dirt strip parallel to the main runway—they didn't want us to tear up or block the main runway." Moreover, the dirt plowed up by the aircraft as it skidded on an unprepared surface would help to smother any fire that might break out.

Baeta decided in favor of a belly landing rather than jumping clear of the B-25 with parachutes. Accordingly, the aircraft was readied, which included securing the top gun turret with a steel cable so that it wouldn't break from its mount and crush the crew in the event of an especially hard touchdown. "When I looked down to the airfield, it looked like the entire country had moved into town. Everyone wanted to see the wheels up landing."

"Normally, when we came back from a mission," Baeta said, "we dived toward the end of the runway, peeled off, threw our wheels down, put our flaps down and landed. I did the same thing on that day." Then, just before touching down, he shut down the engines and feathered the propellers.

The landing was a good one. "We just skidded along—it wasn't very much of a shock. After we stopped, my crew chief came running over and gave me the biggest bear hug you ever saw. I told him I was sorry that I ruined his aircraft." Indeed, that B-25 never returned to service and was instead salvaged for parts and material.

A similar training mission only a couple of weeks later ended much less happily. Quentin Stambaugh, who'd practically had to beg a colonel to send him to a combat unit, was the radioman aboard Elmo Cranford's aircraft during a training mission over Subic Bay on April 17, 1945. "There was a half-submerged Japanese wreck that we made practice bombing runs against."

On that day, Cranford was part of a flight practicing low-level antishipping attacks. "The bombs we carried that day didn't have fuzes because it was just a practice mission," said Stambaugh. "They weren't supposed to explode."

Stambaugh was in the tail gun position and recalled, "We were very, very low when we made a run against what was left of the ship. The bomb bay doors were only a few feet above the water." The bomb was released very close to the wreck and hit it at about the same time the aircraft passed over.

The enormous energy of the bomb's mass and velocity was converted to a sharp, hot blast when its steel casing smashed into the steel hull of the wreck. That blast was harsh enough to detonate the bomb's explosive material even though it carried no fuze. "There was a big bang that rocked the aircraft," said Stambaugh. "And all of a sudden it was full of holes. There were holes to my left and right and behind me. The interphone box by my left elbow was blown away, but I didn't have a scratch on me."

The airplane continued to fly, and Cranford and his copilot brought it back to San Marcelino and landed it safely. "I didn't know it at the time," Stambaugh said, "but a piece of shrapnel punched through the bottom of the aircraft and went through Cranford's seat and into his right kidney."

William Witherell of the group headquarters recorded that more than a hundred blood donors—Type A—left the movie that night to offer blood for Cranford. "Despite transfusions from those found suitable," Witherell said, "the captain died during the night. After two years overseas we have learned somehow to accept the combat loss of a comrade, but a ground or practice flight accident seems harder to take. Affable, popular Captain Cranford is sorely missed by his outfit."

CHAPTER EIGHTEEN

"I Jerked and Ducked Instinctively"

JAPANESE MARITIME TRAFFIC THROUGH THE SOUTH CHINA SEA TO the Home Islands had essentially been stopped by late April 1945. Allied aircraft and submarines dominated the route, and it was simply too risky for the Japanese to put to sea. Consequently, many vessels sat quayside or anchored at various ports and harbors between Singapore and Kyushu.

In particular, there was a concentration of shipping at Saigon, in French Indochina. Located on a river of the same name, Saigon's well-defended wharves protected a number of vessels that George Kenney and his staff wanted destroyed. Attacks by high-altitude bombers had damaged or destroyed parts of the city and the area around the port, but the ships laid up there were relatively unscathed. Low-altitude bombing and strafing attacks had proved problematic as Saigon was beyond the reach of medium bombers based on Luzon, Leyte, or Mindanao in the Philippines

However, the 345th had proved itself adept at long-range operations and was given the nod to hit Saigon. The 499th Bomb Squadron characterized the coming mission as "a continuation of a long series of anti-shipping strikes which have so seriously depleted the Japanese merchant fleet and virtually severed the shipping lanes from the southern area." On April 27, 1945, fitted with additional fuel tanks in their bomb bays, fifteen aircraft—seven from the 499th and eight from the 501st—were sent from San Marcelino to Puerto Princesa on Palawan Island, at the southwest extremity of the Philippines archipelago. The distance from the airfield at Puerto Princesa to Saigon, at eight hundred miles, was at the very limit of the B-25's combat radius.

Nevertheless, the group's commander, Colonel Chester Coltharp, led the fifteen aircraft out of Puerto Princesa the next morning, April 28, 1945, at 0615. Each aircraft carried a load of four five-hundred-pound demolition bombs. Mindful of the distance they had to cover, the pilots leaned their engines to the maximum extent possible to conserve precious fuel. On the route, the crews looked down on the Spratly Islands, which were little more than yellow-white sand spits surrounded by blue-green rings of shallow water. Small as they were, they were still better than life rafts in the event that a forced landing became necessary. Two of the 499th's B-25s did in fact develop mechanical problems and returned to Puerto Princesa.

The coast of Indochina appeared on the horizon just before 1100. Coltharp led the formation to Phan Thiet, approximately ten miles south of Saigon, where they were to rendezvous with more than twenty P-38s. A portion of the fighters were tasked with attacking antiaircraft positions in the target area, while the remainder were charged with protecting the B-25s from enemy fighters.

But they didn't show. While he circled the formation over the enemy coastline, Coltharp made radio contact with the P-38 pilots. Also operating at the limits of their range, they didn't have enough fuel to complete the mission and had just turned back for their base. One of the 345th's pilots called over the radio, "Hope you pea-shooter bastards have enjoyed drawing your combat flight pay today! Do a barrel roll and go on back home while we win the war!"[1]

Coltharp continued the mission without the fighters. He turned the formation north and brought it down to treetop level, hoping to convince enemy observers that Saigon was not the intended target. Once past Saigon, he wheeled the two squadrons back to the south and toward the city's docks. On his hand signal, the 501st's pilots spread into an attack formation of three two-ship flights in a line abreast and one two-ship flight in trail. Behind the 501st, the 499th followed with a three-ship, trailed by a two-ship.

The Saigon River meandered through a flat delta that offered the group's fliers very little cover. Consequently, the Japanese were ready and fired antiaircraft guns of all calibers at the B-25s racing low and fast toward the wharves. In the lead with his wingman, Andrew Johnson, Coltharp spotted a heavily camouflaged, small, engine-aft freighter and destroyed it with a brace of bombs. Behind them, Milton Esty set up his two-ship flight to make an attack on another vessel. Esty's aircraft was hit just as he fired his guns. The stricken B-25 exploded and fell to the ground.

Still low and firing his guns, Coltharp dipped a wing and targeted a larger freighter—also camouflaged. His bomb slammed into the side of the ship, bounced back into the river, and exploded. The blast ripped the enemy vessel open.

Flying just off Coltharp's right wing, Andrew Johnson put two bombs into a twenty-three-hundred-ton freighter. The squadron declared, "Crew members who witnessed the attack reported that the ship must have been loaded with some or other explosives, as it blew up with a violent explosion and disappeared almost immediately."

The antiaircraft fire grew fiercer as the B-25s flashed low over the river. Coltharp's third attack was his deadliest. "Continuing to the south, Colonel Coltharp made a run on one of the two freighter transports docked on the south bank of the Saigon River at the main wharves. The vessel he attacked was approximately 2,000 gross tons. One bomb, his last, was dropped, scoring a direct hit and starting a heavy, black smoke fire which was seen still burning eight minutes later."

Coltharp strafed a set of warehouses and started a left turn toward the coast. At that point, the control cable to his right rudder was shot out, and the top turret was hit. The aircraft was still controllable, but Coltharp's wingman, Andrew Johnson, had been hit by a heavy-caliber round from point-blank range and was afire. Johnson leveled his aircraft's wings and pulled skyward. As they climbed through a thousand feet, he and his crew were set upon by a single enemy fighter, which fired several bursts. Then, still aflame, Johnson's aircraft staggered and fell earthward. Only a few hundred feet before smashing into the ground, a single crewman threw himself clear of the burning wreck. Both hit the ground at the same time.

Coltharp hauled his aircraft around and circled the immolated bits of what had been his wingman's aircraft. Certain there could be no survivors, he continued toward the coast.

Ralph "Peppy" Blount started the attack to Coltharp's left with his wingman, Vernon Townley. He remembered that the antiaircraft fire was "so intense, you could have walked on it!" He searched anxiously for his assigned target, a six-thousand-ton freighter discovered a few days earlier by reconnaissance aircraft. Not spotting it, he instead let loose a bomb and opened fire on a small engine-aft freighter similar to the type that Coltharp had hit. The bomb missed.

Then Blount spied the larger freighter. It sat two miles in front of him. At the same time, Townley's B-25 was hit by antiaircraft fire. Nevertheless, both Blount and Townley continued toward the large ship as the antiaircraft fire continued to target them. "Two strings of tracers, now joined by two more from different directions, started to converge on the [Blount's] cockpit, but passed over the top of the airplane at the last moment!"

Blount lifted his aircraft up and over a line of trees that ran along the east bank of the river. "If they can't see you, they damn sure can't shoot you!" But the tree cover gave out a few seconds later. "As we exploded from behind the trees and made our appearance over the river, the antiaircraft fire met us with such intensity I jerked and ducked instinctively."

Still, Blount pressed toward the enemy freighter. Behind him, Townley followed, his right engine now afire. In range, Blount released three bombs and fired his guns. He was so low that he had to stand his aircraft on a wing to pass between the freighter's twin masts. As he flashed past, his first bomb slammed into the side of the ship, his second fell into the hold, and the third flew over the top. A pair of furious explosions rocked the enemy vessel. As he climbed away, antiaircraft fire caught his aircraft and blew away a portion of its right elevator and the right trim tab.

Townley, his aircraft still burning, likewise dropped three bombs on the freighter. A near miss rocked the ship's stern, while the other two bombs sailed long. But his aircraft, flying at less than a hundred feet, was knocked upside down by another burst of antiaircraft fire. He never let off the firing button, and his guns continued to spit bullets as the B-25 hit the ground a few seconds later and exploded. There were no survivors.

In front of and behind Blount, other B-25 crews bombed and strafed through curtains of antiaircraft fire. The 499th's men hit a series of freighters, luggers, barges, and warehouses and a floating crane. Receiving especial attention were large oil storage tanks still painted with "SOCONY," the acronym for the Standard Oil Company of New York, which had operated an oil terminal at Nhà Bè, near the city. One or more was set afire, and huge masses of flames danced skyward as they burned.

Blount strafed a mix of targets as they presented themselves. Approaching a ship that was apparently under repair, he fired his guns and recalled how the rounds caught a man running on the deck. "The figure appeared to be transformed into a grotesque mannequin, suspended in air, with arms hanging limp, and a massive, bloody hole where a stomach and chest had been only a moment before."

Perhaps mesmerized by the grotesqueness of the sight—and no doubt hindered by the damage his aircraft had already sustained—Blount smashed into the ship's mast. The collision nearly knocked his aircraft out of the sky, but he and his copilot kept the hard-used B-25 flying. The 501st's mission summary report tallied the damage to his aircraft as "two cylinders in the right engine knocked out, the cowling torn off the right engine, a hole, one foot in diameter, in the lower left side of the right engine, the right side of the right engine nacelle badly caved in, a ten-inch jagged hole in the leading edge of the right horizontal stabilizer, the right elevator half knocked off and the right trim tab completely knocked off by flak."

Blount coaxed his staggering B-25 back over the water and thence to Puerto Princesa. The mission logged in at nearly ten hours. It had been brutal and cost the 501st three of its eight aircraft. The 499th suffered no losses.

Despite the damage sustained by the Air Apaches, the crews of the 501st and 499th claimed more than twenty thousand tons of enemy shipping destroyed. It was the group's best single-day performance and earned the 501st a Distinguished Unit Citation.

Ron Pietscher, a pilot recently assigned to the 501st Bomb Squadron, flew on the Saigon mission. "That was a hard one for me. My original crew—the one we formed at Columbia [South Carolina]—lost three men that day. Our pilot, Marlin Miller, was killed, as was the radio operator, Lester William, and our navigator, Aubrey Stowell. Following that, there were only three of us left."[2] Adding to the pain was his assignment to pack the personal belongings of two other squadron mates who had also perished on the mission.

In fact, Pietscher had already been dealing with loss before he flew the Saigon mission. His brother Reed was a P-38 pilot with the 475th Fighter Group, which had dive bombed Japanese positions on Luzon earlier in the month. "On April 19, Walter Radzun, a close friend of my brother and also in the 475th Fighter Group, came down from their base at Lingayen Gulf to advise me of my brother's death the previous day. My brother's plane was hit as he made an attack," said Pietscher. "No one was sure what happened. It might have been shrapnel or a bomb from another airplane. Or shrapnel from his own bomb. Or he might have been hit by Japanese ground fire. But no one knew for certain."

"He called out that he was hit and that he had gas fumes in the cockpit. They told him to start back for base." Pietscher's brother climbed several thousand feet and turned for the 475th's base. "But, for whatever reason," Pietscher said, "he turned back around and started descending. And then he crashed into a mountain. They never found his aircraft or his body."

Misfortune continued to dog Pietscher. "Not long afterward, I was cooking on a camp stove that we fueled with 100 octane aircraft fuel. It blew up and burned me pretty badly—I ended up in the hospital for about a month during May 1945."

The Japanese simply didn't have the airpower to provide their convoys continuous coverage. One Japanese officer declared, "When we requested air cover, only American planes showed up."[3] Nevertheless, there is no denying that the effort was costly to the Americans. The 345th, badly in need of replacements, took on twenty-one new crews during May 1945. Additionally assigned were sixteen A-20 crews whom the Air Apaches were to transition to the B-25.

One of the A-20 pilots, Clifford Lawrence, had trained on both the B-25 and the A-20 while stateside. Once overseas Lawrence flew twenty-five missions as an A-20 pilot with the 3rd Bomb Group. "Then," he said, "several of us pilots were told by our squadron commander that we were being transferred to B-25 units as replacements because of the heavy losses they suffered going after shipping in the South China Sea."[4] Lawrence was subsequently sent to the 345th's 500th Bomb Squadron.

⌒

Melvin Pollock flew combat regularly in February, March, and April 1945. Up until that time he had written assiduously to his father, Manley. But during that three-month period, he wrote only two letters each during February and March and one during April. His tone changed as well. Gone were the subtle—and sometimes not so subtle—undercurrents of complaint and dissatisfaction that had marked some of his earlier correspondence. He noted the hardships but with no bitterness. "Things aren't tough here. Sick of dehydrated food and I'd give $25 to hear a toilet flush. And a white girl would be out of this world."[5]

Indeed, the letters were short and almost breezy. In one he described some Filipino currency he had enclosed and explained, "The Japs paid the Filipinos in this currency. It was so inflated they say it took a lot to buy a bag of rice in the end."[6]

Although he kept his father abreast of his mission count, he didn't share much about combat. On April 24 he wrote, "I flew another mission the other day, so that makes 23. Lots of antiaircraft [fire], but no hits. They're lousy shots. This squadron [500th] really has a good record. Wish I could tell you about it. Oh well, sometime I will."[7]

He also had been in a landing accident and made little fuss over it, even though his two front teeth were knocked out. His B-25 ran off the runway at Manila. "Washed the ship out and drove Jap narrow gauge railway track through the bomb bay."[8] Aside from the loss of his teeth, he was unharmed.

And Pollock seemed more mindful of his father's needs. He set up an allotment that ensured his father received fifty dollars of his pay each month. And he sent additional money when he could. "Take it easy, Dad, old pal, as I'm doing. And be good too. Here's a hundred bucks for your birthday. Let me know you got it."[9]

Chapter Nineteen

"He Also Flew Missions with Several Other Crews"

MELVIN POLLOCK FLEW LESS AS MORE REPLACEMENT CREWS ARRIVED from the States. In fact, when he wrote his father on May 9, he had been on a furlough to Manila and hadn't flown a mission since writing his previous letter on April 24. "I haven't been doing too much flying lately," he wrote. "That's okay by me as I'm not too eager one way or the other. I've still got 23 missions in." He additionally observed, "I sure was crazy over airplanes once upon a time, but when this war's over, those days are gone forever."[1] Pollock was quite reasonably ready to put the experience behind him. Men were still dying, and many of them were his friends.

Pollock's "not too eager one way or the other" attitude toward flying more combat missions was typical of many men who flew sustained operations. And it was completely understandable as each mission presented a new opportunity to die. An official assessment following the war observed, "The development of fatigue and associated neuropsychiatry disorders among flying personnel had a definite effect on air operations. Men, tired and fatigued from long hours of operations, were not eager to engage in aerial combat. Instances were noted where flight leaders of this category, who would never have adopted such tactics during the early period of their overseas duty, restricted their bombing runs and occasionally even salvoed their bombs when faced with hazards such as enemy interception and flak."[2]

When the monsoon rains arrived during early May 1945, San Marcelino was transformed into a mud hole. This was not unexpected, and the Air Apaches were ordered to Clark Field, near Manila, where an advance party had been preparing for the group's eventual arrival for more than two months. As the base sat only about fifty miles to the east, the move to Clark during the second week of May was easier and more orderly than the move to San Marcelino had been.

Prior to the war, Clark had been the Army Air Corps' premier installation in the Far East, with the same sorts of facilities, infrastructure, and amenities typical of a large stateside airfield. Following the fall of the Philippines, the Japanese had likewise used it as a major base. And although much of it had been destroyed during the fighting, much of it had also been repaired or at least put back into service since its recapture. William Witherell, writing the group's monthly narrative, waxed almost poetic about Clark's attribute: "Houseboys, civilian work crews, friendly Filipino laundresses mingled in the area with Filipino guerilla guards. Beer, steak, chicken, fresh eggs and butter became part of the regular daily fare. Two nearby barber shops offered reclining chairs, shampoos and massages. Nearby Fort Stotsenburg offered the facilities of tennis courts and swimming pools. In the officers' and enlisted men's clubs, Army nurses, WACS [Women's Army Corps] and Red Cross workers mixed with the dark-skinned Filipino girls in a nightclub atmosphere reminiscent of the States."

Indeed, although most of the men were billeted in tents, some of the ranking officers lived in permanent quarters. Filipino mess men in white jackets waited on the officers, whose dining experience was further enhanced by an ice machine. The clubs were kitted to a point that they rivaled anything back in the States. And on the flight line, maintenance activities were eased by electric lighting that ran to all the tents.

And despite the fact that the missions they flew were as dangerous as ever, the 345th's men enjoyed other amenities they hadn't at their previous bases. "We had a houseboy, Ramon, who worked only for us," said Otis Young. "He was a good worker, bright and polite. Occasionally, he would mop the shack's plywood floor with kerosene. He claimed it kept the bugs out, never thinking of it as a fire hazard."[3]

Ramon was an obviously clever young fellow. "When one of us would play solitaire," said Young, "he would quietly stand by and watch, so as to learn the game. After a while, when we would waken in the morning, Ramon would be at the table playing solitaire. We very seldom, if ever, had to tell him what to do. He just knew what had to be done and did it."

But as comfortable as Clark was, the sicknesses that had bedeviled the men ever since they arrived in theater never abated. Indeed, throughout their entire time in the Pacific, the 345th's men slept under mosquito netting. The protective nets were an imperative not only to avoid the itching bites but to preclude being laid low by any one of the several diseases that sometimes came with them. "I fell into my cot at Clark one night and fell asleep without my mosquito net," said Roger Lovett, a copilot with the 500th Bomb Squadron. "I was bitten pretty badly and it wasn't long before I got sick. The flight surgeon diagnosed me with malaria and sent me to the general hospital. It was a prewar building that had survived all the fighting."

Lovett stepped wearily out of the jeep that brought him to the hospital, climbed the steps, and staggered to the reception desk. "They asked me how I got there and I told them that a jeep had brought me. But they wanted to know how I got into the building. When they found out that I was able to walk on my own, they turned me away. The fighting on Okinawa was raging and badly wounded men were being evacuated down to Clark. They needed all the hospital beds they had for men who were in much worse shape than me. Anyway, I missed six weeks of flying while I recuperated."

Although the decision had been taken to bypass Formosa, the big island was still regularly hit by air raids. The Japanese had maintained a significant air presence there, and the Americans needed to knock it down and keep it down. That had been largely accomplished by mid-May 1945. In truth, because it was not going to be invaded, there was little left on the island that merited attention by that point in the war. Consequently, the 345th was sent on May 11 "to complete the wiping out of Kagi Town, with preference to be given to the main lumber yard."

Sending an entire medium bomber group after such a target was a fool's errand. A lumber yard on the bypassed island was of little war-making consequence whatsoever. But the Far East Air Forces had aircraft and crews to spare, and so the lumber yard was the day's designated target.

The takeoff and flight to Formosa went without incident, but the group had trouble locating the exact target. The bulk of the unit's aircraft passed south of the Kobi airfield. Except for approximately ten biplanes sprayed with machine-gun fire by one of the 501st Bomb Squadron's gunners and a few bombs dumped into a building, the crews paid little notice to the airfield.

However, the B-25 flown by William Mathews received plenty of attention from the airfield's gunners. "His plane was hit by a burst of 40 mm [gun]fire," the squadron reported, "and temporarily knocked out of control, skidding into the ground on Kobi runway."

A massive clot of dirt enveloped Mathews's aircraft as the rest of the 501st sped along. And then, incredibly, he hauled the bomber-cum-tractor airborne again. "His right prop[eller] tips were bent by the impact with the ground," the squadron noted. "Four nose guns had been knocked out by the flak burst and 118 holes were later counted in the right engine cowling alone." The mission summary report described how Mathews sensibly "abandoned his attack on the primary target and headed out to sea." While closing the distance on a formation of 499th Bomb Squadron aircraft, his B-25 was attacked by a Zero. The enemy pilot broke off without firing his guns after the top turret gunner sent a burst of .50-caliber rounds in his direction.

Meanwhile, the 501st formation pressed on with its attacks. "Some planes in the squadrons ahead of us," the squadron stated, "had evidently misjudged the target, as they were bombing various towns and villages in the Kobi area." However, the 501st did little better and dropped bombs into Kobi town and into the villages at Puk-Lang, Tairan, and Tamio. When finally spotted, the lumber yard was dutifully bombed and strafed.

Ultimately, William Mathews and his crew coaxed their crippled craft back to Laoag on the northern tip of Luzon, where they landed with no injuries. Curiously, the squadron's leadership was unimpressed with

Mathews's airmanship, as the mission summary report declared, "There were no actions in the opinion of this officer that merited awards." Men had been richly recognized for doing far less than Mathews did on that day.

—◆—

One of several pets the Air Apaches adopted overseas or brought with them from the States was a little black-and-white terrier mutt. Jack Williams of the 500th Bomb Squadron recalled that John Loisel's crew acquired it just before flying their B-25 to Hawaii, on the first leg of their trip to New Guinea. "For only three bucks, John Loisel, Dick Pease, Bill Lambert and I acquired the dog from a pet store in Sacramento."[4]

The crewmen watched over their new puppy very carefully as they flew across the Pacific. They named it Ramses after the Egyptian pharaoh famous for having hundreds of progeny. "Obviously," said Loisel, "we had hopes for our little dogadier. He grew up fast and became a real feisty mutt. He and the rest of us arrived in New Guinea in November 1944 and finally joined the 500th in late December."

"The one thing Ram will always be remembered for was his love of flying," Loisel recalled. "Not only did Ram fly with our crew, but he also flew missions with several other crews. It was a standard joke in the squadron that Ram was accumulating points faster than any other 500th crew member so that he could complete the magic number needed for rotation back to the States."

Jack Williams remembered, "Ram developed a widely held reputation as a food taster. Ram would follow us into the mess hall where we'd always put some of our food on the floor for him to eat. One evening he just turned his nose up at our offering and walked away. Seeing this, somebody in the mess called out, 'Hey, look, even the dog won't eat this stuff tonight.' Fortunately, he usually ate the food. He also frequently ate cigarettes, dirty socks and anything else he could steal from neighboring tents."

Ramses moved with the rest of the 500th through the Philippines and finally to Clark. There Loisel completed the last of his missions and received orders home. "I took Ram with me to the processing center, where I fully expected to fly home. However, when I got there I was told that I would be returning Stateside by ship."

Loisel was determined to keep his faithful friend with him; the two had endured much together. Accordingly, when he boarded the ship, Ramses was tucked into his duffel bag. "Alas, someone turned me in and I was called up to the bridge where the captain informed me that I could not keep the dog." Ramses was put on a launch headed back to shore. "When I last saw him," Loisel said, "Ram was in the rear of the boat looking back at our ship as if to say, 'What do I do now?' I have no idea what happened to him after that."

James Baross recalled another pet, a mongrel that one of the men had adopted. "It became his friend and he decided one day to take it along on a mission. He loaded it in and we all took off. Over the target, strafing, with guns all roaring, the dog decided he just did not want to be a part of that any longer and jumped out the window."[5]

———

The 345th's operations expanded during its time in the Philippines. During the late spring of 1945, aside from antishipping missions, raids on Formosa, and sorties flown in support of ground forces in the Philippines, the 345th also flew weather reconnaissance missions, training sorties, and various types of liaison flights.

One of those liaison flights occurred during the latter part of May 1945. At that time, Japanese forces on Luzon, harried by American air and ground units, were retreating toward the port city of Aparri on the northernmost coast. The 11th Airborne Division was tapped to make a parachute assault and cut off the enemy's escape route. As they developed their plan, the division staff wanted a firsthand look at the proposed landing ground.

The 345th's 500th Bomb Squadron was tasked with giving them that look. Although the C-47 was the typical mount for the airborne troops, they didn't want to tip the Japanese off by using one for the reconnaissance flight. Don Wagner, the pilot assigned to the mission, recalled, "The B-25 was selected so as not to alert them [Japanese] to the coming action. And if fired upon, it could provide some protection."[6]

"With a copilot and a crew chief and eight fully loaded .50-caliber machine guns up front," remembered Wagner, "we flew to a camouflaged runway near Batangas, south of Manila Bay, where the 11th Airborne Division was bivouacked. The landing strip was a hard-surfaced runway, camouflage-painted to match the surrounding jungle. We landed without incident and were parked in a small clearing off the end of the runway."

A weapons carrier brought the 11th Airborne Division's commander, Major General Joseph Swing, together with a pair of colonels—his operations officer and his intelligence officer. Also accompanying them was the lieutenant colonel whose battalion had been picked to lead the attack. Wagner gave the men a quick briefing and put them aboard the B-25. The takeoff and flight up to the Aparri area went without incident.

As they approached the proposed drop zone, Wagner recalled, "the battalion commander came forward over the bomb bay for a good look at where his troops would be jumping. General Swing asked if he could sit in the copilot's seat for a better look-see, and he and the copilot changed places." Wagner noted a few Japanese vehicles hidden in the foliage to the east of their position. "We were flying at about two hundred feet when small arms fire started coming our way. I swung to the west, out of the way."

"General Swing," said Wagner, "asked if my guns were charged and I replied in the affirmative. He looked at me and said, 'Well, let's strafe the sonsabitches!'" Wagner hauled his aircraft back around, dropped to an altitude of just fifty feet, and shredded the Japanese positions with his guns. Fires burned where Wagner had hit vehicles or ammunition. "The General was overwhelmed by the firepower of those .50-caliber machine guns."

Wagner recalled that the general "was so excited that he asked me to make another pass." Moreover, the general wanted to fire the machine guns himself. "I banked the aircraft around," said Wagner, "and lined up on our target. The general was like a kid with a new toy!" On Wagner's cue, Swing reached over and pressed the firing button on the aircraft's yoke. The guns roared and sent rounds ripping through the Japanese.

On the return flight, Swing told Wagner that he couldn't remember having had "more fun." "We landed okay," said Wagner, "and the General thanked us for taking him and his staff to see the drop area." Swing additionally thanked Wagner for the "great combat experience" and remarked that he would "like to do that again sometime."

—————

Warren Brown was a twenty-year-old crewman at Clark Field during the spring of 1945. Like many others, he was sometimes tasked with other duties when not scheduled to fly. On one particular day he was one of twenty men sent to Manila to retrieve jeeps for the group. "I did not tell the one in charge that I had never driven before," he said.[7] "However, I knew you had to step on the clutch before starting and when shifting, and step on the brake to stop. I was anxious to learn to drive."

"We were trucked to the depot on the outskirts of Manila," he recounted, "where each of us climbed into a new jeep that had recently been offloaded from a ship. Our motor pool corporal led the convoy." Brown, with something less than ten yards of driving experience under his belt, managed to position himself at the end of the line of jeeps. He stalled his vehicle several times before finally getting underway. "That's when I learned about easing in the clutch while pressing the gas pedal."

Notwithstanding the fact that he was a quick study, he still had difficulties. "At times the convoy pulled out of sight, leaving me wondering if I was on the right road to Clark Field. After about an hour of this we arrived at Clark with all the jeeps undamaged and with me as a full-fledged driver."

Melvin Pollock's war was more or less over by late May 1945. He had been selected to serve two months of detached service in New Guinea. "A radio man, pilot, and I came down to be instructors for the new guys from the States." His observations in a letter to his father revealed that the war he and his comrades had fought had been a tough one: "My pilot and navigator quit. Nerves. And my radio man was killed. We lost three out of eight in my tent [by the end of the war, five of eight would be dead]. Didn't tell you before as it'd worry you—but now it doesn't make any difference. Out of forty of us, twenty-six are still alive. That's the forty of us that went by train across the States. We had some rough targets and I saw ships [B-25s] go down, but I only was holed once. Plain luck!"[8]

In fact, it wasn't overly unusual for men to quit flying as Pollock's crew mates had. Whether they lived or died was due in large part to luck, regardless of how skilled a crew might be. It was luck that determined whether an engine would fail on a given mission. It was luck that determined which aircraft in a formation enemy gunners or fighters targeted. And it was luck that created the physics—down to multiple digits to the right of the decimal point—whether an antiaircraft shell struck a critical part of the aircraft or passed harmlessly. That being the case, many men were terrified by the fact that they lived or died largely at the caprice of some sort of cosmic dice roll.

Few men talked about the terrors they endured in their dreams or in their imaginations. The specter of a hellish death was omnipresent. It was very real and possible, if not probable. Some men were quite understandably gripped by terrors that compelled them to stop flying combat missions. "One day," recalled James Baross, "while getting ready for take-off, lined up plane-after-plane, the front hatch of the plane in front of us dropped and out came a pair of legs." The legs belonged to David Lilley, who climbed down from his aircraft and walked away. "He was grounded and never flew again," said Baross.[9]

No official stigma or punishment was attached to requests to be removed from combat flying. All aircrew in the United States Army Air Forces were volunteers and could not be forced to fly. Typically, the men were given support positions and the commensurate lower rank and continued to contribute as part of the team.

The group did not see much action during June 1945 and flew combat missions on only nine days. Most of those missions were unremarkable ground-support sorties over Luzon during which evidence of the enemy beneath the jungle canopy was scant to nonexistent. The relatively slack pace permitted the group to focus efforts and resources on training newly joined crews. These were mostly third- and fourth-generation replacements—only a very few original crewmen remained.

One of the last of those originals left the unit near the end of the month. Chester Coltharp, who had so bravely overseen the rescue of two

345th crews from the hotly contested waters off Kavieng the previous year, passed command of the group to Glenn Doolittle. Most men were sorry to see Coltharp go. William Witherell recalled that, his leadership in the air aside, "on the ground he was one of the Army's few perfect gentlemen. His very appearance was refreshing and his manner encouraged his staff to produce its best."

Glenn Doolittle had earned his commission and wings just before the war and had already completed a year of combat operations in the Aleutians. There he flew B-26s and had been awarded the Silver Star for an attack on Japanese shipping in Kiska Harbor during December 1942; at that time, the 345th was only finishing its first month of training in the States. Since joining the Air Apaches at Biak, he had flown bravely and skillfully as evidenced by the addition of the Distinguished Flying Cross to his collection of medals. He was a quiet, good-looking, and efficient man who felt no need to make big changes to the way the group was doing business. For everything he was and everything he had accomplished, he was well liked.

Even before the group had completely settled into its comfortable new accommodations at Clark, Doolittle was ordered to move its flag to a new location. "It became more obvious with each succeeding day," said William Witherell, "that once again this Pacific war of movement was going to make a fool of the 345th. When couriers began to run to Okinawa, and S-2 officers [intelligence officers] began to draw range circles from Ie Shima, we knew our civilized days were numbered."

Indeed, the Air Apaches were directed to prepare for a move to Ie Shima, a tiny island just off the coast of the larger island of Okinawa; both had just recently been seized from the Japanese. From Ie Shima, the Air Apaches could range to southern Japan and Korea. For the first time, the group would be able to bring the war to Japan's Home Islands.

The 345th flew even fewer combat missions during July than it had during June. It spent most of the month training and preparing for the move. Indeed, combat missions were flown from Clark on only two days during the month. On July 11, as one part of a larger group effort, Robert Canning led three other 500th Bomb Squadron B-25s up the east coast of Formosa on a shipping sweep. Aboard his aircraft was

Robert Reeves, a public relations officer from Fifth Bomber Command. Reeves was on the flight to gain a better understanding of how the Air Apaches operated.

Canning, the 500th Bomb Squadron's commanding officer, was not only well liked but a good pilot and leader—and had additionally been a world-class high jumper. "Bob Canning was a good-looking, all-American type of guy," said Irving Horwitz, a navigator with the 500th. "He was about six-foot-two. I was pretty short and we made quite a Mutt and Jeff team. He was a good friend, and very popular. When I got to the end of my tour, I tried to get him to go back to the States with me—he had flown more than enough missions and I thought that it was time for him to go home too. But he didn't want to go back to the States until he was promoted to major." Unable to persuade Canning to accompany him, Horwitz shipped home.

The hunting that day was poor. Canning and his little formation found no shipping as they flew north along Formosa's east coast. This was hardly the show that Robert Reeves, the public relations man, had hoped to see. Upon reaching Kiirun Harbor on the northern tip of the island, Canning reversed course and looked for targets of opportunity ashore. Almost immediately, they attacked the lighthouse at Sancho Point, leaving it and several nearby rock dwellings badly damaged.

Canning continued south but, likely due to the seeming absence of the enemy, loped along at a leisurely cruising speed on a steady course. At Hokuho-O Point, the formation took heavy fire. The 500th described what happened: "Airplane 169, piloted by Major Canning, our squadron commanding officer, was fatally hit by what was believed to be 40-millimeter antiaircraft fire from Hokuho-O Point, and after cartwheeling in the air, crashed and burned at 1145 near the shore at 2435N-12152E."

The report is curious because the location given is roughly fifteen miles from the coast. William Lambert, who manned the top turret of Canning's wingman's aircraft, remembered that he had been shot down inland.

We were flying over a valley with a stream and a lot of trees. I was flying in the top turret with Captain George Schmidt. We were on the left wing of our commanding officer, Major Canning. I was looking at Canning's plane and suddenly it flipped over and dove straight down and hit the ground, exploding. The picture will always remain in my mind.

Captain Schmidt assumed the leadership of the mission and we all turned to fly back over the same area to bomb and strafe and kill the enemy that killed Major Canning and his crew.[10]

Regardless of where it happened, Canning, his crew, and Robert Reeves were dead. "Orders promoting [Canning] to major were received while he was out on the mission," said Horwitz. "The boys got together and made a big, gold oak leaf—a major's insignia—out of foil. They were going to present it to him when he landed. He never came back."

"I was standing in formation for an awards ceremony back in Texas when I heard what happened," Horwitz remembered. "I almost passed out. That news really hit me hard."

———

Stan Muniz, a radio operator with the 500th Bomb Squadron, was part of Paul Kent's crew on July 12, 1945. The men were assigned to fly a weather reconnaissance mission over the South China Sea. Muniz wasn't happy about it. "It meant that we would be flying alone back and forth along the China coast over that always rough water. To make matters worse," he said, "I would have to encode the weather report given to me by our passenger, a weatherman. About every half hour I would radio this information back to our base in the Philippines over 750 miles away."[11]

Muniz's concerns were not unfounded. "We knew that not only did our base receive our messages, but so did every Japanese listening post, trying to get a fix on our position, so they could send some fighters out to shoot us down." Tapping out the messages using Morse code was not easy, but Muniz had to do it as expeditiously as possible so that the enemy would not have time to locate and intercept the aircraft.

To help ensure that his messages were received over such long distances, Muniz used the aircraft's trailing antenna, essentially a lead-weighted cable reeled from the bottom of the aircraft a precise distance, depending on which frequency was used. Extending and tuning it was a time-consuming task. Consequently, once deployed and working, it was not retracted.

Happily, the mission was uneventful, and the aircraft motored back toward the Philippines through alternating patches of bright sunshine and clouds with heavy rainfall and lightning. "I was busy encoding the last weather report," said Muniz, "when suddenly everything inside and outside our B-25 lit up like a million Fourth of July sparklers. There were arcs of blue-white electricity from one point to another all over. The arcs were jumping from the radios to the walls, down to the floor and up to the fuel tank in the radio compartment. A quick look out of the waist window revealed big spinning circles of fire going around the props and dancing along the tops of the wings."

Muniz quickly deduced that the phenomenon was St. Elmo's fire, an unusual but generally harmless discharge of electricity caused by high voltage differentials between clouds and aircraft. Muniz's pilot, Paul Kent, was not so sanguine about the disconcerting display. "He said the cockpit was full of sparks and his instruments had gone crazy," said Muniz. "At the same time, I had already started to reel in the trailing wire antenna, as I knew that was the source of the problem. I tried to tell him all this but apparently he wasn't hearing me. He just kept telling me to shut down everything, right now!" Kent was concerned that the discharges might ignite one or more of the aircraft's fuel tanks.

Muniz obeyed his pilot, and just as he knew it would, the St. Elmo's fire dissipated when the wire antenna was brought back aboard the air- craft. The recovery back to the 345th's base at Clark was uneventful after a flight that exceeded ten hours. "We landed at Clark about an hour later," said Muniz, "just in time to stop a search plane from going out to look for us. Since we had suddenly gone off the air and I had not sent out any distress signal, we were thought to have gone down."

Muniz was happy to be done with the mission. "If given a choice, I would rather go on a combat mission anytime and leave the [weather] recon missions to someone else. Fortunately, and thank goodness, I never did fly another before returning stateside."

Although the group continued to fly training and other types of flights, the mission during which Canning and his crew were killed on July 11 was the last combat mission the Air Apaches flew out of the Philippines. The men started tearing down their tents during the middle of July, and their experience with such moves was apparent. "In spite of the heavy rains and other difficulties," said William Witherell, "the movement was accomplished in an efficient manner. Morale was good as the men felt that we were making a long stride toward a final victory by moving to a base that would enable us to carry the fight to the enemy's own land and water."

Most of the men and the heaviest equipment were put aboard Navy LSTs for the trip to Okinawa and thence to Ie Shima. The trip passed uneventfully, and the men particularly enjoyed the Navy food, described by the 498th as "fresh meat, eggs, celery, apples, oranges, all crisp and cold just out of the cold storage locker. Then there was the good Navy bread and fresh butter—all we could eat!"

Still, there was a palpable—and understandable—fear of kamikazes. The 345th's experience aboard the *Nelson* and *Waite* the year prior aside, enemy suicide pilots had killed thousands of men off the coast of Okinawa during the previous several months. In the end, the ships went unmolested, and the support elements joined the aircrews and aircraft at Ie Shima during the last few days of July.

What they found was nothing like what they had enjoyed at Clark. "It was just one big field of mud with here and there some patches of weeds," noted the 498th. "The mud was of a peculiar quality with which we had no experience before. It was at the same time as slippery as grease and as sticky as warm tar." Nevertheless, the Air Apaches were old hands at setting up operations, and combat operations commenced on July 29.

CHAPTER TWENTY

"Well, I'm Done For"

AT THE START OF AUGUST 1945, THE 345TH BOMB GROUP WAS BIGGER than it had ever been. More than 1,900 men—404 officers and 1,510 enlisted personnel—were still settling into their work and living areas on Ie Shima. Aircraft on hand included seventy-three B-25Js and a single B-25D. And there were enough fliers on the unit's roster to form 118 separate crews.

The unit was flush with both men and aircraft because it needed to be. The invasion of the Japanese Home Islands, planned for November, was expected to be a bloodbath. The enemy that the Air Apaches had been battling for two long years had defended far-flung outposts with a fanaticism that bordered on insanity. "My heart dropped," said George Givens, when it became clear that the 345th was going to participate in the invasion of Japan. "I thought, well, I'm done for." Many of his comrades shared his stoic grasp of reality.

Indeed, some authorities estimated that the invasion of Japan would cost up to half a million American dead or more. The Japanese would lose many millions more lives—both military and civilian. In anticipation of the invasion, the military placed an order for half a million Purple Heart medals. In truth, no one knew how costly the subjugation of Japan might be.

It was known, however, that the invasion would be less costly if Japan's ability to fight was first beaten down from the air. And of course, as always, the 345th was tasked with helping administer that beating. Together with a group of fighter escorts, the group was scheduled to hit targets in Korea on August 1. The fighters failed to show, and the Air Apaches—not permitted to proceed to Korea without an escort—were compelled to hit a coastal town on Kyushu, the southernmost of Japan's main islands. It was the 345th's first strike against Japan, a goal toward which a great many of them had strived since putting on a uniform. And it was a goal that had cost many of them their lives.

However, the raid was anticlimactic. The crews hit a series of unremarkable targets before heading back to Ie Shima, anxious to arrive before a quickly advancing typhoon. The storm blew in on the heels of the recovering B-25s and thoroughly soaked the men and their gear but caused no lasting harm. It took time to dry out, and the 345th hit no targets until several days later.

"Near the end of the war," said Roger Lovett, "the replacements we received started coming in as individuals rather than as entire crews. Training in the States was slowing down in anticipation of the end of the war, and there weren't as many crews available. A lot of the people who arrived were guys who had been stuck behind a desk, or in the training command, for most of the war. They showed up at units like ours with the hope of getting some combat time before it was all over."

Lovett was slated to fly as a copilot on the mission of August 5, 1944. "I was assigned to fly with a captain that I'd never even seen before," he said. The target was a collection of factories, aircraft and munitions storage depots, and waterfront installations at Tarumizu. It was also suspected that the fearsome rocket-powered Yokosuka MXY7 Ohka suicide bombs were manufactured there.

Tarumizu was situated across Kagoshima Bay from the large city of the same name, located at the southern tip of Kyushu. The strike was to be a joint effort that included elements of both the Fifth and Seventh Air Forces. Lovett remembered, "There were 325 planes scheduled for the attack—B-24s, B-26s, B-25s, P-47s and P-51s. A lot of them—including us—were carrying napalm. And we were scheduled to go in last."

The takeoff from Ie Shima and the subsequent rendezvous and flight north to Kyushu were routine. "We could see the smoke and fires from the attacks of the earlier aircraft as we got close," said Lovett. Hubert Hendrix was a P-51 pilot from the 348th Fighter Group. Like Lovett, he was impressed by the effects of the raid: "When we made our low-level approach, huge columns of deep, black napalm smoke were rising above the landscape and obscuring the mountains immediately beyond our target. I glanced up and saw a flight of P-47 Thunderbolts releasing their bombs in a straight-down dive. Those bombs had to be very close to where we were heading. We had to fly through all that smoke and wonder where those bombs were, because we had to go on instruments until we got in the clear on the other side."[1]

"The attack routing had us coming up from the south," said Lovett, "and then turning west, so that we attacked from the east. Our attack altitude was supposed to be at 1,000 feet, which was 950 feet higher than any attack I'd ever made up to that point." Lovett was in the last three-ship element of the 500th Bomb Squadron's nine aircraft. "We spread out, line abreast," he said, "and we were the last aircraft on the right side. When the formation started a gentle left turn toward the target, this new captain kept sliding us under the next aircraft to our left so that we had a face full of bomb bay. That was obviously a very bad place to be. I had to take the controls from him three different times to get us back into the proper position."

The fires started by the earlier attacks had turned the sky into a roiling volcano of black smoke and orange fire. Visibility was nil, and the 500th's B-25s were rocked by the oven-hot updrafts created by the inferno below. "It was very hard to see anything," said Lovett. "It was just black out there. I finally dropped our napalm in the middle of all that fire and smoke."

"I turned around to get confirmation from the navigator that the bomb bay was clear," said Lovett, "and that none of the napalm canisters had gotten hung up. And right about that time the captain shouted, 'You've got it.' He had lost sight of everyone and was disoriented and in danger of losing control of the aircraft."

Lovett was caught off guard. "I simultaneously turned around, brought the bomb bay doors up, grabbed the control yoke and checked the instruments." He wrestled the aircraft back to straight and level flight and peered into the murk, desperately hoping against a collision with one of his squadron mates.

The aircraft popped out of the smoke shroud a few anxious moments later—it was like stepping out of a darkened room into bright daylight. "We caught sight of the rest of the formation," said Lovett, "and got back into position. That was probably one of the most nerve-wracking incidents in my entire flying career."

The next day, August 6, the 345th sent its squadrons on two separate shipping sweeps against a convoy off the coast of Korea. There, along the way and on the return, a number of targets at sea and ashore were hit at a cost of two aircraft and their crews.

On the following day, August 7, 1945, the group sent another attack to Kyushu to hit transportation targets. Quentin Stambaugh, a radio operator with the 498th Bomb Squadron, was nearing the end of his combat tour. "I went to the operations clerk and told him that I wanted to fly with Robert Neal and his crew because they were also approaching the end of their time in combat. They had a lot of experience."

"I flew with a new pilot—they didn't put me with Neal," said Stambaugh. "Instead, my friend Robert Goulet flew with them as their radio operator. We flew a mission to hit a bridge and an industrial area on Kyushu." As it developed, Neal's ship went down. "The Japanese came and got them," Stambaugh said, "and later decapitated them."

Although Stambaugh didn't know it at the time, the B-29 bomber *Enola Gay* had dropped an atomic bomb on Hiroshima, Japan, the previous day, August 6, 1945. The devastation was unlike anything ever seen: an estimated one hundred thousand people were incinerated, and the center of the city was flattened. Another B-29, *Bockscar*, dropped a second atomic bomb on Nagasaki, Japan, on August 9, 1945. The results were similar, with up to seventy-five thousand people killed.

The Air Apaches didn't understand the science behind the atomic bomb—no one did. But they did understand its potential, as noted by the group headquarters: "The first news of the atomic bomb began to come over the radio. Amateur scientists came up with wordy explanations. The laymen knew that if the reports were true, a savage weapon was ours to be used in the hastened defeat of a savage enemy."

Yet none of them really knew, as noted by the 499th Bomb Squadron, "if the reports were true." It declared, "On August 9th, news of the new and extremely powerful atomic bomb crept into the squadron. The majority of the men, however, met the story with considerable skepticism and only the most prolific of rumor mongers continued to spread stories of its devastating effects on Japan."[2]

And then, nothing happened.

The Japanese remained belligerent. Consequently, on August 10, 1945, the Air Apaches launched a shipping sweep through the Tsu Shima Strait, which separated southeast Korea and the Japanese islands of Honshu and Kyushu. Japanese shipping activity was reported on the uptick since the previous day when the Soviet Union declared war on Japan. The reports were not in error, and the group attacked and sank a destroyer, together with a half dozen transports and freighters of various sizes. Another warship and several other vessels were damaged.

Aerial resistance was non-existent except for a halfhearted attack by a single-engine fighter. But the warships put up intense antiaircraft fire. The 500th Bomb Squadron observed an unusual antiaircraft device thrown up by a lugger that "consisted of a rocket-like affair which may have trailed a cable." The 501st B-25 piloted by George Vincent was knocked down by antiaircraft fire and exploded upon hitting the water. Another 501st aircraft, crewed by Earl Wilkinson, was hit and forced to ditch partway back to Ie Shima.

On that day, Quentin Stambaugh was the radio operator aboard John Kelly's aircraft. "The squadron attacked in two-plane elements and we were in the wingman position," he said. "Normally, we flew close together and started our attack from a couple of miles away at four or five thousand feet. The pilots started a dive and pushed the power up to nearly full throttle. When the ship was within range, the pilots sprayed them with the .50-caliber machine guns. Then," Stambaugh continued, "after leveling off just above the water—and getting pretty close to the ship—the bombs were released so that they either flew right into the ship or skipped into it."

"My pilot had never flown a mission against shipping," said Stambaugh, "and we lagged much too far behind the lead aircraft." This was problematic as the trailing pilot couldn't fire his guns for fear of hitting the lead aircraft. Consequently, the enemy gunners endured only half the fusillade they otherwise would have faced.

"We were so far behind our leader that my pilot should have just turned away," said Stambaugh, "but he kept flying at the target after our leader dropped his bomb." The bomb fell short and detonated before it hit the enemy ship. "We were directly above it when it blew up," said Stambaugh, who was in the tail gun position. A geyser of water erupted from the surface of the ocean and slammed into the aircraft's underside, tipping it like a toy. "Water shot like a fire hose through the hole down which shell casings were supposed to fall when we fired our guns. At the same time, I was thrown up from my seat and my head smashed into the Plexiglas canopy."

The impact with the canopy wrenched forward Stambaugh's helmet, and gashed his lip and face. "I could taste blood," he said, "and I was soaking wet with water in my nose and eyes and mouth—like a dunked donut. I couldn't see, and I thought we had crashed into the water. I reached up to release the canopy so that I could get out, but I couldn't find the handle."

A few seconds passed before Stambaugh realized the aircraft was still flying. "The plane was vibrating and the skin on the right vertical stabilizer was peeled back far enough that a man could walk through it. We kept flying low and got out of there pretty quick." Once clear of the enemy ships, Kelly started an easy climb during which Stambaugh checked himself over. Aside from the gash on his face, he was wet but otherwise unharmed.

"Not long afterward, we were jumped by a pair of Jap fighters and we had to dive back low over the water—our propellers were just barely above the waves." The enemy pilots made a lackluster pass at the B-25, during which Stambaugh fired a few rounds. Evidently discouraged or simply not eager for a fight, the Japanese fighters winged away as Kelly climbed again and pressed back toward Ie Shima. "After about an hour," said Stambaugh, "we spotted a man in a raft. We didn't know if it was an enemy pilot or one of ours, but we circled him while the navigator got a fix on the location. He passed it to me and I got on the radio and sent it out. We continued to circle until a PBY arrived and landed to pick him up."

In the meantime, Earl Wilkinson had set his damaged B-25 down in the water. All of the crew escaped but were unable to retrieve their life raft. Donald Wright of the 499th had flown on Wilkinson's wing ever since he had been hit; he dropped another raft to them, but it was too damaged to be used. Nevertheless, Wright's navigator got a good fix on the position and transmitted it to Air Search and Rescue. When Wright finally landed back at Ie Shima, he had flown a near-record eleven hours and forty-five minutes.

Wilkinson and his crew spent the next several hours floating in the water. As each hour passed with no sign of rescue, they grew increasingly disheartened as they knew the odds of being saved degenerated steadily over time. Nor was there any guarantee that the Japanese wouldn't spot them rather than their own countrymen.

Their despondency quickly turned into elation when an SB-17G—a search and rescue variant of the B-17 bomber—appeared and parachute-dropped one of the recently fielded A-1 life boats close by. When the men splashed over to it and climbed aboard, they felt that the well-provisioned and well-equipped boat might well have been a yacht. Although not quite so luxurious, the yellow-painted, laminated mahogany boat was twenty-seven feet long and weighed nearly two tons. It was equipped with sails and two separate engines. If need be, the crew could survive at sea for months.

Safely back on the ground at Ie Shima, Quentin Stambaugh had his face patched up before debriefing the mission with the rest of the crew. "Afterward, I told them [operations personnel] I wanted my mission whiskey," he said. "Up to that time, I had never drunk whiskey after a mission. I didn't like it and I didn't want it. But after that mission, I sure did."

The clerk poured a double shot of whiskey and pushed it across the table at Stambaugh. "I told him I didn't want a shot—I wanted it all. I'd flown 39 missions and I wanted all the whiskey they owed me. So, he pulled out a logbook in which they tracked that stuff and he started making marks and pouring shots in an empty bottle until finally he just gave up and shoved two bottles of whiskey at me."

Stambaugh grabbed his prize and went back to his tent. "I shared it with two friends. We mixed it with canned grapefruit juice and drank it all in about twenty minutes, and then passed out." The three men did not die of alcohol poisoning but did stay unconscious for a long time. "I finally woke up and guys were shaking me and slapping my face. They said, 'Stummy! Stummy! You've got 103 points—you've got enough points to go home!' I had flown my last mission."

Wilkinson and his crew aboard the A-1 lifeboat likely awoke about the same time as Stambaugh on April 11, 1945. Bleary-eyed, they watched the horizon for several hours after daylight but saw nothing. Although they were safe for the moment and their position was generally known, there was still no sign of rescue.

The submarine USS *Plaice* was not aware of any downed crewmen in its patrol area. A log entry made at 0916 noted that its crew had "sighted what appeared to be a small boat through [the] high periscope, bearing 119 degrees true. Closed to investigate on four main engines. Looked like sampan with two sails."

Wilkinson's sore and exhausted crew didn't spot the submarine. They fussed with the rescue radio—the Gibson Girl—and other equipment while also administering first aid to each other. The men aboard the *Plaice* were still unsure what they had spotted and were wary of a Japanese trap. "Manned both 40-millimeter guns," noted the log's 0931 entry. "As we approached, could see several figures moving about, but making no signs of recognition, or waving. A balloon ascended from boat. Realized it could be antenna for Gibson Girl, or a signal for locating boat, but could see no reason for using it at this late period when we were in plain sight."

The captain of the *Plaice* took no chances. "At about 1,500 yards range," the log recorded, "put rudder over hard right and circled. Fired three 40-millimeter shells as a warning. All overs [passed overhead the A-1 lifeboat]. Still no signs of recognition."

Despite the submarine crew's observation, the cannon rounds certainly did catch the attention of Wilkinson's men. Looking up, they spotted the *Plaice*, grabbed whatever was at hand, and waved it wildly. This was noted by the submariners, who were closing at flank speed. "Could discern then that they were friendly," observed the log. "Maneuvered close aboard and picked up five survivors."[3]

By the time that Wilkinson's crew had been rescued and Stambaugh and his friends got sober, most of the 345th's men had flown their last missions. Although the group made several more raids during the next four days, little about them was remarkable.

And then, the Japanese gave up.

On August 15, 1945, for the first time in history, Emperor Hirohito addressed his subjects via radio. In a thin, reedy voice he directed his people to accept the unconditional terms of surrender the Allies had crafted at the recent Potsdam Conference. Notwithstanding isolated attacks against Allied forces by diehard hotheads or by combatants unaware of the order, the Japanese obeyed their emperor. From that point, there was little to do except wait for the surrender to be formalized.

The United States broadcast a set of instructions to Japan. The emperor was ordered to send military and government representatives to Ie Shima, from where they were to be flown to Douglas MacArthur's headquarters in Manila. There, they were to sign the surrender documents that would technically end the war, although the final, more formal ceremony—intended for a broader audience—would take place at a later date. The message read, in part,

> *The party will travel in a Japanese airplane to an airdrome on the island of Ie Shima, from which point they will be transported to Manila, Philippine Islands, in a United States airplane. They will be returned to Japan in the same manner. The party will employ an unarmed airplane. . . . Such airplane will be painted all white and will bear upon the side of its fuselage and the top and bottom of each wing green crosses easily recognizable at 500 yards. The airplane will*

be capable of in-flight voice communications, in English, on a frequency of 6,970 kilocycles.[4]

P-38s of the 8th Fighter Group and B-25s of the Air Apaches were selected to escort the aircraft carrying the Japanese representatives to Ie Shima. The 345th's men recognized it as the great honor it was—a tribute to the hurt they had done the enemy and to the sacrifices they had endured. "For three days," noted the 345th's headquarters, "we had been alerted to escort the Japanese peace envoys to Ie Shima enroute to Manila for instructions from General MacArthur."

Many of the 345th's aircrews wanted to be part of the historic mission. However, at least a few did not. "I got a note from Major Jack McClure," said Quentin Stambaugh. "A courier delivered it to my tent. It said, 'Going out to meet the Japs tomorrow. Would like to have you fly radio with me.'" Stambaugh considered the offer for a few minutes. He was finished with his combat missions and ready to go home. Even though the shooting was finished, he knew that the simple act of flying was risky in its own right. And there was no telling what might happen during a mission to escort a Japanese surrender delegation.

"I sent a return message on the back of the note," he said. "I wrote, 'Thanks, but no thanks, Major. I've had enough.' I gave it back to the courier and was glad not to be going, although I was somewhat proud that Major McClure thought enough of me to ask me to be his radio operator for a pretty important mission."

The Japanese prepared two Mitsubishi G4M "Betty" bombers as instructed. The armament was removed, both were painted white with large crosses on their wings, fuselages, and tails. Although the crosses were supposed to be green, they appear black in extant color photos—or so dark green as to appear black. Regardless, the job was poorly done with seemingly cheap paint; the red "meatball" insignia, or *hinomaru*, was still faintly visible. So prepared, and with the necessary personnel aboard, the Japanese bombers took off from Kisarazu, near Tokyo, on the morning of August 19, 1945.

"August 19th," the group headquarters recorded, "six of our planes loaded with the great and near-great of the group searched three assigned areas in pairs for the plane loads of Jap peace emissaries that had left Kyushu in the early morning." It was nearly noon when Jack McClure spotted the two enemy aircraft. Escorted by the P-38s, he rendezvoused with them and, after exchanging a series of confused radio calls and hand signals, led them to Ie Shima.

Long lines of men snaked their way to the runway. "It seemed like everyone on the island was there that day," said George Givens.[5] "There were MPs [military police] everywhere. And cameramen, too. The MPs were there to make sure everyone behaved—they didn't want any of our men to misbehave or shout, or curse. The GIs could get out of hand if given a chance."

"A huge crowd lined the runway," Givens said. "I was down by the end where the Bettys turned off before they taxied to the parking apron. The Japanese were mostly generals and diplomats. There were no disruptions and it seemed to me that everything was done with dignity."

After a short time the Japanese envoys were directed to climb a ladder into MacArthur's C-54, which carried the name *Bataan*. A short time later the brilliantly polished silver aircraft took off and turned south for the Philippines. Back on the runway, the crowd of American servicemen straggled back to their living and working spaces.

MacArthur, at his headquarters in Manila, instructed the Japanese as to American expectations. Under the terms of surrender the Japanese were not in a position to negotiate, and what discussion there was focused on clarifying specific points. MacArthur's behavior and countenance were observed to be professional and no-nonsense, as those of a man definitely in charge. The Japanese were returned to Ie Shima the following day.

When the enemy aircraft left the island for Japan late that afternoon, the 345th sent B-25s to escort them part of the way. George Givens was aboard one of the aircraft. He recounted,

After we were airborne for a while, one of the Japanese airplanes started easing toward us on the left side. I was on that side at the waist gun position. As he got closer the Japanese pilot met my eyes and he smiled at me. I patted my .50-caliber machine gun and smiled back. He got so close to us that his wing was tucked a few feet under ours. I called my pilot on the interphone and asked if he knew what was going on. He said that he saw everything and seemed uncon- cerned. After a while, the Japanese pilot eased away. Not too long after that, we turned back to Ie Shima.

—◆—

With the war essentially over, Melvin Pollock reflected on his experience to his father. "One thing, I'm still alive and that's a lot more than I can say for some of my old friends. And believe me, I didn't know if I was going to go the distance a few times. Maybe you've been worried that something didn't happen to me in the last days of the war. Well, old Dad, don't worry, as I'm perfectly all right."[6]

In one of his later letters he was very matter-of-fact about his time in combat. "I strafed Japs jumping off a sinking DE [destroyer escort] and saw about twenty fall dead. So now I know I've killed, but it doesn't bother me. They'd have killed us if they could've. That's the way it goes in war I guess."[7]

—◆—

On Hainan Island, Ben Muller, James McGuire, Gene Lawliss, and Eugene Harviell were nearly dead. Still captive in their bamboo cage, they were little more than skeletons. "I weighed about 80 pounds," said Ben Muller. "Another two weeks, I'd have been dead for sure. I got malaria. I got beriberi. I got pellagra. I got amoebic dysentery."[8]

As sick as Muller was, Eugene Harviell was in worse shape. Like Charles Suey, he was injured when his aircraft was shot down, and he received no medical care for his wounds. He died on August 10, 1945, of neglect and starvation. Of the five Americans originally held on Hainan, two had perished. At 40 percent, this was higher than the average mortal- ity rate of 27 percent for all POWs held by the Japanese. They had been captive less than five months.

The fortunes of the remaining three men changed dramatically fol- lowing the atomic bomb attacks on Hiroshima and Nagasaki on August 6 and 9, respectively. Japan agreed to surrender on August 15, 1945. "They put us in a little hospital," said Ben Muller, "and they said there had been an 'automatic' bomb dropped."[9]

News of the barely fathomable destructive power of the atomic bombs—and the cessation of hostilities thus forced on the Japanese—worked to the benefit of Muller and his comrades. The men received a letter from a Japanese doctor, Colonel Miyao, notifying them that they were to be moved to a hospital where they would receive better care. The doctor, who had previously offered them absolutely nothing, wrote, "The war was stopped recently," and "I congratulate you your heartfelt joy from your Christian spirit, because you can go back to your each [*sic*] lovely home. . . . If you want anything, tell me or write me about it. I will try to send you as far as I can." Muller was moved into a small hospital. "I was so bad and weak that they put a Jap nurse beside me in another bed and transferred blood from her arm to my arm—a transfusion."[10]

On August 27, 1945, six days before the official surrender ceremony aboard the USS *Missouri*, Captain John Singlaub of the Office of Strategic Services (OSS), leading eight other men, parachuted onto Samah. He was tasked with coordinating the repatriation and evacuation of the Allied POWs there.

Such a job—among thousands of bitterly angry fighting men who had not yet formally surrendered—demanded calculated bluster, intelligence, and courage. Few men, if any, were better suited for the task than Singlaub. A veteran of clandestine activities behind Nazi lines, he had recently been assigned to operations in China during early 1945.

Once on the ground at Samah, he and his team, armed only with pistols, confronted two truckloads of Japanese soldiers. Singlaub ordered the enemy lieutenant commanding the small force to take him to the ranking officer. He was subsequently brought to the Japanese headquarters, where he immediately took the high ground and brusquely issued a series of commands that cowed the Japanese officers into obeisance. A subsequent meeting with the senior Allied POWs—Australian and Dutch officers—left Singlaub stunned.

They were emaciated, badly scarred from beatings, and sickly. They literally stank of starvation. There followed a visit to the POW camp and its hospital. Singlaub was not prepared for what he saw. "Here the stench of dysentery and festering wounds was nearly overpowering. The patients lay on primitive bunks fashioned from crates and scraps of plywood, segregated by their affliction—the beriberi patients to one side, the men with dysentery isolated at the far end. . . . The worst of the beriberi cases were grotesque. The men's bellies and limbs were swollen to elephantine proportions, their scrotums distended like terrible orange melons."[11]

The Japanese were forced to acknowledge the authority of the small OSS party and of the Allied personnel who followed during the next several days. Although they were initially unwilling to do anything to help the POWs, Singlaub threatened them into action. The gates of the prison camps were thrown open, and the guards were sent away. Food and medical attention were brought to the former prisoners. Ben Muller, already convalescing under Japanese care, recalled the transition. "This little hospital had a little circular [area], not a platform, by the front door where the flagpole was. They lowered the Jap flag and raised the American flag. That was great. I remember that."[12]

Soon after Singlaub's arrival, the evacuation of the POWs, including the three surviving 345th men—Muller, McGuire, and Lawliss—got underway by both sea and air.

~ ~

Max Mortensen, a 500th Bomb Squadron pilot who had flown with the group from beginning to end, flew an aerial reconnaissance of the wracked and ruined nation into which the United States had turned Japan. Aside from his crew, the aircraft carried John Graham Dowling, a reporter for the *Chicago Sun*. Dowling was awestruck by what he saw at Nagasaki, the target of the second, and last, atomic weapon ever used in combat. "We saw half a city laid waste. Not in ruins as after an ordinary bombing or shelling but smashed flat. Even the ground and stones were turned into a dust and still burning, still stinking of death weeks after the atomic bomb was turned against them."

"Before this," wrote Dowling, "Nagasaki had been that comedy place in that tinpan alley song: 'Back in Nagasaki, where the women chew tobaccy, and the ladies wicky wacky woo.'" The reeking, radioactive, and ruined city upon which the 345th's men looked down was no longer the silly city of the Tin Pan ditty.

Dowling also saw and understood the devastation wrought not by atomic weapons but by the sheer weight of American might and will. "This flight not only provided a startlingly clear picture of a disrupted enemy industry and war machine, of smashed cities and sunken or beached ships, but also gave us a feeling of a beaten countryside and confused people, of Japanese faces flying by in the kaleidoscope of our speed. I remember them waving, running, crouching, gaping, or just standing. We even saw one Japanese soldier taking a picture of us with a candid camera. We were that low and he was that close."[13]

Marvin "Murph" Leventon was aboard the same aircraft that day. "It was hard to believe how one bomb had caused so much destruction," he said. "It was so different from the bombs we dropped. We also found a POW camp nearby. The prisoners jumped up and down and waved. We circled back and dropped a note to let them know the war was over—it was a good feeling to see them so happy."

With the war essentially over, William Witherell captured the collective and reflective spirit of the men. "For all intents and purposes, the crude and barbaric war in the Pacific was over," he wrote. "Our group arrived in this theatre in time to count cadence with its bombs and bullets for the real aerial march north from New Guinea, through the Philippines and onto the very soil of the enemy. We lost both fliers and ground men. We made our camps in the hellholes of the world."

Witherell struck a tone of defiant pride and blunt honesty. "We were the 'soft' Americans on a warpath that had led to the Emperor's palace. Some of our leaders were great, many were mediocre and not a few should have stayed home. Despite commitments that were often overambitious, the sheer force and power of our spirit and our weapons had made a record of which we can be justly proud. And we are proud."

And they had cause to be so. In all the war, few groups had so distinguished themselves. The Air Apaches—making daring and deadly low-level attacks in resplendently marked aircraft—fought themselves into the nation's history as the most iconic bomb group of the Pacific War.

EPILOGUE

NO DOUBT, ON COMING HOME, THE VAST MAJORITY OF THE 345TH'S MEN shared experiences similar to Joseph Solomon's. "It was great to be home! In the service we talked about what we were going to do when we returned. We made so many imaginary plans."

But the reality of life overcame many of the newly returned men. "About a week after my return," said Solomon, "I started to get restless. The euphoria had lasted about a week. It seemed like something was missing and I realized I missed the service, missed all the buddies I spent the last three years with—even missed the tents, the outdoor living and the army chow. Where were those dreams that we'd had back in New Guinea and the Philippines?"

Solomon and his comrades were hardly the first to miss the friendships, the routines, and the sense of purpose created by military service. "Some of the fellows I knew never made it back and the ones that did became recluses and restless like myself," he said. "This is when I learned that it was harder to adjust to our return than it was to adjust to the service."

But young men are resilient, and Solomon sorted himself back into the peacetime world. "As time passed, I adjusted, as most of us did. I found that a part of that adjustment was to make my memories of the war and my time in the Southwest Pacific a part of my new life."

Many Air Apache men, however, were never able to reconcile themselves to their wartime experience. Once home, they did what they could to forget the war and to leave that time—and everything associated with it—behind. To the end of their days, they declined all contact with their former comrades.

Lincoln Grush, like many of the men, didn't talk about his experiences for many years. "I lost quite a few buddies. You'd go to sleep at night in your tent with ten guys, and the next night, there would be only three or four." He hopes that future generations will remember the sacrifices made.

J. R. Jones and his vivacious redhead, Elnora Bartlett, were married on September 7, 1944, in Houston. After he left the service the following year, they both studied at Indiana University in Bloomington and earned degrees. They subsequently moved to Houston, Elnora's hometown, where he ultimately went to work for the Shell Oil Company. She became a teacher.

Both continued their love of music and other entertainments. Their marriage was a happy one and produced two children, a boy and a girl. Sadly, J. R. suffered a massive heart attack and died too young in 1973. Bone cancer took Elnora in 1985.

Talmadge Epps went back to the States without his Australian wife, Ruth. Wartime exigencies kept her and twelve thousand other war brides from leaving Australia. It wasn't until April 1946 that he received a phone call at work that the Red Cross had brought his wife home to Pennsylvania. The two set up house and raised three children.

Through his life, although a proud advocate of the Air Apaches and the military in general, Epps wanted more than anything for the nation's young people—and especially his own children and grandchildren—to understand that freedom isn't free at all. Rather, the liberties we all enjoy are too often paid for—necessarily—with the lives of our sons and daughters. Perhaps we all understand this to varying degrees, but Epps knew it from keen and bitter experience as he saw, literally, too many sons perish in ways horrific and cruel.

Indeed, too many 345th men were shot down over water or impossibly rough terrain or dense jungle. Their remains were essentially irretrievable, and their families were left with little more than memories. Such was not the case with James Underwood, who smashed into a mountaintop in the predawn darkness of January 9, 1945, while en route to support Douglas MacArthur's landing at Lingayen.

The 501st Bomb Squadron reported that Underwood crashed on Sibuyan Island, part of the Philippine archipelago. Government efforts during 1947 and 1948 failed to find any trace of him or his crew.

Philippine natives ultimately found the wreckage high on the rugged mountainside of a completely different island, Mindoro, in 1962. A U.S. team eventually reached the crash site in 1963 and found pieces of the wreck, as well as Underwood's dog tags and a few bones. Underwood's son, James Briggs—who carried the last name of his mother's second husband—said, "My family was never told even the mere fact that my father's crash site had definitely been found." Indeed, there is no evidence that the government ever tried to contact Underwood's family or the families of the other crewmen.

In fact, a Filipino native had found skeletal remains and brought home Underwood's flight school ring—engraved with his name—and a handful of family photos. After he told the Red Cross of his find, U.S. authorities recovered both the ring and the photos. Again, no attempt was made to contact the family. Finally, in 2014, a box with the ring and photos and other evidence was found in a back room at the National Archives by a workman who carried it to a researcher. Only because James Briggs had been actively working to find documents and artifacts relating to his fallen father was the researcher able to present his father's ring, ID tag, and photos to his mother almost exactly seventy years to the day after Underwood was lost. Most families weren't so fortunate.

Soon after returning from overseas, James Baross married his sweetheart. They were on their way to Buffalo, New York, to begin their honeymoon when a tire went flat during a blinding rainstorm. "I got out to change it, in the pouring rain, and was about to jack up the car when a car stopped and a man climbed out, saying, 'Get back in the car. You've done enough for us. I'll do this for you.' I had my uniform on with the ribbons and wings so he could see I had been overseas. What a wonderful thing for him to do. I have often wondered about him."

After his honeymoon, Baross was sent to Plattsburg Convalescent Hospital where he was diagnosed with extreme anxiety reaction, known today as posttraumatic stress disorder, or PTSD. Most of the group's combat men no doubt suffered similarly to a certain degree. He spent a month or so convalescing before returning to school and eventually recovering from the most intense aspects of the illness. His reflections on his wartime experiences mirrored the thoughts of many 345th men:

"While it is hard to picture myself doing now those things that I was called upon to do during wartime, I did what I was called upon to do, and did those things the best I could. And I feel good about that."

Melvin Pollock, who had written so faithfully to his widowed father, left the service and moved around quite a bit as he worked different jobs and attended art school. He was eventually smitten by a Wisconsin beauty, Lucille Mikoda, whom he met in his hometown of Adams, where she owned and operated a café with her sister. The two were married in 1948 and were straightaway blessed with two children, a boy and a girl.

In November 1951, Melvin was away doing steeplejack work at the power plant in Winona, Minnesota. One day a man stopped by the house and then left with Lucille's father. Sometime later, Lucille looked through the window and saw the man approach the house again. This time he had with him Melvin's father, Manley.

Before the men even reached the door, Lucille came to a stark and horrified realization. "I knew," she said. "Oh, I knew then he wasn't coming back. I felt like my life was over." Melvin, who had worried about "going the distance" while fighting in the Pacific and who didn't "give a damn for the medals if I can come back in one piece, with the war over, and civilian life waiting for me," had fallen to his death.

Preparatory to being sent home after the war, George Givens and others in the 345th were moved the few miles across the water from Ie Shima to Okinawa. "A couple of us decided to hitchhike to Naha," said Givens. "It had been the biggest city on the island but was pretty much leveled during the fighting. We wanted to see it anyway."

"A Marine Corps colonel in a jeep had his driver stop to pick us up," Givens recalled. "And we drove only a short distance when we came to a hill on one side of the road that was just covered with white crosses. They were our men who had been killed fighting on the island. The colonel stepped out and we did too. He just looked at all those crosses and tears streamed down his face. Finally, he saluted, and we did too."

When Ben Miller returned home to the family farm in Adams County, Indiana, after more than three years of military service, it took only seconds for his dog, Spot, to realize who he was. During the succeeding several days, they were inseparable; Miller rode his bike with his dog's hind legs in his back pockets and his front legs wrapped around his neck. He worked at General Electric full-time and often put in several hours each day on his parents' farm. He married, raised a family, and was active with the American Legion, the 345th Bomb Group Association, and his church.

Harry "Sam" Chused, not previously mentioned in this book, was a navigator and bombardier with the 345th. His wartime service and his postwar life were marked by steadfast dedication, hard work, some amount of tragedy, and a greater amount of love. Indeed, his experience was similar to that of many of the thousands of other 345th men also not mentioned in this book. Mentioned or not, they were no less remarkable than any others.

A college man when the war broke out, Chused had no great desire for the hardship or terror that the conflict promised and chose to serve in the U.S. Army Air Forces, reasoning that the war might be over by the time he was fully trained. During that training he became close with Julius "Jukey" Cohen. Chused and Cohen enjoyed their time together, including breaks in training during which they went to Chicago to visit with Cohen's high school sweetheart, Lenore. During the summer of 1944, Cohen married Lenore, and a few months later, both Chused and Cohen were sent overseas.

Both men joined the 345th in the Philippines. Like virtually every Air Apache man, they mastered their fears and performed their duties quietly and diligently. Chused was devastated when Cohen was shot down and killed on April 6, 1945. Lenore, whom Jukey had left pregnant, shared that sense of loss and anguish. Chused was himself shot down twice. The first time, his aircraft crashed ashore in the Philippines; the next time he was wounded and plucked from the water by a submarine dangerously close to the Japanese coast.

Once home, Chused studied optometry on the GI Bill. As he studied, he made time to visit with Lenore and her new baby girl. Those visits turned from mutual mourning into something else, and the two were married in May 1946. Chused became a doctor of optometry, went to work, and steadfastly built a successful practice and a warm, happy home with Lenore. Together the couple raised Jukey's daughter and four more children with love and grace and discipline. That love and grace and discipline shaped the children—and eventually their grandchildren and great-grandchildren—into a family of which Chused and Lenore were justifiably proud. The story of unassuming Harry "Sam" Chused and his progeny underscores the best of what America's World War II veterans achieved when they came home.

In the end, most of the 345th's men likewise hung up their uniforms, put away their footlockers, and got on with their lives. Families, jobs, mortgage payments, and the great industrial miracle that was postwar America were their new realities. The terrors of treetop-level strafing runs and kamikazes seemed far gone and otherworldly. Few of them thought of their service as extraordinary relative to the other 16 million men who had served during the war. It was simply something they had done, just as a neighbor had slogged through the fighting on the far side of the Rhine, or a boss had led an artillery battery on Okinawa, or an alcoholic brother-in-law had won the Silver Star fighting Erwin Rommel in North Africa.

Happily, the half million Purple Heart medals manufactured in anticipation of the invasion of Japan were never awarded for that purpose. Instead, they have been used to decorate veterans of every conflict since. Indeed, today's military men are receiving Purple Heart medals originally intended for their grandfathers and great-grandfathers.

And those old Air Apaches—those who are still alive—mourn the fact that even a single one of those half million Purple Heart medals has ever had to be awarded.

ACKNOWLEDGMENTS

ANY ATTEMPT TO WRITE A BOOK OF THIS SORT WITHOUT THE HELP OF others would produce little more than a thin skein of official figures, dates, and dry mission summaries. The only way to give such a story the heart it needs is to incorporate the firsthand memories of those who actually lived it. To that end, I was greatly aided by several of the surviving veterans. For that, I am grateful. However, time is a merciless mistress, and sadly most of the veterans are gone. Happily, my efforts were blessed by the generosity of others—families, friends, and fanatics—who had the foresight to preserve the experiences of many Air Apaches and who graciously shared them with me.

Jim Bina, the son of a 345th veteran, a veteran himself, and a big part of the 345th Bomb Group Association, gave me much guidance and a thorough review of the manuscript. His keen eye kept me from committing mistakes that would have detracted from the book—for that I thank him. My friend and colleague Dr. James Perry also gave the manuscript a good look and, as he always has, made genuinely useful remarks.

Special thanks go to the 345th Bomb Group Association, which allowed me to quote from its newsletter, *The Strafer*. Published for more than thirty years, it has captured many fascinating accounts from the group's veterans. Also, alone among the group's four squadrons, the 500th Bomb Squadron published a newsletter, *Rough Raider*, which was similarly useful and from which I was also permitted to quote.

Marcia Pollock Wysocky kindly allowed me to use the letters of her late father, Melvin Pollock. Those letters are part of her own excellent book, *Two Fathers, One War: A Daughter's Story*. They are especially valuable because her father's thoughts and observations are contemporaneous—unfiltered and unburnished by time and experience. As such, they afford a raw and frank look at the war through the eyes of someone who was actually living it as he wrote.

René Palmer Armstrong wrote *Wings and a Ring*, a second edition of which has just been released. The book outlines the love story of J. R. Jones and Elnora Bartlett. Organized around their correspondence, this book likewise provided a wonderful and unique look at the war—a look that would never be found in official accounts. Thanks to Ms. Armstrong and Suzanne Jones Neff for allowing me to borrow from such a remarkable romance. Thanks also go to Senath Rankin, who captured the recollections of Jay Moore in their outstanding book, *A True Flyer*. Moore's accounts are especially colorful, and he pulled no punches in describing his war. His perspective as a rank-and-file pilot was quite useful.

There were two memoirs to which I turned over and over again. James P. Baross's *The War Years* is a frank, well-written account from a man who left college to serve as an enlisted flyer. Similarly, Ben Miller's excellent *A Farm Boy Goes to War* includes many unusual stories about his time working in the 499th Bomb Squadron's communications section. Both provided insights and anecdotes that lent more context to the overall narrative. I thank the families of both these men for sharing these chronicles.

Aside from the veterans whose stories appear herein, many Air Apache friends and families were gracious with other assistance and material. Among them was Perry Hurt, who shared his father's memoirs, letters, photos, and diary; the Epps family, who provided much material about their father's service; Kelly McNichols, who shared the letters of Wilmer "Buck" Fowler and also provided me much information about the 500th Bomb Squadron; Randy Wagner, who generously shared records of his father's experience; Bob Kantor, whose experience as a 345th intelligence officer gave me perspective; Elizabeth Miller, Jon Anderson, Terry Weisshaar, Everett Hatcher, Ron Beattie, and Stephen Quesinberry, who shared their own 345th material; and John Turner, who provided the Ray Link letters. Pam Gay at the San Diego Air & Space Museum was also helpful with information about the Kavieng mission.

Especially poignant was the story of Robert Jensen and his new wife, Ruth. It was shared with me by their son, Robert Pearson, who was still unborn when Jensen and his crew perished near the end of the war. The story is one that proves that the hurt of the war carried—and carries—on for decades afterward.

My agent, E. J. McCarthy, has always been, and continues to be, a blessing. And the fine folks at Stackpole have ensured that the book is as good as it could be. Many thanks.

I know that I have surely forgotten to thank someone. I am sorry and ask for your understanding.

Finally, our beloved German Shepherd, Frankie, who gave me and my family so much companionship and comfort over so many years, died as I finished this manuscript. Her spleen tried to match the size of her heart, and it failed. We are devastated and heartily agree with Will Rogers, who declared, "If dogs aren't allowed in heaven, then I want to go where they are."

Jay A. Stout
San Diego
2018

Notes and References

Unless noted otherwise, the official quotes for specific missions are derived from the group and squadron mission summary reports for that particular day. That being implicit, and in order to save clutter and page count, I did not footnote those quotes. Neither did I footnote quotes from the monthly group and squadron histories written primarily by Aldridge Nichols and William Witherell. These histories and mission summary reports—in fact, the group's official history—are readily available from the Air Force Historical Research Agency at Maxwell Air Force Base, Alabama.

For readability, I often spelled out acronyms in the mission summary reports. For instance, "A/P" was changed to "airplane," and "A/A" was changed to "antiaircraft fire." The reports were also sometimes lightly edited for grammar, spelling, and clarity, as were selected letters, diaries, interviews, and so forth. This improved the book's readability without detracting from its accuracy or the intent of the original document's creator.

The 345th Bomb Group Association's newsletter, *The Strafer*, can be accessed online from the association's website (http://345thbombgroup.org). The 500th Bomb Squadron Association's *Rough Raider Newsletter* is not accessible online. Many of the missing air crew reports (MACRs) can be found online at Fold3.com.

Chapter 1: "It Couldn't Be Much Worse"

1. George C. Kenney, *General Kenney Reports: A Personal History of the Pacific War* (Washington, DC: Air Force Historical Studies Office, 1987), 35.

2. Ibid., 39.

3. Ibid., 45.

4. Ibid., 152.

5. Telephone interview, Irving Horwitz, January 27, 2017. All subsequent quotes from or references to Horwitz are derived from this interview.

6. Letter, Wilmer Fowler to Edna Fowler, January 6, 1943.

7. William A. Miller, "One Cold Night in '42," *The Strafer* (December 1992): 6.

8. Jim Mahaffey, "Bats Outa Hell, 499th Squadron," *The Strafer* 28, no. 3 (September 2010): 7.

9. John C. Hanna, William R. Witherell, and Max H. Mortensen, *Warpath: A Story of the 345th Bombardment Group (M), the "Air Apaches," in World War II* (Atglen, PA: Schiffer Publishing, 1996), 89.

10. Letter, Wilmer Fowler to Edna Fowler, April 23, 1943.

11. Hanna, Witherell, and Mortensen, *Warpath*, 90.

12. Ibid., 94.

13. Jay Smith, "R-2600 Lockland Investigation," Case History of R-2600 Engine Project Lockland Investigation, http://www.enginehistory.org/Piston/Wright/R-2600/R-2600Lockland.shtml (accessed June 16, 2018).

14. Talmadge Epps collection, courtesy of the Epps family. All subsequent quotes from or references to Epps are derived from this material.

15. Benjamin F. Miller, "499th Squadron," *The Strafer* (June 1997): 2.

16. Hanna, Witherell, and Mortensen, *Warpath*, 94.

17. Headquarters, 498th Bombardment Squadron (M), *The Falcons, History of the 498th Medium Bombardment Squadron, United States Army Air Corps* (Oxford, MS: Mullen Publishing Company, 1945), 22.

18. Bob Hackett and Sanders Kingsepp, "IJN Submarine RO-102: Tabular Record of Movement," Imperial Japanese Navy Page: Sensuikan! http://www.combinedfleet.com/RO-102.htm (accessed June 18, 2018).

19. Hanna, Witherell, and Mortensen, *Warpath*, 96.

20. Ibid., 97.

21. Headquarters, 498th Bombardment Squadron (M), *The Falcons*, 24.

22. Karl James, The Track—*A Historical Desktop Study of the Kokoda Track*, Department of Environment, Water, Heritage and the Arts, 2009.

23. "Aussies Said to Have Hanged 213 PNG Native Villagers in WWII," *Pacific Islands Report*, October 1, 2007, http://www.pireport.org/articles/2007/10/01/aussies-said-have-hung-213-png-villagers-wwii (accessed June 21, 2018).

24. Benjamin F. Miller, "499th Squadron," *The Strafer* 17, no. 3 (September 1999): 7.

25. MACR #15105, Headquarters, 500th Bombardment Squadron (M), 345th Bombardment Group (M).

26. Letter, Wilmer Fowler to Edna Fowler, July 14, 1943.

Chapter 2: "That Made Him Very Happy"

1. George C. Kenney, *The Saga of Pappy Gunn* (New York: Van Rees Press, 1959), 22. Unless otherwise noted, all references to Gunn are derived from this source.

2. Wesley Craven and James Cate, Plans and Early Operations, vol. 1 of *The Army Air Forces in World War II* (Washington, DC: Office of Air Force History, 1983), 375.

3. Kenney, *General Kenney Reports*, 44.

4. Paul O'Brien, "Bombing Diary," *Flying* (March 1944): 140.

5. Garrett Middlebrook, *Air Combat at 20 Feet: Selected Missions from a Strafer Pilot's Diary* (Bloomington, IN: AuthorHouse, 2004), 159.

6. Ibid., 184.

7. René Palmer Armstrong, *Wings and a Ring: Letters of War and Love from a WWII Pilot* (Mustang, OK: Tate Publishing & Enterprises, 2011), 40.

8. Ibid., 48.

9. Ibid., 52.

10. Ibid., 204.

11. Ibid., 64.

12. Ibid., 67.

13. Douglas Cheever Busath Collection (AFC/2001/001/50445), Veterans History Project, American Folklife Center, Library of Congress.

14. Kenney, *General Kenney Reports*, 293.

15. Ibid., 244.

16. Ibid., 255–56.

17. Ibid., 263.

18. Ibid., 278.

19. George J. Odgers, *Australia in the War of 1939–1945: Ser. 3. Air*, rpt. ed. Air War Against Japan, 1943–1945 (Canberra: Australian War Memorial, 1968), 2:70.

20. Kenney, *General Kenney Reports*, 208.

21. MACR #754, Headquarters, 499th Bombardment Squadron (M), 345th Bombardment Group (M).

22. Armstrong, *Wings and a Ring*, 84.

23. Ibid., 330.

Chapter 3: "The Enemy Was Taken Completely by Surprise"

1. Dan Van der Vat, *The Pacific Campaign: World War II, the U.S.-Japanese Naval War, 1941–1945* (New York: Simon & Schuster, 2006), 291.

2. Kenney, *General Kenney Reports*, 313.

3. Eric M. Bergerud, *Fire in the Sky: The Air War in the South Pacific* (Boulder, CO: Westview Press, 2000), 358–59.

4. Jim Busha and John Bronson, "A Punch in the Nose," *Warbirds* (October 2012): 25.

5. Oral history interview of Melvin Best by Ed Metzler, Center for Pacific War Studies, Archives for the National Museum of the Pacific War, Texas Historical Commission, September 4, 2006.

6. Bergerud, *Fire in the Sky*, 642.

7. Lex McAulay, *Into the Dragon's Jaws: The Fifth Air Force over Rabaul, 1943* (Mesa, AZ: Champlin Fighter Museum Press, 1986), 25.

8. Ibid.

9. "Bombs Lay Rabaul Open," *Abilene Reporter-News*, October 14, 1943, 1.

10. "Jap Air Offensive Costs Loss of 104 Planes," *Salt Lake Tribune*, October 18, 1943, 4.

11. Kenney, *General Kenney Reports*, 107.

12. Lee Jefferson, William T. Y'Blood, and Jacob Neufeld, *Reflections and Remembrances: Veterans of the United States Army Air Forces Reminisce about World War II* (Washington DC: Air Force History and Museums Program, 2000).

13. Armstrong, *Wings and a Ring*, 175.

14. Edward Frederick Langley Russell, *The Knights of Bushido: A History of Japanese War Crimes during World War II* (New York: Skyhorse Publishing, 2016), 49–50.

15. V. Douglas Wrynn, "Massacre at Palawan," *World War II* (November 1997): 56.

16. Russell, *The Knights of Bushido*, 236.

17. Hal Gold, *Unit 731 Testimony* (New York: Tuttle Publishing, 2011), 166.

18. Telephone interview, John Baeta, January 13, 2017. All subsequent quotes from or references to Baeta are derived from this interview.

Chapter 4: "The Squadron Was Attacked"

1. McAulay, *Into the Dragon's Jaws*, 39.
2. MACR #1339, Headquarters, 500th Bombardment Squadron (M), 345th Bombardment Group (M). Migliacci's accounts of the fates of the various crewmen are derived from this source.
3. Patrick Lindsay, "A Tribute to Peter Figgis," PNGAA Library, https://www.pngaa .net/Library/Figgis.htm (accessed June 25, 2018).
4. Ken Wright, "Organisation of Coastwatching in the New Guinea [of] WW 2," Naval Historical Society of Australia, May 12, 2015, https://www.navyhistory.org.au/ organisation-of-coastwatching-in-the-new-guinea-ww-2/2 (accessed June 25, 2018).
5. Kenney, *General Kenney Reports*, 316.
6. Armstrong, *Wings and a Ring*, 119–20.
7. Ibid., 114.
8. Ibid., 116.
9. Ibid., 143.
10. Sarah Moore, *Flying Colors* (Wellesley, MA: Branden Books, 2015), 36.

Chapter 5: "The Pilots Did Not Appear Eager"

1. U.S. Military Intelligence Service, "Tactical and Technical Trends," Number 26, June 3, 1943.
2. MACR #1071, Headquarters, 500th Bombardment Squadron (M), 345th Bombardment Group (M).
3. MACR #1219, Headquarters, 501st Bombardment Squadron (M), 345th Bombardment Group (M).
4. Donald Hitchcock, "The Jap That Got Away," *The Strafer* (March 1992): 4.
5. "USAAF 'Bloody Tuesday' Attack on Rabaul Harbour," *World War II Today*, http://ww2today.com/2nd-november-1943-bloody-tuesday-attack-on-rabaul-harbour (accessed June 25, 2018).
6. Kenney, *General Kenney Reports*, 319.
7. Ibid., 321.
8. Ibid.
9. Odgers, *Australia in the War of 1939–1945*, 2:98.
10. Ibid.
11. Armstrong, *Wings and a Ring*, 103.
12. Ibid., 135.
13. Ibid., 103.

Chapter 6: "I Turned Back to Pick Him Up"

1. MACR #1146, Headquarters, 500th Bombardment Squadron (M), 345th Bombardment Group (M).
2. Ibid.
3. U.S. Air Force Historical Study No. 95, *Air-Sea Rescue* (Maxwell AFB, AL: USAF Historical Division, Air University, 1953), 68–92.

4. MACR #1248, Headquarters, 498th Bombardment Squadron (M), 345th Bombardment Group (M).
5. Ibid.
6. Ibid.
7. Ibid.
8. Armstrong, *Wings and a Ring*, 158–59.
9. Ibid., 175.
10. Ibid., 215.
11. Busha and Bronson, "A Punch in the Nose," 24.
12. Armstrong, *Wings and a Ring*, 183.
13. Ibid., 198.
14. Ibid., 208.
15. Ibid., 259.
16. Interview with Lincoln Grush, February 26, 2017.
17. Armstrong, *Wings and a Ring*, 257–58.
18. Ibid., 277.
19. Ibid., 107.
20. James P. Baross, *The War Years: WW2* (Riverside, CA: Self-Published, 1998), 33.
21. Armstrong, *Wings and a Ring*, 200.

Chapter 7: "We Think We Destroyed the Mission"
1. Diary, George Hurt, January 22, 1944.
2. Jim Mahaffey, "Bats Outa Hell, 499th Squadron," *The Strafer* 29, no. 2 (June 2011): 3–5.
3. Carroll R. Anderson, "Mission to Kavieng," *American Aviation Historical Society Journal* 10 (summer 1965): 88.
4. Diary, George Hurt, February 15, 1944.
5. Tal Epps, "John Murphy Remembered," *Rough Raider Newsletter* (May 2001): 9.
6. Anderson, "Mission to Kavieng," 96.
7. Ibid., 92.
8. Ibid., 94.
9. Ibid.
10. Ibid., 92.
11. Ibid., 97.
12. Tom Phillips, "The Saga of the Kavieng Cat," *Centennial of Naval Aviation* (winter 2010): 5. All subsequent quotes from Gordon are from this source.
13. Epps, "John Murphy Remembered," 9.
14. Armstrong, *Wings and a Ring*, 236.
15. William DuBose, "James 'Webb' Dubose," *Rough Raider Newsletter* (November 2005): 6–7.
16. William DuBose, "My Brother Webb," *Rough Raider Newsletter* (November 2003): 5.

Chapter 8: "Many Strange Faces"
1. 500th Bomb Squadron Association Newsletter, February 2004, 4.
2. Armstrong, *Wings and a Ring*, 231.

3. Ibid., 247–50.

4. Baross, *The War Years*, 20.

5. Ibid., 23.

6. Ibid., 29.

7. Ibid., 41–42.

8. Ibid., 65.

9. Diary, George Hurt, March 5, 1944.

10. Baross, *The War Years*, 50–51.

11. Ibid.

12. Diary, George Hurt, March 13, 1944.

13. Armstrong, *Wings and a Ring*, 110.

14. Ibid., 241.

15. Ibid., 150.

16. Ibid., 281.

17. Michael J. Claringbould, *Black Sunday: When the U.S. Fifth Air Force Lost to New Guinea's Weather* (Australia: Aerosian, 1998), 26.

18. Armstrong, *Wings and a Ring*, 276.

19. Ibid., 314.

20. Claringbould, *Black Sunday*, 38.

21. Jay A. Stout, *Unsung Eagles: True Stories of America's Citizen Airmen in the Skies of World War II* (Havertown, PA: Casemate Publishers, 2013), 178–79.

22. Claringbould, *Black Sunday*, 87.

23. Kenney, *General Kenney Reports*, 388.

24. Armstrong, *Wings and a Ring*, 291.

25. VP-34 War Diary, April 1944, 3.

26. Claringbould, *Black Sunday*, 100.

Chapter 9: "I Hate to See Them Go"

1. Armstrong, *Wings and a Ring*, 341.

2. Ibid., 347.

3. Baross, *The War Years*, 25.

4. Ibid., 26.

5. Armstrong, *Wings and a Ring*, 350.

6. Wesley Frank Craven and James Lea Cate, *Matterhorn to Nagasaki: June 1944 to August 1945*, vol. 5 of *The Army Air Forces in World War II* (Washington, DC: Office of Air Force History, 1983), 325–26.

7. Armstrong, *Wings and a Ring*, 140–41.

8. Ibid., 222.

9. Ibid., 119.

10. Mae Mills Link and Hubert Anderson Coleman, *Medical Support of the Army Air Forces in World War II* (Washington, DC: Office of the Surgeon General, United States Air Force Medical Service, Office of the Air Force Surgeon General, 1955), 849.

11. Headquarters, 345th Bomb Group, *History of the 345th Bomb Group, June 1944: Narrative of Local Interest Doings*.

12. Armstrong, *Wings and a Ring*, 79.

13. Ibid., 129.

14. Headquarters, 345th Bomb Group, *History of the 345th Bomb Group, June 1944.*

15. Ibid.

16. R. E. Blount Collection (AFC/2001/001/15748), Veterans History Project, American Folklife Center, Library of Congress.

17. Howard D. Thompson Collection (AFC/2001/001/68214), Veterans History Project, American Folklife Center, Library of Congress.

18. Robert Scudder, "Good Was My Copilot," *Rough Raider Newsletter* (August 2002): 8.

19. Interview, McKinley Sizemore, Illinois Veterans & Community Classroom Project—Student Interview Projects, Carlyle Junior High School, 2014. All subsequent quotes from or references to Sizemore are derived from this source.

20. Cal Peckham, "Thank You Captain O'Brien," *Rough Raider Newsletter* (May 2002): 4.

21. Sil Mawrence, "My Time with the 500th," *Rough Raider Newsletter* (November 2001): 21.

22. Jerry Chealander, "A Close Call," *The Strafer* 30, no. 2 (June 2012): 8.

23. Benjamin T. Muller, "A Really Close One!," *Rough Raider Newsletter* (May 2000): 10.

24. William J. Cavoli, ed., "Memories of Roy Smith," *Rough Raider Newsletter* (November 2001): 11.

25. Armstrong, *Wings and a Ring*, 121.

26. Ibid., 314.

27. Ibid., 356.

Chapter 10: "Torn to Death"

1. Scudder, "Good Was My Copilot," 7–8.

2. Diary, George Hurt, July 2, 1944.

3. Lisa Sprague, "Dear Dad," *Rough Raider Newsletter* (November 2001): 20–21.

4. Armstrong, *Wings and a Ring*, 311.

5. Clarence Bryk, "An Interview with Mr. Benjamin Teofilo Muller, Radio Operator/Tail-Gunner, United States Army Air Corps," Center for Pacific War Studies, Oral History Program, October 20, 2002.

6. Senath Rankin and Jay W. Moore, *A True Flyer: Memories of a World War II Air Apache* (Morrisville, NC: Lulu.com, 2015), 121.

7. Ibid., 124.

8. Ibid.

9. Baross, *The War Years*, 35.

10. Benjamin F. Miller, *A Farm Boy Goes to War: WW II Memories* (Decatur, IN: Self-Published, 2015), 40.

11. Rankin and Moore, *A True Flyer*, 124.

12. Miller, *A Farm Boy Goes to War*, 40.

13. Letter, Ray Link to Mrs. A. J. Link, n.d.

14. Baross, *The War Years*, 36.

15. Rankin and Moore, *A True Flyer*, 159.

16. Bert Rosenbaum, "498th Squadron," *The Strafer* (June 2002): 2.

17. Miller, *A Farm Boy Goes to War*, 38.
18. Baross, *The War Years*, 36.
19. Ibid., 53.
20. Ibid., 55–56.
21. Rankin and Moore, *A True Flyer*, 135.
22. Wesley Frank Craven and James Lea Cate, *The Pacific, Guadalcanal to Saipan: August 1942 to July 1944*, vol. 4 of *The Army Air Forces in World War II* (Washington, DC: Office of Air Force History, 1983), 4:200.
23. Craven and Cate, *Matterhorn to Nagasaki*, 327.
24. Hanna, Witherell, and Mortensen, *Warpath*, 30.
25. Rankin and Moore, *A True Flyer*, 136.
26. Diary, James P. Baross, September 9, 1944.
27. Letter, Ray Link to Mrs. A. J. Link, September 25, 1944.
28. Rankin and Moore, *A True Flyer*, 141.

Chapter 11: "Love to All and Write Real Often"
1. Letter, Ray Link to Mrs. E. A. Buchanan, October 3, 1944.
2. Benjamin F. Miller, "499th Squadron," *The Strafer* 26, no. 2 (April 2008): 9.
3. Letter, Ray Link to Mrs. E. A. Buchanan, October 15, 1944.
4. Kent Sanborn, "Kent Sanborn's Story," *The Strafer* 17, no. 3 (September 1999): 10.
5. Ken Gasteb, "Remembering Leyte—1944," *The Strafer* 27, no. 2 (June 2009): 2.
6. Letter, Ray Link to Mrs. A. J. Link, November 2, 1944.
7. Gasteb, "Remembering Leyte—1944," 3.
8. Miller, *A Farm Boy Goes to War*, 44.
9. Benjamin F. Miller, "499th Squadron," *The Strafer* 26, no. 2 (April 2008): 9.
10. John William Stone Collection (AFC/2001/001/10277), Veterans History Project, American Folklife Center, Library of Congress. All subsequent quotes from or references to Stone are derived from this interview.
11. Stout, *Unsung Eagles*, 181–82.
12. Miller, *A Farm Boy Goes to War*, 45–46. Miller's experiences during the kamikaze attacks and the aftermath are included in these pages.
13. Gloria Grush, "Pilot Lincoln Grush's Story," *The Strafer* 33, no. 1 (February 2016): 6.
14. Ken Haller, "498th Falcons," *The Strafer* 23, no. 2 (June 2005): 7.
15. Pete Prunty, "Remembrances of the Waite," *The Strafer* 18, no. 3 (September 2000): 9.
16. Ibid.
17. Fred Deady, "Heroic Action on the SS *Morrison Waite*," *The Strafer* (March 1992): 3–4.
18. Letter, Reggie Dunnavant to parents, November 26, 1944.
19. Rankin and Moore, *A True Flyer*, 141.
20. Ibid.
21. Miller, *A Farm Boy Goes to War*, 47.
22. Robert H. Elliot, "Robert H. Elliot," 3rd Attack Group, http://www.3rdattackgroup.org/robert-elliot.php (accessed June 26, 2018).
23. Diary, James P. Baross, December 30, 1944.

Chapter 12: "A Perfect Swan Dive"

1. Joe Mallard, "Same Area, Another B-25 Ditching," *Rough Raider Newsletter* (May 2003): 7.

2. E-mail from Sherry Symington to Lynn Daker, February 27, 2004.

3. William Caputo, "How Well I Remember," *Rough Raider Newsletter* (May 2001): 7. All subsequent references to the mission by Caputo are derived from this source.

4. Stout, *Unsung Eagles*, 185.

5. Joseph W. Rutter, *Wreaking Havoc: A Year in an A-20*, Texas A&M University Military History Series 91, 1st ed. (College Station: Texas A&M University Press, 2004), 144.

6. Stout, *Unsung Eagles*, 186.

7. Howard D. Thompson Collection (AFC/2001/001/68214), Veterans History Project, American Folklife Center, Library of Congress.

8. MACR #16290, Headquarters, 500th Bombardment Squadron (M), 345th Bombardment Group (M).

9. Diary, James P. Baross, January 13, 1944.

10. "Statement on Missing Aircraft," Kenneth W. Smith, January 15, 1945, and "Report on Extent of Search," Roland Lamb, January 15, 1945.

Chapter 13: "It's All for the Best, Dad"

1. Note citations to letters typically include the writer, the recipient, and the date. As these elements are noted in the main body of the chapter, they are not included here.

Chapter 14: "We Seemed to Be Awfully High"

1. Donald Wagner, "San Marcelino," *Rough Raider Newsletter* (May 2005): 7.

2. Telephone interview, Al Stone, January 21, 2017. All subsequent quotes from or references to Stone are derived from this interview.

3. George Givens, "From Columbia AFB to Overseas—Pre-combat Training," *The Strafer* 34, no. 1 (February 2017): 9.

4. George Givens, "From Columbia AFB to Overseas—San Marcelino," *The Strafer* 34, no. 2 (May 2017): 6.

5. Telephone interviews, Roger Lovett, February 12 and 19, 2017. All subsequent quotes from or references to Lovett are derived from these interviews.

6. Kenney, *General Kenney Reports*, 471.

7. Ibid., 521.

8. Helene E. Maw, *Freedom Is for Those Willing to Fight for It: Stories of Men in War* (Victoria, BC: Trafford Publishing, 2002), 27–33.

9. Telephone interview, George Givens, February 10, 2017. Unless otherwise noted, all subsequent quotes from or references to Givens are derived from this interview.

10. Telephone interview, Marvin "Murph" Leventon, January 27, 2017. All subsequent quotes from or references to Leventon are derived from this interview.

Chapter 15: "He Was Even More Handsome in His Uniform"

1. Ruth Pearson, "A Few Great Years with Bob Jensen," November 2008. All subsequent quotes from Ruth Pearson are sourced from this memoir.

2. Letter, Thomas Bazzel to Ruth Jensen, March 23, 1945.

3. Duke Doering, "George Blair, B-25 Bomber Pilot, Remembers World War II," *Black Hills Journal*, December 6, 2016, http://blackhillsjournal.blogspot.com/2016/12/george -blair-b-25-bomber-pilot.html (accessed August 31, 2017).

4. "Weekly News Letter to Johnny," *Abilene Reporter-News*, June 10, 1945, 49.

Chapter 16: "Jap Fighters Making Long Range Passes"

1. The log of the USS *Chub* can be found online at http://navsource.org/archives/08/ pdf/0832915.pdf.

2. MACR #16235, Headquarters, 499th Bombardment Squadron (M), 345th Bombardment Group (M).

3. Maw, *Freedom Is for Those Willing to Fight for It*, 33–36.

4. Telephone interview, Quentin Stambaugh, October 6, 2017. Unless otherwise noted, all subsequent quotes from or references to Stambaugh are derived from this interview.

Chapter 17: "I Inflated My Mae West"

1. Ben Muller and Hayden Reese, e-mail exchange, May 2004.

2. Bryk, "An Interview with Mr. Benjamin Teofilo Muller."

3. Muller and Reese, e-mail exchange.

4. Bryk, "An Interview with Mr. Benjamin Teofilo Muller."

5. Bob Tutt, "A-Bomb Gave POWs a Boost," *Houston Chronicle*, August 19, 1995.

6. Tom Pledger, "Hasho POW Camp, Hainan Island," Center for Research, Allied POWs under the Japanese, http://www.mansell.com/pow_resources/hainan.html (accessed June 28, 2018).

7. Muller and Reese, e-mail exchange.

8. Bryk, "An Interview with Mr. Benjamin Teofilo Muller"

9. Muller and Reese, e-mail exchange.

10. Bryk, "An Interview with Mr. Benjamin Teofilo Muller."

11. Baross, *The War Years*, 62.

12. Ed Bina, "Air Arena," *The Strafer* (March 1991): 1.

13. Stan Muniz, "Friends Again," *Rough Raider Newsletter* (May 2005): 8.

Chapter 18: "I Jerked and Ducked Instinctively"

1. Ralph E. "Peppy" Blount, *We Band of Brothers* (Austin, TX: Eakin Press, 1984), 364–71.

2. Telephone interview, Ron Pietscher, January 28, 2017. All subsequent quotes from or references to Pietscher are derived from this interview.

3. Craven and Cate, *Matterhorn to Nagasaki*, 497.

4. Clifford Lawrence, "Great Models," *Rough Raider Newsletter* (May 2000): 7.

5. Letter, Melvin Pollock to Manley Pollock, March 29, 1945.

6. Letter, Melvin Pollock to Manley Pollock, February 26, 1945.

7. Letter, Melvin Pollock to Manley Pollock, April 24, 1945.

8. Letter, Melvin Pollock to Manley Pollock, September 4, 1945.

9. Letter, Melvin Pollock to Manley Pollock, March 14, 1945.

Chapter 19: "He Also Flew Missions with Several Other Crews"

1. Letter, Melvin Pollock to Manley Pollock, May 6, 1945.
2. Link and Coleman, *Medical Support of the Army Air Forces in World War II*, 855.
3. Otis Young, "Remembering Clark Field," *Rough Raider Newsletter* (May 2000): 2.
4. Jack Williams, "Rameses," *Rough Raider Newsletter* (May 2002): 6.
5. Baross, *The War Years*, 66.
6. Don Wagner, "Special Mission," *The Strafer* 23, no. 1 (March 2005): 9.
7. Warren Brown, "Nothing to It," *Rough Raider Newsletter* (August 2000): 7–8.
8. Letter, Melvin Pollock to Manley Pollock, June 25, 1945.
9. Baross, *The War Years*, 66.
10. Bill Lambert, "Not a Milk Run," *Rough Raider Newsletter* (November 2003): 5.
11. Stan Muniz, "My Exciting Recon Mission," *Rough Raider Newsletter* (May 2004): 7.

Chapter 20: "Well, I'm Done For"

1. Hubert Hendrix, "Recalling War Mission from Half a Century," GoUpstate, August 20, 1995, http://www.goupstate.com/article/NC/19950820/News/605186823/SJ (accessed June 28, 2018).
2. Hanna, Witherell, and Mortensen, *Warpath*, 169.
3. Ken McClure, ed., "Navy Rescues Air Apaches," *The Strafer* 17, no. 1 (March 1999): 7.
4. U.S. Department of State Bulletin, "Directions to Japanese Officials for Meeting in Manila," August 15, 1945, 9:52 a.m.
5. Telephone interview, George Givens, April 28, 2018.
6. Letter, Melvin Pollock to Manley Pollock, August 24, 1945.
7. Letter, Melvin Pollock to Manley Pollock, September 11, 1945.
8. Bryk, "An Interview with Mr. Benjamin Teofilo Muller."
9. Tutt, "A-Bomb Gave POWs a Boost."
10. Bryk, "An Interview with Mr. Benjamin Teofilo Muller."
11. John K. Singlaub and Malcolm McConnell, *Hazardous Duty: An American Soldier in the Twentieth Century* (New York: Summit Books, 1991), 94.
12. Bryk, "An Interview with Mr. Benjamin Teofilo Muller."
13. John Graham Dowling, "Even Stones Pulverized in Nagasaki," *Chicago Sun*, August 27, 1945.

BIBLIOGRAPHY

Anderson, Carroll R. "Mission to Kavieng." *American Aviation Historical Society Journal* 10 (summer 1965): 88–101.

Armstrong, René Palmer. *Wings and a Ring: Letters of War and Love from a WWII Pilot.* Mustang, OK: Tate Publishing & Enterprises, 2011.

"Aussies Said to Have Hung 213 PNG Villagers in WW II." *Pacific Islands Report.* October 1, 2007. http://www.pireport.org/articles/2007/10/01/aussies-said-have -hung-213-png-villagers-wwii (accessed June 30, 2018).

Baross, James P. *The War Years: WW2.* Riverside, CA: Self-Published, 1998.

Bergerud, Eric M. *Fire in the Sky: The Air War in the South Pacific.* Boulder, CO: West- view Press, 2000.

Birdsall, Steve, and John Preston. *Flying Buccaneers.* Garden City, NY: Doubleday, 1977.

Blount, Ralph E. "Peppy." *We Band of Brothers.* Austin, TX: Eakin Press, 1984.

"Bombs Lay Rabaul Open." *Abilene Reporter-News.* October 14, 1943.

Bowman, Martin W. *The USAAF Handbook: 1939–1945.* Stroud, Gloucestershire, UK: Sutton, 1997.

Boyer, Allen D. *Rocky Boyer's War: An Unvarnished History of the Air Blitz That Won the War in the Southwest Pacific.* Annapolis, MD: Naval Institute Press, 2017.

Busha, Jim, and John Bronson. "A Punch in the Nose." *Warbirds* (October 2012): 25.

"Case History of R-2600 Engine Project Lockland Investigation." Case History of R-2600 Engine Project Lockland Investigation. http://www.enginehistory.org/ Piston/Wright/R-2600/R-2600Lockland.shtml (accessed June 30, 2018).

Claringbould, Michael J. *Black Sunday: When the U.S. Fifth Air Force Lost to New Guin- ea's Weather.* Australia: Aerosian, 1998.

Cook, Haruko T., and Theodore F. Cook. *Japan at War: An Oral History.* New York: New Press, 1992.

Craven, Wesley Frank, and James Lea Cate. *Matterhorn to Nagasaki: June 1944 to August 1945. Vol. 5 of The Army Air Forces in World War II.* Washington, DC: Office of Air Force History, 1983.

———. *The Pacific, Guadalcanal to Saipan: August 1942 to July 1944. Vol. 4 of The Army Air Forces in World War II.* Washington, DC: Office of Air Force History, 1983.

———. *Plans and Early Operations. Vol. 1 of The Army Air Forces in World War II.* Wash- ington, DC: Office of Air Force History, 1983.

Doering, Duke. "George Blair, B-25 Bomber Pilot, Remembers World War II." *Black Hills Journal*. December 6, 2016. http://blackhillsjournal.blogspot.com/2016/12/george-blair-b-25-bomber-pilot.html.

Dowling, John Graham. "Even Stones Pulverized in Nagasaki." *Chicago Sun*. August 27, 1945.

Elliot, Robert H. "Robert H. Elliot." 3rd Attack Group. http://www.3rdattackgroup.org/robert-elliot.php (accessed June 30, 2018).

Gold, Hal. *Unit 731 Testimony*. New York: Tuttle Publishing, 2011.

Gunn, Nathaniel. *Pappy Gunn*. Bloomington, IN: AuthorHouse, 2004.

Hackett, Bob, and Sanders Kingsepp. "IJN Submarine RO-102: Tabular Record of Movement." Imperial Japanese Navy Page: Sensuikan! http://www.combinedfleet.com/RO-102.htm (accessed June 30, 2018).

Hanna, John C., William R. Witherell, and Max H. Mortensen. *Warpath: A Story of the 345th Bombardment Group (M), the "Air Apaches," in World War II*. Atglen, PA: Schiffer Military History, 1997. Reprint.

Headquarters, 498th Bombardment Squadron (M). *The Falcons, History of the 498th Medium Bombardment Squadron, United States Army Air Corps*. Oxford, MS: Mullen Publishing Company, 1945.

Headquarters, AAF, Office of Flying Safety. *Pilot Training Manual for the Mitchell Bomber, B-25*. Los Angeles, CA: Periscope Film, 2007.

Hendrix, Hubert. "Recalling War Mission from Half a Century." GoUpstate. August 20, 1995. http://www.goupstate.com/article/NC/19950820/News/605186823/SJ (accessed June 30, 2018).

Hickey, Lawrence J. *Warpath across the Pacific: The Illustrated History of the 345th Bombardment Group during World War II*. Boulder, CO: International Historical Research and Publishing Company, 1984.

Ichimura, Hiroshi. *Ki-43 Oscar Aces of World War 2*. Oxford, UK: Osprey, 2009.

"Jap Air Offensive Costs Loss of 104 Planes." *Salt Lake Tribune*. October 18, 1943.

Kenney, George C. *General Kenney Reports: A Personal History of the Pacific War*. Washington, DC: Air Force Historical Studies Office, 1987.

———. *The Saga of Pappy Gunn*. New York: Van Rees Press, 1959.

Lindsay, Patrick. "A Tribute to Peter Figgis." PNGAA Library. https://www.pngaa.net/Library/Figgis.htm (accessed June 30, 2018).

Link, Mae M., and Hubert A. Coleman. *Medical Support of the Army Air Forces in World War II*. Washington, DC: Office of the Surgeon General, United States Air Force Medical Service, Office of the Air Force Surgeon General, 1955.

Maw, Helene E. *Freedom Is for Those Willing to Fight for It: Stories of Men in War*. Victoria, BC: Trafford Publishing, 2002.

McAulay, Lex. *Into the Dragon's Jaws: The Fifth Air Force over Rabaul, 1943*. Mesa, AZ: Champlin Fighter Museum Press, 1986.

Middlebrook, Garrett. *Air Combat at 20 Feet: Selected Missions from a Strafer Pilot's Diary*. Bloomington, IN: AuthorHouse, 2004.

Miller, Benjamin F. *A Farm Boy Goes to War: WW II Memories*. Decatur, IN: Self-Published, 2015.

Millman, Nicholas. *Ki-61 and Ki-100 Aces*. Oxford, UK: Osprey, 2015.

Moore, Jay W., and Senath Rankin. *A True Flyer: Memories of a World War II Air Apache*. Morrisville, NC: Lulu.com, 2015.

Moore, Sarah. *Flying Colors*. Wellesley, MA: Branden Books, 2015.

O'Brien, Paul. "Bombing Diary." *Flying* (March 1944): 140.

Odgers, George J. *Australia in the War of 1939–1945: Ser. 3. Air*. Vol. 2. Rpt. ed. Air War against Japan, 1943–1945. Canberra: Australian War Memorial, 1968.

Phillips, Tom. "The Saga of the Kavieng Cat." *Centennial of Naval Aviation* (winter 2010): 5.

Pledger, Tom. "Hasho POW Camp: Hainan Island." Center for Research: Allied POWs under the Japanese. http://www.mansell.com/pow_resources/hainan.html (accessed June 30, 2018).

Pollock Wysocky, Marcia L. *Two Fathers, One War*. North Charleston, SC: CreateSpace, 2013.

Russell of Liverpool (Edward Frederick Langley Russell). *The Knights of Bushido: A History of Japanese War Crimes during World War II*. New York: Skyhorse Publishing, 2016.

Rutter, Joseph W. *Wreaking Havoc: A Year in an A-20*. Texas A&M University Military History Series 91. 1st ed. College Station: Texas A&M University Press, 2004.

Sakaida, Henry. *The Siege of Rabaul*. St. Paul, MN: Phalanx Publishing, 1996.

Singlaub, John K., and Malcolm McConnell. *Hazardous Duty: An American Soldier in the Twentieth Century*. New York: Summit Books, 1991.

Stout, Jay A. *Unsung Eagles: True Stories of America's Citizen Airmen in the Skies of World War II*. Philadelphia: Casemate, 2016.

"USAAF 'Bloody Tuesday' Attack on Rabaul Harbour." *World War II Today*. http://ww2today.com/2nd-november-1943-bloody-tuesday-attack-on-rabaul-harbour (accessed June 30, 2018).

Van der Vat, Dan. *The Pacific Campaign: World War II, the U.S.-Japanese Naval War, 1941–1945*. New York: Simon & Schuster, 2006.

"Weekly News Letter to Johnny." *Abilene Reporter-News*. June 10, 1945.

Wright, Ken. "Organisation of Coastwatching in the New Guinea [of] WW 2." Naval Historical Society of Australia. May 12, 2015. https://www.navyhistory.org.au/organisation-of-coastwatching-in-the-new-guinea-ww-2/2 (accessed June 30, 2018).

Wrynn, V. Douglas. "Massacre at Palawan." *World War II* (November 1997): 56.

Y'Blood, William T., Jacob Neufeld, and Mary L. Jefferson. *The U.S. Army Air Forces in World War II: Reflections and Remembrances: Veterans of the United States Army Air Forces Reminisce about World War II*. Washington, DC: Air Force History and Museums Program, 2000.

Index

A-20 light attack bombers, 5; on Black
    Sunday, 163; at Clark Field, 229,
    230, 231–35; conversion of, 28; at
    Hollandia, 154, 155, 158; at Manam
    Island, 164; of 3rd Bomb Group,
    316–17
A-24 dive bombers, 2
A/A. *See* antiaircraft fire
ack-ack. *See* antiaircraft fire
Admiralty Islands, 148, 153
aerial burst bombs, 91; at Samate and
    Jefman airfields, 181
Aichi Type 99 "Val," 115–16
Air Apaches. *See* 345th Bomb Group
Air Medal, 244
Ajoe Island, 194
Alamo Scout, 257
Albert, Nathan, 304
alcohol, 175–76, 262; Stambaugh and,
    338–39
Aleutian Islands, 327
Alexishafen, 35, 103–4
Alicante airfield, Philippines, 211–12,
    214–16
Amarillo Army Air Field, Texas, 242–43
Amatsukaze, 275, 289, 293
Amberley Field, Australia, 14, 15
Ames, William, 128–29
Anacker, Lyle, 78–83
Anderson, Carroll, 130–31
antiaircraft fire (A/A, ack-ack), viii, 93;
        at Alicante airfield, 215; at Cape
        Gloucester, 115; at Clark Field, 231;
        501st Bomb Squadron and, 336; at
        Hollandia, 156; at Kavieng, 131; at
        Lembeh Strait, 201; at Los Negros

Island, 227; parafrag bombs on, 90;
    at Rabaul, 96; at Saigon, 312–13,
    314; in Salamaua, 22; at Samate and
    Jefman airfields, 182; strafing of, 90;
    at Tacloban Airfield, 217; at Toyohara
    Airfield, 259; at Uligan Harbor, 170;
    unexploded ordinance from, 202–3; at
    Wewak, 65–66; at Yulin Bay, 290
Apache Theater, 198–99
Aparri, 323
Arawe, 111
Arkansas Traveler, 134–37
Army Air Corps, 5–7
Arnett, Fred, 131
Arnold, Gordon, 237
Arnold, Henry "Hap": Kenney and, 36–37;
    of USAAF, 1
artificial horizon, 160
Astaire, Fred, 152
Astrolabe, 160–64
atomic bomb, 335–36; devastation from,
    346; on Hiroshima, 335; on Nagasaki,
    335
Australia: alcohol from, 176; Amberley
    Field in, 14, 15; bombers based in,
    2; Coastwatch outpost of, 83–84;
    furloughs in, ix, 30–31, 87–88, 109–
    10, 197, 272; Jones, James, on, 108–9;
    POWs from, 301; 3rd Division of,
    21; women of, 109–10. *See also* Royal
    Australian Air Force

B-17 bomber, 27–28
B-18s, 5
B-24s: bombardier on, 157; crash landings
    of, 166; at Hollandia, 154–55, 158;

at Rabaul, 50; of USAAF, 275; at Wewak, 41, 43

B-25s, 2; armor on, 205; for Army Air Corps, 5–7; bomb bay of, 186, 205–6; bombing strategies for, 23–24; bomb load of, xv, 62; cameras on, 206; carburetors of, 51; at Clark Field, 229, 233–34; crew of, 7–9; difficulties flying, xiv; as escort for Japanese surrender representatives, 342–43; .50 caliber machine guns on, 25, 28–29, 34, 52, 79, 169–70, 205, 278, 323; at Formosa, 258–60; of 498th Bomb Squadron, 168, 170–71, 192; fuel tanks on, 7, 13–14; at Hollandia, 158; improvements to, 205–6; line-abreast attack by, 51–52; low-level flight of, 100–101; NA-62 and, 6; naming of, 12, 87–88; painting of noses, 88, 237; pilots of, 7, 52; POWs and, 237; at Rabaul, 45–50; 75-millimeter cannon on, 168–69, 192; speed of, 7; for strafing, 25, 28–30; taxiing of, 183; .30 caliber machine guns on, 34, 150, 169–70; of 38th Bomb Group, 170; of 345th Bomb Group, 5; for transporting men and equipment, 111, 188–89; water landings of, 22–23; Wright Cyclone R-2600 engines on, xiii, 5, 6, 7, 206. *See also specific topics*

B-26s, 2, 6

B-29s, 335

Baatan Peninsula, 256

Bacelli, Fred, 220

Baeta, John, 72, 169; at Clark Field, 235; in San Marcelino, 308–9; water landings by, 267–69

Bagabag Island, 165

Bagwell, William, 227–28

Baird, Julian, 163–64, 165

Baker, Dick, 162

Bankson, Buell, 10–11

Bardwell, Lloyd, 200–201

Barnes, Cecil, 171–72

Baross, James, v, 145–50, 236–37; on Albert, 304; on Biak Island, 190, 199; Bianconi and, 172; on Lilley,

326; PTSD of, 349–50; Welch and, 193–96

Bartlett, Elnora. *See* Jones, James R. "J. R."

Bartlett, H. R., 150

Bataan, 342

Bats Outta Hell. *See* 499th Bomb Squadron

Battle of Empress Augusta Bay, 90

Battle of Leyte Gulf, 212

Battle of the Bismarck Sea, 29

Battle of the Coral Sea, 17

BC-778 "Gibson Girl," 291, 339

Beaufighters, of RAAF, 50, 52, 58–59

Bedell, Gordon, 162

Bena Bena, 39, 41

Bennett, Sam, 306–7

Bennington, Dora, 87–88

beriberi, 303

Berman, Marty, 172

Best, Melvin, 44, 52

Best, Robert, 155

Betty. *See* Mitsubishi G4M bomber

Betty's Dream, 87

Biak Island, 171, *191*; caves on, 192; crash landing at, 198; theatre on, 198–99; 345th Bomb Group at, 188–203, 225; water at, 189–90

Bianconi, Owen, 171–72

Billig, Harold, 201

Bina, Ed, iv, v, vii, 195; on Albert, 304

Bird's Head, 180

Black Day of August 17th, 40

Blackmore, Charles

Black Panthers. *See* 501st Bomb Squadron

Black Sunday, 163, 166

Blair, George, 213, 296; water landings by, 276

Blanche Bay, 77–83, 90–91, 96

Blount, Ralph "Peppy," 68, 175; at Saigon, 314–15

Bluegill, USS, 275

Blum, Arthur, 300

Bobay, Francis, 218, 219

Bockscar, 335

Bogia, 171

Bold Venture, 273

bombardier: on B-24s, 157; on B-25s, 8

bomb bay: of B-25s, 186, 205–6; shackles in, 255

bombs: fuzing of, 63–64, 255, 265; loading on planes, 255; with wrapped steel wire, 61–62. *See also specific types*

booby-trapped dead bodies, of Japanese, 189

books, 151–52

Boom-Boom, 12

Borgen Bay, 64–65; Cape Gloucester and, 113–14; water landings of damaged planes at, 119

Borneo, 204; raw materials from, 257

Bornstein, Millard, 268–69

Boulton, William, 58

boxing match death, 17

Boyce, Bill, 289

Boyd, John, 285–86

Braun, George, 129, 133

Brick, Daniel, 151

Briggs, James, 349

Britt, Robert "Bear," 143

Bronson, John, 49–50

Bronson, Theodore, 286

Brown, Charles, 37–38

Brown, Warren, 325

Browngardt, Arthur, Jr., 234

Brownson, USS, 116

Bryant, Clifford, 14

Buffington, James, 236

Busath, Douglas, 36

Bushido (samurai warrior code), 70–71

C-46s, 249

C-47s, 30–32, 111; in Ferry Command, 246; Peckham and, 177; to San Marcelino, 253–54, 261; at Tacloban Airfield, 252–53

C-54s, 342

Cabell, William, 95

cameras, on B-25s, 206

Camp Doomben, 17

Camp Stoneman, 13

cannibalism, by Japanese, 69

Canning, Robert, 327–29

Cantanzarita, Francis, 186

Cape Batangas, 267

Cape Gloucester, 111–20; 500th Bomb Squadron at, 112–19; 501st Bomb Squadron at, 113–19; 498th Bomb Squadron at, 112–19; 499th Bomb Squadron at, 114–19; MacArthur and, 111

Cape Torokina, 89–90

captives: decapitation of, 69, 335; murders of, viii–ix, 68–69, 105, 107, 236, 264. *See also* prisoners of war

Caputo, Phil, 49, 234

Caputo, William, 227, 229–30, 232, 235

caves: on Biak Island, 192; on Luzon, iv

Cavin, Ed, 131–34

Cavoli, William, 129–37

Cebu Island, 222

Celebes, 199, 201–2

censorship of mail, 121, 172; kamikaze attacks and, 222

Cesna, Carl, 139–40

Challifoux, Wallace, 236

Chambers, Franklin, 265, 268, 295

Chance, James, 216

Chealander, Jerry, 178

Chelang Point, 273

Chiappe, Tony, 133, 134

Choshu, *250*, 258

Christmas, 225

Chub, USS, 283–85, 290–95

Chused, Harry "Sam," 351–52

Clark, James, 42

Clark, Joseph "Jocko," 26

Clark Field, Philippines, iv, 229–36, *250*; jeeps for, 325; kamikaze at, 212; MacArthur and, 229; 345th Bomb Group at, 319–20

clothing, 173–74, 202; of POWs, 302

Cohen, Julius "Jukey," 351–52

Cohron, Henry, 117, 120

Coltharp, Chester, 53–54, 92, 134, 137, 308, 326–27; at Clark Field, 230; at Saigon, 312–14; at San Marcelino, 251; in South China Sea, 277, 280; as True's replacement, 175

Convention Relative to the Treatment of Prisoners of War, 72

Cooper, George, 22–23, 55–56
copilot, on B-25s, 8, 170
Corsairs, 256
Crabb, Jarred V., 4–5; Kenney and, 38
Craig, Johnson, 192
Cranford, Elmo, 266, 309–3110
crash landings, 171; of B-24s, 166; by
    Baeta, 308–9; at Biak Island, 198; by
    Kortemeyer, 118–19; at Lingayan,
    260; at Manam Island, 164–65;
    of P-38s, 166; at Saidor, 162; at
    Tacloban, 253; on training flight, 151.
    See also water landing
Curtiss-Wright Aeronautical Corporation,
    Wright Cyclone R-2600 engines by,
    14–15
Cyclops, 155

Dagua, 42–43
Daker, Lynn, 188, 200, 202–3, 229–30, 232,
    234, 235
Davis, Howard, 79
Davis, Lawrence, 23
Deady, Fred, 221
Dean, Casey, 54
Dear John letters, 122
decapitation, of captives, 69, 335
Decker, Wendell, 218, 232
DeCobellis, Ernest, 187
DeCobellis, Fred, 187
DFC. See Distinguished Flying Cross
Dick, Fred, 217–18
Dinah, Mitsubishi Ki-46, 54
Dirty Dora, 87–88
disease: beriberi, 303; dysentery, 102, 303;
    malaria, 190, 303, 320
Distinguished Flying Cross (DFC), 244; of
    Doolittle, 327; of Gunn, 27–28
Distinguished Unit Citation, for 501st
    Bomb Squadron, 315
Dittum Dattum, 12
Dobodura, 48, 90, 98, 122; Port Moresby
    to, 111
Dodinga Bay, 194
dogs, 124–26; of 500th Bomb Squadron,
    322–23

Doman, Francis, 129
Doolittle, Glenn, 218, 327
Doolittle, Jimmy, 7
Doom Island, 182–83
Dougherty, John, 140–41
Douglas, Lloyd C., 152
Dowling, John Graham, 345–46
Draper, Robert, 232–33, 292–94
Du Bose, James, 93, 138
Dulag, 225–26
Dunnavant, Reggie, 222, 236
Durand Airfield "Seventeen-Mile
    Airdrome," 18
dysentery, 102; of Muller, 303

Eager Beaver, 31–32
Eaton, Burton, 80
18th Army, of Japanese, 153–54
8th Fighter Group: at Clark Field, 229,
    230; as escorts for Japanese surrender
    representatives, 341
Eighth Fleet, of Imperial Japanese Navy, 17
11th Airborne Division, 323–25
Ellard, Fred, 37–38
Elliot, Robert, 224
engineer, on B-25s, 8–9
Enola Gay, 335
Epps, Talmadge "Tal," 15, 20, 21, 137, 348;
    on furlough, 30, 109–10; luck of, 272;
    replacement crews and, 143–44
Erima Plantation, 43
Erskine, Robert, 196, 201, 288
Esty, Milton, 277, 313

F-5B, 161
Fabrica airfield, Philippines, 211–12, 216
Falcon. See 498th Bomb Squadron
Fatso, 87
Ferry Command, 245–46
Fife, James, 294
Fifth Air Force, 22; on Black Sunday, 163,
    166; at Formosa, 258; at Hollandia,
    154–59, 180–81; Kenney of, 21; at
    Rabaul, 47–48, 72, 99, 100; rescue
    service of, 105–7; South China Sea
    and, 260; at Tarumizu, 333–35;

Te-Go and, 224; training unit of, 142; at Wewak, 40

Fifth Bomber Command, 38, 193; exhaustion in, 173; public relations of, 328; on San Marcelino, 249

.50 caliber machine guns, on B-25s, 25, 34, 52, 79, 169–70, 205; Gunn and, 28–29; Sizemore on, 278; Wagner on, 323–24

50-mission men: of 345th Bomb Group, 142, 193–97; Jones, James, as, 172–73

Figgis, Peter, 83–84

Fighter Grid, 163

Finschafen, 153, 162–63; propaganda leaflets at, 37

1st Marine Division, xiv, 114

Fisher, Julius, v

500th Bomb Squadron "Rough Raiders," xii–xvi, 123–24; alcohol and, 175; at Alexishafen, 35; at Alicante airfield, 214–16; at Baatan Peninsula, 256; at Biak Island, 188; at Blanche Bay, 77–83; Britt of, 143; at Cape Gloucester, 112–19; at Clark Field, 229–30, 233–34; dog of, 322–23; in Formosa, 258, 306–7, 327–29; at Hainan Island, 299; at Hansa Bay, 103–5; at Hollandia, 158; at Indochina, 264–67; at Jackson Airfield, 18; at Kavieng, 128–29; at Lembeh Strait, 199–201; at Los Negros Island, 227–28; Lovett in, 262–64; in Luzon, 236, 323–25; at Mako town, 305–6; at Manam Island, 164; at Manokwari, 184; at Manus Island, 124; Mawrence of, 178; at Mindanao, 225; at New Hanover, 139, 140; nickname for, 88; Pollock in, 248; at Rabaul, 49, 91–100; at Samate airfield, 182; in South China Sea, 281, 285; Stone, A., in, 254–56; strafing by, 35; submarine and, 139; at Tarumizu, 334–35; at Vunakanau, 56, 58; at Wewak, 41–42, 65–68, 150–51

501st Bomb Squadron "Black Panthers," iv, xiii, xv; A/A and, 336; at Alexishafen, 35; at Alicante airfield, 214–16; at

Biak Island, 190; at Cape Gloucester, 113–19; at Clark Field, 235–36; Distinguished Unit Citation for, 315; at Formosa, 259, 321; furloughs of, 197; at Hainan, 286–89; at Hollandia, 158; at Kavieng, 131; at Lembeh Strait, 199–201; nickname for, 88; at Rabaul, 49, 91–100; at Rapopo, 74–77; at Saigon, 311–16; at Salamaua, 24, 25; at Samate and Jefman airfields, 181; at Schwimmer Airfield, 18; in South China Sea, 275–80, 285; strafing by, 34–35; at Vunakanau, 55, 59; at Wewak, 65–68

Flannigan, Thomas, 151

Flaps (dog), 124–26

Flounder, USS, 283–85

food, 43–44; at Biak Island, 190; for POWs, 301, 345

Formosa, *250*, 320–28; 500th Bomb Squadron at, 306–7, 327–29; San Marcelino and, 258–60

Fort Oranje, 196

Fort Stotsenburg, 232

40th Troop Carrier Squadron, 31

43rd Bomb Group, 60

417th Bomb Group, 229

475th Fighter Group: on Black Sunday, 163; P-38s of, 316

498th Bomb Squadron "Falcon": at Alexishafen, 35; at Alicante airfield, 214–16; B-25s of, 168, 170–71, 192; at Blanche Bay, 91; at Cape Gloucester, 112–19; at Clark Field, 230, 231, 236; at Hansa Bay, 103–5; at Hollandia, 155; at Indochina, 264–67; at Jackson Airfield, 18; at Kavieng, 131–33; Nakajima Ki-43 and, 286–87; nickname for, 88; at Rabaul, 49, 91–100; at Ragitsuma, 38–39; at Rapopo, 74–77; at San Marcelino, 273; in South China Sea, 279–80, 285, 286–87; Stambaugh in, 297–98; at Vunakanau, 51–59; at Wewak, 41, 65–68

499th Bomb Squadron "Bats Outta Hell," xiii, xv; at Alicante airfield,

214–16; Bankston of, 10–11; bombing inaccuracy of, 288; at Cape Gloucester, 114–19; at Clark Field, 231, 232–34; Durand Airfield, 18; at Finschafen, 162–63; at Formosa, 259–60, 321; at Hainan Island, 286–88, 299; at Hollandia, 158; at Lembeh Strait, 199–201; lost plane of, 14; at Manam Island, 164; at Manokwari, 184; at Manus Island, 124–25; at New Hanover, 139; nickname for, 88; at Rabaul, 91–100; at Rapopo, 74–77; at Saigon, 311–16; at Samate and Jefman airfields, 182; in South China Sea, 267, 275, 280–81, 285; strafing by, 36; Thompson of, 22; training in, 308–10; at Vunakanau, 55–56, 59; at Wewak, 65–68

"Fourteen-Mile Airdrome," 18

Fowler, Edna, 12, 25, 31

Fowler, Wilmer "Buck," 9–10, 12, 25; death of, 31

Fox, Jack, 28–29

Fox Tare Charlie tanker, 282

Frazier, George, 217–18

Frazier, Tom, 268

Freeman, Thomas, 130

Frey, Arthur, 129, 151

friendly fire, at Cape Gloucester, 117

furloughs: in Australia, ix, 30–31, 87–88, 109–10, 197, 272; to Manila, 251; of Pollock, 244

fuzing, of bombs, 63–64, 255; malfunction of, 265

Gaalong Point, 292

Garbutt Airfield, Australia, 15, 30–31

Garoka, 39–40

Gasteb, Ken, 209

Gath, Philip, 67

Geer, Ray, 78, 104–5

Geneva Convention, 72

Gentry, Robert, 162

George, Jack, 22, 96

Germany, viii; USAAF and, 3

Gibson Girl, 291, 339

Giffin, Earl, 35, 114–15

Gilgore, Merton, 54

Girdler, Edgar, 222

Givens, George, 252–54, 266, 295; as escort for Japanese surrender representatives, 342–43; on Okinawa, 350; at South China Sea, 269–70; after war, 350

Goehring, Donald, 227–28

Good, Floyd, 176–77, 184, 185, 186

good-luck charms, 176–77; of Jensen, Robert, 274

Gordon, Nathan, 134–37

Goulet, Robert, 335

Greenling, USS, 84

Gremlin's Holiday, 131–33

Grier, Bauduy, 265–66, 268, 295–96, 298

Grush, Lincoln, 121, 219–20, 347–48

Guadalcanal campaign, 4

Guavina, USS, 276, 296

Gullette, Frank, 104

Gunn, Paul "Pappy," 26–29, 34

gunner, 278; on B-25s, 9; radio operator as, 269–70; training for, 243–45

Gusap, 151

Haikou, POWs at, 303–3

Hainan Island, 275; 500th Bomb Squadron at, 299; 501st Bomb Squadron at, 288–89; 499th Bomb Squadron at, 286–88, 299; POWs on, 343; rescue at, 287–95

Haller, Ken, 220

Halmahera Islands, 193–94, 211, 252

Halsey, William "Bull," 100

Hamilton Field, California, 14

Hamner, John, 236–37

Hamp. *See* Mitsubishi A6M fighter

Hanna, John Clifford, 257

Hansa Bay, 103–5, 153, 167

Hardeman, Donald, 277

Hardy, George, 79, 80, 82–83

Harrell, Wood T., 303

Harviell, Eugene, 290; as POW, 302, 343

heat, of New Guinea, 173–74

Hecox, Thane, 78, 128–29, 138

Henderson, Robert, 83, 84

Hendrix, Hubert, 334

Henghai Bay, 273

Hensel, Karl, 294
Herbst, Lawrence, 131–32
Here's Howe, xii–xvi
HI-88J convoy, 275–81
Hickam Field, Hawaii, 13, 14
Hicko, Edward, 81
Hirohito, 72, 340
Hiroshima, *250*; atomic bomb on, 335
Hitchcock, Donald, 95
Hochella, Michael, 128, 140–41
Hokuho-O Point, 328
Hollandia, 153–59; Fifth Air Force to, 180–81; Jones, James, at, 172; parademo bomb malfunction at, 185–86
Home Islands, 188; Formosa and, 258; invasion of, 332–33
Honshu, 336
Horwitz, Irving, 4, 188, 202–3; on Canning, 328, 329
Howard, Charles, xiii, 37, 73
Howard, Jack, 140
Huff, Robert, 132–33
Hurt, George, 124, 128–29, 140, 148–49; on parademo bomb malfunction, 185; on Siegrist, 151

Ie Shima, 317, 327, 331–50; Japanese surrender and, 340–43
Imperial Japanese Navy, 17
Indochina, 257, 264–67, 275. *See also specific sites*
instrument flying, 160
internment camp, for Japanese, 72
Isler, Weldon, 130

Jackson Airfield "Seven-Mile Airdrome," 18
Jacobson, Hilding, 201
Japanese: booby-trapped dead bodies of, 189; cannibalism by, 69; 18th Army of, 153–54; freighters of, 186–87; HI-88J convoy of, 275–81; internment camp for, 72; kamikaze of, ix, xi, 212–13, 218–22, 229, 331; left over at Biak Island, 190–92; pilots, 212–13; POWs of, 300–303; racism of, 70; raw materials for, 257; samurai warrior code of, 70–71; ship identification for,

282; surrender of, 340–43; Te-Go by, 224; torture by, 69–70; Zero fighters of, 37, 42. *See also specific topics*
Japanese submarine, 16–17
jeeps, in Manila, 325
Jefman airfield, 180–83, *191*
Jensen, Floyd, 171
Jensen, Robert, 271–72, 274; death of, 273–75; good-luck charms of, 274
Jensen, Ruth, 271–72, 274–75
jinx, 177
Johns, Cary, 222
Johnson, Andrew, 313
Johore Maru, 78
Jones, Cecil, 177
Jones, Jack, 277–78, 279, 280
Jones, James R. "J. R.," 32–33, 43–44, 66, 87, 101–2; on Australia, 108–9; Black Sunday and, 163; at Cape Gloucester, 117–20; on censoring mail, 121–22; exhaustion of, 137–38, 172–73; going home, 183; good-luck charm of, 177; on heat of New Guinea, 173; on Hollandia, 172; Hollandia and, 156; on letters to family of slain servicemen, 180; on movies, books, and music, 151–52; at Nadzab, 162; on Nadzab, 144–45, 174–75; on replacement crews, 143; after war, 348; wounding of, 120
Jones, R., on Wewak, 180
Jordan, Kenneth, 279
Joy Baby, 165
Just, Henry, 177

Kagi Town, *250*, 320
Kagoshima, *250*, 333
kamikaze, ix, 212–13; from Clark Field, 229; *Morrison R. Waite* and, 220–22; in Okinawa, 331; *Thomas Nelson* and, 218–22
Karkar Island, 162, 164
Karnis, Edward, 267
Kasten, Edmund, 196; crash landing of, 198
Kavieng, 127–38; Coltharp at, 175; water landings at, 132–37

Kawasaki Ki-43 "Oscar," 234; 498th Bomb Squadron and, 286–87; in South China Sea, 286–87, 294

Kawasaki Ki-61 "Tony," 42, 54; at Alicante airfield, 215, 216; at Samate airfield, 182; at Wewak, 66–67

Keesler Army Airfield, Mississippi, 241–42

Kelly, John, 336–37

Kenney, George C., 1–4, 21, 65, 73; Arnold, H., and, 36–37; Black Sunday and, 163; on bombs, 61; China Sea and, 260; Crabb and, 38; Gunn and, 29; Hollandia and, 157–58; MacArthur and, 2; Philippines and, 206–7, 229, 258; phosphorous bombs and, 98–99; at Rabaul, 47–48; Saigon and, 311; True and, 86; Wewak and, 40

Kent, Paul, 330–31

Khan, Kublai, 212

Kiiru Harbor, 250

Kinkasan Maru, 78

Kirkland, Elmer, 131, 171

Kiska Harbor, 327

kitchen sink, 202

Kizzire, William, 106–7

Knoll, Henry, 42, 67

Kobi, 250

Koch, Joseph, 127

Koenig, David, 83

Kokoda Track, 19

Korczynski, Mike, 30–31, 79

Korea, 333, 335, 336

Kortemeyer, Henry, 117–19, 120; at Nadzab, 162; at Samate airfield, 181–82

Kramiskas, Alfred, 92–93

Kusebauch, Anton, 179

Kyser, Kay, 12

Kyser, William, xi–xvi; at Cape Gloucester, 116

Kyushu, 333, 335, 336

Lady Lil, 87

Lae, 29–30, 153, 161

Lahug Airfield, 222

Lamarr, Hedy, 87

Lambert, Bill, 322, 328

Landon, Jack, 215

Lane, Jimmy, 265–66

Langoan Airfield, 199

Larsen, Robert, 35, 55, 66–67

Latawiec, Frank, 116

Lawliss, Merritt "Gene," 300–303

Lawrence, Clifford, 316–17

Lay, Allan, 200

Lee, Richard, 287–95

Leggett, William, 213, 215, 216–17

Lembeh Strait, 191, 199–201

Leonidas Merritt (Liberty ship), 207

Leventon, Marvin "Murph," 270, 346

Lewis, Robert, 130

Lewis, Thomas, 162

Leyte, 206, 208, 210; Saigon and, 311

Liberty ships, 206–11, 218–20

Lilley, David, 326

Lingayen: 475th Fighter Group at, 316; MacArthur at, 235; Thompson, F., at, 260

Link, Ray, 190, 199, 204; death of, 222; Dunnavant and, 236; Liberty ships and, 209

liquor. See alcohol

Logui #2 airstrip, 24

Loisel, Cyriaque, 281–82

Loisel, John, 322

Long, Robert, 104

Loochow Peninsula, 299

Los Negros Island, 148, 211–12, 227–28

lovers, 32–34; pictures of, 204; slain husbands of, 183. See also wives

Lovett, Roger, 260–64, 288–90; at Formosa, 306–7; malaria of, 320; at Tarumizu, 333–35

Love Walked In, 152

low-level flight: of B-25s, 100–101; in Saigon, 314; at ships, 278; by 345th Bomb Group, 150, 204

luck, 176–77, 326; of Epps, 272

Luzon, 230, 250; caves on, iv; 500th Bomb Squadron in, 236, 323–25; Saigon and, 311; 345th Bomb Group in, iv, 225. See also San Marcelino

MacArthur, Douglas, viii, 21; Cape Gloucester and, 111; Clark Field and,

229; on crew personnel rotation, 197; Hollandia and, 153, 157–58; Japanese surrender and, 340–43; Kavieng and, 127; Kenney and, 2; at Lingayen, 235; in Manila, 340, 342; New Guinea and, 36, 37; Philippines and, 229; Rabaul and, 45, 47, 60, 89, 152–53; as SWAPA, 1

MacCready, David, 131

machine guns: .50 caliber, 25, 28–29, 34, 52, 79, 169–70, 205, 278, 323; .30 caliber, 34, 150, 169–70

Macropoulos, Constantinos, 210, 219

MacWilliam, James, 162, 164–65

Mae West life vest, 202, 266; of Blair, 276; of Muller, 300

Magee, Milford, 54

Maggi, Bartolino "Bart," 305–6

Mahaffey, Jim, 124–26; on alcohol, 176

mail, 121–22; censorship of, 121, 172, 222; death notices by, 179–80

Makassar Strait, 27

Mako Town, *250*, 304–6

malaria, 190, 303; of Lovett, 320

Mallard, Joe, 227–28

Manam Island, 164–65

Manchuria, SS, 13

Manders, John, 93–94

Mangum, Thomas, 286

Manila, 27; furloughs to, 251; jeeps in, 325; MacArthur in, 340, 342

Manokwari, 184

Manus Island, 124–26

Markham Valley, 36, 144

Marks, Marshall, xi

Marlinan, 39–40

Marsili, Anthony, 287

Mathews, William, 321–22

Mawrence, Sil, 178

Mays, Ellis, 162

McCall, Garvice, 54

McClellan Field, 13

McClure, Jack, 279, 341

McClure, Kenneth, 124–26

McDole, Glen, 68–69

McGowan, Bud, 98

McGuire, James, 289–90; as POW, 302

McKinney, Arthur, 259

McKinney, John, 215

McLean, John, 124–25

Medal of Honor: of Gordon, 137; of Wilkins, 98

Merritt, James, 165

Messerschmitt Me-109 "Mike," 67

Metzel, Charles, 237

mid-air collision, 161, 194–95

Middlebrook, Garrett, 30

Migliacci, James, 82–83, 84

Mikoda, Lucille, 350

Miller, Ben, 16, 20, 189–90, 207; on Biak Island, 192; on music, 210; on *Thomas Nelson*, 218–20; after war, 350–51

Miller, Marlin, 315

Miller, William, 10

Mindanao, 214, 225; Saigon and, 311

Mindoro Island, 235, 236; Underwood and, 349

Mios Waar Island, 181

Missouri, USS, 344

Mitchell, George, 116, 148–49

Mitchell, William "Billy," 6

Mitsubishi A6M fighter "Hamp," 57–59; at Clark Field, 234; at Rabaul, 95; at Samate airfield, 181

Mitsubishi A6M fighter "Zero, Zeke," 53, 57–58; at Blanche Bay, 78, 79–81; at Cape Gloucester, 117; *Chub* and, 293–94; at Formosa, 321; at Hollandia, 155; of Japanese, 37, 42; at Lembeh Strait, 201; at Rabaul, 95, 96; at Rapopo, 77; at Wewak, 66–67

Mitsubishi G4M bomber "Betty," 53–54, 106; for Japanese surrender representatives, 341, 342

Mitsubishi J2M Jack II, 286

Mitsubishi Ki-21 "Sally," 59

Mitsubishi Ki-46 "Dinah," 54

Miyao (Colonel), 344

Mokmer, 189, *191*, 196

Monaghan, Daniel, 162

monsoons, 319

Moore, Jay, v, 188, 189, 196; on Biak Island, 190; on clothing, 202; on crash landing, 198; in Philippines, 222–23

Moore, Orbry, 42, 93–94, 98

Moresby Wreck, 110; Peckham and, 177

Morison, Eliot, 99

Morotai, 204, 211, 218

Morrison, Harold, 221

Morrison R. Waite (Liberty ship), 207–11, 218–19; kamikaze and, 220–22

Morse code, 149

Mortenson, Max, 78, 92–93, 98, 179–80, 200, 345; at Hansa Bay, 105; at Kavieng, 128; kitchen sink and, 202

movies, 151–52

Muller, Benjamin, 178–79, 187, 299–303; as POW, 343–44

Muniz, Stan, 305–6, 329–30

murders, of captives, viii–ix, 68–69, 105, 107, 236, 264

Murphy, John, 79, 80, 81, 130

music, 151–52, 210

Muster, Henry, 222

Myers, Charles "Chuck," 286

NA-21, 5

NA-39, 5

NA-40, 5–6

NA-62, 6

Nadzab, 35; beauty of, 188; Bianconi in, 171–72; indoctrination training at, 252; Lovett at, 261; Pollock at, 248; Stambaugh in, 297; 345th Bomb Group at, 144–64, 174–75

Nagasaki, *250*, 345–46; atomic bomb on, 335

Nakajima Ki-27 "Nate," 55–56, 58

Nakajima Ki-43, 181

Nakajima Ki-44 "Tojo": at Alicante airfield, 214–15; at Clark Field, 234; at Indochina, 264–66

Nakajima Ki-49 "Helen," 56

Natamo Point, 114, 115

Nate. *See* Nakajima Ki-27

National Museum of the Air Force, iv

navigator: on B-25s, 8; bomb bay duty of, 186; training for, 238–41

Neal, Robert, 335

near miss stories, 178–79; with parafrags, 307

Nelson, Walter, 236

Netherlands (Dutch) East Indies, 257, 258, 260, 275

Neuenschwander, Darwin, 42

New Britain, xii, 29, 45, *57*, 74. *See also specific sites*

New Guinea, *11*; difficult geography of, 154; heat of, 173–74; MacArthur and, 36, 37; Pollock in, 325; to San Marcelino, 252. *See also specific sites*

New Hanover, 138–40

Nha Trang Bay, 275

Nichols, Aldridge, 144, 174, 175, 193

Nightwine, Ted John, 107

Nimitz, Chester, 47

90th Bomb Squadron: of 3rd Attack Group, 30; at Rapopo, 60

Nirdlinger, Eugene, 193–96

Nolan, John, 194–95

North American Aviation, 5–6, 205; Fox of, 28–29

Nusbaum, John, 57

O'Brien, John, 177

Office of Strategic Services (OSS), 344

Officers Candidate School, 241

Ohnemus, Roman, 160, 214, 215; at Clark Field, 230, 233

O'Hop, John, 287

Okinawa: Givens on, 350; kamikaze in, 331

Olsen, John, 229–30, 232, 235

Operation CARTWHEEL, 47, 152–53

Operation RECKLESS, 153

O'Rear, Theodore, 54

Orland Loomis (Liberty ship), 206–7

Ormoc Bay, 217, 218

Oro Bay, 50–51

Oscar. *See* Kawasaki Ki-43

OSS. *See* Office of Strategic Services

Ow, Lee, 20, 21–22

Owen Stanley Range, 18, 21, 48, 110

P-38s: at Alicante airfield, 214–15; on Black Sunday, 163; at Clark Field, 229, 234; crash landings of, 166; as escorts for Japanese surrender representatives, 341, 342; of 475th Fighter Group, 316; head-on collision of, 161; at

Hollandia, 155, 156, 158, 159; at
Kavieng, 130–31; at Manam Island,
164; from Mios Waar Island, 181;
at Rabaul, 50, 95–96; at Saigon,
312; at Samate, 181; at Vunakanau,
56, 58–59; at Wakde Island, 179; at
Wewak, 66–67
P-39s, xiii–xiv, 2
P-40s, 2, 42, 107
P-47s: 499th Bomb Squadron and, 43; at
Hansa Bay, 103–4; at Manam Island,
164; at Manus Island, 126
P-51s: at Formosa, 259; at Tarumizu, 334
Palawan Island, 311
Pallotta, Rico, 277
Paquette, Wilford Joseph, 107
Paracel Islands, 267
parademolition (parademo) bombs, 62;
malfunction of, 184–86; on Samate
and Jefman airfields, 180–81
parafragmentation (parafrag) bombs, 35,
62–63, 256; on A/A, 90; toggling
near-miss with, 307
Parker, Frank, 43
parties, 174–75
PB4Y-2 Privateer, 292, 294
PBM Mariner, 268–69
PBY: Fighter Grid and, 163; of Gordon,
134–37; at Hansa Bay, 105; at Los
Negros Island, 228; at Manam Island,
165; at Selapiu Island, 141
Pearson, Ruth, 109, 143, 272, 348
Pease, Dick, 322
Peckham, Cal, 177
Peregoy, Nelson, 227
Perkins, Morris, 287–95
Pescadores Islands, 304
Peterson, Harlan, 78–79, 81
Phan Thiet, 312
Philippines, 207; as base, 257–58; Formosa
and, 323; Kenney and, 206–7, 229;
Liberty ships to, 206–9, 218–19;
MacArthur and, 229; railroads in,
236; 345th Bomb Group in, 204–12,
351. See also specific sites
phosphorous bombs, 90–93, 95; at Cape
Gloucester, 113; at Clark Field, 234;
Kenney and, 98–99

Pietscher, Reed, 316
Pietscher, Ron, 315–16
pilots: on B-25s, 7, 52; Japanese, 212–13;
training for, 238–48
"Piss-call Charlie," 211
Pitoe airstrip, 211
Plaice, USS, 339–40
Plumb, Charles, 279
Pollock, Melvin, 238–48, 317, 318, 343; in
New Guinea, 325; after war, 350
Port Moresby, xii, 2, 110; to Dobodura, 111;
345th Bomb Group at, xii, 17–23, 34,
43–44, 48
posttraumatic stress disorder (PTSD),
349–50
Potsdam Conference, 340
POWs. See prisoners of war
Pratt & Whitney R-1830 radial engine, 5
prayer meetings, 175
President Johnson, SS, 13, 15–17, 18
prisoners of war (POWs): B-25s and, 237; at
Fort Oranje, 196; on Hainan Island,
343; at Nagasaki, 346; from water
landings, 300–330; in Wewak, 107
propaganda leaflets, at Finschafen, 37
Prunty, Pete, 221
Pruth, SS, 110
PTSD. See posttraumatic stress disorder
Puerto Princesa, 248, 311–15
Purple Heart medals, 332, 352
Pushetonequa, Charles, 198

Q codes, 149–50
Quadrant Conference, 47
Quietly My Captain Waits (book), 152
Quinn, James, 151

RAAF. See Royal Australian Air Force
Raaven, Howie, 242
Rabaul, 45–61, 91–100; completion of
mission, 152–53; MacArthur and, 45,
47; USAAF at, 84. See also Blanche
Bay; Cape Gloucester; Rapopo;
Vunakanau
radar, flying under, 51
radio operator: on B-25s, 8; as gunner, 269–
70; Morse code by, 149; in Nadzab,
145–47; Q codes by, 149–50

Radzun, Walter, 316

Ragitsuma, 498th Bomber Squad at, 38–39

railroads: in Philippines, 236; POW slave labor for, 301

Ramon (Filipino houseboy), 319–20

Ramses (dog), 322–23

Ranger, Richard, 279

Rankin, Hobart, 161; at Samate airfield, 182

Rape of Nanking, 68

Rapopo, 60, 74–77, 94

Redfin, USS, 275

Reeves, Robert, 328–29

Reheis, Herman, 143, 273–74, 288–89

Rhapsody in Blue, 152

Richardson, James, 276

Rickenbacker, Eddie, 1

Riddle, Billie, 188

Rita's Wagon, 202

Rizal, 223–24

The Robe (Douglas, L.), 152

Robinette, Ralph, 106–7

Rosenbaum, Bert, 192

Rough Riders. *See* 500th Bomb Squadron

Royal Australian Air Force (RAAF), 25; Beaufighters of, 50, 52, 58–59; at Rabaul, 50; at Tobera, 52, 57

Rutter, Joseph, 231–32

Sag Harbor Express, 87, 234

Saidor, 161–64

Saigon, 311–16

Salamaua, 21–25; Logui #2 airstrip by, 24

Sally. *See* Mitsubishi Ki-21

Samah, 262, 285–87; POWs at, 344–44

Samate airfield, 180–83, *191*

samurai warrior code (Bushido), 70–71

Sancho Point, *250*

Sandakan, 204

Sanders, William, 165

San Marcelino: Baeta in, 308–9; Formosa and, 258–60; 498th Bomb Squadron at, 273; monsoons in, 319; Stambaugh in, 297–98; 345th Bomb Group at, 249–319; training in, 308–10

Santo Tomas prison camp, 27

Savannah Army Airfield, Georgia, 12

Sawyer, Vernon, 288–90

SB-17G rescue aircraft, 338

Schmidt, George, 328–29

Schwimmer Airfield "Fourteen-Mile Airdrome," 18

SCR-578, 291

Scudder, Robert, 176–77, 184, 186

Sea Biscuit, 87

Sealion, USS, 295–96

Sea Robin, USS, 283–85

Sebastian, Charles, xi

Selapiu Island, 140–41

Selby, William, 182, 183

Selman Army Airfield, Louisiana, 239–42

Sentani, 155

Seven-Mile Airdrome, 18

Seventeen-Mile Airdrome, 18

Seventh Air Force, at Tarumizu, 333–35

75-millimeter cannon, on B-25s, 168–69, 192

shackles, in bomb bay, 255

Shakespeare, William, vii

Shane, William, 219

Shinan Maru, 285–86

Shinto, 71

Showers, Roy, 107

Sibuyan Island, 235–36; Underwood and, 348–49

Sidate, 201–2

Siegrist, William, 151

Silimati Point, 115

Silver Star, 244, 352; of Doolittle, 327; of Gordon, 137; of Gunn, 28

Simms, Mack, 96

Simonelli, Orazio, 141

Simpson, William, 299–300

Simpson Harbor, 46, 50, 76, 92, 96

Sinatra, Frank, 152

Singapore, raw materials from, 257

Singlaub, John, 344–45

Sisson, Clifford, 259–60

6th Army Special Reconnaissance, 257

Sizemore, McKinley, 177, 278, 303–4

The Sky's the Limit (film), 152

Small, John, 105–6

Smith, Roy E., 179–80

smoking, 147–48

Snafu, 80–83, 82

Sneed, Roy, 17

snipers, ix

SOCONY. *See* Standard Oil Company of
    New York
Solomon, Joseph, 347
Sorry Satchul, 78–79
South China Sea, 275; Fifth Air Force
    and, 260; 500th Bomb Squadron in,
    281, 285; 501st Bomb Squadron in,
    277–80, 285; 498th Bomb Squadron
    in, 279–80, 285, 286–87; 499th Bomb
    Squadron in, 267, 280–81, 285;
    Givens at, 269–70; Nakajima Ki-43
    in, 286–87, 294; rescues in, 287–96;
    submarines in, 275–76, 283–85,
    290–95; water landings in, 265–66,
    287–88, 290. *See also specific sites*
So What?, 252–53
Spam, 44
Speicher, Dale, 158, 160, 161
Spratly Islands, 312
Stambaugh, 341; alcohol and, 338–39
Stambaugh, Quentin, 296–98, 309, 336–37;
    at Kyushu, 335
Standard Oil Company of New York
    (SOCONY), 315
Stapleton, Howell, 171
Steele, Heath, 280
St. Elmo's fire, 330
Stine, Homer, xi, xiv
Stone, Al, 251–52, 254–56
Stone, John, 211, 213–14
Stone, William, 217
Stookey, Donald, 67–68
Stout, Jay, vi–vii
Stowell, Aubrey, 315
strafing: of A/A, 90; at Alicante airfield,
    215; B-25s for, 25, 28–30; Blanche
    Bay, 77–78; at Blanche Bay, 90;
    diminishment of, 157; by 500th
    Bomb Squadron, 35; by 501st Bomb
    Squadron, 34–35; by 499th Bomb
    Squadron, 36; at Halmahera Island,
    194; at Lembeh Strait, 201; in Luzon,
    324; at New Hanover, 139–40; by
    Pollock, 343; at Saigon, 313, 315;
    at Tacloban Airfield, 218; by 345th
    Bomb Group, viii, 36; at Toyohara
    Airfield, 259

Subic Bay, 234, 249, 251, 309
submarines: 500th Bomb Squadron and,
    139; rescues by, 276, 296, 339–40; in
    South China Sea, 275–76, 283–85,
    290–95
Submarine Squadron 30, 294
Suey, Charles, 300–330
Sugar Able Love tanker, 282
Sugar Baker Sugar tanker, 282
Sugar Charlie Love tanker, 281–82
Sugar Dogs, 187
supreme commander of Allied Forces in the
    Southwest Pacific Area (SWAPA),
    MacArthur as, 1
Svec, Millard, 83
Swanick (Colonel), 297
SWAPA. *See* supreme commander of Allied
    Forces in the Southwest Pacific Area
Swing, Joseph, 324–25
Symington, Thomas, 227–28

Tacloban Airfield, 217–18, 225–26, 235;
    C-47 at, 252–53
Tadji airfield, 166–67
Tanauan, 225
Tarumizu, *250*, 333–35
Task Force 39, 90
Tatelman, Vic, 87–88
Te-Go, 224
Ternate, *191*, 194, 196
theatre, on Biak Island, 198–99
3rd Attack Group, 39, 41, 165; 90th Bomb
    Squadron of, 30
3rd Bomb Group, 90; A-20s of, 316–17; at
    Rabaul, 96, 97; Te-Go and, 224
3rd Division, of Australia, 21
Third Air Force, 4
13th Air Force, 128, 210
.30 caliber machine guns, on B-25s, 34, 150,
    169–70
38th Bomb Group, 30, 36, 39, 90; B-25s
    of, 170; at Kavieng, 128; at Manus
    Island, 124; at New Hanover, 138–39;
    at Rabaul, 49, 96, 97; at Rapopo, 60;
    at Samate and Jefman airfields, 181; at
    Vunakanau, 54; at Wewak, 41
Thomas, Roland, 182, 196

Thomas Nelson (Liberty ship), 207–11, 218–20; kamikaze and, 218–22
Thompson, Alden, 22–23
Thompson, Francis, 259–60
Thompson, Howard, 233–34, 234–35
308th Bomb Wing, 217–18
309th Bomb Wing, 4, 297
310th Bomb Wing, 230
312th Bomb Group, at Clark Field, 229, 230, 231–32
345th Bomb Group "Air Apaches": aircraft destroyed by, ix; B-25s of, 5, 205; at Biak Island, 188–203, 198–99, 225; at Borgen Bay, 64–65; at Clark Field, 229–36, 319–20; comradely love in, ix; crew replacements for, 142–67, 193–95, 333; as escort for Japanese surrender representatives, 342–43; 50-mission men of, 142, 193–97; in Ie Shima, 317, 331–50; on Liberty ships to Philippines, 206–9; loss rate of, ix–x; low-level flight by, 150, 204; in Luzon, iv, 225; at Nadzab, 144–64, 174–75; nickname for, 150, 198, 237; organization of, 4; in Philippines, 204–12, 351; at Port Moresby, xii, 17–23, 34, 43–44, 48; at Rabaul, 45–61, 48–50; at Rizal, 223–24; at San Marcelino, 249–319; ships sunk by, ix; strafing by, viii, 36; support personnel of, ix; Third Air Force and, 4; after war, 345–52. *See also* 500th Bomb Squadron; 501st Bomb Squadron; 498th Bomb Squadron; 499th Bomb Squadron; *specific topics*
345th Bomb Group Association, v–vi, 351
348th Fighter Group, 334
The Three Little Fishes, 12
The Three Top Terrors, 150, 188, 198
Tobera, 51–52, 57, 84
Todd, Robert, 281
Tojo. *See* Nakajima Ki-44
Tokyo Rose, 248
Tondelayo, 78, 81, 85, 87
Tonkin Gulf, 283–85
Tony. *See* Kawasaki Ki-61
torture, by Japanese, 69–70

Townley, Vernon, 314
Toyohara Airfield, 258–59
Trip, Don, 178
Triton Reef, 267–69
True, Clinton "Fearless," 10, 38, 51–57, 74; at Cape Gloucester, 112–19; completion of duty of, 175; Kenney and, 86; at Wewak, 41
Truman, Harry S., 15
Truman, Robert, 200
Tsili Tsili, 39
Tuguegarao, *250*, 307
Tungku Island, 273
typhoon, 209–10

Uligan Harbor, 104, 170
Underwood, James, 235–36, 348–49
United States Army Air Forces (USAAF): Arnold, H., of, 1; B-24s of, 275; Germany and, 3; at Rabaul, 84; rescues of, 106. *See also specific units*
USO, 12

Van Ausdell, Robert, 104–5
Victory Mail "V-Mail," 121
Vincent, George, 336
Vogt, Sylvester, 55, 117–18
Vojnovich, Sam, xi
Volelkop, 180
Vonflotow, Walter, 216
Vunakanau, 51–60

WACS. *See* Women's Army Corps
Waggle, James, 161, 164
Wagner, Donald "Buzz," 251, 323–25
Wakde Island, 172; P-38s at, 179
Waldo, Jim, 214, 215–17
Walker, Dick, 97
Walker, James, 187, 286, 287–95
Walker, Robert, 37
Wallace, Ralph, 78–82, 87
Waring, Kenneth, 281
water: at Biak Island, 189–90; for POWs, 303
water landings, viii–ix, 22–23; at Astrolabe Bay, 163; by Baeta, 267–69; by Blair, 276; at Blanche Bay, 82–83; at Borgen

Bay, 119; at Hansa Bay, 104–5; at
    Kavieng, 129–30, 132–37; at Lembeh
    Strait, 200–201; at Manus Island,
    124–26; Muller and, 299–300; POWs
    from, 300–330; at Rapopo, 94; at
    Selapiu Island, 140–41; in South
    China Sea, 265–66, 287–88, 290; at
    Wewak, 67–68; by Wilkinson, 338
Wattum Chew, 12
Weich, Bertram, 237
Welch, William, 193–96
Wewak, 39, 40–43, 65–68, 103, 150–51, 153,
    171; Jones, R., on, 180; POWs in, 107
Whipple, Chandler, 43
White Cargo (film), 87
Whitehead, Ennis, 173, 260
Whitman, Richard, xi–xiv, xvi; at Cape
    Gloucester, 116
Whitsell, Robert, 161
Wilkins, Raymond, 97–98
Wilkinson, Earl, 336, 339–40; water
    landings by, 338
William, Leste, 315
Williams, Don, 227–28
Williams, Jack, 322
Wilson, John, 127, 138
Witherell, William, 199, 210, 224, 331,
    346; on Christmas, 225; on Coltharp,

327; on Cranford, 310; at San
    Marcelino, 251
wives, 32–34; of Epps, 272; of Jensen,
    Robert, 271–75; mail from and to,
    121–22; slain husbands of, 183
Wolf Pack, 87
Women's Army Corps (WACS), 319
wood, as commodity, 261–62
Wright, Donald, 338
Wright Cyclone R-2600 engines, xiii,
    5, 6, 14–15; on B-25s, xiii, 5, 6, 7;
    improvements to, 206

XB-21, 5

Yagita, Kiyoshi, 59
Yamakawa, Mitsuyasu, 79
Yarborough, John, 23
Yellow Beach, 113, 114, 116–17
Yokosuka MXY7 Ohka suicide bombs,
    333
Young, Otis, 319–20
Yulin Bay, 285, 288–90

Zahora, Charles, 31
Zeke. *See* Mitsubishi A6M fighter
Zero. *See* Mitsubishi A6M fighter
Zig-Zag Pass, 255, 256